GW01454258

SEMIOTEXT(E) FOREIGN AGENTS SERIES
Co-published with Sternberg Press

Published by Semiotext(e)
2007 Wilshire Blvd., Suite 427
Los Angeles, CA 90057
www.semiotexte.com
ISBN: 978-1-58435-079-8

Sternberg Press / Caroline Schneider
Karl-Marx-Allee 78, D-10243 Berlin
1182 Broadway 1602, New York, NY 10001
www.sternberg-press.com
ISBN: 978-1-933128-78-8

Second Edition prepared by Hedi El Kholti.

Interview with Volker Schlöndorff edited by Iris Klein.

Special thanks for partial funding to Anton Vidokle and e-flux, as well as Christo and Jeanne-Claude.

Special thanks to Hans Haacke, Iris Klein, Chris Kraus, Marc Lowenthal, and Erik Morse.

Semiotext(e) is distributed by The MIT Press, Cambridge, Mass. and London, England
Printed in China by C & C Offset Printing

THE GERMAN ISSUE

SYLVÈRE LOTRINGER
German Issues

To Heidi Paris (1950–2002)

Post-Political Politics

The German Issue is as "untimely" today as it was twenty-five years ago. When it was first published in 1982, the world was still starkly divided into two antagonistic blocks and our intention was to loosen them up in all sorts of ways, as we did earlier with other binary oppositions that regulate culture.[1] The wall that used to separate East and West Berlin at the time was the stark embodiment of the struggle between the two systems, capitalism and communism, and it runs as well through every page of *The German Issue*. But here, instead of sharpening their confrontation, it allows for active crossovers between West and East. It also acts like a Moebius strip, progressing from Wall Street to the Berlin wall and from the United States to Germany—and back. Reality itself conspired to make it go that way since I miraculously found the comic strip that concludes the issue (Heidi-the-blond-Nazi saved by GI's from the Russians soldiers is flown to America) at the back of an old black woman preacher's car as she kindly gave me and my daughter a ride through Central Park during a bus strike in 1991.

The wall of images isn't just a formal conceit: one may have forgotten that after the collapse of the Third Reich, Germany was rebuilt from scratch by America, which rewrote its constitution and imposed its own values over the defeated country. As Wim Wenders said, "America has colonized our unconscious." Dealing with Germany, therefore, was an indirect way of dealing with America on a large scale, the way West Berlin subterraneously communicated with New York. The trajectory from one to the other wasn't oppositional, but continuous.

In the late seventies and early eighties, a number of innovative political experiments were being carried out, especially in Italy and in Germany. What allowed these bold social projects to thrive for a few years was the slow demise of established communist parties which, for a long time, had monopolized and defused any attempt to transform society. These creative political openings unfortunately coincided in both countries with the rise of Marxist-Leninist urban guerilla groups eager to take revolution into their own hands and address the masses through spectacular means. As a result, every attempt to reinvent politics in the margins of traditional institutions was crushed.

The German Issue was originally conceived as a follow-up to the *Autonomia/ Italy* issue that Semiotext(e) published in 1980. Autonomia, a powerful social movement, fluid and rhizomatic in its organization and neo-anarchistic in spirit, tried to drive a wedge between the Italian Communist Party and the Red Brigades—another deadly dichotomy. The ICP was giving up on class struggle to share power with Aldo Moro's Christian-democrats, their "class enemy," prompting the Brigate Rosse to escalate the struggle by other means. The assassination of Aldo Moro gave the ICP a chance to get rid of the Autonomia which was growing at its expense in the Far Left. The leaders of Autonomia were falsely accused of masterminding the terrorist organization and the entire movement was eradicated. It remains one of the most inventive responses in the West to the end of ideologies and the dissipation of classes in late capitalist societies.

The Berlin wall collapsed in 1989, followed by the implosion of the Soviet Union and its satellites. For a while the American empire reigned supreme—the New World Order—only challenged by its own excesses and the process of globalization that it had imprudently initiated. The horrors of "real communism" were disclosed very late and those of capitalism paled in comparison. But the sudden meltdown of the international financial market, which is wreaking havoc on the entire planet, amply demonstrates that it can be no less devastating for being immaterial. In the rush to go forward, crucial questions were left fallow. We gave up too fast on legitimate aspirations that the market economy had left behind, mostly untouched. Bouts of revolt, then as now, from the Zurich revolt of 1968 to the recent riots in Athens, remind us of a lingering disaffection from a system that is reaching its own limits and doesn't seem to have anywhere to go.

The German Issue was not limited to Germany any more than the Italian issue exclusively addressed Italian concerns. Both were meant to investigate the future of politics in late capitalism ("post-political politics"). The two issues complement each other, subjecting a different social landscape to a similar type of questioning. Both issues stand on the threshold of the strange anomie that we are experiencing today.

Die Deutschen Freunde

In 1980 I received a letter from Peter Gente and Heidi Paris, two young publishers at Merve Verlag, a small independent press in Berlin. The letter was written in German, so I put it aside. Maybe they assumed, since my name sounds German, that I knew the language. They obviously didn't know that I was born in Paris and had only arrived in New York eight years before. As it turned out, they spoke French to perfection. It took me a little while, a few weeks probably, before I got the letter translated and set the record straight—in French. Later on, after we became friends, they learned English as well and we worked together on a number of projects, including this issue, which may be what they had in mind when they first wrote to me.

As the child of Polish immigrant Jews, I had a problem with German. I learned Italian at school instead, and it had served me well when I went to Italy in 1979 to gather the material for the *Autonomia: Post-Political Politics* issue. Peter and Heidi had just got a copy from a friend returning from New York and they got very excited. New York then was the center of the world. Peter Gente, an outlaw academic (he didn't write) once active in the 60s anti-authoritarian movement, had already brought the autonomist thinkers to the press, and Heidi, who was more of an artist, and had a sharp mind, got him interested in French theorists, some of whom (Gilles Deleuze, Félix Guattari, Paul Virilio, Guy Debord) had been included in the Italian issue. Neo-Marxist French Theory had been badly received by the German academy ever so fearful of "irrationalists"—Nietzsche included—and it didn't fare any better in the United States among 60s academic radicals. One of the first things I had done with Semiotext(e) was to orchestrate *Nietzsche's Return*.[2] Peter and Heidi welcomed the idea that another press in New York was working along the same fault line as they did. It made them feel less isolated.

West Berlin then was an island in the middle of the European continent. The Western part, divided into three zones, American, British and French, stuck like a thorn on the vast East German backside. While East Berlin belonged to the rest of East Germany, West Berlin remained a mere enclave surrounded by a barbed-wired wall complete with turrets, search-lights and machine-guns. Many people from East Berlin got killed over the years trying to cross it. Built in 1961, the wall was meant to prevent East Germany from hemorrhaging into the capitalist West, but it instantly turned West Berlin into an artificial bubble that could burst at any time. The bubble was wide enough (it included parks and lakes) to give people the impression that they were living a normal life, but exiting from it always met with stern borders and harsh controls. Flying over it all by plane and landing in West Berlin (via Frankfurt) was far easier, but it felt like rushing from the bottom to the surface without decompressing—the Cold War hit you without preparation. Over time, of course, I got used to taking the subway which wound its way in and out of East and West—like *The German Issue* itself—past heavily-guarded East German stations, but this kept reminding me how paradoxical the whole situation was.

Only New York at the time could have matched that experience. It certainly wasn't a normal place to inhabit either. The wall there was invisible, only delineated by the Hudson, but the population inside, teeming and compressed, felt isolated, as well, from the rest of the American continent which distrusted it as much as it envied its fluid lifestyle, unabashed permissiveness and suspicious cosmopolitanism. New York, showcase of the West, was a heaven for freaks and artists who could also be found in Berlin; decadent cities where possible futures were being experimented with daily and negligently tossed to the side. No wonder the Peters and Heidis in West Berlin were as keenly interested in sprawling urban art and scratchy music as we were. Both Merve Verlag and Semiotext(e) were part of a larger cultural scene, and they were meant to meet.

Zealous about publishing, Peter Gente kept a basket of articles he found interesting, which he occasionally assembled into small books. Some of them found their way into *The German Issue*, even though Peter hadn't read them all. He instinctively knew what would be good, and the selection of authors we made together is probably one of the best that could have been done at the time, and certainly remains unequalled to this day. No one then bothered about copyrights; writers would simply give verbal permission to publish. Needless to say, neither of us was interested in money, or benefited from what we published. All we wanted was to make available right away what we considered important.

It didn't take me long to realize that the situation in Germany was quite different from what I had documented in Italy two years earlier. The terrorist issue in Germany had never reached the intensity that it had in Italy, nor was it used to annihilate an entire social movement. The tension had significantly abated three years after the last members of the Red Army Fraction [RAF], Andreas Baader, Gudrun Ensslin and Jan-Carl Raspe, were mysteriously found shot or hung in their cells at the Stammheim prison, near Frankfurt. Whether they killed themselves or had been executed by a police squad only five days after a group of Palestinians commandeered a Lufthansa plane to Mogadishu in exchange for their liberation, we will never know. Ulrike Meinhof, the most clear-sighted intellectual among them, committed suicide in 1976 after being subjected to intense sensory deprivation. Their deaths concluded this somber episode which, for a few years, threatened to fulfill the terrorists' wishes and turn Germany into a fascist state. The Nazi past, obviously, was still present in everybody's mind, but other, more pressing issues that they raised through their violent actions, like First World imperialism and the exploitation of the Third World, are still with us.

The issue of political terrorism had deeply divided the Left in Germany. Unlike the Red Brigades, which originated from the Fiat factories in Northern Italy, the RAF members came out of the student movement and they could count on a certain amount of sympathy among them. The 1977 kidnapping and ruthless assassination of Hans-Martin Schleyer, an ex-SS who became head of the Federation of German industries, ended up alienating their last supporters. There was a clear sense of relief among various people I met, including ex-terrorists,[3] in the more diffused movement who had watched, powerless, as political violence got out of hand. Eager to get on with their lives, most of them would make up the new tertiary class and participate in the democratic process, especially within the "Green" party. All that remained from the terrorist period were fierce street fights that lingered on—mostly in Berlin, where many houses remained vacant—between the Squatters' movement and the police.

Putting together the issue on Germany without knowing German could be considered a serious handicap, even some kind of a joke, but I looked at it in another way. It made a true collaboration with my new friends possible. I had to trust them blindly since some pieces were commissioned or translated before I could even read them. Obviously, I had them look at previous issues published in New York so they could figure out what I was really after. Sharing the same intellectual references was a huge help. It was our common *lingua franca*. Not being able to speak German also forced me to get our material directly from the people themselves and go from there, following up on some of their leads, instead of relying on existing studies. I conducted substantial interviews with some of the people in Germany whom I considered important for the issue, the way I had done in New York with Christo, William Burroughs and Walter Abish.

Peter and Heidi had been publishing Heiner Müller—now widely considered the greatest German dramaturge, and successor of Bertold Brecht—and had arranged for us to meet in the apartment they still kept at Güntzelstrasse (the original Merve Verlag group used to live there) where Müller, who lived in East Berlin, also rented a room. Müller was interested as well in French Theory and wasn't yet very well-known outside Germany, so we both knew that our dialogue would be used to give him some more visibility in the world outside. (It was translated into several languages.) It also gave me a chance to exorcize some of the issues I had with Germany, since I lived through the war as a child in Occupied France.

Making *The German Issue* and staying with my friends in Berlin for several consecutive summers, as I did, made it less of an obsession, and more of a living reality. I had to learn how to look at what was happening around me and not just struggle with it in my worst nightmares. Keeping Germany at arm's length, with the distance of language, certainly helped. It made me realize that the new generations of Germans may have been torn by a similar ambivalence toward their own past. We had all reacted to it with whatever weapons we had at hand, language included, and it was fitting that it was through language as well, and not just with deadly weapons, that something could be done about it. □

1. Sex and genders in the *Polysexuality* issue, 1980; madness and art in the *Schizo-Culture* issue, 1978, etc.

2. Semiotext(e), *Nietzsche's Return*, 1978. Edited by Sylvère Lotringer.

3. Horst Mahler, lawyer and ex-member of the RAF, whom I met as well, has since become the head of the Nazi party in Germany and a Holocaust denier.

VOLKER SCHLÖNDORFF
Burying the Past

Sylvère Lotringer: It was a wonderful coincidence that we should meet here, in neutral grounds, as we are just about to republish *The German Issue*, originally issued in New York in 1982. Just one year before, in 1981, you directed a film, *Marianne and Juliane*,[1] which touched upon some of the same aspects of German politics that were documented in this issue, namely German terrorism.

Volker Schlöndorff: Actually I only produced *Marianne and Juliane*. It was directed by Margarethe von Trotta, my wife. The German title of the movie is *Die bleierne Zeit* ("Leaden Times"). It did not refer to "the lead in the bullet" as most people assumed—the Italian translation was "*Anni di piombo*," and in French "*Les Années de plomb*." In fact it came from Hölderlin,[2] a German poet born in the eighteenth century, who said that "these are leaden times," describing feelings of heaviness and oppression, visualizing them with "skies that feel like lead above you." And this was exactly the feeling Margarethe and I—our entire generation in fact—had in the 1950s, under the so-called Adenauer era. We had the feeling that we could not breathe, it weighed on us with such crushing force. It was one of the reasons why so many of us took off.

SL: And why you took off too. You don't seem to have liked the "Deutschland Modell" much.

VS: Definitely not. *Die bleierne Zeit* (AKA its English title *Marianne and Juliane*) in fact, was Margarethe von Trotta's second film, after she had been co-writer and co-director of *The Lost Honor of Katharina Blum*. It was, of course, a time when we were all politically very involved, often on the side of Heinrich Böll, against the hysteria of the media and the police, as well as against the nuclear arms race. It all culminated in the fall of 1978, when we reflected on the events with *Germany in Autumn*, a collective film by Fassbinder, Alexander Kluge, myself and others. All these movies were extremely popular with young and even middle-class audiences, because they were so different from the print and TV news. Not so much "leftist," rather just liberal in a good old "humanistic" way. When the Red Army Fraction prisoners in Stammheim were found dead in their cells—in my opinion they killed themselves—we decided to film the funeral in Stuttgart. The day before, we went to check the location, to scout where we would be able to place the camera, and so forth. We also went to the little funeral chapel and took some photographs there. The man from the funeral chapel had told us, "Come along, come along, I'll show you," and indeed he did; he opened the caskets and there was Andreas Baader, also Gudrun Ensslin and Jan-Carl Raspe. They didn't just look like corpses but almost like skeletons. Just prior to their death, they had been on a two-month hunger strike. To top it all, they had undergone an autopsy—their heads had been cut off, decapitated, in order to take out their brains. People were not aware that it was a standard procedure at the time, especially in the case of suicide. Anyhow—the heads were sewn back on, and the scars looked like a crown of thorns; it was altogether a rather strange experience, as you can imagine. When we left the chapel, a young woman suddenly stepped before us, and she looked just like the Gudrun Ensslin we had seen a moment before in the casket! She was just as young and sported the same regional accent as Gudrun had when she was alive. It was Gudrun's sister Christiane. She addressed us right away with a plea: "You've got to help me, please. They don't want to allow Gudrun and Baader to be buried on top of each other in the same grave. The administration gave us two graves for three caskets and usually, if there is a couple, they are buried together in the same grave. But now the administration of the cemetery says that this is only valid if you have a marriage certificate."

SL: This is amazing. One is never finished with bureaucracy.

VS: And she continued, "But it is well-known that they were a couple, that Baader was with Gudrun Ensslin—after all, the entire German Republic hated this couple—and yet they told me that it is not enough. You've got to help me." So Christiane put up this whole fight, and it reminded us right away of Antigone. Before this fight about the common grave for Baader and Ensslin, there had been another fight as to whether the three of them could be buried at all in the cemetery. The reasoning behind the argument was that it was asking too much from people who had their relatives buried in the same graveyard that they would lie next to a terrorist. How could a terrorist be buried next to my grandfather?

SL: They could be indoctrinated in their tomb.

VS: Manfred Rommel, son of the famous General Erwin Rommel and Lord Mayor of the city of Stuttgart then, finally made the decision. The dead prisoners were going to be buried there, so half of Antigone's fight was done. A little later I went on with Alexander Kluge to check out more location sights, and Margarethe was left behind. She ended up talking much longer with Christiane Ensslin and this talk was at the origin of the movie *Marianne and Juliane*.

SL: In a sense, this burial was like Germany itself. Death is not enough, it goes on.

VS: It goes on, yes.

SL: In year 2000 you directed another film—it was you who did it—called *The Legend of Rita*. It somehow picked up where the other film left off.

VS: Yes. It was this whole group of films: *Germany in Autumn*, *The Lost Honor of Katharina Blum*, the *Stammheim* movie by Reinhard Hauff, and, of course, Margarethe's film, *Marianne and Juliane*. Six months after the wall came down, we learned in the newspaper that eleven of the most wanted West German terrorists were in hiding in East Germany. This information was dropped by someone from the Stasi[3] [the East German secret police]. The Stasi person just showed up one day in Bonn and said, "I have some information you might be interested in. What is it worth to you?" Of course, his immunity had to be included in the bargain. And the information went that way. "Years ago, perhaps eight, we took in eleven terrorists, and gave them a 'legend'—hence the name of the movie *The Legend of Rita*—which means a new life, a new identity. We put them all over the country; in factories, administrative jobs. We put them up in apartments—they were very hard to get for East Germans at the time—but from then on they had to live the life of the working class. And they were not allowed to have any contact with each other." We wondered: why would the GDR [German Democratic Republic, more commonly known in English as

East Germany] do such a thing? Of course, we knew that they were craving to be recognized as a loyal state among other states; that they were eager to have a seat in the United Nations. So why would they harbor terrorists? There was also the next huge question, "How would the terrorists—in reality, they only were young anarchists out to break all the rules of the bourgeois class—*how* would they bear, how could they *tolerate* living in such a Stalinist society as East Germany?" It was just mind blowing! By today's accumulated information, it seems that this exchange had been prepared a long way back, perhaps as far back as 1968 or 1967. The Stasi had infiltrated the student movement in Berlin from the very beginning.

SL: Paradoxically then, these rebels now were forced to experience what they had been fighting for.

VS: Yes, but of course that was not their original intention at all. The way the refugees themselves tell the story is that they went to the Stasi officers in East Germany with whom they already had some contact. They had always used the route through East Germany to go from West Berlin to Beirut, Lebanon— there was a daily flight from East Berlin to Beirut—and from there on to the rest of the world. All it took was to catch the subway from West Berlin to Friedrichstrasse, and then they were home free. The Stasi had been watching them, and they asked, "You've got to help us. We are a group of eleven who do not want to go on with the violence. We don't want to go on with the ter- rorist fight. But we don't want to give ourselves up to the authorities in the West either." Unfortunately, unlike in Italy with the Brigate Rosse and the *repentiti*,[4] (those who repented) there was no such amnesty program in West Germany. So they pleaded, "Please help us go to Africa, to an Arab country, to Cuba, or to any of your brother states." The East German authorities thought about it and responded, "Yes, we agree to help you, but we can't send you elsewhere. That would be too dangerous. You have to stay with us so we can keep an eye on you. But other than that, we will give you anything you need."

SL: So it became some kind of live experiment. They did not know exactly what was in the offing. They became the guinea pigs of their own politics.

VS: Yes, it was very different. All of a sudden they were in a factory. They had to pretend that they came over from the West because any East German could tell right away that you were a West German, and vice versa. Their socialization, their childhood, just everything about them, would add up to the total sum of a different upbringing and personality. Once in a factory, they would betray themselves in a matter of minutes. So they were given these fake identities, and stories to boot. They had an uncle who died and he had always considered East Germany the better state; he told them that there was much more repression in the West, that the capitalist system was intolerable and so they had come on their own to live here. Now the factory worker in Dresden, for example, to whom they told that story, wouldn't believe a word, of course.

SL: There was no precedent that people would choose to move from West Berlin to East Berlin.

VS: No, nobody would do this. So already this pretense was difficult to maintain. But they also did not know how to behave. Say that there was some sort of a fundraising for Nicaragua. The collection list would go around, everybody would have to sign it and the "new East German" would contribute five Deutschmarks; then the list would be passed on to the next worker. Later the party member with the list would storm out of the room screaming, "Are you crazy? Why did you sign up for five Deutschmarks?" The "new" East German then said, "Well, it's for Nicaragua, you know, it's for solidarity." "But don't you see? We all put in only fifty pennies, half a mark! That money will never get there anyway! And besides, you make us all look very bad by putting up five marks!"

SL: The "real" East Germans had no illusion about the system.

VS: They certainly hadn't, no. Of course, there were eleven cases and hence eleven different stories. Most of the eleven who crossed over couldn't tolerate it, they were very unhappy. Almost all of them got married in some way or other, they got involved and tried to live a normal life. But only one or two really enjoyed it there. And that is the heroine we picked for the movie, *The Legend of Rita*, of course, as this was far more interesting. When the first signs of the wall coming down showed up, she was arguing with the workers in the factory, "What are you doing? What we have here is such an achievement, this is the social experiment mankind has been waiting for! Don't give in to the West just for all these consumer goods, you will deeply regret it." All of a sudden Rita became a kind of Rosa Luxemburg. And a co-worker told her, "Well, I would do it just for the jeans." And she shot back, "What's more important—a pair of jeans, or your backbone?" Of course a rhetorical question, ultimately the pair of jeans were more important.

SL: But it was not as if the East was tightly cut off from the West. In East Germany they watched the television from the other side, and there was no way they could get all these products. The good life was just at hand, and they couldn't get any part of it.

VS: Exactly. Because of the television and of the commercials on television, the East Germans had the wrong idea of the West. It was like a virtual reality, like *The Truman Show* by Peter Weir. If you mistake what you see on television for real, if you can't differentiate between the reality you are living and what you see on television, well then you are in for a tough awakening the day you are confronted with real problems. That's what happened after the fall of the wall, when East Germans discovered quite a different West than the one they had imagined.

SL: Commercials were the best possible capitalist propaganda. Consumerism, anyway, had been a direct answer to class struggle. If one managed to erase social classes, capitalism would win. The fascists tried this before in a time of crisis. They managed to abolish classes by forging a personal allegiance to the Führer. The experiment proved much too costly and half of Europe was destroyed. They had to find another way to achieve the same goal.

VS: East Germans wouldn't listen to the words, they only saw the images—the washing machines and the cars, the clothes—and they would said, "OK, it is the money that we want—the Deutschmark." And that's what they went for in the end.

SL: *The Legend of Rita* was released in the year 2000.

VS: Yes, but it had taken ten years to make the movie. Nobody wanted to partake in it.

SL: It only worked after the wall fell.

VS: It was afterwards, yes.

SL: Then it became a reflection on what had happened to Germany as an experiment in socialism.

VS: Yes.

SL: A reflection on the relation between socialism and capitalism. The question raised *with* Germany, as one puts down a question mark with a pen, also concerned the entire world at the time.

VS: Yes, that's right.

SL: The film also became a film about the victory of the market over socialism. And whether there could be a future to socialism at all as long as it kept being thwarted by these kinds of violent confrontations.

VS: There was a moment of fleeting hope at that time that one could keep the best of both worlds. You know, the famous "socialism with a human face," envisaging all kinds of mitigations between the two systems. Some people would say, "Let's try a confederation: we'll keep a kind of moderate socialism in the former GDR and we'll just associate the two states into a confederation." Well, that was pure daydreaming as reality quickly proved. The seventeen million East Germans would have quit their confederate state ASAP and all would have moved over to the capitalist state.

SL: And you think that they could possibly have stayed?

VS: Yes, they could have done it at the very moment the wall came down and if a confederation had been created. But the East Germans started crossing over by the hundreds of thousands and it became an urgent matter to switch the monetary system immediately and introduce the Deutschmark in East Germany as well. Otherwise almost everyone would have gone to where the Deutschmark was.

SL: That was why the wall had been built in the first place—to prevent people from leaving.

VS: Initially, yes. It certainly was not out of any political conviction, or did not involve freedom in any political sense—a parliamentarian system and a freedom to vote for your delegates. I don't think that was one of their major concerns. Only the freedom to consume, the freedom to travel—it was a very important concern, though.

SL: So the wall went down, but immediately something else went up to replace it.

VS: Well, we didn't know that at the time. When the wall came down we thought, in Willy Brandt's words, "We'll grow together what belongs together."

We will merge again. And that was the feeling so many of us had during the first years. But it soon turned out that the wall was more in the mind, exactly like in 1945 when some people claimed that this was Germany *hour zero*, and that we would/could start a whole new society. Well, you couldn't do it because you had people from the former society. And they had all these thinking patterns and the mentality of the previous one. And it became more and more evident as the years passed. And now, twenty years later, it is an extremely strong feeling, a real conviction: there are indeed two different sets of minds. Even the generation born after the wall came down, over the last twenty years, idolizes the society from the past. That's the way parents and schools transmitted the historical experience, embellishing what they remembered of it. Now, instead of the wall you have a sort of mental barrier. Not for everyone, but for the majority of East and West Germans. Let's look back at this experiment where you take twin brothers at birth and you separate them. You raise them in two different systems and after forty years you bring them together again. The purpose was to determine the influence of the environment and the influence of genetics in the development of the person.

SL: They did these kinds of experiments with children in the eighteenth century.

VS: And here we got the result on a large scale—seventeen million people on one side and sixty million on the other. And you can tell, well, "Das Sein bestimmt das Bewusstsein" [One's existence determines one's consciousness]. The influence of the social system was so strong that even after forty years these brothers still are different.

SL: Now another paradox: East Germany was based on the fact that they didn't inherit anything from the Nazi state. They were trained to feel that West Germany inherited the past and they were immune from it. While putting this issue together and talking to many people, I realized that there was much more awareness among the younger generation in the West about what had happened in WWII. In East Germany, which was much more controlled and repressive, they made people believe that they shared no responsibility for it.

VS: Well, yes, again it was a question of teaching. In East Germany the emphasis was put not on the Holocaust, but on anti-fascism. And even though they produced movies on Buchenwald, they said that Buchenwald was liberated by a Communist cell within the "Lager" [camp], and not through any Jewish resistance, or the Americans. The heroes of the Resistance were invariably the anti-fascists. They were convinced that, "We are the inheritors of the anti-fascists, so we are free of guilt."

SL: The same happened in France. Originally tainted by the German-Soviet Pact of 1941, the French communists ended up taking the lead of the Resistance inside France, while the Gaullists were trying to impose their legitimacy from London. As a result...

VS: …everybody in France was…

SL and VS [in chorus]: … in the Resistance!

SL: Yes. It took them fifteen years to acknowledge that France had collaborated with the enemy. So paradoxically, East Germany and France had something in common: they did not feel responsible for what had happened.

VS: The other facet was that East Germany claimed that it purged its administration of former Nazis, which most likely was true. A lot of Nazis, realizing that they would be prosecuted in East Germany, left in a hurry to the West, where they felt more protected. So indeed there were less Nazis in East Germany than in other countries. Some of them, of course, like everywhere else, were integrated into the police, and were immediately incorporated into the existing system. I can only say this from hearsay, because I didn't grow up in East Germany. But the astonishing thing was what happened after the wall came down. In East Germany there were about sixty thousand Vietnamese workers, and thousands of Cuban and African students. They all had been protected by the government as an act of solidarity. These were "our" brothers. But after the wall came down, there was this sudden outburst of racial incidents in East Germany. Now this, according to the book, shouldn't have happened at all. They had all been given an anti-fascist education and they all had been raised to feel solidarity with the Third World, especially with the Socialist brother states. You could have imagined there would be incidents against the Russians, but nothing of that sort happened. And there it was: black people, and especially Vietnamese, could not go out into the streets at night anymore in certain places. The hatred that had been repressed or controlled by the State for forty years totally exploded. "They take our jobs, they take our women, whatever—and they have too much fun in life, especially the Cubans and the Africans." It was this kind of hatred that apparently had accumulated. The most tragic was the case of these sixty thousand Vietnamese. The GDR had sent weapons to help North Vietnam during the war, and in exchange they sent Vietnamese to work at East German factories—you might say as slaves, since they had not been consulted. They had been allowed to bring their families, though. And now, as the wall came down, people from the Republic of Vietnam didn't want to take them back. They had the clear feeling, "We are unwanted here, but we can't go home either." A lot of them ultimately lost their jobs and started to traffic with cigarettes. They were criminalized almost instantly. And nowadays, when you say "a Vietnamese," it is almost always synonymous with trafficker or criminal.

SL: In the conversation I had with Heiner Müller, the great East German dramaturge, he made a point of telling me that East Germany was much more open to the Third World than the West, and that Moscow looked like a Napoleonic camp with all the Asians that you find there.

VS: He was speaking in favor of the socialist state. Nowadays, even in Russia or in Moscow, Asians have a very hard time and the fascist movement is much stronger in the former anti-fascist state [the GDR] than in the former Federal Republic.

SL: It is a strange experience re-reading this conversation with Müller now. We were both aware that we weren't just talking to each other, but that everything we said would be simultaneously addressed to the West and to the authorities in East Germany. He deliberately used a coded language, often praising East Germany for its obvious failings. What he said about his theater perfectly applied to our dialogue: "I can say one thing and mean the contrary." He was very good at it while showing his hand and bluntly admitting many things that the functionaries of the party may not have liked. It was a tight-rope exercise, but we both realized the limits and the possibilities it offered. He was used to dodging censorship, and he could count on his audience to react to his plays as he would have wanted them to. It makes his language more difficult to understand among those who didn't share that kind of experience, of course. He knew that his notoriety in the West was used to legitimate the East, and he had to watch closely whatever he said publicly. But this earned him the privilege of circulating freely—most of the time—on both sides of the wall. Still he chose to remain in East Berlin. This tension and indirectness was necessary for his work. His passport was always revocable and, I remember in one of my visits, waving at him from a distance as he accompanied me to the border. Actually I felt pretty sad about it. You are one of those people who left Germany, but it was West Germany.

VS: Yes.

SL: Maybe it happened by chance, but you recognize…

VS: No, it was not chance at all, it was deliberate. In the 1950s, because of these "leaden skies" mentioned before, a lot of young Germans tried to escape the country. On the one hand, they did not like to share the guilt, they did not like to be Germans, but they wanted to be Europeans. It was a way to unload.

SL: Once outside, they often pretended to be Swedish or Norwegian—everything but German. They were a bit like Jews in that respect. They had to hide who they were.

VS: Yes, and America was far away. There were no cheap flights to go there at that time, the cheapest way to go was on the transatlantic boat. But borders were open. You could go to France or Italy. So it was half the old "Wanderlust" by Goethe, you know, going to Italy like Hans Werner Henze the composer, or Enzensberger, and many others who went to Italy. For me, living on the Rhine river and the Rhine valley, near Frankfurt, Main, Mainz, the next logical step was France—it was just across the river. And we were attracted to Paris. We thought of "Paris, l'amour," of course, adolescently, but also of a freer country, a freer society, unburdened by the past. Well, once I was there, I went to a Jesuit boarding school. I loved it there, especially being Protestant, I did not have to follow all the religious rituals. I was the only Protestant, but there were quite a few Islamic youngsters, Moroccans and Tunisians, in that school, and they didn't have to go to mass either. So we sat together and they started introducing me to colonialism. Hence the realization that I had come from a country with a dark past, but as they stated, "Not everything in France is as bright as you think." The Indochina war was still going on—the French-Vietnam war—and another one had just started in Algeria. Morocco had just gained its independence, and war literally happened in France. So I realized I could neither escape history, nor the fact that politics was part of our lives. And that was the reason why very quickly I became radicalized—because of the Algerian war. Even though as a German I really had no responsibility in it whatsoever, and I could have said, "You do whatever you want," when we received *The Question*, the book by Henri Alleg about torture in Algeria, I took fifty copies in my suitcase and smuggled them into the Lycee Henri IV and started to distribute and sell them under the table. Naively, idealistically, because I thought that we had once let that happen in Germany, and that this should not happen again wherever, in no country in the world. And "La Mouffe" [the popular Mouffetard district in Paris] was right around the corner. A lot of Algerians were also living in Maubert, these kinds of districts. Some sixteen of them, one morning, were found floating in the Seine river, murdered, of course. So you had a very strong feeling that this time you couldn't just be an onlooker, you had to partake. This was not just my sentiment, but one I shared with all the students I was with. And it was an extremely radical movement then in 1959–1960; it was much tougher than what happened with the German terrorism and the RAF later on and on a much larger scale. So at the time when the terrorism and violence started in Germany, I felt I had been immunized already. I had seen it before.

SL: Believe it or not, I left France for the same reasons. I didn't feel entirely at ease there either and only understood why I left much later on. Actually this issue on Germany helped me figure out a few things, settle my accounts, but in a kind of positive way, opening myself up to the reality I was investigating. It was no coincidence that this was the last magazine issue that I did. I was very active as well in the French student movement at the same time as you were and participated in the resistance against the war in Algeria. And I did it pretty much for the same reason as you did, although I had been brought up in France and you were coming from Germany.

VS: The German Left in general, and the terrorists in particular, always suspected that what was on the other side of the wall, in East Germany or in all the socialist countries for that matter, was not *really* socialism. Otherwise, instead of becoming terrorists in the West, they could have just gone to the East. And they had constantly been invited to do so. "If you are not happy here, why don't you go to the other side?" the conservative and bourgeois liberal press kept asking them. And I must say, in retrospect, that it was a very valid argument. We didn't want to hear it, though. This was the argument of our parents. But of a generation who, in part, had spent time in prison camps and came back from Siberia and elsewhere. So they knew better what the system was like and that it wouldn't work. But the Left would not accept the argument at all. There was a complete blindness, especially in West Berlin, on the true nature of the system in the East. Nobody would even admit the existence of the gulags. They were convinced that it was different, that it couldn't be compared with what had happened under the fascists. They wanted to have the revolution in West Berlin. And had they succeeded in overthrowing the municipality of West Berlin, they would have automatically become part of the GDR. They would have become what they did not want to be. So the whole revolution, the movement at the Free University and so forth—I already was a filmmaker, I was not part of it—was lacking in credibility. I don't think they ever wanted to take over and take responsibility, initiate a real revolution. All they wanted was to annoy the government.

SL: But isn't it incredible that in Berlin you had it all—there was a wall dividing the East and West, socialism and capitalism. The wonder is how could anyone believe in East Germany at the time? One could not get out of West Berlin without crossing the whole length of East Germany, and the police were controlling everything along the road. You couldn't stop anywhere, even for a second, without the police jumping on you. How could it be possible that people who were so conscious of the past would be so blind to the present?

VS: They saw it the other way around. Since they were walled in, the wall was not really in the GDR, it was, in fact, around West Berlin. They thought that revolution might be possible within these walls, within this fortress. I don't think anybody in Munich, Frankfurt or Düsseldorf thought that revolution could overthrow the government. But in this small entity, in this enclave of West Berlin, the "revolutionists" thought it was possible. Did they believe they would have a sort of ideal socialist state just within West Berlin and outside would be Soviet socialism? I don't think anybody thought that far ahead. I don't think they really meant it.

SL: They were just being rebellious.

VS: They were rebellious, yes. It was a cultural revolution. The rebellion was against the parents, against the generation of teachers, against structures within the university more than within the society, because the workers were pretty happy there. *They* didn't want to be liberated.

SL: Berlin had a special status in Germany at that time. A lot of young men settled in West Berlin as a way of avoiding conscription.

VS: That was the other big issue. And a whole different chapter. Let's call it: "German pacifists." The ones who say, "*You* go and fight Al-Qaeda, *you* go and fight so and so, *we* are pacifists." It's like watching a murder perpetrated on the other side of the street and saying, "You can go over there and stop them, but I am non-violent, I stay on this side." This was a huge fact, as you mentioned, that the majority of the students came to West Berlin because there they would be exempted from the military service, from the draft—at that time there still was a general draft. They were pacifists. They did not want to enter the army, not even in peace times, but they also were under the unrealistic illusion that you could free the Third World with pacifist means. And that is perhaps one reason that led the RAF to more violent actions. A very small portion of them said, "Violence is general in the world, therefore we partake in it, and we will use it." Now the RAF did not want to overthrow the German government. They were anti-imperialists, they were fighting for Palestine, for example.

SL: But the RAF was not alone. A lot of people among the alternative movement who were not in favor of violence still considered the terrorists as their comrades. The same thing happened in Italy. The Red Brigades had an entourage that, at least at the beginning, offered them solidarity and protection. This stopped later on, when they felt blackmailed and manipulated by the terrorists.

VS: Yeah. Even in retrospect I don't quite understand how it could have become so violent and so radical.

SL: It was not just in Germany at the time, it was...

VS: … a worldwide phenomenon.

SL: It was the last outburst of communist ideology. Communist parties were just about selling out everywhere. There was no communist party in Germany, the Italian party was allying itself with the Christian-Democrats (it was the "historical compromise"). In France, everything closed down after May 1968, the communist party remained Stalinist, but had lost credibility. One hundred and fifty years of class struggle and the belief that it was possible to overcome capitalism were coming to an end. It was "the end of ideologies," as the French called it.

VS: In 1967–68, the students, myself included, really the entire generation, indulged in the idea that we could totally change our ways of life, and totally change society. A year or two later, this kind of fell flat on the nose. As a consequence, the vast majority went into some kind of resignation, a few committed suicide while others went in the opposite direction. They believed that we had not been violent enough. What they needed were guns. It took a while to get there and all the fights were meant to stop this escalation. The only reason why Margarethe and I, Heinrich Böll and others, got involved was that we could see their actions escalating from a little *Kaufhausbrand*—a little arson in a department store—to liberating Andreas Baader from prison. A guard was shot during the escape. Nobody had planned to have an armed faction. It escalated and escalated and at some point you could hear the gasp, "But nobody wanted this." Hitler had a plan from the beginning, including the Holocaust, the invasion of France, Poland and all that, but the student's movement did not have a plan.

SL: Italian terrorists sprung from the workers in the Fiat factories. They were orthodox Marxists-Leninists who took it where the Communist Party had left it. It was a *hysterical* reaction to its renunciation of the class struggle.

VS: It was hysteria on both sides, and not just the government. The vast majority of the population was so happy to have finally achieved—via the so-called "economic miracle"—a certain well-being, traveling, and so forth. They were very self-satisfied, no more questions asked. And all of a sudden comes this generation which keeps asking questions. "What did you do in the war? What's under the carpet?" So that made them angry. And when, on top of that, they grabbed a gun and resorted to violence, it was more than they could take. The media got into it and the government just followed. Sadly, the original force behind it were the people. They exploded immediately. All that mentality which had been swept under the carpet now exploded with a big noise.

SL: The big noise was the silent majority.

VS: Yes.

SL: You made films on the division of Germany. Now twenty years after the wall was removed, do you think there are questions about that experience that we couldn't have asked at the time?

VS: I didn't ask the question. It came to me. I left New York for Berlin after the wall came down in 1990–91. I came to make movies, but instead of that I ended up helping to reform and to renovate the East German film studios which used to be the former UFA (Universum Film AG) studios of the 1920s. It was just an enterprise as any other, an industrial enterprise in East Germany. We had 710 people on the payroll, and all of a sudden, I was in charge of this project. And the question was: how come they lived forty years under socialism, and *nothing* worked? You know the old story: "We pretend to work and they pretend to pay us." But well then, why didn't you plant flowers, why weren't the streets ever paved? "Well, we didn't have anything to do it with." There was a total lack of initiative. There was the feeling that nothing should change. And I came to realize that this socialism that we had dreamt of not only had destroyed the economy, the habitat and the environment—it had really destroyed the people, it had broken their back, their sense of initiative, of individual responsibility. It took a couple of years until I came to the conclusion that we don't have any choice but to stay with the market economy. The market economy seems to address people far better. The mistake was *planification*. I don't know if it works elsewhere.

SL: But that was *bureaucratic planification*.

VS: I suddenly became a fervent believer in the free market. And then last year the financial collapse made me wonder whether a free economy could work without a certain degree of regulation. That's where I am standing now. Therefore, the fall of the wall, the collapse of the socialist system, on the economic side strictly speaking, keeps reminding us that this may not be the solution. This experiment has been going on for eighty years in Europe, and it didn't work, whatever the circumstances. But we cannot accept the way it currently is either. We saw that from the financial crisis. So what might be a new way? I think the search for a third way is the result of the fall of the wall. The necessity of running production and distribution of goods in the world in another way. There must be another way. □

— *Saas-Fee, Switzerland, June 7, 2009*

1. *Marianne and Juliane*, 1981, is a film directed by Margarethe von Trotta. Its original German title is *Die bleierne Zeit*, which can be translated as "the heavy ('leaden') times." The film was released in the UK as *The German Sisters*. The screenplay is a fictionalized account of the true lives of Christiane Ensslin, a politically active journalist and militant feminist, and her sister Gudrun, who chose the path of armed struggle and joined the Red Army Fraction [RAF] and was found dead in her prison cell in Stammheim, near Frankfurt, in 1977. In the film, von Trotta depicts the two sisters Juliane (Christine) and Marianne (Gudrun) through their friendship and journey to understanding each other. *Marianne and Juliane* was von Trotta's second film and established her position as a director of the New German Cinema. She was the first German filmmaker to be awarded the Golden Lion, the main prize of the Venice Film Festival.

2. The quote comes from Hölderlin's poem, "The Passage to the Country." Christian Friedrich Hölderlin (1777–1843) was a major German lyric poet who spent most of his life tormented by mental illnesses. In Italy, "leaden" was interpreted as the lead in the bullets used by armed groups of the extreme Left, especially the *Brigate Rosse*. This important shift towards the years of terrorist violence can also be found in the French "Années de plomb" and finally seeped into the German.

3. Stasi. Contraction of "StaatsSicherheitsdienst." Designates the political police directed by the department of Internal Affairs of the GDR [German Democratic Republic].

4. The Red Brigades (*Brigate Rosse* in Italian, often abbreviated as the *BR*) were a terrorist communist-inspired group responsible for political assassinations and bank robberies during the "Years of Lead." *Pentiti* designates people in Italy who, in the late '70s, agreed to "repent" and collaborate with the judicial system to fight terrorism. Their correct technical name in Italian is *collaboratori di giustizia* ("collaborators with justice").

Editor for German Issue	*Sylvère Lotringer*
Editorial Committee (Berlin)	*Peter Gente*
	Frank Mecklenburg, Heidi Paris
Associate Editors (New York)	*Jim Fleming, Etienne Li,*
	Frank Mecklenburg, Marc Parent,
	Dagmar Stern, Brigitte Vial
Issue Design	*Martim Avillez, Sylvère Lotringer,*
	Michael Oblowitz
Design Consultant	*Gil Eisner*
Translation	*Dagmar Stern (Editor), Ruth Crowley,*
	John Johnston, Andy Gould,
	Susan Ray, Howard Stern
Assistant Editors	*Karen Hornick, Bill Fisher, Peter Walker*
Production	*Catherine Poussard, Kate Doyle, Nathalie Martin*
Production Assistants	*Kathy Acker, George Alexander, Zoe Beloff,*
	Kanak Dixit, David Blanchard, Hans Brockmann,
	Susan Flato, Paul Foss, David Haik,
	Cesar Loaiza, James McLaughlin, Mister,
	Fred Nolan, Roman Paska, Mark Polizotti,
	Tim Simone, John Richardson, Maurizio Torrealta,
	Ulrich Thiele, Lisa Vasami
Cover Photographs	Front: *German Information Center*
	Back: *Paul Virilio*
Cover Design	*Martim Avillez, Michael Oblowitz, Catherine Poussard*

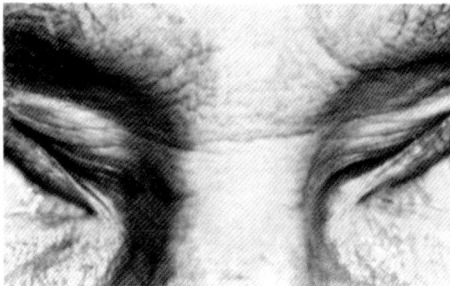

General Editor	*Sylvère Lotringer*
Editor-Manager	*Jim Fleming*
Editorial Committee	*Denise Green, Denis Hollier,*
	Sylvère Lotringer, Roger McKeon,
	John Rajchman, Pat Steir
Design Committee	*Martim Avillez, Kathy Bigelow, Diego Cortez,*
	Denise Green, Joseph Kosuth, Michael Oblowitz,
	Pat Steir

Special thanks to Henry Ries for the many photos of the Berlin Wall

THE GERMAN ISSUE

semiotext(e)

I: writing on the wall

II: wall of fire

III: wall-to-wall

IV: the atlantic wall

V: off the wall

HERBERT ACHTERNBUSCH
America

Thanks to Heiner Müller I enjoyed a three week stay in America (financed by the Goethe Institut), in the California cities of Holy Francisco and Last Angeles. He recommended me to Tom Luddy. Tom Luddy is the boss at the Pacific Film Archives in Berkeley, and I owe it to him that I finally received a professional evaluation of two of my films. He recognized, namely, that they are great films because they consistently expand from an obscure beginning to a logical end. He said that under the friendly California sun which laughed in a friendly way as only poached trout do in Germany. He wore a small yellow feather, a canary yellow feather, on his grey Hammett hat. His facial features are enigmatic, his mouth not talkative. His mind likes to emit the name Wim. Whenever I was with Tom I knew exactly where Wim was: writing his script, and what he planned for the next few days: scriptwriting. When I planned to meet him at Coppola's house, Wim called a half hour before midnight to say that he would meet me somewhere at half past. It was Friday and he didn't have time because he had to finish his Hammett script by Monday. On Monday I met him at Coppola's office, in the hallway, more grown-up than ever, and he had no time because he had to finish his script by Friday. Which he has

---

Herbert Achternbusch is a Bavarian writer and filmmaker known for his non-conformist positions.

CHRISTO
Wrapping Up Germany

Sylvère Lotringer: What induced you to undertake the apparently incongruous project of wrapping the Reichstag?

Christo: Until now, all my projects have been situated in the Western world and within only one system. For the Reichstag project, we had to negotiate simultaneously, and for the first time, within two different systems. What I was mainly interested in, was to work in a place where the separation between both Berlins was obvious. I am fascinated by the physicality of this separation, its demonstrative character. It is not a frontier border in the countryside, but a city, one of the biggest and the most remarkable in the world from an urban point of view, which is divided like that.

SL: What have been the consequences of this division, from an urban point of view?

been writing now for over two years. I had the impression that Coppola keeps his eye on him. Tom said that Wim will become an American, that he knows his way around America better than Tom himself, but it was said with an undertone that suggested no American in America wants to know his way around like a German. Damn it, I was standing too close to this lowerlip Coppola, I offered him a punch (sic) of snuff and already he was talking about his Octoberfest visit when he ate snuff in the pissoir. I recommended my Octoberfest film to him because he seems to know all too well how it runs. His old house was nice and green, and there was a restaurant below called Wim and there was a Wimburger which I downed (downed because it was so huge), and I swear that I ate no other burger during my visit because I too thought I was stricken with Wimeritis. How can a man who radiates such seriousness produce so much trivia? Herzog had tattooed on his shoulder a skull which stuck out its fleshy tongue, and he had trouble with Fox. Brandner[1] followed an actor with a dark look. I didn't belong here, I listened to the noises, let myself be driven over the Golden Gate Bridge, enjoyed Frisco as it awaited its decline, huddled together. The Bay is said to be clean once again and stocked with fish. At this crossing the Mafia caused a car accident, and Kurosawa has already chucked two stars from his new film, and I also had time to myself. Yes! Yes! No! No! The Director of the Goethe Institut showed us the redwoods, those mammoth trees that just stand there and let people look under their skirts and are shamelessly tall. And then, for the second time, I met a Negro painted white; he was from Iran, he was from France, he was from Germany, where he almost has a harder time than I do raising money for his films, for his austere films, films so beautiful that other films look like frivolous

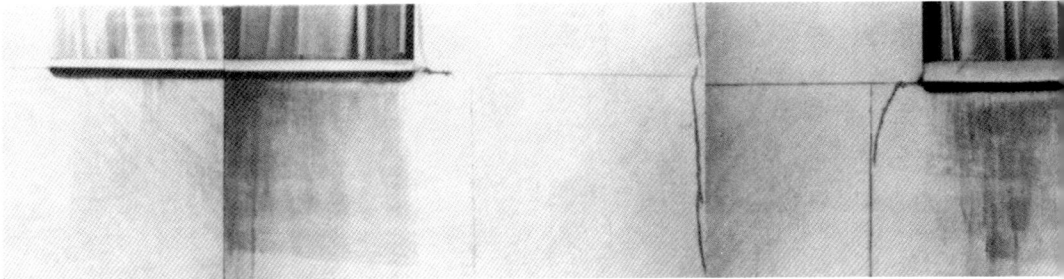

C: On one side is East Berlin, which includes the former administrative headquarters of the city. The Eastern part has been entirely rebuilt according to a totalitarian urban plan, like in Bulgaria or Hungary, with spacious but empty avenues sort of Kafkaesque, obviously conceived for groups, never individuals. On the other side is West Berlin, which corresponds to the old residential neighborhoods. It has been rebuilt in the flamboyant style of capitalism, with neon lights, concrete, and glass walls.

SL: In a word, the window dressing of the West. What about the Reichstag?

C: Besides its enormous dimensions, there is nothing unusual about it. Its structure is completely trivial. It looks like a Nineteenth Century casino.

SL: What's important is obviously its symbolic value.

C: Its symbolism is, in fact, mostly inappropriate. Hitler hated the Reichstag, which symbolized German democracy. After the 1933 fire, he had his parliament installed in the big opera house. It was only in 1943-44 that Goring, who presided over the Reichstag, held the last Nazi parliamentary session there. Furthermore, in Albert Speer's project to planify Berlin, it is obvious that the Reichstag would have been one of the first buildings to disappear. Which did not keep the Russians, in a famous photograph taken a few days

underwear. How is it possible that such frivolous films are made in Germany? Because it is possible, I said. The only right answer. In LA, too, a good-for-nothing from the Film Subsidies Board was prowling around, I don't remember the name, Today or Yesterday. I called these little films Filmburgers, which amused the Yankees. For no matter how glued on their smile is — glued on to be pulled off — they let themselves be carried away and laugh. Even in my films they laughed at scenes and at sentences where the German audience pretended to think. But to get back to this Iranian director who makes the best German films, he suddenly appeared and everything got easier for me. Because he didn't like America, it was easier for me to find something to like. (In Germany we don't have even one postage stamp that says writing is the source of democracy.) I liked the elephantitis of young American women. LA's diffuseness was nice. The mocking emptiness of Universal, however, was not. (I thought to myself, though, that I want to see the Fox Studios again.) Asked by the wife of the Goethe Institut director, this filmmaker said that "Knife in the Ass" is an anarchic animated film. At a public discussion we said nothing because once someone talked about the absent Hauffs and Bohms,[2] and, as Herzog rightly pointed out, these Americans couldn't comprehend that there isn't only *one* German cinema. Therefore, the Goethe Institut should be thankful that this Bavarian and this Iranian didn't sing but drank whiskey. Moreover, the discussion took place before our films were shown, and you have to be a real driveler just to be able to talk about films, and if I have to talk with someone after seeing my film, then he is also a real driveler. Of course we were supposed to be representatives: the film festival of the reserve troups, as the third squadron we were supposed to mark off the terrain for the heroes, to

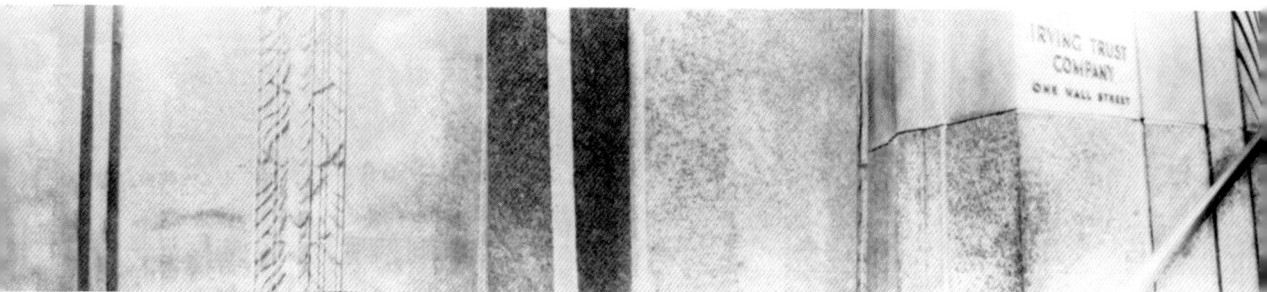

before the end of the war, from representing a katiouchka machine-gun next to a rocket on which was written: "Vo Reichstago" (for the Reichstag).

SL: Even when inappropriate, symbols can be deadly. There have been ferocious fights over the Reichstag.

C: The Reichstag was not important, from a military point of view, in the battle of Berlin. Of course, not far away were Hitler's bunker and Göring's Chancellery, the latter linked to the Reichstag by a tunnel which was supposedly used to set fire to the building in 1933. Two Nazi commandos defended the Reichstag like mad, step by step, floor by floor, with the same lack of purpose as the Russians who lost two thousand men in attempting to take hold of it. I have the feeling that they were sacrificed for a mere photograph, the famous photograph of the Russian soldier waving the Soviet flag on the roof of the Reichstag. I have a photograph of the inside of the building where one can see inscriptions in Cyrillic.

SL: Which shows that the Russian soldiers knew how to write. What happened to the Reichstag after the war?

C: It remained in ruins until the end of the Fifties. In 1960, Bonn's government spent

10

some sixty million dollars restoring it. They wanted to make a historic building out of it, a kind of meeting place for the future parliament.

SL: The Reichstag is no longer the seat of Federal Germany's parliament?

C: No. The Russians refuse to allow the structure to be used for political purposes. No minister of the Federal Republic is allowed to enter it, only members of the four allied countries. A year ago, Schmidt* came with Andreotti, the Italian prime minister, to show him the Reichstag. The Soviet jeeps kept him from coming close to it. To allow him to enter the Reichstag would have set a political precedent.

SL: So it isn't used at all.

C: It is used as a historical museum of the city of Berlin. Sometimes, scientific congresses are held there, but never political ones.

SL: As I understand it, there are no more reasons to set the Reichstag on fire. Wasn't it a Bulgarian who was accused of setting it on fire?

C: The accused was a Dutch anarchist, but Georgi Dimitrov, a Bulgarian communist leader and a very important figure of the Comintern, the Communist International, was

11

demonstrate the unlimited possibilities in German film, we two nihilists who always escape the tentacles of positive ass-licking by means of horror, these know-it-alls without spark. What could you talk about if it wasn't even certain that the films would arrive from one day to the next. Ron Holloway tried hard to get the prints, the Goethe Institut let him use their telephone so that he could shake the Export Union out of their coma, and the secretary Erika paraded in front of him so that his gaze didn't freeze with his waiting ear. He accompanies a package of German films with charming patience through various American cities, building up an organization in Minneapolis which — instead of a distributor — is supposed to help place the films of progressive filmmakers directly with the cinema owners. The traditional wheeler dealers say it will never work. With his wife Dorothea, Holloway prepared a brochure for which he was author, editor and manager. Only after it was finished did the FFA (Film Subsidies Board) graciously provide the printing costs. FFA is in fact the abbreviation for Film Fetus Board because it acts more as an abortion clinic than a funding board. Who is the scriptwriter Peter Steinbach, Herzog asked quite rightfully. He is pictured in the brochure sitting over a cup of coffee, looking glumly at a self-made film. The Bavarian and the Iranian were carried away by the excellent projection of their films at the Castro in San Francisco. The theatre has stood there proudly since 1913 with its 1500 seats. That was something else compared to the dingy or luxurious mini-theatres in Munich. The name of the Iranian director, who makes the best German films, is Sohrab Shahid Saless. Is he the first that would support me for Chekhov? At the Vox (sic) Venice cinema I saw his documentary film "Die langen Ferien der Lotte H. Eisner" (The Long Vacation of Lotte H. Eisner). Watch out for creativity, I

also allegedly involved in the attempt. Dimitrov wasn't just anybody. He was a bright lawyer who spoke very good German. The Nazis wanted to use Dimitrov's trial for propaganda, but he undertook his own defense and turned the trial into an all-out attack against the Nazis. Dimitrov made a famous retort to Göring, who had accused him of being a Bulgarian savage: "When your King was still speaking German to his horses, the Bulgarians already had an alphabet and wrote poetry."

SL: Was Dimitrov accused of having inspired the attempt?

C: Not of inspiring it, but of having physically perpetrated it. The German legislation at that time made it impossible to condemn the nationals of another country. The Bulgarian Tsar, who was of German descent, deprived Dimitrov of his Bulgarian citizenship; but Stalin, in a bold move, immediately conferred on him Soviet citizenship! Later, Dimitrov became the first president of the Democratic Bulgarian Republic. A monument was erected in his name.

SL: And you erect a monument to the Reichstag. Weren't the Germans shocked by the fact that you too are Bulgarian? A Bulgarian sets the Reichstag on fire, another comes to wrap it up...

heard her say again and again. The Nazis sent her to Paris on vacation, but she never wanted to return to her fatherland. She is poor, but rich in spirit, which the FRG* today still doesn't know how to use. Sohrab told her about me, my films. "...and I have the feeling I would like them. I'd like to show them all at the Cinemathéque française. How is it that your films aren't distributed in Paris like those of Werner Herzog, Wim Wenders and Fassbinder?" Her letter is postmarked with a Swiss stamp on which Thomas Mann looks back severely at Germany. Yes, how is that? It looks as if the German cultural institutes will not have enough money to provide French titles for my films. Yes, we come from the land of culture. (And the Goethe Institut is more an artists-in-residence enterprise than a cultural institution.) Don't forget, it is embarrassing enough to appear in foreign countries, because I am not at the beginning only H.A. but also the representative of a culture. I come from a 700 year old family which has always produced oppositional peasants and only two bootlickers, a bishop and a high level administrator in the 17th century. And now here I am, feeling all too strongly the impropriety of public life. I quickly got the Yankees on my side with my clownery. Or I sent them packing with questions about Germany. (And America? If America is a dog, I said, then we have the dog shit.) I do not feel responsible for Germany. I do not care how many states this monster had in the past or has in the present. The potential injustice in any state cannot be so great that the people do not identify with it. The German people have only really accepted one form of state, dictatorship. I tried to relax in California, which I was able to do for hours while watching the Pacific. If you asked the girls whether the sun was always so delightful here, they were happy. My room was also robbed once. And I got to know a

C: I am not keeping my Bulgarian origins a secret. But the *Pravda* editorial that condemned the Reichstag project didn't even mention that I was a refugee from Eastern Europe.

SL: And what about the Bulgarians, did they think it was an oblique way to do homage to Dimitrov?

C: On the contrary. My brother was questioned by the authorities of the Bulgarian State Department of Culture about the Reichstag. Dimitrov, in Bulgaria, is a little like Washington.

SL: Are you interested in what the Bulgarians think of this project?

C: Yes, but I am much more concerned with the Soviet government's reaction, for they have a direct effect on the present negotiations.

SL: Why must you take the Soviet government's reactions into account?

C: Technically, the whole structure of the Reichstag falls within the British zone. But in fact, the facade, to a depth of 28 meters, is under Russian control.

SL: Is it guarded by the army?

cowboy with whom I drank a bottle of Tequila-Tokillyou. Even Wolfgang Ebert appeared, who didn't want to be a car in San Francisco. And I stayed away from drugs and laughed uncontrollably anyway when Sohrab had his calf humped by a dog named Badweiser, even though he tried to be friendly toward the little bitch. The best American beer is also called Badweiser. I told jokes and made faces and represented German culture. I had my newest play in my pocket, GUST, a 34 page monologue by an old man who summarizes his life while his wife goes through her silent struggle with death. He was fit for life, a spend-thrift, and saved the above mentioned 700 year old family. I wrote the play in Austria, it was too loud here, too inhuman and ugly. Sentences I have been storing up for 35 years. And whenever I found someone who was culture-starved in America, I spoke these sentences about the play. And if someone was cunning, he recognized my own situation. (Electric power line = Germany / the leather cap = my artistic creativity). Gust once went to his cousin Otto's, a farmer in Nattenberg. There were clouds on the horizon, and it rained. It got BLACK, they had to hurry, they had to get to work so that he could still see something while disconnecting the electric power. He has to remove roof tiles because he has to climb up the roof pole, except that he can crawl and slide over the tiles. But of course he didn't consider that the barn is much higher than the pole, and as he crawls out, he is standing with his leather cap touching the line. Jesus, he thinks to himself as he turns a bit. Christ Almighty, he thinks to himself as he touches his ear. Those damn wasps, he thought to himself. There must be a wasps' nest there, he thought to himself. Stung me alright! His ear was electrified just as if a wasp stung him. And as he makes a cut, he sees that he is pressing on a wire with his cap. Then he meekly

C: By Vopos.

SL: The Reichstag therefore can't be wrapped.

C: This is why I want to wrap it. And to do so, I must negotiate with the Soviets. It is impossible for individuals to deal directly with the army. Hence, the three Western allies — the Americans, the French, and the English — are presenting my project to the Russians.

SL: What were the arguments stated by *Pravda* to condemn your project?

C: It is asserted that what I was doing offered nothing to the masses, to the workers; that it was the prototype of wanton, formalist and decadent art.

SL: Maybe *Pravda* is not entirely wrong. Wasn't that the reason for your leaving Bulgaria?

C: I participated, against my will, in the Agit-Prop. We were to spend every weekend in the kolkhoz and take a hand in "artistic" activities in the service of the party. I hated that. I left my country at the age of 22 (my son's age) on the spur of the moment because I was suffocating. I wanted to escape the terrible provincialism and to experience a freer professionalism. I didn't leave for the sake of love, but because the art world in Bulgaria meant academicism and socialist-realism.

14

retreats, then he carefully disconnects the wire with a laugh. What would have happened without the cap! That bit of insulation. What would have happened if he had touched it with his bare head? Man alive. He could have been dead. And he thought it had felt like a wasp sting. I even cried out. Jesus, he had said, there's gotta be a wasps' nest there. And I was touching the power line. Wasps, huh!

23.11.1979

Names which I misspelled in the rush: Goethe / Schurmann / Badwiser □

Translated by Marc Silberman

1. Austrian actor and film director.
2. German film directors.

SL: What would have happened to you if you had stayed in Bulgaria?

C: Since I was a very talented student, I would have most probably been sent to the Soviet Union to conclude my specialized training as a socialist-realist. To go to Leningrad or Moscow to study was the highest award.

SL: You might have ended up wrapping the Red Square...

C: There are no propitious circumstances, as far as work is concerned, in the East. Nevertheless, I grew up in a communist country and I feel very personally and emotionally concerned with the relations between the East and the West.

SL: Which brings us back to the Reichstag project. Is it to be as "wanton," as far as the relationships between the East and the West are concerned, as it is accused of being?

C: It is clear that by asking the Russians, the Germans, the French, the English, and the Americans for permission, we are led to a totally new interpretation of the project, which none of the others ever provoked. With the wrapping of the Reichstag, we will find ourselves in a remarkable situation in which it shall be possible for a work of art to be perceived simultaneously from East and West Germany. From a visual point of view, a communication will be established by means of these structures, and it will keep chang-

15

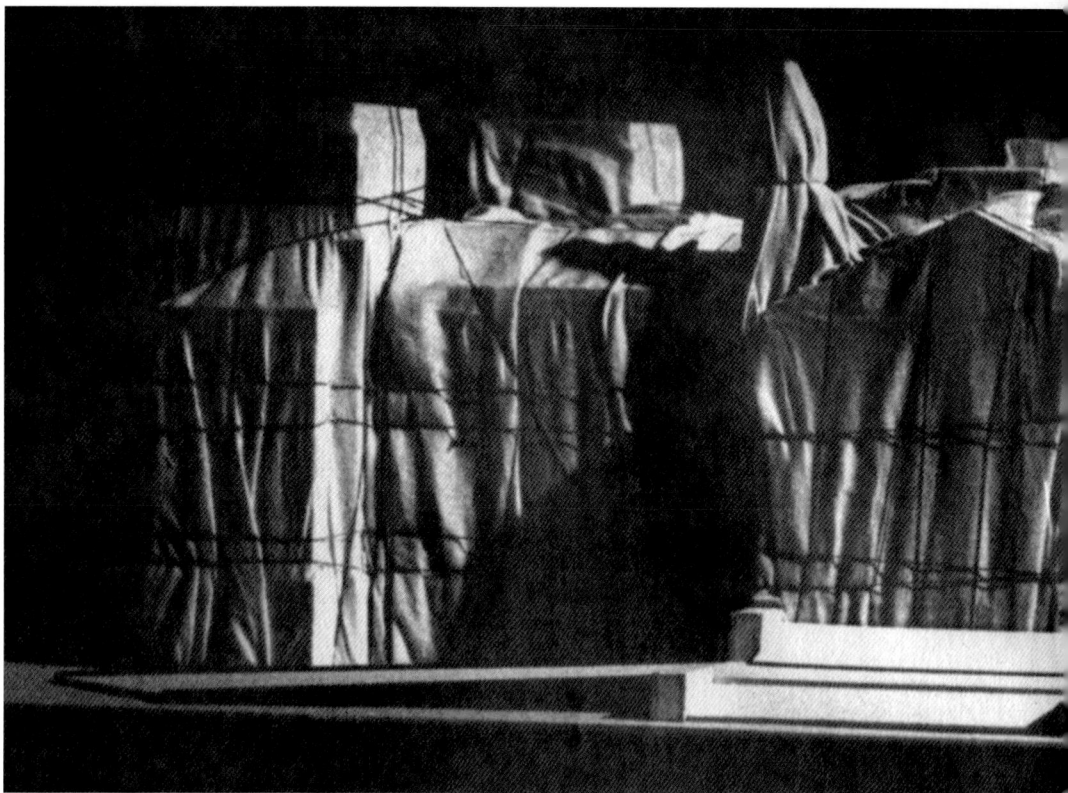

Christo / Jeanne-Claude

ing during the two weeks of the installation. Wrapping the Reichstag corresponds to a real event. That means a profound transformation of the space. All my projects, not only this one, maintain an intimate relationship with a space and its meaning, not unlike what happens in the works of urban-planning architects, with whom I am often compared. If you want to build a highway, a school, or a bridge somewhere, you have to take into account what the people will see there. You must ask yourself whether this can become an object of communication or not.

SL: Your projects, "Central Park" here, "Running Fence" in California, or "Iron Curtain" in Paris, are always a means of rendering space perceptible. The wrapping of the Reichstag will undoubtedly go much further. It has the capacity to crystallize the relationships between two worlds. To render the *political* space perceptible. This can also be very risky.

C: That is what all my opponents claim. According to them, Germany's division, artificial from the start, has ended up separating both sides, not only physically, but mentally. Günter Grass fears that the East Germans might see in this gesture a blasphemy against their sense of heritage, especially the older people, who are not accustomed to modern art and remain very attached to historical references.

16

SL: Do you think this objection is valid?

C: There is, in fact, a lot of information circulating between both Germanies, mainly through the television network, which is hard to control. Consequently, the risk is an imaginary one. A senator opposed to my project even declared at the Bundestag that the Russians might call it an invasion of their territory and close the check points with West Berlin if the drapes that cover the Reichstag were to puff out in a gust of wind. These are not serious objections. In fact, no one wants to create any kind of tension. Anything that might favor the contacts between both sides is perceived by both sides as positive. Thus, everybody will benefit from this project.

Of course, there's always the possibility that something may go wrong. Chance has always been a factor in all of my projects. The international situation can tighten up and both sides can become hysterical. The Russians, however, are not the ones who are creating the problems, but a conservative group from West Germany.

SL: From West Germany or West Berlin? Within which jurisdiction is the Reichstag?

C: The Reichstag building is under a special regulation. It is under the jurisdiction of the Federal Republic of Bonn, which also insures its management. The Reichstag is a direct responsibility of the Bundestag's president, the second most important authority after

17

CHRISTA WOLF
Change of Perspective

1

I've forgotten what my grandmother was wearing when the dreadful word "Asia" brought her to her feet again. I don't know why she's the first person I remember, during her lifetime she never sought the spotlight. I remember all of her clothes: the brown dress with the crocheted collar, which she wore at Christmas and for all family birthdays; her black silk blouse; her large-checked apron; and the black-mottled knit jacket, which she wore in the winter when she sat in front of the stove reading the local newspaper. She didn't have anything suitable to wear for this journey, it's not my memory's fault. She could use her small buttoned boots; they always dragged two centimeters on the floor when they hung from her short, slightly crooked legs, even when she sat on an air raid shelter cot, even when the floor was just dirt, as it was on the April day I recall here. The bomber formations which had flown over us in broad daylight toward Berlin couldn't be heard anymore. Someone had pushed open the door of the air raid shelter; in the blinding

Christa Wolf is a leading East German author. She is best known in English for *The Quest for Christa T.* (Farrar, Straus & Giroux, 1971).

the President. Both of them are now members of the party opposed to Chancellor Schmidt, which does not make things easier.

SL: You have received the support of Willy Brandt* and the left wing of the Social Democrat party.

C: In 1976, when I started working on this project, the president of the Bundestag was a Socialist. Now the president, Dr. Schückler, is a member of the Bavarian party, an ultra-conservative, one of Strauss' men. Perhaps we made a tactical mistake in polarizing this project. We were seeking allies on both sides. We have some Christian Democrat supporters but not as many as in the Socialist party.

SL: What's the next step then?

C: To get permission to go ahead with the project. That's always the hardest thing to obtain. After the October 1980 elections, it looked as if we were going to win. By the end of May 1981, however, everything fell through. It was the second time they refused to grant permission.

SL: How many refusals before you abandon a project?

triangle of sunlight at the entrance, three paces from my grandmother's dangling button boots appeared a pair of high black boots, occupied by an officer of the Waffen SS, who had retained in his blond head every single word my grandmother had said during the air raid. No, no, I'm not leaving here even if they kill me, an old woman is no loss. What? asked the officer. Tired of life? You want to fall into the hands of these asiatic hordes? The Russians cut off women's breasts!

Then moaning my grandmother got up again. Oh my God, she said, what did mankind do to deserve this. My grandfather addressed her angrily: Why do you always have to open your big mouth! And now I see them distinctly as they go into the courtyard and each one takes his place by our handcart: grandmother in her black cloth coat and the light and dark brown striped kerchief, which my children still used as a scarf, leaning with her right hand on the handle at the back; grandfather in his cap with earflaps and herring-bone jacket, standing next to the shaft. Time is of the essence, night is near and so is the enemy, only each one comes from a different direction: night from the west and the enemy from the east. In the south where they meet, where the small city of Nauen is located, the sky is ablaze with fire. We believe we understand the fiery writing, the *Menetekel*[1] seems to be clear and loud: toward the west.

But first we have to find my mother. Often she disappears when we're supposed to move on, she wants to go back, and she has to go forward, sometimes both demands are equally strong in her, and then she finds an excuse and walks away saying: I'm going to hang myself, and my brother and I still live in the realm in which we take her literally, we run into the small wooded area in which my mother has no business, we catch each other looking

C: Each case is different. At present I'm working simultaneously on four projects. I'll simply put the Reichstag aside for a year or so.

SL: History will have to wait.

C: Not for long. I'm preparing a big scale model in three dimensions which will be exhibited at the Cologne museum. We'll take advantage of the show to renew our contacts with the senators.

SL: Why is Willy Brandt favorable to the project?

C: Because such a project, according to him, can only be realized in a nation which has reached maturity. Germans, he says, will be able to look at it as at a mirror. Even if the project carries historical references in a somewhat questionable situation of pride, it shall raise comments that will give the Reichstag a new currency in the future. The project will electrify the place, give it a new energy, and not just the energy of memory which it has now, since people go there like they visit an historical monument. This is the reason why we were supported by lawyers, bankers, journalists, professors, and "establishment" people who are not especially interested in art. Beyond its proper aesthetic dimensions, they saw in the project an exceptional public dimension. They felt

into the treetops, we avoid looking at each other, we can't speak anymore about our unmentionable suspicions, we are also silent as my mother, who gets bonier and thinner every week, comes from the town, throws a small sack of flour on the cart and rebukes us: You two run around in the countryside and drive people crazy, what were you thinking of? And who is supposed to convince the farmers to relinquish their foodstuffs, if not me?

She grabs the front of the cart and my brother and I begin to push, the sky adds its eerie fireworks and I hear the almost inaudible sound with which the humble train Reality derails and plunges wildly forward into the middle of the thickest, unbelievable Unreality, so that a laugh escapes me, whose inappropriateness I sense intensely.

I just can't make anyone understand that I'm not laughing at us, God forbid, at us established, upright people who live in the two-story house next to the poplar tree, at us peepshow people in a pickle. Fishes, fishes, little fishes in the sea, my wife Isabel doesn't want what I want. But none of us wanted to be Kaiser or even Pope and certainly not God, one of us was very happy selling flour and butter in the store downstairs and dill pickles and coffee, another one learned English vocabulary lists at a table covered with a black, wax tablecloth and looked out of the window now and again at the city and the river, which lay very quietly and properly there and never expressed the wish that I should leave them, very patiently my little brother screwed together small wonders with his erector set and insisted on making them roll and move senselessly with strings, while upstairs in her kitchen my grandmother fried hash browns with onions and majoram — which disappeared with her death from the face of the earth, and my grandfather hangs his cobbler's thread over the sash-bolt and

that once the project was carried out, many ideas and effects which would otherwise remain unsuspected, could be realized.

SL: Is the present situation very different from the conditions in which the project was initiated?

C: Nine years ago, when we actually started the project, nobody was interested in the Reichstag. It had sunk into oblivion, like a wound not to be touched. In the Seventies, however, the Germans suddenly began to reinvent National-Socialism. The Hitler period became an extraordinary creative resource for a whole generation of filmmakers and writers. As far as the terrorists were concerned, the Thirties became a fundamental reference. All of a sudden, because it was identified with that period, the Reichstag took on a great importance.

SL: Your project came right on time. In fact, it was ahead of it.

C: I wasn't aware of all that in the beginning. This aspect appeared later. The project really was bigger than my idea; it's because the situation is so fertile.

SL: With the digging up of the National-Socialist past, there has also been, as much on the Left as on the Right, in both the East and the West, a reappearance of the idea of the

unties his blue cobbler's apron so that he can cut a dozen grooves into every piece of breadcrust for his toothless mouth to chew.

No, I don't know why we've gotten into this pickle. And I don't for the world know why I'm laughing about it, even when my uncle, who is pulling the second handcart in our tiny caravan, angrily asks again and again: I just want to know who's funny around here! Even if I understand how disappointed one has to be so that the fear of his being laughed at isn't even over when he finally is out of danger. Even if I had really wanted to do him a favor, to assure him that I was laughing about myself: I couldn't lie, and I distinctly felt I was absent, although I could have easily been confused with one of the figures leaning forward into the wind and the darkness. When you are absorbed in yourself, you don't see yourself, but I saw all of us, as I see us today, as if someone had pulled me out of my shell and placed me next to myself with the command: look!

I did it, but I didn't like it. I saw us leave the main road, grope around in the darkness on the side roads and finally come upon a lane which led us to a gate, to a remote farm, to a stooped slightly trembling man, who was hobbling in the middle of the night to the stables, who was incapable of being surprised by anything, so he greeted the dispairing, exhausted little caravan blithely. Hey, you Sodom and Gomorrha? It doesn't matter. There's always enough room in the smallest hut for a happy, loving couple. As we followed Kalle across the yard, my mother said despairingly, that man isn't too bright and my grandfather laconically explained: He's crazy — that really was the case. Kalle called my grandfather "master," whose highest rank had been private in the Kaiser's infantry regiment, cobbler's apprentice by Mr. Lebuse in Bromberg

Prussian State. An exhibition on the subject, which raised quite a few controversies, was lately held right near the Reichstag. Did this have an effect upon your project?

C: What's new is the idea of seeking the origins of Prussia, which only remains in the spirit of discipline without which the paradoxical separation of both Germanys wouldn't have been possible. One must not forget that East Germany is a Prussian State. The masses couldn't have lived through such a situation without an incredible disposition to obey. Communism did not give birth to this police state; it was already running in the people's veins. If the division had occurred in a "softer" area, like Bavaria, the results would have been completely different. This paradox is inscribed in the German nation. Its effects on the project are also unpredictable. Once it is wrapped, the concrete object will develop its own autonomous relationships.

SL: In short, you started out with an art object, a project concerned with space, and you find yourself with a political litmus test, or a detonator. A time-bomb.

C: The Carter administration was pretty nervous about this project. I was told by Vice-President Mondale at the time that they already had enough problems with Berlin without the ones I was going to add.

and linesman with the railroad for the borough of Frankfurt on the Oder. Master, said Kalle, you better take that spot back there in the corner. Then he disappeared, whistling. The people sleeping in the bunkbeds already had behind them the divying up of the tea and the unavoidable liverwurst sandwiches, I could smell it. I tried to hold my nose closed with my arm while I was sleeping. My grandfather, who was almost deaf, began to recite the Lord's Prayer as he did every night, but at the "and forgive us our tresspasses as we forgive our tresspassers" my grandmother shouted into his ear that he was disturbing the other people, and the two started to fight. Everyone in the room could hear them, where in the past only their creaking old wooden bed was a witness and the picture of angels in a black frame, saying: Don't give up, even when everything seems lost.

Kalle woke us up at daybreak. You can drive a wagon, can't you, he asked my uncle. Mr. Volk who owns this farm wants to leave lock, stock, and barrel, but who will drive the oxcarts with the fodder sacks? I, said my uncle, and that's the way it went, even though my aunt insisted that oxen were dangerous animals and that he shouldn't risk his neck for these people. Shut up, he barked. How else do you expect to get out of here? We were all allowed to ride on the oxcart and our handcart was attached to the back of it. Clever, said Kalle, but don't think that the oxcart is faster than your handcart. Mr. Volk came personally to shake his new driver's hand, he wore a hunting cap, a waterproof woolen coat and knickerbockers. Mrs. Volk came to offer encouragement to the women, who now belonged one way or the other to her servants and addressed them with well-meaning, educated sentences, but I couldn't stand her because she just used the familiar form of "you" when she

SL: Due allowance being made, your undertaking reminds me of the conceptual artist Andre Cadere's arriving uninvited with his "art stick" at galleries and museums and letting them decide whether it is art or not. Like him, you install a little artistic machine in the midst of the institutional gearwheels, but your device has taken a worldwide political dimension. Besides, it's more than the political aspect, it's the relationship you share with the financial powers which troubles people. Since your projects need considerable amounts of money, you are often accused of being a capitalist. How does that make you feel, coming from a socialist country?

C: I am constantly accused of being a capitalist. Not only by the Russians, and because of the Reichstag, but because of all my big projects and by artists as well.

SL: Does one have to be educated in an Eastern country to really understand capitalism and to know how to mobilize economical forces for artistic ends?

C: My education in Bulgaria has certainly been very important for my present work. Since the art world there was ossified, I started to associate with other people, engineers, lawyers, workers, architects, so that even now I see very few artists. The world of galleries and museums is like a vacation for me. I go there for pleasure.
The misfortune of many American and Western artists is that they were taught to

spoke to me and she allowed her dachshund, Little Bee, to sniff our legs, which probably smelled like liverwurst sandwiches. My aunt realized that we were dealing with refined people, my uncle wouldn't have done it for just anybody. Then we heard gunfire right behind us and we took off rapidly. My grandmother said, God doesn't forsake his flock.

But I dreamed my last childish dream that night: I am not my parent's child, I was exchanged with another child and really belong to the merchant Rambow in Friedrich Street, but he is too shrewd to voice his claim openly although he sees through everything and he uses measures to lure me so that I am finally forced to avoid the street in which he waits for me in his store's doorway with enticing gumdrops. In my dream that night, I was able to distinctly inform him that I had lost all fear of him, even the memory of fear, that this was the end of his power over me and that from now on I would come everyday to him to get two bars of chocolate. The merchant Rambow quietly accepted my terms.

No doubt he was vanquished because he no longer had any function. I hadn't been exchanged with another child, but I wasn't myself anymore either. I never will forget when this stranger entered into my body, took hold of it, and discreetly began to control me. It was on that cold January morning when in haste I had left my town in a truck on the way to Küstrin and when I was amazed at how gray this city was in which I had always found everything full of light and color, which I needed. Then someone inside me said slowly and distinctly: You'll never see it again.

I can't describe my astonishment. There was no appealing this verdict. The only thing I could do was to remember for myself truly and honestly what

scorn economics. Economics is one of the most important inventions of the 20th century. Since I studied Marxism closely, I am able to use the resources and structures of capitalist society. I am able to apply what I learned, to manipulate the system here, but in a very cynical way, aiming toward absurd ends which no one can appropriate.

SL: I have always thought your projects constitute a kind of *simulation* of the capitalist system, a mock-epic of Capital. "Running Fence" is the conquest of the West played out again, but for no purpose. The contracts are negotiated one at a time, but no land is bought; you are content to go once again through the forms which enabled capitalism to secure expansion on a continental scale.

C: I don't think that there is a capitalist or a socialist system. Technically, the way communism is practiced is not that different from what exists here. In both cases, it's really a matter of state capitalism. Marx discovered an extraordinary machinery.

SL: You think the difference between the two regimes is negligible?

C: There certainly are important differences; otherwise I wouldn't be here. Capitalist society offers a natural organic anarchy which it knows how to use for its own purposes. Communist society, on the contrary, is structured in a very rigid way: it has an almost

I knew, to watch the ebb and flow of rumor and hope rise and fall again, in the meantime I should continue doing what I was doing as the others expected of me, to say what they wanted to hear from me. But the stranger inside me ate around herself and grew and would soon take complete command of me. Already she was kicking inside me sometimes, so that they looked at me askance: She's laughing again. If we only knew why.

2

I was supposed to tell about the *liberation*, the hour of liberation and I thought that nothing would be easier to do. Despite all the years which have passed, this hour was riveted in my mind and, in case there were reasons for not mentioning it until now, twenty-five years should have obliterated them or at least diminished them. I just would have to give the order and the apparatus would start working and as if by magic everything would appear on the paper. A procession of clear, very distinct pictures. Contrary to my expectations, I got stuck on the question of what my grandmother was wearing on the journey and from there I digressed to the stranger, who one day had changed herself into me, has already become another person and pronounces different verdicts and finally I had to accept the fact that there would be no chain of pictures: the memory is not a photo album and the time I was freed did not depend solely on the dates and chance movements of the Allied Troops, but rather also on certain difficult and long-lasting movements within myself. And if time obliterates reasons, it also brings forth an unending string of new ones and makes the designation of a particular hour rather more difficult; you want

tsarist rigidity, in any case it is very archaic. Even biologically speaking, because they are so old, the Soviet authorities are incapable of accepting movement.

SL: What strikes me is the singular relationship each project maintains, not only with location and space, but also with their history. It is never a question of manipulating a system in general, but of diverting, in a very specific way, the elements of a particular cultural situation.

C: A new element emerges from every place, every city, every space, and one has to start from scratch in order to discover how to get the project accepted. The essential thing is to remain humble, to listen to all advice, for you never know in advance what is the right approach. Furthermore, the people I talk to all know the locations better than I do. In fact, that's really the reward. The location is always richer than I can imagine.

SL: For my part, I am very sensitive to the *humor* such a humble attitude implies. For example, I find very appropriate the fact that your first "concrete" construction, a huge metallic "pyramid" (the Mastaba of Abu Dhabi), will be erected in the middle of the desert, in the United Arab Emirates. And that it will be made of thousands of oil barrels. You chose the cradle of nomadic civilization, which has become the pillar of the Western economy, as the place to build a huge tent — made not of cloth, but of

to say precisely from what you were freed and if you are conscientious perhaps also for what purpose you were freed. Then you think of the end of a childish fear, the merchant Rambow surely was a good man, and now you look for a new beginning, which brings nothing but approximations and that's the way it's going to stay. The end of my fear of dive bombers. You've made your bed, now lie in it, Kalle would have said, if he were still alive, but I assume he's dead, like so many of the people in this tale (death obliterates reasons, yes).

Dead like the worker Wilhelm Grund, after dive bombers shot him in the belly. That's how I saw my first death, at sixteen and I must say that was really late for those days. (The infant which I handed down as a stiff bundle from the truck to a refuge woman doesn't count, I didn't see him, I only heard his mother scream and run away.) It was sheer luck that Wilhelm Grund was lying in my spot because only chance had kept my uncle in the barn with a sick horse that morning, instead of going together as we usually did with Grund's oxcart to the main road before the others. I had to say to myself, we should have been here and not there where we were safe, even though we heard the shots and the fifteen horses went wild. Since then, I've been afraid of horses. But more than horses, since then I've been afraid of the faces of people who have had to see what no human being should ever see. Gerhard Grund, a young farm worker, had such a face when he opened the barn door, took a few steps and then collapsed: Mr. Volk, what did you do to my father!

We were the same age. His father lay at the edge of the road in the dust next to his ox and stared into the sky, if you insist: into Heaven. I saw that there was no life left in his stare. It did not acknowledge his wife's crying, the whimpering of his children. This time they had forgotten to tell us that this

stainless steel. Now this is a serious form of parody, a humorous inveigling of a location and of a culture. History's tragedy doesn't return as a farce, as Marx said, but as an ambiguous ritual, maybe the only one which we can still share. In a way, your wrappings always summon up the altar of history. Conquest of the West, but without the Indians; pyramid of solitude, but without the nomads; tribunal of the Reichstag, but without the Jews. When you showed me the photographs of your scale model, a huge and spectral Reichstag wrapped up in its grey shroud, I couldn't help thinking of the end of history. Not Hegel's: it is not humanity finally reaching its self-realization, it's a building which is no longer used.

C: I want to wrap the Reichstag in a very thick cloth, almost 50% thicker than the surface of the stone. The cloth will obviously efface all details and accentuate the proportions. The building will become much more organic. The symmetry, which is very banal, will be upset by the new forms created by the roof. The movement of the cloth, puffed out by the wind, will give a feeling of grandeur.

SL: The ritual of packaging in a society which has consumed everything, even its own symbolism. Collective symbols, shameful practices, defunct traditions are thus not only exhumed, but elevated in the open air into esthetic experiences, turned into ambiguous

was nothing for children to see. We've got to get away from here quickly, said Mr. Volk. They would have grabbed me and dragged me to the edge of the woods the same way they grabbed this dead man by the legs and shoulders. For everyone, even me, the canvas from the farm's fodder floor would have been our coffin, as it was for him. Like the farm hand Wilhelm Grund, I would have been placed in the ditch without a prayer and without a song. They would have cried for me too and then they would have continued on their way like we did because we had no choice. For a long time nobody would have said a word, as we were silent, and then they would have had to ask themselves what they would have to do to remain alive, and precisely as we did now, they would have torn large branches from the birch trees and camouflaged our wagons, as if enemy pilots would be deceived by the little travelling birch forest. Everything, everything would have been the same, except that I would no longer have been there. And the difference, which meant everything to me, wouldn't have meant anything to most of the others. Gerhard Grund already sat in his father's place and spurred the oxen on with his whip and Mr. Volk nodded encouragingly: Good boy. Your father died like a hero.

I actually didn't believe that. That's not the way a hero's death was described in the newspapers and in the school books and I informed them that, according to my convictions, a husband and father of four should not die this way. There's a war on, said Mr. Volk, and certainly there was and it had to be that way, but I could point out that there was a deviation here from the ideal of a death for the Führer and the Reich. And I didn't wonder whom my mother meant when she embraced Mrs. Grund and said, damn them. These damn criminals.

objects of conviviality. It means paying back society in its own coin and confronting history with the hallucination of its own existence. It would not be such a bad thing after all if the Germans could confront the ghosts of their past under the funeral mask, displaced and parodied, of their own grandeur. □

Translated by John Johnston and Marc Parent

Because it was my watch, I got to signal the next wave of attacks, by two American fighter planes. As I had expected, the birch forest came to a halt, a very visible easy prey on the otherwise bare road. Whoever could run, jumped from the wagons and threw himself into the ditch at the roadway's edge. I did too. Only this time, I didn't bury my face in the sand, but rather I lay on my back and continued to eat my sandwich. I didn't want to die and I certainly wasn't tired of life either and I knew what fear was better than I wanted to. But people don't die twice on the same day. I wanted to see the man who was shooting at me, because I suddenly realized that a couple of individual men were in every aircraft. First I saw the white stars under the wings, but then as they turned for another assault I saw very close by the heads of the pilots in their cockpits, finally even the naked white spots of their faces. I was familiar with prisoners of war, but this was the attacking enemy face to face, I knew that I was supposed to hate him and it seemed strange to me that I asked myself for a second if they enjoyed what they were doing. Soon they stopped.

When we returned to the wagons, one of the oxen, whom we called Heinrich, fell to his knees in front of us. Blood gushed from his neck. My uncle and grandfather took off his harness. My grandfather, who had said nothing while standing next to Wilhelm Grund, emitted curses now from his toothless mouth. The innocent creature, he said hoarsely, these bastards, damned cursed dogs all of them, all of them are alike. I was afraid that he was going to cry and wished that he would curse his head off. I forced myself to look at the ox for a while. I saw no reproach in his eyes, but why did I feel guilty. Mr. Volk gave my uncle his hunting rifle and pointed to a spot behind the animal's ear. We were sent away. I jumped and turned around when I heard the shot. The

ox fell with a heavy thud. The women had to work all evening to prepare his meat. It was already dark by the time we drank broth in the straw. Kalle, who had bitterly complained that he was hungry, greedily and noisily drank from his bowl, wiped his mouth with his sleeve and began to sing contentedly. Damn you, you crazy man, my grandfather blurted out. Kalle fell onto the straw and hid his head under his jacket.

3

You don't have to be afraid when everyone else is. It's comforting to know that, but the sense of comfort was still to come for me and I want to relate what my memory wants to surrender today. It was the morning of May 5th, a nice day, panic broke out again when we heard that the Soviet tanks had surrounded us, then we got the word: march rapidly to Schwerin, to the Americans, and whoever was still capable of questioning the action must have found it strange how everyone was rushing toward the enemy who had been threatening our lives for days. Of everything that could still happen to us, nothing seemed desirable or even bearable, but the world strongly resisted coming to an end and we were not prepared to survive a thwarted end of the world. Therefore I understood the horrible words, which a woman screamed when she was told that the Führer's long-sought-after secret weapon could now be used only to destroy everyone, the enemy and the Germans. Then so be it, the woman said.

There was a dirt path running along the last houses of the village. A soldier was washing his hands at a pump next to a red brick Mecklenburg

STEPHAN HERMLIN

Germany, 1932 and Thereafter

A new kind of obscurity had arisen in the midst of horrifying news reports, uncertain anxieties, appeasing speeches. Sects were springing up overnight, spreading and displaying their colorful weeklies on the racks of newsstands. The horoscope had begun to determine the lives of millions. The leader of the most influential sect could fill the Berlin Sportpalast whenever he called a meeting. He corresponded with the spirits of Frederick the Great and Bismarck; and they announced through an ear trumpet connecting them to the earth that the future belongs to the forces of nationalism.

The newspaper of this sect was distinguished by especially fantastic headlines which drew everyone's attention. One morning last summer, or the previous one before

Stephan Hermlin, a poet and novelist, lives in East Germany. He joined the communist youth organization in 1931.

farmhouse. He had rolled up the sleeves of his white undershirt and stood with his legs apart and shouted to us. The Führer is dead, like someone who would yell: Nice weather, today. The tone of his voice shocked me more than the recognition that the news was true. I continued to trot alongside our wagon, heard the hoarse cries of the drivers spurring on their beasts, the groaning of the exhausted horses, saw small fires at the edge of the road in which documents of Wehrmacht officers were mushrooming, saw piles of guns and bazookas accrue mysteriously in the ditches along the side of the road, saw typewriters, suitcases, radios and all sorts of expensive technical military equipment senselessly line our path and could not stop repeatedly recalling in my innermost self the sound of the soldier's words, it was just an ordinary remark, but according to my feelings it should have echoed horribly between Heaven and Hell.

Then the paper appeared. Suddenly the entire road was flooded with paper, they kept wildly throwing paper out of the Wehrmacht wagon, forms, mobilization orders, reports, proceedings, reports of a regional Wehrmacht commando, everyday paperwork as well as secret matters and secret statistics of men killed in action, which no longer interested anyone since they were just thrown at out feet. As if the desert of paper were something odious, I didn't stoop down to pick up a single sheet, which I later regretted, but I did pick up the canned goods which a truck driver threw to me. The motion of his arm reminded me of the motion which I often repeated in the summer of 1939 as I threw cigarettes to the dusty troop transports, which passed our house day and night on their way east. During the intervening six years I had stopped being a child, summer was coming again but I had no idea what I was supposed

the catastrophe, I read such a headline: "On August 19th England will sink into the sea." The accompanying article explained that the Lord God would no longer tolerate the aggregated sins of the British plutocrats, particularly those they committed against Germany. He had decided to let the island sink into the rising tides. The grim seriousness of the prediction sounded cheerful but my smile would disappear quickly. I waited with a certain impatience for the designated day. As a sense of inevitable defeat permeated me, I read the blunt words of the news account that England had sunken into the sea. I realized that it would be useless to try to persuade the people who believed it. The fact that all other newspapers, undisturbed by the report, would continue to bring the latest news from England, even the displaying of English newspapers with their accounts of the Royal Court, and the most recent results of the tennis tournament at Wimbledon, as well as an invitation to England in order to see with one's own eyes that the island still existed — all this would have been dismissed with a wordless smile of superiority. For those people who had decided from now on to follow the master and to be thus informed of the truth, every proof to the contrary would be tantamount to the devil's work. The very contradiction of others, their far greater number and the power of their counter-evidence would strengthen the blinded in their conviction — for there is a blind pride of the minority for whom the proof that they alone possess salvation seems to lie precisely in their own insignificance and lack of persuasive power. They would live from now on in

to do with it.

The supply column of a Wehrmacht unit had been abandoned on a side road by its escort. Whoever passed it took whatever he could carry. Order in the caravan was lost, many were beside themselves from greed as they were earlier from fear. Only Kalle laughed, he dragged a large quantity of butter to our wagon, clapped his hands and cried gleefully: Oh my God. What a mess!

Then we saw the people from the concentration camp. The rumor that they were being driven behind us had been following us like a specter. The thought of these people from Oranienburg oppressed us. The idea that we were also fleeing from them didn't even occur to me then. They stood at the edge of the forest and they looked cautiously in our direction. We could have signalled them that everything was safe, but nobody did it. Cautiously they approached the road. They looked different from all other human beings I was accustomed to seeing until then and I wasn't surprised that we instinctively drew back from them. But our withdrawal gave us away, it showed that, despite everything which we had promised ourselves and each other, we knew the score. All of us, we unfortunate souls, who had been driven from our homes and possessions, from our farms, from our farmhouses, from our grocery stores and musty bedrooms and well-polished living rooms with the Führer's portrait hanging on the wall. We knew: those people there, who had been designated animals and were now approaching us slowly so that they could take their revenge upon us, we had let them down. Now these ragged people would put on our clothes, put our shoes on their bloody feet, now these starving people would grab the butter and sausage which we had just captured. And to my amazement, I felt that that was just and realized for a split

a self-chosen reality unattainable to all others. Shocked, I had a presentiment of the breaking apart of the world as I knew it, into a multiplicity of illusionary realities, each of which would derive its justification from itself and among which no common denominator or dialogue could anymore be found.

I had not thought of Erich M., who had been my friend, for at least seven years. I saw him for the last time seven years ago and had then quickly forgotten him. He was the youngest son of a proletarian family in whose living-room-cum-kitchen I sat as often as possible. In those days I spent much of my time in living-room-cum-kitchens in Berlin. I met new people who intimidated me even though they were not unfriendly; for me they were complete mysteries, even when they only spoke of mundane things. Erich's father had fought on the side of Spartacus,[1] he spoke rarely, looked exhausted and suffered, Erich said, from pulmonary disease. Both of Erich's brothers worked as specialists in the Soviet Union for Elektrosawod. It was the time of the first five-year plan. With speechless enthusiasm I looked in the illustrated journals at the pictures of new cities which Le Corbusier and Ernst May had built; every week I read the *Moskauer Rundschau* (Moscow Panorama), which was written in good German. It was edited by Karl Radek and printed on cheap paper. When Erich's brothers occasionally spent a vacation in Berlin, I persuaded them to visit my group. How lovely those evenings were, happily anticipated days in advance, which we could hardly wait for, where everyone

second that we were guilty. I forgot it again. The concentration camp inmates didn't throw themselves onto the bread, but rather onto the guns in the road-side ditch. They loaded themselves up with them, they crossed the road without paying any attention to us, climbed laboriously up the slope on the other side and took positions there, gun in hand ready for an attack. Without making a sound, they looked down at us. I couldn't stand looking at them. They should scream, I thought, or shoot into the air, or shoot at us. For God's sake! But they just stood there quietly, I saw that some were unsteady and could barely manage to force themselves to hold the gun and stand there. Perhaps they had been hoping for this day and night. I couldn't help them and they couldn't help me. I didn't understand them and I didn't need them, and everything about them was foreign to me.

Someone shouted from the front that we were all to dismount, except the drivers. It was a command. A deep sigh passed through the caravan because it could mean only one thing. We were just a few steps from freedom. Before we could get moving, the Polish drivers jumped down, wound their reins around the uprights of the wagons, laid their whips on the seats, gathered together in-to a small troop and began to head back toward the east. Mr. Volk, who im-mediately got bluish red, blocked their way. At first he talked calmly to them, but soon he was screaming. He screamed about a conspiracy, a preconceived plot and a work boycott. Then I saw Polish guest workers push a German landowner aside. The world had really changed, only Mr. Volk didn't know anything about it yet. As he was accustomed, he grabbed his whip, but he couldn't strike anyone because someone was holding his arm firmly. The whip fell to the ground and the Poles continued on their way. Mr. Volk pressed his

greeted everyone else with a hello and happy laughter. Almost all of my young comrades were unemployed. Many of them had come from professional training schools to the Labor Exchange, in front of which they often loitered in the hope that it would find them jobs. I was an outsider for a while; the glances that fell upon me were distrustful or ironic. Then I proved myself. It was the time of a latent civil war, and I did not run away from the SA people[2] and police. Moreover, it wasn't the street and parlor battles that I feared. I was made much more uneasy by the so-called house and courtyard agitation, the ringing of strangers' doorbells, the necessity of beginning a conversation with peo-ple one had never seen before. I had to fight against the fear which such encounters caused and subdue them forcefully, but the fear always rose again. My friends didn't know anything about it. They had observed me and now treated me as one of their own. Whenever Erich's brothers joined us, our enthusiastic curiosity knew no bounds. We never got tired of asking questions. They told us about their daily lives in Moscow, of the enormous achievements in production, and of want and sacrifice. They were never afraid to call shortcomings by their proper names. They explained statistics: their plans and counterproposals, their food rations. The Soviet Union did not want to minimize poverty and hunger in our eyes; they were the heritage of the past, of a corrupt society, of war and civil war which had been forced upon the people. We were also experiencing hunger at that time. It was the result of the self-indulgence of the few. Over there, a country

hand against his heart and leaned heavily against a wagon and let himself be comforted by his sarcastic wife and Little Bee, the dumb dachshund. While Kalle shouted from above, "Piece of shits, piece of shit." The French people who stayed with us shouted greetings at the departing Poles, which they understood as little as I did, but they understood their tone of voice and I did too and it hurt me that I was excluded from their shouting, waving, and hat tipping, from their joy and their language. But that's the way it had to be. The world consists of victors and the vanquished. The former may give vent to their emotions. The latter—we Germans—would have to suppress our feelings in the future. The enemy should not see any weakness in us.

Moreover, then it arrived. I would have preferred a fire-breathing dragon to this light-weight Jeep with the driver who chewed gum and the three lazy officers who in their limitless arrogance had not even unsnapped their holsters. I made an effort to ignore them and told myself that their relaxed laughter, their clean uniforms, their indifferent glances, their whole damned victor's mien had been ordered especially to assure our humiliation.

The people around me began to hide their watches and rings and I also took my watch from my wrist and casually slipped it into my coat pocket. The guard at the end of the gorge, a very tall man, under his incredible steel helmet at whom we had always laughed loudly during the weekly newsreels, pointed out to the few people who were armed where they should throw their weapons and the others frisked us civilians with a few skilled police movements. Petrified by indignation, I let them frisk me. Secretly I was proud that they believed that I might carry a weapon. Then my overworked guard asked business-like in English: Your watch? He wanted my watch, the victor, but he

which knew no unemployment was preparing for a superfluity for everyone. There was a housing shortage, but already cities were being built, which I named, in my dreams and later in my poems, the "white cities" because I perceived them as white and perfect in the photographs of *UdSSR im Bau* (Soviet Union Under Construction) and the *Arbeiter-Illustrierte* (The Workers' Illustrated Magazine). We had enough housing, but daily hundreds of people were evicted because they could no longer pay their rent. We laughed at the reports of Russian misery in the bourgeois newspapers; it was an uncontained laugh, because we knew that everything over there would improve quickly, while capitalism was in its end phase with us.

In the beginning of February, only a few days after Hitler had seized power, I was walking through a side street of the Kaiserallee when I heard drumming and singing. I stood still and saw in a few seconds a singing troop of Hitler youth turning into my street. In the questionable German of many a soldiers' song, they sang, "So that the Fatherland would not succumb. They died in battle at La Bassee." I had never heard the song before. The melody and text remain etched in my memory, even though years and years have passed, as well as the quick turning of the left flank men around the corner. The flank man in the second row singing loudly and wearing a brown shirt and a brown cap on his head was my friend Erich M. He saw me and turned bright red, and at the same time, I sensed that I turned pale. He stared straight ahead. It had only taken a

didn't get it because I managed to convince him that his buddy, the one over there, had already gotten it from me. As far as the watch was concerned, I had gotten away scott free. Then my sensitized ears perceived the sound of still one more approaching airplane engine. Of course, it didn't matter to me anymore, but habit made my eyes follow its flight path, my reflexes forced me to throw myself onto the ground as it began to dive, the nauseating dark shadow flitted across the grass and trees one more time, one more time the repulsive sound of bullets penetrated the earth. Even now? I thought amazed and noticed that you get used to being out of danger in a second. With sheer malicious pleasure I watched an American artillery man aim an American gun and fire on an American airplane, which quickly began to climb and then disappeared behind the forest.

Now I should be able to describe what it was like when silence fell. For a while I remained prone behind a tree. I believe it didn't matter to me that from that moment on perhaps no more bombs or machine gun bursts would hail down upon me ever again. I wasn't curious about what was going to happen now. I didn't know what a dragon was good for after he had stopped breathing fire. I had no idea how Siegfried was supposed to behave when the dragon asked for his wristwatch instead of devouring him. I didn't want to see how Mr. Dragon and Mr. Siegfried would get along with each other as civilians. I didn't have the slightest desire to go to the villa, occupied by the Americans, for every pail of water, particularly not to get into a fight with the black-haired Lieutenant Davidson from Ohio at the end of which I envisioned being compelled to explain that my pride dictates that I hate him. And I had no desire at all to speak with the man from the concentration camp, who sat with us by the

couple of hours or days to transform him into this. I was seventeen years old and did not understand, but I learned to understand a long time after he had passed by me. He was the first one; I saw innumerable people follow him. The urge to be among the stronger people cannot be tamed. On how many battlefields had these people, when threatened by defeat, changed their flag?

Seven years and a few months had passed since this street encounter, when I suddenly thought of Erich M., whom, as I have already said, I had completely forgotten. It was night, and we were lying in a narrow pass. We had, in the previous days, marched almost non-stop in various directions. We were no longer sure where we were. Straggling soldiers, as well as civilians, who disappeared as suddenly as they appeared, had joined us. We listened for the noises of tanks not far from us. Lately they had become unexpectedly audible. During the day the sky was full of German airplanes; we heard bombardments in the distance. A squadron of Morane planes fled from a couple of Messerschmidts. The war was causing us to disintegrate. In my empty village, I noticed a poster on the wall: "*Nous vaincrons, parce que nous sommes les plus forts.*" German tanks could appear from every direction, some, it was said, attacked from the deep south. The main thrust of the Germans no longer came from the north. They were attacking from Mezieres and the forest of Mormal, that is, from the east. They advanced to the coast, they divided the British troops from the French troops. I saw the stars in the sky,

fire in the evening, who had a bent wire-frame pair of glasses on and never stopped saying the unmentionable word "communism" as if it was an ordinary word like "hatred" and "war" and "destruction." No the last thing I wanted to know about was the sorrow and confusion with which he asked us: Where were you all those years?

I didn't want to be liberated. I lay underneath my tree and everything was quiet. I was lost and thought that I should remember the tree's branches partially obscuring the beautiful May sky. Then a tall Sergeant came up the slope after he had finished his duty and had a squealing German girl in each arm. All three walked together toward the villa and finally I had a reason to turn around a little bit and cry. □

Translated by Dagmar Stern

1. The warning "writing on the wall," from the Old Testament.

the round light of a flashlight on a map not far from me. The voices of a few officers murmured constantly near me, as during my childhood, when I loved to have the conversations of adults around me, conversations which I did not understand and did not want to understand. I loved their sounds. Out of the incomprehensible dialogue, only one sentence found its way through my exhaustion. "They have taken Lens," someone said, "Bethune and La Bassee." A monstrous uniformity of history became visible; every twenty years the same places that were otherwise never mentioned surrendered; again and again, the same fate appeared, like heaps of rubble. Villages and small town seemed to exist only to be conquered, to be forgotten, and lost and in suffering, the people lived on toward their future suffering.

I entered the hall behind the Palais Bourbon. The ground did not stop quaking, the shots from Spain had faded out, after the Sudetenland came Prague, the Memel area and Albania were occupied; I had already seen how bombs fall, oaths dissipate into smoke, bonds break; I kept my eyes glued on my friends, we were in the most difficult of all battles, our intention was to divert the war's path. Statesmen gave speeches in which one had to find a clause, a subordinate clause, which contained the ominous, subtly spoken threat. It was easy to despair. Already around me I saw many demoralized, cynical, or despairing men. I was not desperate. I always heard within me the Lutheran words: "We must succeed." That is the way it stayed. I lived with a sense of belonging to an avant-

"Disappearance is our future."
Paul Virilio

HEINER MÜLLER
The Walls Of History

Sylvère Lotringer: You live in East Berlin, but you are in the unusual position of being able to travel freely to the West. How much of a wall is there between East and West?

Heiner Müller: When I go from the Friedrichstrasse checkpoint to the zoological garden in West Berlin, I feel a great difference, a difference in civilization, a difference of ages, of time. There is a different time level, a different time space. You really go through a time-wall.

SL: I asked some German friends, yesterday, about East Berlin and they said: "We love it. It's like going back to the fifties."

HM: Most people coming from West to East Berlin keep comparing them on a horizontal level. It doesn't work that way. The problem is the misery of comparing. You just can't compare things.

The Time-Wall

SL: So East Berlin is something of its own?

Heiner Müller is a major East Germany dramatist. His plays circulate on both sides of the Wall.

garde, which alone offered mankind the only possible way, and even if I often quoted Rosa Luxemburg's "Socialism or Barbarism," the latter alternative always remained unbelievable, unfathomable for me. I shoved the threatening "or" aside, the naming of the great goal seemed to want to dispel the fearful thing into non-existence.

I entered the room in a high fervor of trust; we held a congress against war and Fascism, the last one. We still had three or four months' time. All European languages buzzed around me. It seemed as if every smile was turned on me with affection, sympathy, trust, perhaps it was because I was so young; I was one of the youngest delegates. I saw Paul Nizan with a troubled brow leaning on the executive committee's table, I saw Andersen-Nexo, I saw Aragon, to whom, every few days, I brought information about the Spanish refugees in the Rue du 4 Septembre. Clouds swam through the auditorium, a stormy joy penetrated me, filled me up. I looked for my friends' table, a sign with the designation "Allemagne" stood in the middle of the round table. I saw faces of the people I knew. Rudolf Leonhard, Franz Dahlem, Siegfried Radel[3] waved to me. Heinrich Mann pointed to the empty chair next to his, he called me "young man," I fell silent out of joy and embarrassment. How many dead people were gathered around me and why did Reichstag representative Radel carry his head under his arm . . . . □

Translated by Dagmar Stern

HM: I was very impressed by the remark of a young man who was writing an essay on my work. He remembered that he never quite understood why the German Wehrmacht didn't succeed in entering Moscow during the Second World War. They just stood there. They couldn't go further. He didn't believe in military or strategic reasons. He didn't believe in geographic reasons. He didn't believe in ideological reasons. There simply was a time-wall. They were not on the same track. A few years ago, I was asked by *Le Monde* in Paris to write something about the cultural situation in East Berlin. I tried to explain it to the French public and it wasn't easy. People brought up here have at least an image, or a hope, for another society, for another kind of living. This image is linked to the end of the commodity world. In the West, this world is in full bloom and you can never really get accustomed to that. Many of my friends moved to the West — writers especially. They tried to write there, but it's really a problem. You can never forget the image of another world. That becomes their schizophrenia.

SL: If living in East Berlin, or in East Germany is something altogether different from living in the West, how would you define it in itself, especially as a writer?

HM: Everything you write in the East is very important for the society or the society believes it's very important. You have a hard time being published here because it has such impact.

SL: You mean that in West Germany you can publish almost anything because it has no impact?

1. The far Left of the SPD, destroyed following the defeat of the German revolution of 1918-19 which brought the of the German Empire.

2. Paramilitary wing of the Nazi party, founded in the early 20's. Their power was eventually reduced by Hitler in 1934, during the "Night of the Long Knives."

3. Leonhard was the pseudonym for Robert Lanzer (1889-1953). He left Germany after the collapse of the Weimar Republic and became a member of the French Resistance. Dahlem (1892-1982) was on the Politburo of the German CP since 1929. Radel (1893-1943) was on the Central Committee of the German CP until he was murdered by the Gestapo.

GUENEY DAL

Little Ankara

When building the Wall prevented 60,000 East Berliners from reaching their places of work in West Berlin, foreign help was called for. Among other emigrants, 100,000 Turks settled in West Berlin as "guestworkers." Most of them live in Kreuzberg in ghetto conditions. All in all, there are four million foreign workers in West Germany.

Gueney Dal, a free-lance Turkish writer now working for Radio Free Berlin's program called "Guestworkers," calls the invasion "the Crusades in reverse." His first book, translated into German is, *When Ali Hears the Church Bell Toll.*

How is it possible for church bells to reach the ears of an Osmanli? They sound no echo in his ears, yet millions have left their homes to listen. Hundreds of thousands of workers wait for permission to hear the bells: they toll for work permits and for Deutsch Mark, planting the chimes of a foreign culture in their heads. They accept it as their fate.

HM: It's an artificial freedom, an artificial free space for ideology, for the arts and for literature. The artificiality of this freedom is based on the fact that West Germany couldn't function if foreigners, people from the south, from poor countries didn't do the dirty work or the service work. In our countries, in our bloc, we are on the contrary in some sort of osmosis with the Third World. Russia is just a very small part of the Soviet Union. Its population is minimal in relation to the Asian provinces, the Asian regions. There is much more Third World inside the Soviet Union than in the United States. The Third World is like a big waiting-room, waiting for history. There is a line by Jim Morrison: "Live with us in the forests of Asia..."

SL: Do you think history has become a Third World notion at this point? Are we through with our own history?

HM: There are two ideas or concepts of history. There is no more history in Western Europe. The European concept of history is over.

SL: There is no belief in progress anymore?

HM: There can't be any progress in the West. The problem is just to hold on and not to lose what we already have.

SL: This is the degree zero of history. Maybe we finally managed to get rid of history.

HM: Michel Foucault wrote that since the 18th century, the first theme or the first preoccupation of European thinking has been the question of the revolution. Now, he says, a new question is arising.

Working on an assembly line is like treading water: you can kick and splash all you like, you're always in the same spot. Exhausted, you want to rest a second, can't get your arse up, but you've got to graze where you're tethered. They didn't say for nothing that assembly lines eat people and shit cars. The tyranny of an alien civilization and culture imprisons us.

The first generation here has it the toughest. Coming from a feudal society and believing in fairy tales, they view the machines they service as magic boxes capable of fearful wrath. How often have I heard them invoke the name of Allah under their breath before turning on television, praying He will protect them from evil spirits residing in that box. Everything that spews forth German instills Angst of the unknown.

Our problem is not the Wall; our problem is the Berliner. Many in this shrunken half of a once-mighty city vent their rage and daily frustrations on us: 'Ugly creatures, garbed in screeching colors, cursed with shrieking voices and blessed with hordes of kids, a plague God has visited on us. Instead of thanking heaven they didn't die of starvation and are permitted to live in our land, they dare to strike against our holy German laws. These barbarians ought to be sent back where they came from — the sooner, the better.'

All the old prejudices still slumber inside Germans, and the danger of an awakening still exists. They try to forget the past, but it's like a cancer. They've gone through near-

SL: Is revolution something we can still desire?

HM: Yes. This is, however, a very privileged question. You can't afford to ask this question if you have nothing to eat. The division between ideologies isn't very important. Ideologies are merely masks. What is important is the difference of interests or needs. The Western paradise is based on hell for the Third World. We are indeed living in what you called "Limbo" the other day.

SL: Many political thinkers in the West feel that Russia is being threatened by its Asian side. The split between Russia and China may be indicative of a total reshuffling of forces.

HM: Politicians in the West tend to overestimate the conflict between China and Russia. This conflict will be short-lived. The development of China along Western lines is actually diminishing the danger of a real confrontation. I don't believe Mao-Tse-Tung's experiment has been defeated or that the debate is over. When one class in China reaches the saturation point, contradictions gain momentum again.

SL: After the "end of ideologies" in the West, more people begin to question the validity of the ideological conflict deliberately played up by the two rival blocs. Capitalism and Socialism may prove to be simply two different ways of controlling the sphere of production and insuring the discipline of work, especially in the post-industrial era.

HM: I recently met a Russian writer who spent two months working in a kolkhoz somewhere in the Ukraine. After a few days, he devised a new

fatal operations, but something is left of the original sickness.

Who knows? Maybe our six- or eight-year-olds will make it. Like it or not, they've become Germanized. Already we need translators to communicate with our own children. They not only speak German — I bet they dream *auf Deutsch.* □

Photograph and text by Henry Ries

DIETER DOMBROWSKI

BOUGHT FREE

I tried to escape from East Berlin in 1974. They caught me. At the border, they searched the furniture van and discovered me. After five months of detention, I was sentenced to four years in prison.

Twenty months and four different prisons later, I was free. Mother had contacted a West Berlin lawyer. She was the first of our family to leave East Berlin where all of us were born. My father is dead. The family is now equally divided: Mother, myself, a brother and a sister living here, and two brothers and two sisters still in East Berlin. Two of them are in jail.

Well, Mother's lawyer contacted *Herr* Vogel, the East Berlin lawyer. West Germany paid somewhere between 40,000 and 50,000 Marks — none of us knows the exact

organization of work that would eventually bring better results. He described it to an old peasant who replied: "You know, we don't live just to work. Work takes up a great deal of our lives, so we try to live during our working time, too!" The division of life and work, which is typical of the capitalist organization of production is over in the East. What authorities here consider to be a weakness in production presents, in fact, a very positive aspect. The division between life and work is bound to disappear.

SL: It may be breaking down in the West, as well. Absenteeism is rampant, too, among Italian factory workers. Theoreticians of the Workers' Movement, like Mario Tronti, were quick to recognize it as a positive symptom. So, on the one hand, we have a wall separating different types of society, but, on the other, both seem to have evolved in a similar direction.

HM: At the base though, not on top.

SL: So, maybe the wall or the two parallel tracks will meet somewhere in the infinity of the near future...

HM: It won't happen above, from the level of politics. The wall can only be abolished slowly, through basic changes.

The Nightmare of History

SL: What's the relation of people in East Germany to the West? Paradoxically the West here in Berlin is not outside, but inside the East.

HM: You have to realize that the vast majority of our population watches the

amount, but that's supposed to be the going rate for a semi-skilled worker — and here I am!

Before the Wall, Mother used to take us to the *Kranzler Eck* here at the *Ku-damm*[1] for *Kaffee und Kuchen*—and now I treat my buddy, Thomas, to a beer and Petra to ice cream at the same spot. Petra is my fiancee. She came with her whole family from East Berlin in 1976, father, mother, three younger brothers and sisters and their poodle. And Thomas is here since '75; he tried to escape through Yugoslavia, was caught, turned over to the GDR* police and sentenced to two and a half years. After serving one year, he was bought free too.

I used to be a paper-hanger and painter in East Berlin. Now I'm studying to become a dental technician. All professional schools here were filled, so I enrolled in one in Hamburg. I commute by car; leave Sunday evening, back Friday afternoon. It's only 150 miles each way. Never had any problems with East German border guards; I don't feel any apprehension. After all, I have proper West Berlin papers!

Money is no problem. As long as I'm a student, the West German government pays the full amount of my unemployment compensation which equals the monthly paycheck I earned as house-painter in the GDR; they also pay for one monthly roundtrip plane ticket to Hamburg and for all my social security and insurance deductions —

West German TV program.

SL: Is it accessible to the rest of Germany?

HM: Only two small areas do not receive it.

SL: How does West German TV affect the population in East Germany?

HM: The most political part of the program is the advertising. It is political in two different ways. On the one hand, it means accumulating, not unhappiness, but needs.

SL: Is it creating needs?

HM: Yes, it's creating needs. But, on the other hand, it is weakening any possibility of building an opposition from the Left. The standards of the dreams here are mostly Western in terms of foods, goods and products. This is paradoxically a great factor of stability for our society.

SL: You actually mean that Western fantasies are a stabilizing factor in East Germany?

HM: Yes.

SL: Because they are produced on the other side of the wall?

HM: Yes.

SL: In psychoanalytic terms, fantasies are some sort of a frame or window. Variations within the structure of the frame are virtually infinite, but if you go

altogether, I get a little more than 1,800 Marks per month. Although all my insurance and deductions had been collected by and paid to the GDR government, the *Bundes Republik Deutschland** honors these payments in full, as if I had lived and earned my money here all the time. I hate to refer to our government as the "BRD" like they do on the other side, since we don't have to be ashamed of the word "Deutsch" on this side.

One of my sisters was also arrested for attempted border-crossing without proper papers; she's now been in prison for two years, and we hope she'll join us soon.

My oldest brother tried, too. Together with his wife and daughter, he stood in line at a legal border-crossing in East Berlin. When he reached the guard, he showed his GDR passport and, though he had no proper permit to cross, demanded in a loud voice: "We want to go through to West Berlin." Of course, he knew what could happen. All of us know what will happen, but we also know that this is the only way to get out of East Germany. By this action, we unmistakably demonstrate our desire to get out; we accept the consequences of one or two years in prison; we count on the West German government to buy us out. Naturally, if we couldn't rely on that, we'd never attempt this method.

I'm a member of the Christian-Democratic Union* and politically active on behalf of all those who want to leave the East. The party is bulky and too lazy, so I act entirely on

through the frame and act out your fantasy, you die. Is that what the wall is for East Germans: a window-frame?

HM: It's a good image for it.

SL: But for it to be a stabilizing factor, people shouldn't have the temptation to cross the wall of their fantasy.

HM: The common attitude here, or the common fantasy, is to go to the West from time to time and to come back. Most people here know that it's easier to live on our side.

SL: Is it really?

HM: Yes. It is.

SL: How would you account for that?

HM: You have to work much harder in the West. The whole rhythm of life is much slower here, much more convenient. And social security is far better.

SL: So people here feel they've got the best of two worlds?

HM: No, no. I don't think people here feel that way. West Germans believe they've got a better deal, and they do have it from their own viewpoint. A majority of the West German population finds its identity in the standard of the "Deutschmark." There's no other national identity in the West. You also need Deutschmarks here if you want to buy other kinds of goods. Our own currency can't be used in special shops. The real danger for us is that the Deutschmark would become our standard as well.

"Remember what Hegel said: no German can lie for very long without believing it."

Heiner Müller

my own when I display large posters on top of one of these observation platforms. That's where I met Thomas, and we've been demanding freedom for various dissenters who are jailed in East Berlin. Of course, I don't expect any direct results, but we're very visible to East Berliners, and our posters and demonstrations reassure them of our support. They also attract questions from West German visitors and from foreigners and give us a chance to explain the political significance and our moral obligation.

As a Berliner, I cannot accept the division of my city as final. Of course, I recognize the need for the Wall from their point-of-view. Without it, half the population would have crossed over into the West. But I'm optimistic about Berlin, and if I had the money I'd buy a house here. After all, my whole family lives here. Well, all of us do live in Berlin. □

Photograph and text by Henry Ries

1. The 5th Avenue of West Berlin.
2. West Germany.

SL: The wall is inside East Germany too. The fantasy is at hand, but do people have equal access to the Western dream?

HM: I'm now earning money in West Germany and it's transferred here so I get checks for shopping in these special shops. A lot of people must get Deutschmarks through relatives and friends because the Intershops are always crowded. There is obviously a kind of schizophrenia here on the economic level.

SL: You don't feel that a segment of the population has access more readily to these goods?

HM: Functionaries, members of the party or the government have a harder time to get Deutschmarks. They are the underprivileged class in this respect.

SL: Very few people in the West would believe that.

HM: I think they're wrong, at least as far as the German Democratic Republic is concerned. Maybe our country is special. There is much less corruption among the leading class here than in any other Socialist country. This may be part of the Prussian tradition. There was very little corruption in Prussia. It was always relatively strict.

SL: Prussian identity is now surfacing again in West Germany. Many people feel somewhat uneasy about it since it awakens heavy memories. It also upsets the wall that separates the two worlds. What do East Germans feel about this Prussian revival? Are they willing to recognize a common bond, a national identity with their counterpart in the West?

SABINE ZURMÜHL

Lesbian Brigades

Sabine Zurmühl: When talking about homosexuals, one thinks immediately of the network of bars characteristic of gay subculture. Are there such places in the GDR* and have you been in them?

A: A few times, yes. I've been in the former *Cafe Peking*, now the *Schonhauser Ecke* in East Berlin, and also the *Senefelder*. Until around 6 o'clock people go there with their

In *Man and Woman Intimate*, a sex-education book published in the German Democratic Republic in 1973, the term "homosexuality" appears under only one heading — "Abnormality." Love between women is not officially prohibited, but it is considered incommensurate with socialist morals. A West German feminist spoke with a lesbian woman about her life in East Germany.

HM: The interest shown in the West for Prussia and for Prussian history is just an effort to take it away from the East. This is the first motive behind the Prussian revival and the countermotive here is to hold on to it, keep it alive for our own purpose. It's the old German brother conflict all over again. The war between brothers, between relatives is a major theme in German literature. It begins in Tacitus with Armenius standing on one side of the river and his brother on the other side together with the Romans. His brother tries to convince Armenius that the Romans are the best chance for Germany and for civilization. Why fight them? But Armenius denounces him as a slave of the Romans. They start quarrelling and throw spears at each other. That's how it all began — an old German situation.

SL: On what side are the Romans?

HM: The Romans are on both sides!

SL: Do you really believe that the Prussian idea is part of a strategy meant to question East German identity?

HM: I wrote several plays on German history. The most polemical deals with Prussian history. It is not easy to have it performed here because it's too critical against Prussian or German traditions. So I wouldn't say that reviving Prussian history or even reinstating monuments that have been put away is necessarily a bad thing. People need to have access to their own historical background. The memory of the nation shouldn't be discarded. The best way to kill a nation is to extinguish its memory and its history.

SL: We are at the point where the idea of history has become pretty unclear.

families. Then they leave and the crowd changes. It's all unofficial. People who don't know about these cafes also wander in. They're somewhat shocked when they begin to realize what's happening. In the *Cafe Peking* there are really a lot of women, where in the *Senefelder*, mostly gay men hang out. Women are more or less tolerated there.

SZ: Can you dance in the cafes?

A: No, dancing isn't allowed. Also there's no music. We can only drink coffee or brandy, and meet one another.

SZ: Then it's pretty hard to just go somewhere and have a good time...

A: After I got to know a few women, we arranged private parties on someone's birthday, or when a woman moved into a new apartment. Small women's parties, where we could be open in our relationships. Most lesbians live their everyday lives completely "normally." They work; they hide their homosexuality. They're mostly "Sunday lesbians." Sometimes there are dance parties on the outskirts of town. They're held in bars or restaurants where a room can be rented under another name, like "women's brigade party." No one objects to women's brigades, on the contrary...

Isn't there a danger that history may return in an artificial way, as a pure construction: made-up memories, forged identity? Do you think the idea of Prussia has become hyperreal: the revival of history when history has already disappeared?

HM: In order to get rid of the nightmare of history, you first have to acknowledge the existence of history. You have to know about history. It would come back in the old-fashioned way, as a nightmare, Hamlet's ghost. You have to analyze it first and then you can denounce it, get rid of it. Very important aspects of our history have been repressed for too long.

SL: In the East?

HM: Yes. In the West, it is another part of history that's been repressed and still is repressed. Repression is no way to get rid of it.

SL: What's been repressed in the West: is it the Nazi period?

HM: Yes, for the most part.

SL: And what's been repressed here?

HM: Mainly the positive aspects of Prussian history. We kept talking only about the negative aspects. There were a lot of illusions about the role of the working class during the fascist period here.

SL: East Germany has had a definite tendency to throw the blame of fascism on West Germany. Do you think this has to do with the fact that East Germany actually paid the price of the war whereas the West didn't?

SZ: Do you have any clubs or associations where people can just get together?

A: No, we don't. If a group is formed in an apartment among friends and acquaintances, then it must be kept private. It can't go public, because the authorities would become involved immediately. They're scared shitless that political dissatisfaction could crop up there. If they learn that a lot of homosexuals meet in a bar, then you can be sure that there is a secret service agent sitting among them. The *Cafe Mokka* in Friedrichstrasse was closed down because it had become a meeting place for Western and GDR homosexuals. They made an intershop out of it.

SZ: Wasn't a medical institution working with a group of lesbian women until recently?

A: Yes, for about two years. Between 8 and 15 women were in the group. The medical center had departments for depressives, mentally disturbed people, child psychology, psychiatry, etc. They wanted to find out how lesbians live. The women met every two weeks for two to three hours at a time. All group discussions were tape-recorded, but what they did with the interviews never came out.

SZ: Did the questions show that homosexuality was considered pathological?

A: At the beginning that was certainly suggested. The medical team did hormone tests

HM: Most people who had something to hide about their past went to the West.

SL: Getting rid of the criminals, you got rid of the crime?

HM: Yes.

SL: Do you think West Germany is now coming to terms with the repression of its own history?

HM: I don't think so. The problem with West Germany is that there is still a political vacuum. This vacuum is filled by a silent majority that hasn't really changed its ideas or its opinions on politics, or history, or the past. It just remains silent. The stability of the West German State relies on this silence which remains unbroken, except for a few extremist groups on the left or the right.

SL: When history returned in West Germany, it wore the mask of terrorism.

HM: Yes.

SL: That terrorism was so extreme in Germany...

HM: ...has to do with its isolation.

SL: Does the fact that terrorism has virtually ceased to be a threat mean that West Germany now has a chance to come to terms with its own history? Do you think the problem is still there?

HM: You can see it everywhere in West Germany, in the attitude against the

and blood analyses. They spoke about a possible "cure." But the women in the group were not interested in that. At first the doctors believed lesbians came from problematic social backgrounds. They found out that this wasn't the case, although their conclusions were rarely presented to the participants.

SZ: Do you have the impression that there are more lesbians in certain professions than in others?

A: No. They work in all possible fields. I know a crane operator, a machine worker, a teacher, a post office employee, a woman who works at the police station, a theology student, all of whom are lesbians, I know many in the arts, in the literary and theater scenes who live a bit more openly.

SZ: Do you know women who have lost their jobs because they are lesbian?

A: No, simply because women never reveal themselves as lesbians at work.

SZ: There must be women who share apartments and live together...

A: If you have a relationship with a woman, you have to be willing to live in the one-room apartment to which you are entitled as a single person. Many relationships have broken up because of that. Lesbian women frequently marry gay men in order to get a larger

Turks or the Greeks or Blacks. It's just a continuation of the attitude against the Jews. The minorities are still the target of all the hatred and frustration.

SL: You don't have a similar problem in the East?

HM: Maybe at first. For years, it was very dangerous to say anything against Jews here. It's still dangerous to say anything against Blacks living here — working or studying. They are much more privileged here even in terms of money.

SL: Is it another form of guilt?

HM: It has nothing to do with guilt. It's a sense of solidarity with the weak, the underprivileged, the underdogs.

SL: And you believe this is not mere propaganda, but some deep feeling in the population?

HM: I don't know if it's a deep feeling but remember what Hegel said: no German can tell a lie for very long without believing it. Besides, there's a real sympathy towards El Salvador or Nicaragua, in a very complicated way. They identify with Chileans or with the people of El Salvador as people who feel suppressed here.

The End of History

SL: When I went to other countries of the Eastern bloc, I noticed that East Germans assumed the same role there as West Germans in the rest of Europe. They were considered rich, privileged people.

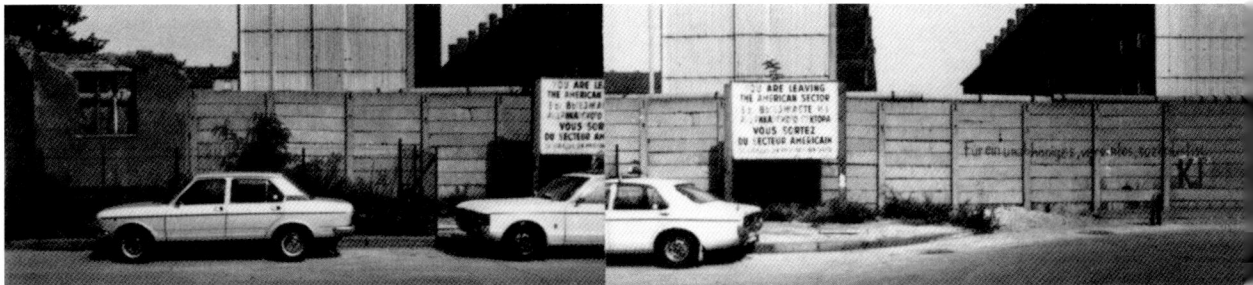

apartment.

SZ: Is it possible to meet other women, for example, through personals columns in newspapers?

A: There's a newspaper here called the *Wochenpost*. I often sent announcements to their "correspondence" column when I was desperate for contacts. It didn't always work out, because people just couldn't know for sure if it was written by a lesbian. "Woman seeks woman penpal" is the only thing you can say. Either you get back a threat, or a positive answer. I met with a woman for over a year and up to the end we didn't admit our lesbianism to each other. Recently the messages in the personals columns have been further restricted. Now we have to communicate in an even more hidden style, and use just the phrase "pen-friendship." "Woman penpal" is considered too explicit.

SZ: What about women in the small towns?

A: They're even worse off. They live completely in the closet. They're dying to move to Berlin. They think they'll have it better here. But there's no way a lesbian can lead an open life in the German Democratic Republic. □

Translated by Joan Reutershan   **49**

HM: In our bloc, only Germany has had a long tradition of industrial work, except maybe Czechoslovakia. There is none in Poland, none in the Soviet Union, none in Bulgaria, none in Rumania. And Hungary is just beginning.

SL: East Germany is to the other countries of the Eastern bloc what West Germany is, say, to Italy.

HM: Italy is the future of Western Europe because of the stage of the conflicts. It will take ten years for West Germany to get there.

SL: What is the future in the East?

HM: For young couples here, the child comes first, and next comes the car. People have to wait eight years to get a car. This is the image of the future.

SL: Socialist Utopia married to Western consumerism.

HM: This is the present outlook, and one of my writing problems. I don't have any interest in this way of life, and I can't bring myself to write about it.

SL: This allows you to encompass simultaneously the two sides of the wall.

HM: I like to stand with one leg on each side of the wall. Maybe this is a schizophrenic position, but none other seems to me real enough.

SL: Is this why you're being called "Müller-Deutschland"?

HM: This is a very personal joke. But there may be some truth in it.

SL: How do you deal with the contradiction?

Alternative Politics

Klaus Vogelsang (painter)
For the first time I have the feeling that there's a party whose political goals and understanding of democracy I can identify with.

Romy Haag (travesty star)
Young blood's always good.

Conny Konzack (concert impresario)
Of course. It's a definite hope for Berlin. They can tip the scales, force the big parties to be more citizen-oriented and examine their own petrified structures and thought.

In June 1980, the new Alternative List, a "rainbow" of opposition (pacifists, non-dogmatic leftists, environmentalists, anti-nukes, etc.), was elected to the West Berlin assembly with a surprising 7½% of
the votes.

HM: I believe in conflict. I don't believe in anything else. What I try to do in my writings is to strengthen the sense of conflicts, to strengthen confrontations and contradictions. There is no other way. I'm not interested in answers and solutions. I don't have any to offer. I'm interested in problems and conflicts.

SL: How can you have conflicts and contradictions between times or developments that never meet?

HM: The "silent majority" here is very interested in Western standards while younger people in the West are moving in our direction. One day, alternatives on both sides will meet. The surface movements — the silent majorities — never will.

SL: Do you really believe the "Alternative Scene" can have a lasting impact in Germany?

HM: The main function of alternative movements in the West is to establish in its midst islands of the Third World. West Berlin has become the third biggest Turkish city in the world. In ten years, West Germany will be a second Turkish or Greek or Italian state. This is a very positive phenomenon. It will prepare the ground for change.

SL: Berlin, London . . . grandeur and decadence of Western empire. History returns through the back door . . . .

HM: Toynbee used to say that a tree is weakening itself by growing. This is the beginning of decadence. I visited Moscow for the first time a few months ago. It was a very strange sight. In the elevator of my hotel — a huge building from

"I love the wall. There's the possibility to get shot from both sides."
Annette Humpe

the Stalinist era — there were people from all the Asian provinces. The whole city looked like a camp of nomads — a Napolean camp. It reminded me of the later phase of ancient Rome, ruler of the Greeks, but permeated from the inside by Greek culture. This dissolution is the hope.

SL: Because it may simultaneously dissolve the walls?

HM: At least it may free the elements that were originally brought together by imperialism.

SL: We may be getting close to the point where the various walls will give way to a lot of smaller ones.

HM: It's better to have millions of little walls than one or two big walls.

SL: That's what the end of history is about. History was a big wall to be gone through . . . .

HM: That's a European concept of history — very linear.

SL: The wall of history is totally visible here. I'd rather see it that way than hidden in people's minds.

HM: What I like about the Berlin wall is that it is a sign for a real situation, the situation the world is in. And here you have it in concrete. One can see the end of history more clearly from here.

SL: The Berlin wall becomes the fantasy of history realized, a living monument to a now defunct concept. Or an aesthetic object, like Christo's "Running Fence." Could you envisage it that way?

Katharina Thalbach (actress)
Yes, if they get an absolute majority.

Y Sa Lo (actress)
Alternative politics should be an alternative to politics. But that's as impossible as an alternative to life or something.

Thomas Brasch (writer)
Parties are useful only when they dissolve themselves.

Günter Grass (writer)
That's a question not directed only at the AL. I support the Social Democrats in the campaign and would like the AL, if they get into Parliament (and probably will), to become a sort of coalition partner for the SPD, on its understanding of the domestic politics of the city and also of Berlin's whole situation. I see that as a real possibility. But I don't think — this is true not only of AL but of every group — that you can take only your own interest into account, however justified that might be in other cases, in formulating your whole political platform in a city like Berlin with its precarious situation. Berlin's connection with the Federation, the Allies' responsibility for Berlin must take precedence.

HM: Yes, I can.

SL: Did you always put history at the center of your preoccupations as a writer?

HM: I have always been an object of history and so I try to become a subject. That's my preoccupation as a writer. Drama in Europe has always been linked to history, especially because of its geographical position. Germany has been an object of history, more so than France or Italy.

SL: I spoke recently with Klaus Wagenbach.[1] He thought there has been a definite mutation in Germany, that people have overcome the temptation of violence, the temptation of war — an opinion which is far from being shared by the rest of the world.

HM: It is an illusion.

SL: Do you think the beast is still alive and kicking?

HM: I'm sure about that. It's just waiting for another opportunity.

Writing and Treason

SL: That's a very Brechtian idea. Is that why you write for the theatre?

HM: I still believe German audiences understand only military language. You have to fight them in the theatre — otherwise they don't understand anything.

SL: How effective can the language of the theatre be?

TIP: How does it feel to be the spoiler in this election? Aren't you promoting the interests of the Christian Democrats?

AL : That's not our concern. Our concern is to become a political factor in this city, with one leg in Parliament and one leg outside it. We refuse to be forced into a corner about lesser and greater evils. The similarities between the SPD and the CDU are too great for that. We have a clear mission to represent the extra-parliamentary groups whose interests are systematically excluded.

TIP: What will that be like in Parliament?

AL: We want to use Parliament as a forum, to give expression to our movement there too.

TIP: In the past that was the classic historical role of the KPD.*

AL: The concept has historical connotations, true. At some point Lenin talks about bourgeois parliaments as forums. When we talk about a forum, we mean a broader context. We assume that basic interests of groups which are called minorities are never mentioned there — neither in committee nor in debates. The crucial question is, what to do once we're in? All the other parties have a repertory of parliamentary rules which they

HM: In our country, theatre allows you to have 500 or 800 people together in one room reacting at the same time, in the same space, to what is going on onstage. The impact of the theatre here is based on the absence of other ways of getting messages across to people. Films are not as important either because there's so much control. They also require much more money than the theatre. As a result, theatre here has taken over the function of other media in the West. I don't believe theatre has as great an impact in West Germany for instance. You can do anything on the stage there, but it doesn't mean anything to the society. Here the slogan of the Napoleonist era still applies: theatre is the revolution on the march.

SL: That's why you chose the theatre as your medium?

HM: Maybe it was not a choice. When you are an object of history, you need other figures to talk about your problems.

The first image I have from my childhood goes back to 1933. I was four years old. I was asleep. Then I heard some noise coming from the other room and through the keyhole, I saw that some men were beating my father. The S.A., the Nazis were arresting him. I went back to my bed, pretending to sleep. Then the door opened. My father was standing in the doorway. The two men beside him were much bigger than he was. He was a very small man. Then he looked inside and he said: "Oh, he's sleeping." Then they went away with him. That's my guilt. I pretended I was sleeping. This really is the first scene of my theatre.

SL: The first nightmare of history.

can use to make our life difficult. The CDU already declared that it was ready to exclude us from the spectrum of democratic parties — which we take as a compliment, given their understanding of democracy.

Take the committee on internal security as an example. That committee discusses very sensitive issues, and that's a place where the parliamentary rules could be used to exclude us. Then our choice would be to take a long and painful legal way or to use unconventional methods: exert pressure on institutions through demonstrations. We will definitely use the possibilities we have there. But we're always dependent on the strength of the Extra-Parliamentary Movement.* If we were to work only within Parliament, in an isolated way, we'd lose sight of our political connection.

TIP: What about the squatters? You want to legalize squatting. If you get into the Chamber of Deputies, you'll have to work for a parliamentary majority on this question. What concrete plans do you have?

AL: We were thinking about neutralizing property.

TIP: What does that mean?

AL: The decisions would no longer be made by the government or private property

HM: Yes. My next memory also has to do with my father. I was visiting him in the concentration camp with my mother. It was in 1934. We were standing outside the gate. He was led to the gate by two guards. He looked very small again. His clothes were too big for him. My mother talked to him through the wire. I couldn't talk. Then he was led away. One of the guards said: "Don't worry. Your father will be home soon." He had a very rosy but sad face. He was wearing a uniform. I still have a problem with uniforms. We went home and later on my mother told me that I talked during my sleep for days or weeks. I couldn't understand why he didn't jump over the fence.

The third memory is when he left East Germany. He had problems with Stalinism here.

SL: He was first arrested for being a Communist?

HM: Yes. He left East Germany in 1951 and I met him in West Berlin. He had been put in a camp while he was being questioned by the Allies. They didn't want to acknowledge him or to recognize him as a political refugee because he had been a functionary of the Social Democrats in East Berlin. He was suspicious for them too. Then they discovered he had some kind of bacteria, something he never had before. So he was put in a hospital and isolated. We talked through a glass door. He was standing on one side of the glass and I was standing on the other side. That was the next image.

SL: You didn't follow him to the West?

HM: No.

SL: Why didn't you?

owners. It means establishing an institution that would assume the function of neutralization, and preserve the space the squatters have won. The squatters could eventually govern themselves under the umbrella of such an institution.

Our main interest is not in passing new laws or generally in expanding government activity. On the contrary: emancipation from the State, citizen's initiatives, self-rule take precedence for us.

TIP: How do you conceive of your role in parliament?

AL: Here we come to the question of what the AL is and how it sees its vote. Does it see itself exclusively as a coordinator? Is it just an initiator in the content of the new social movement, or is it something more? For instance an organization that develops comprehensive social strategies, where the new social movements are only an aspect. We are witnessing the increasing estrangement of movements from each other. An example: the trade union movement, which supports nuclear power plants, and the anti-nuclear plant movement. The AL could perhaps work as mediator to reduce or eventually overcome this alienation. □

Translated by Michael Lazarin

HM: I didn't really think about it then. Maybe I identified with the East Berlin or the Russian system more than he did. For the most part, I wanted to be alone. I suppose it was a good way of getting rid of your parents.

There was another memory from 1936 or '37. In school, we had to write an essay on the autobahn. We were told that the best text would be sent to Berlin. It could get a prize or a medal. I came home. My father was jobless. My mother wasn't home. She was working in a factory. I told my father about the essay. He said: "No problem. Don't worry about the medal." Two hours later he said: "Let's eat," and he prepared a meal. Then he said: "I will help you write it." And he helped me. Then he said: "You must write that it's a good thing the Führer is building the highway because my father, who is jobless, may be able to get work there." And I wrote that down. That was the experience of treason and of weakness, but another kind of weakness than before. There was a break between us from then on.

SL: Did you get the medal?

HM: I got a prize.

SL: And your father?

HM: He got the job with the highway.

SL: Because of the essay?

HM: Yes. The authorities liked the text. They were looking for some examples that could be used as an alibi, and since I mentioned my father's problem, they gave him the job.

Dr. Jaeger

Berlin, City of Records

Poor, too old, plagued by crime; or, permeated by culture, rich in woodlands and water, with the greatest variety of media of all the German cities and the longest subway? By looking at the facts, everyone can paint his or her own picture of Berlin. Dr. Jaeger, the chief administrative advisor of the Federal Science Service, furnishes some stark contrasts. Commissioned by Deitrich Bahner, the Berlin CDU deputy, Jaeger compiled a set of facts delineating Berlin's extremes: "Berlin — City of Records." Some of his findings, comparing Berlin to the rest of Germany, are presented below.

Highest percentage of municipally-owned land: 47.8%
Highest death-rate per 1000: 18.8 deaths per 1000.
Highest surplus of women: 1244 women per 1000 men.
Highest number of single person households: 50.5%.

SL: So you repaid your debt through a treason. Is that why you didn't follow in your father's footsteps?

HM: This is one of the main reasons.

SL: But at the time, this treason occurred through writing.

HM: Yes.

SL: Did you think at that time of becoming a writer?

HM: Yes.

SL: Was that your very first text?

HM: Yes.

SL: But it was the wrong "lane."

HM: Yes.

SL: Were you a communist at that time?

HM: At least I thought I was. I believed in communism, but Stalin had nothing to do with it. I learned about Stalinism through my father.

SL: Your father got in trouble with the Nazis because he was a communist, and with the communists because he was anti-Stalinist.

HM: Then there was the great paradox of his life in the West. He started working for the West German administration. His job was to pay pensions to

Highest immigration increase (independent of number of inhabitants): c.36,000.
Lowest municipal tax: 246,55 DM ($107.19) per inhabitant.
Lowest real estate tax; c.523 DM ($2.27) per inhabitant.
Second highest crime rate (after Frankfort).
Greatest number of drug deaths (without taking the population into account, otherwise Frankfurt is greater) 1979: 64.
Greatest Federal/Regional subsidy for theater (independent of number of inhabitants): 50 million DM ($21.7 million).
Highest cultural expenditure per inhabitant: 904.00 DM ($411.00)
Greatest number of museums (independent of number of inhabitants): c.45.
Greatest amount of municipal expenditure for science and research per inhabitant: 637.00 DM ($276.95) in 1977.
Greatest amount for social welfare per inhabitant (after federal social welfare legislation): 423,85 DM ($184.28).
Highest number of hospital bed occupancy per inhabitant: 13.5 per 1000.
Greatest hospital bed utilization: 87%.
Greatest average duration of stay per patient in hospital: 22 days.
Greatest mortality rate of mothers during childbirth: 10 mothers per 16,678 living infants.

57

"Aha, the Jews are still the best Germans."

Amos Grunebaum

MARGARETE ISRAEL

Jewish Like Me

I guess you know that we Berliners are considered to be curious and whenever something goes on we've got to stick our nose in it. We like to sit by the window and watch — God forbid, we could miss something! Well, I don't have much time to spare, but that's something I really miss. When I look across from my balcony I don't see anybody leaning out of his window. We're barely 300 feet away, but their windows are always closed. Well, I kept puzzling and puzzling, because they're the same nosy Berliners, after all. Either they're strictly 1000 percenters who don't want anything to do with us 'bad capitalists' or whatever else we in the West are supposed to be, or they're just plain scared, scared somebody would wave and another would wave back, something that's almost automatic among people. Either way, I'm absolutely convinced that any contact from window to window is strictly *verboten* for those who live in East Berlin near the Wall.

widows of Nazis, to widows of generals and to the old officers of the Wehrmacht.

SL: Widows of Nazis got a pension?

HM: According to the law of the Weimar Republic, widows of civil servants like Göring, get a pension and a very high one too. It's much more difficult for communists or widows of communists to get a pension in West Germany.

SL: Did you consider it an irony of history that your father had to assume that responsibility?

HM: Yes.

SL: Did you feel there was some sort of immanent justice?

HM: Yes. Another retribution.

SL: Your writing about history — is that another way of dealing with the debt?

HM: My main existence is in writing. The other level of existence is just perfunctory.

SL: When your writing is being performed, does it take another dimension altogether? You mentioned earlier that the theatre, as opposed to fiction, is a very collective phenomenon.

HM: I have a real difficulty writing prose. I don't believe in literature as a work of art to be read. I don't believe in reading. I couldn't imagine writing a novel.

Well, we've lived here since early 1978 and nothing has ever happened. Only now and then a mine would blow up, and that makes a hell of a racket. Probably rabbits or cats that trigger it in the death-strip down there. And quickly the *Vopos*, the People's Police, come racing up to check and rake everything nice and smooth so they can see any possible footprint. One time I yelled across: 'Bastard, idiots!' but they paid no mind. Only their guard dogs barked back. As for the church, nobody can get in from either side. It sits smack in the middle of that death-strip, and guess what it's named? 'Church of the Reconciliation,' so help me! Only Jesus can look across and He doesn't dare wave, either.

My father-in-law had a hell of time under the Nazis, with a name like Israel. And if you'd see my mother-in-law and her nose, you'd say, she sure is Jewish. It's a funny thing, when you see a Jew, you automatically look at his nose, but none of us is Jewish, despite the name. My husband's family had to prove three generations back that they were nice clean Aryans, not that I give a damn. Once, handing my paper to the East German border guard, he said: 'Well, Israel! Are you just as aggressive?' And me, shooting right back: 'Only when I'm attacked!' That's a Berliner for you. □

Photograph and Text by Henry Ries   59

SL: The essay you wrote on the autobahn, is it the only piece of prose you ever wrote?

HM: No, it was the first piece. I've only written very short prose works.

SL: Where does your distrust of prose come from?

HM: Writing prose you are all alone. You can't hide yourself.

SL: You've got to assume personally the responsibility for your writing?

HM: I don't think I can write prose in the third person. I can't write: "Washington got up and went to 42nd Street."

SL: That was the main objection of the Surrealists to fiction. They couldn't bring themselves to write: "The Marquise went out at 5 o'clock..."

HM: I can only imagine writing prose in the first person. Writing drama you always have masks and roles and you can talk through them. That's why I prefer drama — because of the masks. I can say one thing and say the contrary.

SL: You don't want to assume an unequivocal position. Is that why you like to dramatize contradictions?

HM: I want to get rid of contradictions and it's easier to do it with drama. I had a very strange experience while I was writing a short prose text dealing with the suicide of my former wife. (She killed herself in 1966). First I wrote in the third person: "He came home and he saw..." Then I realized that this was

MAURICE BLANCHOT

The Word Berlin

Berlin represents, for everyone, the problem of division. From one point of view, it is a strictly political problem for which, we must keep in mind, there are strictly political solutions. From another point of view, it is a social and economic problem (and therefore, also political, but in a wider sense), since it represents the confrontation of two economical-social systems and structures. From yet another point of view, it is a metaphysical problem: Berlin is not only Berlin, but is also the symbol of the division of the world, and something even more: a "point in the universe," the place in which the question of a unity which is both necessary and impossible confronts every individual

---

Maurice Blanchot is one of the most important contemporary French writers and philosophers of literature. The following text, translated from the Italian, was never published in France.

the attitude of a coward, so I switched to the "I": "I came home and saw her..." Another part of the text is a memory from the end of the war. I was a prisoner of war in an American camp near Schwerin. I only stayed there two days. I managed to exchange my ration of meat over the fence for a civilian jacket. Then I put it on and went to the gate. I talked to the American guard and he showed me photographs of his family and children. I talked to him for a while. Soon I was standing on the other side of the gate. We shook hands and I went away. This was the war for me. Then I was alone for a long time. I was just walking through the open country when I met a young German soldier. He was my age, 16. I'll never forget his face. He looked like a hen. He had a hen's face. He was clinging to me. He needed company. He needed a leader. It was terrible. I tried to get rid of him for days. I treated him very badly. It was the first time I ever wanted to kill anybody, just to get rid of him. He was so weak, he was looking at me like a slave. In the text about the suicide of my wife, I tried to write about this experience too. I described the murder of this boy. I didn't actually commit it but in this text, I killed him three times. It was a very strange sensation just to write: "I took the spade and I split his head; I saw the blood gushing." It's a very different kind of writing experience than having ten murders in a drama. It's much more personal.

SL: The paradox is that, grammatically speaking, anyone can appropriate the first person. Whoever writes or reads "I" becomes "I".

HM: For me, the first person is very personal. The space between I and I is so vast...

SL: ...that you need to dramatize it.

who resides there, and who, in residing there, experiences not only a place of residence but also the absence of a place of residence. And this is not all. Berlin is not a symbol, but a real city where human dramas unknown to the inhabitants of other large cities are lived out: the word division, in this case, means laceration. And there is still more to consider: from within the same cultural framework, Berlin poses, in very unusual terms, the problem of two contrasting cultures, of two language systems which are totally unrelated to each other even though they are the same identical language; thus Berlin itself questions the false sense of agreement on the existence of intellectual security and the possibility of communication, arrived at by men who live in close proximity to one another, and based upon the fact that they all partake of the same language and of the same historical past. And this is still not all.

The problem of division — of fracture — as Berlin poses it not only to Berliners, not only to Germans but, I believe, to every thinking human being — and it does so in an impelling, I mean painful, way — is a problem which we are not capable of formulating adequately, in its *complete* reality; the most we can do is to formulate it in a *fragmentary* way (which does not even mean in a partial way). In other words, every time it occurs to us to bring up a problem of this nature (after all, there are other such problems), we must

61

HM: Yes.

SL: There is a definite relationship between prose and the theatre then. The theatre is an overcoming of prose and prose a repression of the drama of subjectivity. You dramatize subjectivity in history in order to do away with the first person. Does it mean that the thematics of your play is always personal?

HM: Not on the surface, but there's always something very personal in it. Maybe that's why I don't like to talk about my plays. I don't think a play can be good unless you burn all your intentions in the writing process. So there's no need, no impulse to talk about it. If you talk about your project beforehand you lose your impulse to write it. And after it's finished, it's like talking about a corpse, a dead body. By writing it, I got rid of it.

The Age of The Innocents

SL: Are your plays then a way of getting rid of history, rather than talking about it? But "history" is such an abstract word. Your memories of your father, of the war, of the concentration camp, of the American camp, all these walls and fences, are these really the roots of your preoccupation with history?

HM: I think so. The confrontation with power, this is history for me as a personal experience. Take my version of Sophocles' *Philoctetes*, for instance. In my own play, I have Philoctetes killed by his friend, Neoptolemus. The argument moves as follows: Philoctetes hates Odysseus. But Odysseus realizes that they need Philoctetes in order to end the Trojan war. He asks Neoptolemus to convince Philoctetes to go along with them. Neoptolemus doesn't want to lie

remember that to speak about it honestly means to speak about it in such a way as to allow the profound gap in our words and thoughts to speak out as well, in such a way as to allow expression to the impossibility of speaking about the problem in terms presumed to be exhaustive. This means: 1) that even omniscience, if such a thing were possible, is of no use in this case: the essence of a situation like this one would escape even a God, who would be supposed to know everything; 2) that in general it is not possible to control, survey or contain in one sweep the problem of division, and that, in this case as in others, panoramic vision is not correct vision; 3) that the deliberate selection of a fragment of the situation is not a skeptical withdrawal from the problem or a weary rejection of a complete synthesis (though it could be that); but a patient-yet-impatient, mobile-yet-immobile method of research, and the affirmation — furthermore — that the meaning of the problem, the integral nature of its meaning, is not to be found immediately in ourselves and in what we write, but that it is something yet-to-come and that, in the act of examining this meaning, we grasp it as pure analytical futurity; 4) this means, in the end, that repetition is a necessity. Every fragmentary word, every fragmentary analysis demands infinite repetition and plurality.

I shall add two (fragmentary) observations. The frantic political abstraction which Berlin represents had its peak expression on the day when the wall was built, an act

so he tells Philoctetes that he's been commissioned by Odysseus. Philoctetes misunderstands Neoptolemus' motives and the prospect of an agreement between Philoctetes and Odysseus vanishes. Philoctetes wants to kill Odysseus, but Neoptolemus ends up killing Philoctetes. Odysseus tells him then that Philoctetes' corpse is just as good as the living body. He shows the corpse to the troops of Philoctetes and he tells them that he was killed by the Trojans when they realized they couldn't persuade him to fight with them.

SL: So Odysseus is the power of the State and his cunning is inherent to this power.

HM: These are three attitudes to history, to politics: Odysseus is the pragmatic one and Neoptolemus is the innocent. He kills because he's innocent. Philoctetes is beyond history because he is the victim of politics.

SL: The innocent always ends up with dirty hands.

HM: Yes.

SL: Were you playing the innocent when you worked on the autobahn essay?

HM: I think so, yes.

SL: That's why you had to clean your hands by writing drama?

HM: Yes.

SL: If the problem with history is very much a problem with power, should one assume that history is finished?

which was dramatically concrete. Up until 13 August 1961, the absence of a sign of visible separation — even though before that time a series of regular and irregular controls had already given warning of the enigmatic advance of a line of demarcation — gave to the act of partitioning an ambiguous character and meaning: what was it? A border? Certainly: but it was also something else; something less than a border, given the fact that people could cross over it en masse, escaping the controls; but it was also something more than a border, since to cross over it meant to pass not from one country into another, not from one language into another, but within the same country and language, from "truth" to "error," from "evil" to "good," from "life" to " death"; and this meant to undergo, almost without realizing it, a metamorphosis (but without having more than a partial understandiang as a basis for deciding just where those brutally opposite fields of "good" and "evil" lay). The nearly overnight construction of the wall substituted the violence of decisive separation for indecisive ambiguity. The world outside of Germany realized, in a way which varied in degrees of intensity and superficiality, the dramatic changes prefigured in that event: changes not only in human relationships but also in the economic and political field. But one thing, I believe, escaped everyone's understanding (and perhaps even that of many Germans): the fact that the reality of that wall was destined to throw into the realm of *abstraction* the unity of a large, living, 63

HM: Power is getting to be more and more spectacular and unreal. It becomes power-play. Its theatrical elements are increasingly clear. Nobody's really got power anymore and this is something you can play around with.

SL: The representation of power is more and more divorced from actual power.

HM: It's more and more an empty frame. It doesn't carry any content anymore. It's just like a tennis match.

SL: Power now is internalized. It is in people's heads. By the same token it has become more democratic. How can you work out such a modern conception of power through antiquity, through a thematics that refers to a more traditional conception of the State and a cunning deliberation on the part of the statesman, Odysseus?

HM: In my version of the play, the Trojan war is just a sign or image for the Socialist revolution reaching the stage where it ends up in stagnation, in a stalemate situation. Odysseus didn't want to enter the war; he was compelled to do so. Nobody really wanted it but now they are all in it and the only way out is to go deeper into it in order to put it to an end. There is no ideology anymore but you can't end the war by destroying the enemy.

SL: How does this relate precisely to the Socialist revolution?

HM: I wrote the play about the stalemate situation of Soviet Socialism, and more generally about the Russian revolution in the context of world revolution. Lenin's idea that the German revolution was near because revolution was

organic city, a city that was not and is not — and here in fact is where its profundity really lies — just one city, or two cities, or the capital of a country, or any important city whatsoever, or anything else except for that vanished center-of-a-city. So then, the wall succeeded in *abstractly concretizing* the division, in rendering it visible and tangible, and thus, in forcing us into thinking of Berlin, with the very unity of its name, no longer as some essence which had lost its unity, but as the sociological reality of two absolutely different cities.[1] The "scandal" and the importance of the wall lies in the fact that while it represents concrete oppression, it always remains essentially abstract, reminding us of what we consistently forget: that abstraction is not simply an incorrect way of thinking, not just an obviously impoverished form of language, but that abstraction is our world, the world in which, day after day, we live and think.

By now we have at our disposal an enormous number of writings on the situation of Berlin. It shocks me to realize that among all these writings, at least for the non-Germans, it was in two novels that the best approach to this situation was found: two novels which were neither political nor realistic. I will not attribute the credit for this solely to the talent of Uwe Johnson, but to the truth of literature. In this case, it was the difficulty itself of writing such literature which accounted for the author's successful approach to the situation; rather, it was the impossibility, for the author, of writing

bound to happen first in industrial countries didn't prove true. The German revolution failed and he had to give up on the idea of revolution or implement it in one country only. And since there was no other object, it meant colonizing your own population.

SL: That was the beginning of the dilemma. Does it mean that history will exist as long as blocs exist? Your hope, I understand, is that each bloc will eventually crumble from inside.

HM: I think the existence of blocs and the way the blocs understand themselves, the identity of the blocs, is based on the illusion of history.

SL: Oppositions always play in a conservative way. History is conservative.

HM: A critic saw in my last plays an attack on history, the linear concept of history. He read in them the rebellion of the body against ideas, or more precisely: the impact of ideas, and of the idea of history, on human bodies. This is indeed my theatrical point: the thrusting on stage of bodies and their conflict with ideas. As long as there are ideas, there are wounds. Ideas are inflicting wounds on the body.

SL: Ideas produce dead bodies. As long as you have history . . .

HM: . . . You have victims.

SL: There are three basic historical roles: the role of the cunning, pragmatic statesman, the role of the innocent killer, and the victim who is part of and plays his role in history. I don't think there is a choice to be made between the three.

"In the climate of deterrence, the military no longer confront each other. They turn against their own population."

Paul Virilio

books like these, in which the question of division is involved — and hence, the necessity, on his part, of capturing that impossibility in the writing of his novels: this is what brought the literary operations so close to the unique problem of "Berlin"; the best approach to the subject was realized precisely by virtue of that gap which literature had to leave open, with its dark unrelenting tension — the gap between reality and the literary expression of the meaning of that reality. Perhaps the impatient reader and critic will be able to say that in works like these the relationship to the world and to the responsibility of making a political decision in respect to that world is something which remains out of reach and indirect. Indirect, yes. But we might also ask ourselves in fact whether, in order to get closest to the "world" via the word and, above all, writing, the indirect path might not be the right path, and the shortest. ☐

Translated by James Cascaito

1. The wall pretended to substitute the sociological truth of a situation, the matter of fact, for the more profound truth which could be called — by oversimplifying, of course — the dialectic of this situation.

HM: No, there is no choice. My choice is outside the play.

SL: Innocence is not such a good position either. The guilt of the killer is incommensurate to the deed. Do you think Germany is now playing the part of the innocent?

HM: The turning point in German pre-fascist history occurred in 1932. The chief managers of the German industries met in Dusseldorf and Hitler made his famous speech, which really was a Marxist speech. He declared that the living standards of the white race can be improved only if the living standards of the other races decreased. You cannot hold this position by economic means only, he said. You need military means as well. They understood perfectly this kind of language, and he got the money he needed for the war. This was the last bulwark against socialism.

SL: Hitler was no innocent. But he turned Germany into a nation of killers. Do you think Germany can only dare face its own past through the mask of Greek culture?

HM: I wouldn't want to write another antique play or adaptation now. In the early sixties, you couldn't write a play on Stalinism. You needed this kind of model. People here understood it very quickly. But maybe in the West it just reads like a strange story, a mere version of the antique drama.

SL: What is it about East Germany that you have to go back to the Greeks in order to talk about the present?

HM: At the time of the antique drama, Greek society still relied on the laws of

HEINER MÜLLER

Obituary

She was dead when I got home. She was lying on the cement floor in the kitchen, half on her belly, half on her side, one leg drawn up as if asleep, her head near the door. I bent down, lifted her face off its side and spoke the word which I called her when we were alone. I felt like I was on a stage. I saw myself leaning on the door frame, looking half bored half amused at a man who was kneeling on the cement floor of his kitchen at three in the morning, bent over his possibly unconscious possibly dead wife, who was holding up her head with his hands and speaking with her like a doll for no other audience than myself. Her face was a grimace, the upper row of teeth at an angle in the gaping mouth as if her jaw were dislocated. When I lifted her up, I heard something like a groan that seemed to come from her intestines rather than from her mouth, in any case from a distance. I had often seen her lying there as if dead when I came home and lifted her up with fear (hope) that she was dead, and the horrible sound was reassuring, an

the clans. The step from the clan to the city, to the "polis," marked the beginning of the class society. Now East Germany's goal is to put an end to this kind of society. So the two turning points can be related ideologically in our minds.

SL: Is it paradoxically a positive factor for you as a dramatist to write and be performed in a country where things cannot be as explicitly discussed as in the West? Is that an intrinsic part of the mask?

HM: There's a remark by Hölderlin (I'm always trying to use quotations) on the function of drama at the time of Sophocles. Words should take effect, Hölderlin writes. Words are murder. A text has two levels of transmission: one is information, the other, expression. The expression is much stronger and words much more effective here than in the West because information is repressed. Here words aren't just a vehicle for information, you derive information from expression. This is a better situation for drama. When I am in the West for any extensive period of time, I become aware of the inflation of information. Nobody can possibly read the newspapers in one day. And when you do it, you don't really get any information because there is so much of it. This is a way of misinforming people by informing them.

SL: You inform people to death, but information is divorced from expression. Everything being strictly codified in the East, do you feel that this opens up a range of expression virtually unknown elsewhere?

HM: People in the East know what is going on between the words. They bring in their own experience. People in the West don't. For them it's just an empty space.

answer. Later the doctor explained: a kind of belch caused by moving the body, the last bit of breath pressed out of the lungs by gas. Or something like that. I carried her to the bedroom, she was heavier than usual, naked under her robe. When I placed the load on the sofa bed, a denture fell out of her mouth. It had probably been loosened in the death agony. Now I knew what had distorted her face. I hadn't known that she wore dentures. I went back to the kitchen and turned off the gas stove, and then — after looking at her empty face — to the telephone. I thought, with the receiver in my hand, about my life with her, that is, about the various deaths she had sought and missed for thirteen years until this successsful night. She had tried it with a razor blade; after she cut one vein she called me over to show me the blood. With a noose, after she had locked the door but — either out of hope or absentmindedness — had left a window open which was accessible from the roof. With mercury, from a thermometer which she had broken for that reason. With pills. With gas. She wanted to jump from the window or balcony only when I was in the apartment. I called up a friend, I still didn't want to know that she was dead and a matter for the officials, then the emergency number. ARE YOU CRAZY PUT OUT YOUR CIGARETTE IMMEDIATELY YOU'LL BE KILLED YES AT LEAST TWO HOURS ALCOHOL HER HEART DIDN'T YOU NOTICE THAT YOUR WIFE WHERE IS THE LETTER WHAT KIND OF LETTER DID SHE LEAVE A LETTER WHERE WERE YOU BETWEEN WHEN AND WHEN TOMORROW NINE O'CLOCK ROOM TWENTYTHREE SUMMONS

67

SL: Can you estimate in advance, when you write, the weight of this silence or are you surprised after the fact by the power of allusion in your plays?

HM: It's always a surprise. I write more than I know. I write in another time than the one I'm living in.

SL: Where are you writing from? Is it the time of Odysseus or the time of Philoctetes?

HM: I'm in the time of Philoctetes, although I can't stand to live in that time. Heinrich Mann said of his brother, Thomas Mann, that since he wrote *Buddenbrooks,* he never saw him suffer anymore. Here I have the reputation of being a pessimist. I am mainly accused of having a pessimistic attitude towards history. I never understood that because in life I have no problems. The problems are in my writing, not in my life.

SL: The other day you told me that when you write it's some sort of a black box.

HM: A black space. I don't like to have detailed concepts. I don't want to know the plot before I find it. I never look for a plot. I find it before I look for it. That's what I like about writing: it's a risk, an adventure, an experience. When I'm finished with it, then I can think about it but that's quite another thing altogether.

SL: History, then, is not something you can connect to in a personal way. It's by writing yourself out that you have an immediate access to history.

HM: Yes.

THE CORPSE WILL BE PICKED UP AUTOPSY DON'T WORRY YOU WON'T NOTICE ANYTHING. Waiting for the hearse, in the next room a dead woman. The irreversibility of time. Time of the murderer: obliterated present in the grip of past and future. Go into the next room (three times), look at the body ONCE AGAIN (three times), she is naked under the blanket. Growing indifference toward that thing with which my feelings (grief sorrow lust) have nothing more to do. Draw the blanket again over the body (three times) which will be cut open tomorrow, over the empty face. The first traces of poisoning the third time: blue. Back to the waiting room (three times). The first thought of my own death (there is no other), in the small house in Saxony, in the tiny bedroom, three low stories high, five or six years old me, alone about midnight on the unavoidable chamber pot, the moon in the window. THE ONE WHO HELD THE CAT UNDER THE KNIVES OF THE PLAYMATES WAS I/ I THREW THE SEVENTH STONE AT THE SPARROWS' NEST AND THE SEVENTH WAS THE ONE THAT HIT IT/ I HEARD THE DOGS BARKING IN THE VILLAGE WHEN THE MOON WAS FULL/ WHITE AGAINST THE WINDOW ROOM ASLEEP/ I WAS A HUNTER OF WOLVES HUNTED WITH WOLVES ALONE/ BEFORE FALLING ASLEEP SOMETIMES I HEARD THE HORSES SCREAMING IN THE STALLS. A feeling of the universe during the night trek along the railroad tracks in Mecklenburg, my boots too small and my uniform too big: the droning emptiness. CHICKEN FACE. Somewhere on the way through the aftermath he attached himself to me, a gaunt figure

SL: What about the narratives we discussed earlier? It may not be at this level that you're writing, but if you didn't have the experience of history at such a personal level then your writing would probably be very different.

HM: There's one definition of the theatre by Gertrude Stein that I like very much: writing for theatre means that everything that's going on during the writing process belongs to the text. When you write prose you have to sit down for a while and just write but drama you can't write sitting. It's more body language than prose.

SL: (abruptly) The fact that you keep quoting people, is that another way of using masks?

HM: Maybe. (He laughs).

SL: Both the quoting and the drama are in some sort of a relationship. After all, Sophocles also is a quotation.

HM: Yes.

SL: Is that the way you deal with subjectivity?

HM: Yes.

Death Speaking

SL: Your relationship to your own history, or to history — is it something that's affected by your own writing?

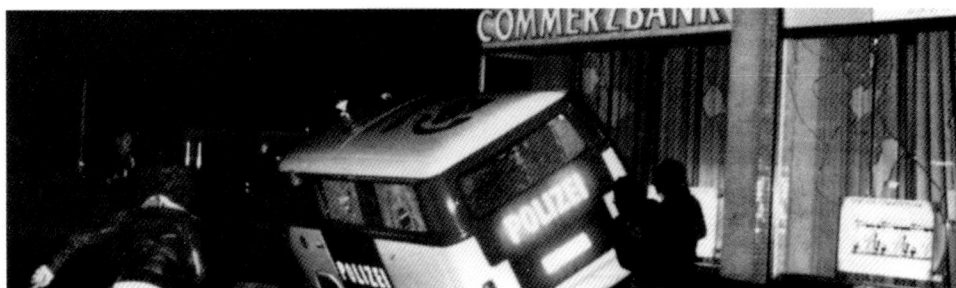

in a flapping military coat which dragged on the ground, a too big cap on a too small bird's head, bread bag hanging at his knees, a child in field-grey. He ran along next to me, silent, I can't remember that he spoke a word. Only when I walked faster or even ran to get rid of him did he emit short wretched noises between his panting breaths. Several times I thought that I had finally gotten rid of him, he was only a dot on the plain behind me, then not even that; but he caught up in the dark and when I woke up, in a barn or in a field, he was lying next to me again, rolled in his shabby coat, his bird's head level with my knees, and if I was able to get up and away before he awoke, I soon heard his wretched panting behind me. I cursed him. He stood before me, looking at me thankfully with swimming dog's eyes. I don't remember anymore whether I spit on him: you don't beat chickens. Never was my desire to kill a person so strong. I stabbed him with the bayonet he had pulled out of the folds of his coat to share his last tinned meat with me, I ate first so that I didn't have to eat his saliva, pushed the bayonet between his thin shoulder blades before it was his turn, watched without regret his blood glistening on the grass. That was near the tracks, after I had kicked him so that he would take a different road. I struck him with a shovel just as he finished building a wall against the wind which swept across the plain we had to sleep on. He didn't resist when I pulled the shovel out of his hand, not even when he saw the blade coming did he squeek out a cry. He must have expected it. He only raised his hands over his head. I saw with relief in the rapidly

HM: The first preoccupation I have when I write drama is to destroy things. For thirty years Hamlet was a real obsession for me, so I tried to destroy him by writing a short text, *Hamlet-Machine*. German history was another obsession and I tried to destroy this obsession, this whole complex. I think the main impulse is to strip things to their skeleton, to rid them of their flesh and surface. Then you are finished with them.

SL: You prefer body language, but you don't like corpses to putrify. Actually, it's an attitude you often find in "primitive" societies. They eat the body of the deceased because they want the bones to be clean. Do you find that theatre has primitive roots?

HM: The formula for theatre is just birth and death. The effect of theatre, its impact, is the fear of change because the last change is death. There are two ways to deal with this fear: as comedy, by deflating the fear of death; and as tragedy, by elevating it.

SL: To go back to Philoctetes — it means that even when you're dead you're not rid of history. Death itself can be used. Death is a process and it's only when you get to the bone that you lose the identity that can still be used for all too human purposes.

HM: I was very astonished when I talked to Klaus Michael Gruber.[2] He said he would like to perform not one of my plays (he doesn't like them) but one of my poems. The content of this poem is as follows: I'm coming back from some foreign country to Berlin; I take a taxi from the airport and I'm looking at this dead city of Berlin. For the first time I feel the need or the desire to take out my

spreading darkness how a mask of black blood obliterated the chicken face. On a sunny May day I pushed him from a bridge that had been bombed. I let him go first, he didn't turn around, a shovel in his back was enough; the bomb hole was twenty meters across, the bridge was high enough for a fall to death, asphalt below. I watched the path of his flight, his coat ballooned like a sail, the side rudder his empty bread bag, the fatal landing. Then I walked over the bomb hole; I needed only to spread my arms, carried on air like an angel. He has no place in my dreams anymore, since I killed him (three times). DREAM. In a house overgrown by trees, the walls burst by trees, I go up the stairs above which a huge naked woman with heavy breasts is strung up, arms and legs spread wide. (Maybe she is even holding herself in this position without ropes: hovering.) Above me the enormous thighs, opened like a scissors which I walk further into with each step, her wild black bushy pubic hair, the rawness of her vulva. □

Translated by Marc Silberman

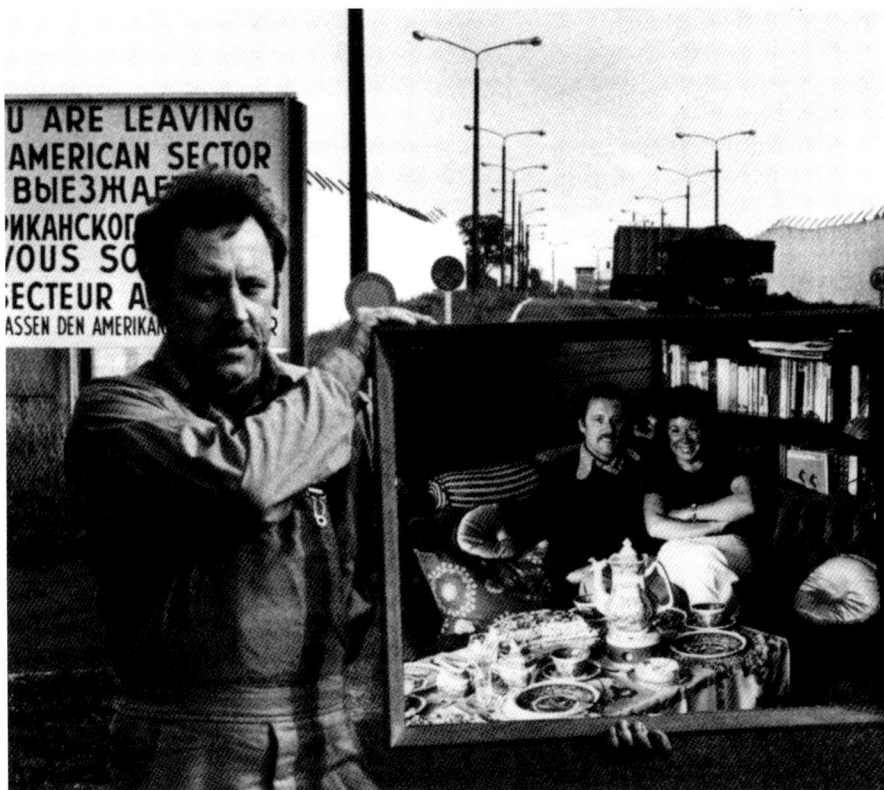

KLAUS BARTZSCH

The Provocation

It isn't so much apprehension I feel when I drive my load of garbage into the German Democratic Republic. It's certainly not fear. I say, I feel provoked! And I'll tell you why I feel provoked: Every time I drive my truck — and that's a special 42-ton truck, built to the tune of 350,000 Marks, loaded with 20 tons of garbage compressed in our latest, six-story, city-block long, multi-million ecological marvel of a sanitation depot which doesn't pollute, doesn't smell, is fully automated, monitored by TV and finally approved, if not fully accepted, by the locals around here, which includes me — as I was trying to tell you, when I drive my 42-ton baby through this opening in the Wall — and that's all that goes through here, no pedestrians, no traffic, no Allies of any color, just our gar-

dead wife from her grave and to look at what is left of her. I want to see the bones I never saw before.

SL: So the trouble with history is . . .

HM: that it's covered with flesh and skin, surface. The main impulse is to get through the surface in order to see the structure.

SL: But you first have to take the body out of the grave. You have to bring it in the open. You have to lay bare the bones of history in order to make sure that history is dead.

HM: Yes.

SL: In "primitive" societies, the dead are very much a part of life. They still belong to the tribe. They don't have to haunt the living to death because they never cease to communicate with them. Our societies, on the other hand, are based on the repression of death. This repression has to be dealt with, especially in Germany where death and history have become so indistinguishable that history could only return in terror, as a bringer of terror and death. So maybe what you do with the theatre is to make sure that death is a part of life again so that the body of history stops infesting German life.

I was very struck yesterday, talking to a pop star, Annette Humpe, by the fact that there's an incredible amount of ambivalence on the part of Germans in relation to their own country. There's a feeling, especially among the young generation, that they have to deal with something that they don't quite feel responsible for but don't quite know how to get rid of.

bage trucks — and when I think what they squeeze out of us just for 'allowing' to dump our garbage in 'their' country, because they can blackmail us into paying almost any price since they know we have no place left here in West Berlin to dump it, when I think they soak us 28.50 Marks for every ton of garbage, and you multiply that by four trips a day per truck for a total of 45 trucks — with 15 trucks we're still in an experimental stage in our plant right now, but the North plant is going full blast with 30 trucks and, once we get going, we'll have that many or more — and multiply that figure by 6 for a week and, finally, multiply that by 52 — I wouldn't be surprised if we pay them over 50 million Marks a year, for the privilege of dumping our garbage!

That's why I feel provoked — and this doesn't include purchase of special trucks, building and maintenance of the compression depots, salaries — oh hell, I better stop, though I should mention that the garbage treaty signed by West Berlin and the GDR* is to run for twenty years! Add to that what we pay for the use of waterways, rail and truck transit, customs, permits, road-use taxes and hundreds of other items and I'd say West Berlin must be paying billions to the GDR every year.

And I bet *they* feel provoked, because they think we have so much more. They're right, we do have more, but that's no reason to slap us with heavy fines for the slightest offense, like an indicator light on the truck that's not functioning. And they are told the

HM: Responsibility?

SL: We call it history. Do you also feel this kind of ambivalence toward German culture? Do you feel that there is something inherent in it that led to the terror of Nazism and to the extermination of the Jews?

HM: In one of the issues of your magazine — I think it was *Nietzsche's Return* — there is an anecdote whose source I couldn't find, although I don't think it was an invention. It was a story about a student who leaves in the middle of a lecture given by Hegel. He said he couldn't stand it anymore because suddenly he got the feeling that death was speaking. The consequence of this radical way of thinking, of thinking in logical terms, has something to do with the concentration camps. This is the negative aspect of going through to the bones. This is still a German problem.

SL: When I came back to Berlin (I happened to be here exactly 20 years ago, just a few days before the wall was built), I was surprised, even somewhat worried, not to feel any sort of hostility towards Germany. It was as if the dead had been buried as far as I am concerned. I felt, however, that it hadn't been buried by the Germans, especially among some writers I happened to meet or read, like Peter Brückner, Thomas Schmidt or Klaus Wagenbach. I felt these were the innocents. And it made me very uneasy because I felt the type of humanist discourse they hold is still a product of guilt. And being Jewish myself, I just don't want to have to deal with guilt anymore. I felt on the contrary close to the new generation of Germans, and I am indeed a German in this respect: I don't want to have to live with guilt, not for fear of death but because I think guilt has to be overcome somewhere.

West is already bankrupt! I must say those people are to be pitied, and I can understand why they feel provoked. I can really feel it, though they never say anything. As a matter of fact, we never talk to each other! At the checkpoint, not a word; at the dumping place inside the GDR, no conversation with the workers who bulldoze the garbage we dump at their direction; returning to the border, their guards silently inspect the empty truck, top to bottom, wheel to wheel, to make sure we're not smuggling someone out; not a single word of greeting, of recognition, nothing. The real fear is that something could happen, a breakdown, a malfunction or a serious accident, involving someone's life! They aren't even as friendly as, say, people in Italy would be. We're truly on foreign soil, even if it *is* Germany.

So a lot of people ask if I feel safe here, if I'm not worried living on an island or fear that Berlin will fall one day. I say: "Nonsense — we live in the safest city in the world!" Considering all the extortions we allow them to squeeze out of us, you don't think they're stupid enough to give us up — only to be stuck with a few square miles of economically worthless real estate and a lot of old people. □

Photograph and text by Henry Ries

ROCHUS MISCH

Why Don't They Make a Movie About Me?

Rochus Misch: I was never a member of the Party, always a member of my church. After being badly wounded in Poland and about to rejoin my outfit, the *Leibstandarte Adolf Hitler,* I was chosen as one of Hitler's bodyguards. It was May, 1940. For five years I was "*Mädchen für Alles*" (girl Friday), as they say. I like to say I followed the orders properly, probably solved all requests rather well. After all, that was my job. I remember the day he got the news about Stalingrad. He was listening to "*Dein ist mein ganzes Herz*" (My Whole Heart Is Yours), sung by Joseph Schmidt. He was a Jew, but Hitler liked to listen to him. That evening, Hitler was very sad but ate it all into himself, as we say in German.

Of course I was there on April 30, 1945, right after Hitler's suicide when guards tried

HM: Yes, because guilt produces crime.

SL: That's right, and I believe that's exactly what you're attempting to do with your writing: going back to the bones of German history to make sure that crime is not lying dormant in guilt and repression.

HM: Yes.

SL: Do you feel that there is a real difference in this respect between the two Germanies? In the East your silence is filled in a certain way but it may paradoxically address a discourse of the West in a much more virulent way.

HM: Quotation again. It's from Ezra Pound in one of the poems translated as *Exile's Letter:* "What is the use of talking and there is no end of talking, there is no end of things in the heart." I think there's too much talking in the West. There's too much murmur, thick layers of murmur. The plays of Botho Strauss, the *Big and Little* for instance — it's just murmur.

SL: It's a cover up?

HM: Yes.

SL: It adds a layer to the grave?

HM: Yes.

SL: You mentioned the other day that a line in one of your plays was read as an allusion to the Polish situation. This may be important for people here, but it is a very literal way of filling the silence. A very deep silence can be full of words.

to burn his and Eva Braun's bodies. How can you do it with just gasoline? You've got to dig a trench and put kindling underneath. The Russians found the charred bodies. After May 2, Goebbels wished me good luck in the bunker, and I escaped through subway tunnels. Walking for miles, I figured it was safe to surface — smack into Russian guns and a kick in the arse. Seven years, three of them in Ljubljanka prison. For twelve nights they beat me to a bloody pulp, with leather straps, holding me on the table. "Where Hitler? That not Hitler cadaver! You know, you in bunker!" They whipped me into unconsciousness.

Of course, we did know a lot. I knew the color code. But nothing about Jews. Not one word! Sure, I handled dispatches (what's a Chief of State without dispatches?), even took a peek when nobody looked, but never a word about Jewish persecution in the Führer's circle. Why should I lie? We knew nothing, none of us, I tell you, not a single one of us. As for the "Holocaust" I can only agree with Joseph Strauss.* That wasn't for real; they are all actors. Had anything like that really happened, the guards would have *verboten* all photographs. I don't believe it. Or so-called newsreels about Buchenwald and Auschwitz, surely it isn't possible; I bet most of that is also fake. Maybe something did happen. But that many people killed! Never, it's mathematically impossible. After all, there was only one crematorium in Auschwitz.

75

HM: Sixteen years ago, I wrote a play on the problems of industrial workers. It was only produced here last year. It deals with a strike and the problem of the wall since the time of the play is '61 — the day when the wall was built and the border closed. The authorities were afraid of the impact of the play and so was the management of the theatre. Everything depended on the reaction of the public. There's one situation in the play when a party functionary from the district town comes to the construction site. He attacks very harshly the local party functionary for being too close to anarchist tendencies that exist among construction workers. He asks him to dismiss a worker well-known for his anarchism: "I won't dismiss him" answers the local representative of the party, "because he's important here and he's a good worker." Then the worker comes and his first sentence to the party functionary is: "My congratulations for the building of the wall. You have won one round, like in a boxing match. But it was a blow under the belt. If I had known that I was building my own prison here, I would have blown up every single wall with dynamite."

And this is a very strange sentence to have right on the stage. At this point the fate of the performance depended entirely on the reaction of the public. If they had applauded or laughed to this sentence, the whole performance would have been in danger. But there was just silence, a very long silence.

They had recognized the power of silence.

This is a quality of the audience. They knew that they shouldn't react. So the performance went on. □

1. West Berlin publisher.
2. Theater director in West Germany.

Gerda Misch: I say if it were only 100, and please excuse the "only," the guilt would be the same. People were murdered, not for their conviction, but for their ancestry; there's no twisting or questioning the numbers. It's simply pretentious to say: "It isn't really that many and it's all propaganda! That people can take this attitude, that's beyond me!"

R: But can you tell me who's behind today's hate campaign, who smears swastikas on Jewish graves, and nobody ever caught? I wonder, wouldn't you? My wife is really very pro-Jewish, I must say.

Q: What do you mean, "pro-Jewish!" I grew up in a left-wing worker's family. In my parents' home, I learned responsibility and to stand by my convictions. I was a member of the SPD* and immediately after '45 rejoined them. I have been active ever since. Yes, there was something hypnotic about Hitler, but I can't comprehend that people didn't see what was happening!

R: I never bothered with politics. I never was in the Nazi party, and I still don't belong to any party now. I mind my own business, in my wallpaper and paint store. I'm too much the realist to bother with politics.

76   **Q:** That's precisely it. If you want to be a realist, you'll have to face your responsibilities.

I've been twice to Israel to see for myself how they built the State of Israel. Never was I made to feel uncomfortable as a German, in fact I made good friends with Israelis. It's remarkable what they've done.

R: It's always the same; hate Germany; I don't like that. After all, what about the bombing of Dresden, Hiroshima? You hear nothing about that. Always harping on Germany. There are crimes committed all over the world. Propaganda, all propaganda! I was at the top; I saw absolutely nothing.

Q: You were "at the top." Why don't you at last forget your *Führer*, your "Big Chief!" I can't listen to it any longer.

R: And what is my guilt? Why did those Jewish soldiers beat me to a pulp, naked, bleeding, making me lose control of my bowels, and always saying, "Where Hitler?" I was so weak. Back under the shower, now face the wall. Aiming a pistol at me, my last chance to tell, last chance to stay alive, they said. And again they whipped me to un-consciousness. Why don't they make a movie about me? ☐

Photographs and text by Henry Ries

Hans-Joachim Klein

SLAUGHTER POLITICS

Jean-Marcel Bouguereau: Who were your first friends?

Hans-Joachim Klein: Anti-authoritarians. They went to meetings, but weren't in any group. They didn't take to being told what to do. When they met me, they didn't immediately say: "Look, a worker. Let's start educating him." They said to each other: "What does a worker like best? — Beer-houses." And they brought me to the beer-houses, the main political forums of Frankfurt. That way we began our discussions naturally, over mugs of beer.

JMB: Is that where you started to get politicized?

Klein: It took time, considering where I was coming from. Just a few months before, I was still the type who'd get into scrapping with the Italian immigrants who came into our pub. For me, these were "guineas." Later, when I'd slip and do the same kind of things, they wouldn't throw Marx and Engels up in my face. They were patient.

Hans-Joachim Klein is a former member of the German urban guerrilla, now in hiding. His account of the German and international terrorist "scenes," published in Germany in 1980, played an important role in the assessment by the German Left of the armed struggle.

WILLIAM BURROUGHS

Exterminating

Sylvère Lotringer: Do you think any form of terrorist action can be justified?

William Burroughs: Some of them are quite rational. Terrorists like the IRA or the Palestinians do make sense. Their motivations are clear, their goals concrete. They can easily visualize what they want to achieve. Then there is another kind of terrorism, international terrorism, which is to me some sort of intellectual sickness. These people don't seem to have a fucking idea of the kind of life they're fighting for. I mean life as it is lived on a day-to-day basis. There's nothing direct in their motivation. Is it some kind of religious belief? Mystics at least believed in another world. They had something to gain. Terrorists don't. I can't understand why they do it.

SL: Ideologies can be very powerful. German terrorists are very strongly motivated

JMB: And what had the students become to you?

Klein: Super-authorities. All through my childhood I'd been fed on that. My father, my teachers, *Bild Zeitung*,[1] everybody told me: "Today they kiss your feet, tomorrow they'll spit in your face." I changed my outlook pretty fast. I discovered a solidarity I didn't know before.

JMB: And what did you do after that?

Klein: I met these guys from the association of objectors. I was supposed to leave for the army, and they tried to convince me not to. It seemed to me more effective to agitate from the inside, so I did my time. It was a fiasco: I spent more time in the hole than anywhere else.

JMB: Was that during the peak of the student movement?

Klein: Yes, I was still in the army when they shot Rudi.[2] He was my idol. In the barracks, my nickname was Dutschke. I put his picture over my bed, which created quite an uproar. They accused me of making partisan propaganda. So next door, a good distance away, I put up a portrait of Luebke.[3] I covered my ass...

JMB: How was Frankfurt at the time — that period when all the political papers had names like "The Red Star," "The Red Morning," "The Red Flag"?

Klein: That was also the time of the boom of the establishment and the first communes, when they were trying neighborhood work with the immigrants. And the experimental neighborhood centers like the *Gallus*. Wilfrid Boese[4]

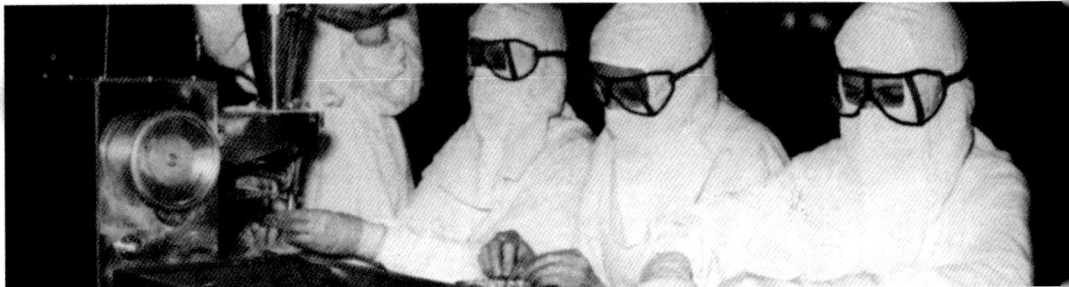

ideologically. They are, after all, a by-product of the 60's anti-authoritarian movement—but a hysterical version of orthodox Marxism.

WB: I never quite understood why people were taken in by Marxism. First of all, Marx's predictions went all wrong. And then Marxism is just one among many ideologies. It was written by someone sitting at his desk.

Today we live in a situation of maximum change, and flexibility is essential. You've got people that *can't* be flexible, that have some nonsense about *isms* and everything, but what the hell does that mean? People who believe such things, fundamentalists, communists, are just dangerous to other people. They are dangerous to the species. Their whole orientation is biologically unsound.

SL: Whatever the motivations, do you believe terrorist strategies have any chance to succeed?

WB: If they want to be terrorists, they might as well be terrorists. But the obvious thing is nuclear or biological weapons.

SL: You mean they don't go far enough?

WB: If they're going to, I don't know. It's not my concern. Still, it's puzzling to me why

himself had been one of its founders. He did street theatre and always played the evil capitalist.

JMB: Then there was that whole period when they were taking over houses, which was very important to you, wasn't it?

Klein: The Mayor's office in Frankfurt undertook to renovate the old neighborhoods. One of the first areas to be affected by what we called deportation was the Westend,[5] where a lot of communes had been set up. We defended our homes, at first symbolically; then, as nothing came out of this, it turned into real street battles. They once mobilized nearly 1,200 cops to seize one house. We ended up starting a militant corps that would go for training on Sundays in the forest. A very elite order. Girls forbidden.

My First Experience of the RAF

JMB: What did you think of the RAF?

Klein: I was for it all the way. Then I had my first experience — a negative one — with the RAF. I helped them find a house, but they absolutely had to leave at the end of the week. They wouldn't. I threatened to throw them out. They threatened me back. I didn't dig that, especially since "Bonnie" Boese had told me similar stories about the way they use people. This kind of manipulation came right back home to them. None of that led me to question the RAF as a whole. I was in complete solidarity with the prisoners, but I really didn't feel like working with them any more. That's also partly why I enlisted with the Revolutionary Cells,[6] and not the RAF.

they don't go any further. Nowadays anyone can make an atom bomb. It's very easy. All it takes is some college physics and, I'm told, $200,000. With what they call a small-yield nuclear device, you can take out an area in New York from Times Square up to the end of Central Park.

Two people would suffice to plan in detail the extermination of a whole population. No one would know who set it off. Emergency plans are ready to be activated. I don't believe they've made all these projections for nothing. Our two men could easily protect themselves from the radiation and wait until people had finished killing each other. Then they would come out of their hiding place.

SL: Can you imagine that happening?

WB: Anything could happen.

SL: How long do you think this planet is going to last?

WB: Some scientist was giving it no more than forty years. I don't mean the planet, but people on it.

SL: Forty years? He may be optimistic.

WB: Any species runs its course, and that's it. Very often the advantage they had in the

JMB: When did you go underground?

Klein: I never did, really. It's just that I was forced to after Vienna.[7] It was my first mission. I'd been badly wounded, and I was recognized; at the hospital they'd had the time to take my picture and finger-print me while I was unconscious. I can only remember it vaguely. Naturally, I meant to return to Frankfurt.

JMB: You didn't want to go underground?

Klein: No, I was the only masked man in the entire commando. It was settled: I was to remain incognito to the end. I had arrived in Vienna at the beginning of December with "Bonnie" Boese.

JMB: Who was Boese exactly?

Klein: He died with his girlfriend, Brigitte Kuhlmann, during the famous Entebbe operation. He was the head of the Revolutionary Cells then. I'd known him for a long time. He was quite a well-known figure in Frankfurt's leftist circles. We worked together in the Red Relief.[8] He knew I had lent a hand to the RAF. Plus I made no secret of what my thoughts were. When the June 2 Movement* executed Schmücker,[9] I had been one of the few in Frankfurt who agreed with Boese that the traitors must be executed.

JMB: You were really rowdy, weren't you?

Klein: Let's just say I wanted some action. I didn't worry about the particulars.

JMB: Were you into weapons?

first place is their ultimate destruction. The dinosaurs got so big they couldn't get enough to eat. There were a number of half-reptile and half-mammal species at one time, not big, about the size of a wolf, with reptile-like teeth. I don't know why they didn't survive. Some of them were quite practical.

SL: We thought we could survive because of our intelligence and technology. That's probably what we're going to be destroyed by.

WB: Intelligence, like technology, is only an instrument. It doesn't exist in a vacuum. It only exists with regard to a purpose.

SL: We seem to be losing our sense of purpose.

WB: To me the only purpose would be to get into space, but not in an aqualung the way they're doing it now.

SL: I heard you would be quite willing to go to the moon.

WB: I would be willing to go anywhere. If flying saucers want to take me out of the solar system, I'd get in right away, without hesitation.

SL: Even with the prospect of no return?

Klein: I was always an avid reader of the *Waffen Journal*, a paper specializing in weaponry.

JMB: For art's sake?

Klein: Out of technical interest only...

JMB: In his book, Bommi Baumann[10] recalls the feeling of power you get from carrying a gun. What's your view on this?

Klein: At the beginning you tell yourself you're going to master the gun, and after a while the gun takes over. When you carry a weapon, you have a different relationship with it. You feel a little stronger. There's something that can come out of this weapon, and you have to see what happens when you disarm a cop; I did it once in Frankfurt — he became a little boy.

After Vienna, I often went around armed in the Arab countries. I felt like a different person, I would think: "Just let them come near me." And the same holds true for anyone who carries a weapon.

In Vienna, when the Austrian police entered the OPEC building, they couldn't do anything more. But they did start to fire. When you've got a gun, you have to use it. It's crazy how a gun compels you to act.

JMB: From that point on, did you lead a double life?

Klein: Yes, I did. I was initiated into all of the tricks of the trade of guerrilla warfare: security, codes, and arms. I learned how to forge papers. And then the rest of the time, I continued my life as a Red Relief militant—by playing down a bit my declarations in favor of armed struggle, as Boese had recommended.

WB: Of course, particularly so. Who wants to come back?

SL: But there doesn't seem to be any other form of life anywhere else.

WB: What makes you think so?

SL: So far we haven't been very successful at detecting it.

WB: Why should we detect it? Particularly if they didn't want us to detect it. Nothing would be easier than to prevent it. We're thinking about life as we know it, which has very definite limitations—temperature, all sorts of things. But that doesn't necessarily apply to any other forms of life.

SL: Terrorists have definite limitations in the face of the universe.

WB: Oh, this is ridiculous. A nineteenth-century type of action, like old bomb-throwing anarchists of the 1910's. At least *they* were into acting, and what a good role it was. Histrionism is a very powerful factor. Everything is a matter of roles, but terrorists refuse to take the stage. They want to remain anonymous. I suspect they're intellectuals who want to prove that their theory is right.

SL: But what if, as you suggested, their bomb-throwing involved atomic weapons, in-

JMB: And after that?

Klein: There was the death of Holger Meins.[11] That's what triggered me: the impotence of legalism had to be done away with. I had to wait a while, though; my time hadn't come. The attempt against Von Drenkmann's life,[12] following Meins' death, pleased me tremendously. Part of the left, on the other hand, was dismayed. The campaign that Holger's death had launched was stopped short by this murder. For a long time after that, so I wouldn't lose the sting of the hatred I felt, I would carry that horrible photo of Holger's autopsy around with me.

Carlos

JMB: While you were still very seriously wounded, you set off again, nearly dead, in the airplane taking the members of the commando and the OPEC ministers away to Algiers. After a stay in the hospital, you stayed in an Arab country for a few months, in a Palestinian camp, usually in the company of Carlos.[13] How would you define him politically?

Klein: That's a tough one.

JMB: But weren't you in close contact with him for months?

Klein: Yes, but all the same, since he doesn't speak German, our discussions were limited. He draws inspiration from what Ho Chi Minh says: "Carry the revolution into every country." So he goes from one country to another trying to stir things up. He tried pretty hard to weasel his way into the Revolutionary Cells and take charge after Boese's death.

"We're reaching the point when instant destruction is making the balance of terror obsolete."

Sylvère Lotringer

cluding the H-bomb?

WB: Besides America, there are few places that have any facilities to make an H-bomb. It is so much more complicated than an A-Bomb. Only three hundred people in the world know how to make one.

SL: At this point a modest A-Bomb would be enough to throw the world in chaos.

WB: Of course, if some people had the idea to use it as a terrorist weapon, that would be their intent: to create total chaos, not to substitute one form of government to another.

SL: In a sense, what has prevented various terrorist groups from going overboard is their political or ideological beliefs.

WB: It is their nineteenth-century thinking.

SL: If they didn't stick to the nineteenth, we certainly wouldn't make it to the end of the twentieth. Although nothing proves that we will.

WB: Also there are all sorts of biological weapons, which seem much more viable really than nuclear weapons. I mean: you can make them in this loft, and they are much less detectable anyway. All you need is some laboratory equipment.

JMB: What did he think of communists?

Klein: He didn't like them. He found them corrupt. Rather than as a Marxist, he defined himself as an international revolutionary, sort of like Che Guevara. He used to tell me all about ETA's operations.[14] He really admired the assassination attempt against Carrero Blanco.[15] He was particularly keen on the accuracy, the technical aspect.

JMB: What did he read?

Klein: *Playboy*...You know, you don't find a lot of books in the Arab countries. He lived out of a suitcase on Rue Toullier — he had a bed, a chest for his weapons, and his suitcase on the floor. And then, what was really important was his bathroom! He's a very anal kind of guy, a cleanliness nut; he's always washing up.

JMB: What was his frame of mind when he planned his operations?

Klein: It's what I call the "slaughter point of view." The more violent you get, the more people respect you. And the better the chances your conditions will be met. One example of this was the attack on the St. Germain Drugstore. The French Embassy in the Hague had been occupied by members of the Japanese Red Army who were calling for the liberation of one of their members who'd been imprisoned in Paris. Since the French wouldn't give in, he went and threw that grenade at the "drugstore."

JMB: Did he himself tell you about that?

Klein: Yeah. Later, Michel Mourkabel put five or six empty grenade containers

SL: Actually bacteriological warfare is in again. The Pentagon recently declared that poison gas could be considered "a cheaper substitute for nuclear warfare." It would, they say, do far less damage in limited wars involving conventional forces in distant parts of the world, "including the pine forests of Germany." I'm sure the Germans appreciated it.

WB: The whole question of selective pestilence is quite within the range of modern technology. They can produce a plague that would only affect white people, or black people, or Mongoloids. Milk is poisonous to some Chinese because they don't have some enzymes that break it down. That's where you start when you want to use a selective pestilence. You start with these differences and then you look at all the diseases to which only certain races are subject, like sickle-cell anemia for blacks. There's a number of illnesses that are either confined to or predominantly Jewish. Tay-Sachs, for example, is almost predominantly a Jewish illness.

SL: It's a lack in chromosomes.

WB: It's an hereditary illness completely crippling and requiring a great deal of care.

SL: It's an equivalent to these neutron bombs that destroy people, not buildings. You can select the target.

in a coat-check room, then called the authorities and told them to go take a look, letting them know he had the contents, and that if the guy wasn't set free he would throw it all into bars or movie theaters. And they freed him right away.

JMB: Did he consider that a good example of the kind of thing that needs to be done?

Klein: He used to say that in order to get anywhere, you have to step over dead bodies.

In Vienna, he pulled off another stunt of the same kind. Right in the middle of the mission, he left his loaded Beretta on a table and walked around the room with his automatic in his hand. I'd read about it in the newspapers and asked him if it was true. He told me he did it on purpose to see if there were any guys from security services in the room. If some guy had tried to grab a hold of the Beretta, Carlos would've caused a massacre, because you can't shoot an automatic with any precision. Same thing with Michel Mourkabel's death on Rue Toullier. He confirmed that he killed him, but *not* because Mourkabel betrayed him, as they said. When the guys from the DST[16] moved in and he started to fire, Mourkabel put his hands up. So Carlos shot him down — because he didn't help. And yet they were good friends.

Then there's that story about the owner of Marks and Spencer in London, Joseph Sieff, who's an old billionnaire. Carlos went over there, he rang the doorbell. The old guy himself answered the door. Carlos asked what his name was, and he shot him.

WB: Yes. And the Jewish population is much more subject to diabetes. No doubt, anyone can get diabetes, but statistically it's much more a Jewish illness than any other race or group. Another bit of information I got from a book called *The Judas Gene*. Someone had planned a real final solution to the Jewish question, this plague that only Jewish people contract.

SL: In as much as there is such a thing as a pure "gene pool," which is highly debatable.

WB: Of course, but the more Jewish they were, the more they were subject to it. Someone who only has a small amount of Jewish blood would be less vulnerable.

SL: The more defined the minority, the easier to exterminate.

WB: Absolutely. I'm surprised the Nazis didn't do more work on that.

SL: That will be for another generation.

WB: Since they really wanted to get rid of all the Jews, well, that was the way to do it. A Jewish plague. They could say they have nothing to do with it quite easily. That's the thing about biological weapons, you can't be sure who's done it.
The more you think about the whole thing, the weirder it gets. After the fall of

JMB: What for?

Klein: He was a Jew. That was the reason.

JMB: ???

Klein: There were more of them, you know, on the list they found at his girl-friend's house in London. Rubinstein was on it, and the violinist Menuhin.

JMB: Did he have something against Jews?

Klein: No, in no way was he an anti-semite. These operations were directed at the Israeli racket.

JMB: Wasn't he afraid his actions would be seen as anti-semitic?

Klein: That wasn't my impression. Wilfrid Boese once proposed to Waddi Haddad[17] that they stage an attempt against Simon Wiesenthal, the one who succeeded in finding Eichmann. The reason for this was that Wiesenthal works closely with Mossad, the Israeli Secret Service. When this project was discussed, Carlos said it was crazy to want to kill this guy, who was anti-Nazi.

Carlos was a very contradictory fellow. After Entebbe, he was real enthusiastic about what the Israelis had done.

JMB: But how could a guy like Boese, an active extreme-leftist militant in Frankfurt, who knows what anti-semitism is, make proposals like that?

Klein: I don't know. The way I see it, it's because they're dependent on Waddi Haddad's group. He's the one who supplies the money, the arms...

France, Hitler had everything going for him. People here would all have done business with Nazi Germany. They liked the idea that the trains were on time. If Hitler had played his cards right, sensibly, he would have had everything he wanted and the whole of modern history would have been different. Then he embarks on this concentration camp nonsense, and the propagandists say, Jesus, we can't be associated with something like this.

SL: He messed it up.

WB: He messed it up. But he might have even gotten away with that if he hadn't invaded Russia. Two pieces of lunacy, one on top of the other, that was too much, too much. Invading Russia was just a straight military mistake he should have learned from Napoleon. You cannot invade a country successfully where there is any amount of room for withdrawal. Remember when the Romans tried to invade Parthia. OK, the Romans marched in, the Parthians shoot some arrows, go away, further, further in. Meanwhile the Romans are dying of thirst and illnesses, and finally they have the Parthians behind them cutting their supply line, it was a disaster. And a foreseeable disaster. The Germans could have profited by Napoleon's example as we could have profited from the French experience in Viet-Nam. They showed that this was a war that couldn't be won. I would

I feel that when you've been in the guerrilla movement for a long time, sooner or later you've got to get rid of a lot of baggage. From your humanity to your political ideals. You sink deeper and deeper into shit. When you take that route, all you can do is keep going straight ahead. You can't get out of it.

That was my problem after Vienna. With a mission like that behind you, you can't just back out. Anyway, you're past the turning point. And backing out like I did, being in hiding for years, well, there's no future in that.

JMB: But that doesn't explain everything.

Klein: In the armed struggle, the only thing they think about is freeing prisoners. And for that they need back-up and logistics. For a mission like the one with Schleyer* you need a tremendous amount of things. You become dependent. For example, the Revolutionary Cells receives $3,000 every month.

And then there's the weapons. They get huge deliveries of them. Haddad, of course, wanted compensation for these favors.

As far as the Revolutionary Cells are concerned, their collaboration with the Palestinians goes back farther than the RAF's. Boese already had his foot in the door at the time of the Olympic Games massacre.[18] He's the one who welcomed the guys in Munich.

To me, it's slaughter politics. One of the guerrilla groups wanted to stage an assassination attempt against the President of the Stammheim* Court. They wanted to fill up a minibus with bottles of propane. They would've got him without a hitch, except they also would've hit a whole bunch of people around him. The connection between the objective and the means gets screwed up.

JMB: At that moment, didn't you show any doubts?

"Every German needs therapy."
Annette Humpe

Klein: I didn't dare express them. That was in the beginning, before Vienna. And I really wanted to take part in the operations.

JMB: But, didn't they do all those things?

Klein: They did other things. There's one thing that really struck me, it's that business with the Japanese Air Line plane in April, '76. It was one of Haddad's ideas. He packed a blue Samsonite suitcase with explosives all around the inside. It was supposed to blow up on the airplane in the middle of the flight.

JMB: Are you sure?

Klein: I was there when they prepared it, and I saw the commando take the suitcase over.

JMB: Well, what was their objective?

Klein: They wanted 5 million dollars.

JMB: . . .

Klein: But it didn't work. "June 2" took the bag over. But the baggage compartment was already crammed full, so the RAF gave it a try — in vain. Some stewardess must have seen that the bag wasn't identified. They brought it back into the hall, where it went off.

All that for 5 million dollars. And these aren't just stories — Boese himself brought the letter to the office of the J.A.L.[19]

JMB: But during those long months when you were in touch only with guerrillas, didn't you ever have the feeling there were people who, even in a limited way, were questioning the sense of these acts and their effects?

have opposed it even on military grounds. And there was no reason for it. It was completely an ideological conflict. We ended up spending God knows how many billions of dollars and we most ingloriously lost the war. There are pictures of people being kicked off the last plane that went out, literally they were stepping on their hands as they tried to get in — these were too much (laughs).

SL: We're relying on the "balance of terror" to exorcize the nuclear holocaust. Do you think this strategy remains effective?

WB: The matter of the situation is now as it has been since the beginning of time. Not since the beginning of warfare, but since the beginning of disagreement. One person picks up a club, and another person picks up a club. So if I hit him, maybe he's going to hit me, and he thinks. In a way, he wouldn't think if I didn't have a club.

SL: But clubs now have a way of becoming invisible, and there is just no time left to think. We're reaching the point when instant destruction is making even the balance of terror obsolete.

WB: It is one of the rules of warfare that people will develop such efficient weapons; they get to a point where it would end the whole game. If you call it a game, the war game, basically there's only one game, and that game is war. All games are hostile by

JMB: But you didn't just see them in the camp. What about in Europe?

Klein: It wasn't easy to discuss things. There was an order from Haddad forbidding us to talk to each other in the camp without authorization.

The Guerrilla Movement and the Left

Klein: I remember how, during a convention in Frankfurt Joschka Fischer, one of the Spontis* of Frankfurt, addressing the guerrilla movement, declared: "Comrades, drop your guns and pull out the cobblestones." They broke up laughing. They don't pay any attention to what the left does.

JMB: You say that some people from the Revolutionary Cells came to that Palestinian camp for training. What did they discuss?

Klein: The Revolutionary Cells had a big campaign going in Germany against the fare hike and the establishment of automatic ticket machines.

JMB: *That's* what they talked about?

Klein: There was always stuff like that going down. That was the petty side of Boese. We spent quite some time discussing plans for forging savings bankbooks or checkbooks. That bankbook fuss kept some guys busy for a year. You could say there were two sections to the Revolutionary Cells, the German and the international one.

JMB: And between the two, were there no disputes?

their nature, because they involve winners and losers. But if anyone achieves what they're allegedly trying to do, which is total victory, they end the game.

SL: So ultimately the enemy must be spared, or somehow propped up again, as happened with Germany after the war.

WB: Yes, you have to. The Germans win one time and then the French come back, whereas if the Germans won completely there would never be another time.

SL: Can you imagine any type of society that wouldn't depend on war games?

WB: There are societies where war is a minimal factor, but those are small groups of people. As soon as you get to what we have now, a heterogeneous population with terrific divergences of interest within the society itself, you've got a situation which cannot be anything other than hostile.

SL: A French political anthropologist, Pierre Clastres, recently argued that war between tribes wasn't an accident, or a natural phenomenon. War was intrinsic to "primitive" cultures, because it was by war only that they managed to prevent the emergence in their midst of a single authority or an overall power structure. Conflict allowed them to remain divided and heterogeneous, immune from the temptation of the State.

Klein: After Boese's and Kuhlmann's deaths at Entebbe, the rest of the international section wanted to stage an act of retaliation in an airport where they had discovered a security gap. But the specialist they needed for this was working for the German section at the time. And in the middle of preparations, the guy they had called for went and snatched the arms cache of the international section. Nothing was left. The worst thing about it was that there were weapons assigned to another group in there as well. There were a number of threats, from Carlos in particular, and the guys brought everything back. The story was over when the other guerrilla group took its turn and stole everything again! It's wild, isn't it?

The Burden of Being Underground

JMB: That petty side you've talked about is a classic form of logic in organizations. Besides, doesn't the burden of being underground play a large part in this?

Klein: It takes up 80% of your time. You've got to watch yourself constantly. You have to code, decode, recode addresses, texts...Besides that, the codes change: you have to keep it all in your head. I can't give any details on that. All I can say is, you waste so damn much time. A meeting is a whole big deal. Not to mention all the security measures you have to take to eliminate the possibility of being tracked down. You fall into habits. I've noticed that when we were at a hide-out, we tended to whisper when discussing anything, even when there wasn't the slightest chance anyone could hear us.

JMB: All that must contribute to limiting political discussions, right?

WB: Why war was there, who put it there, who cooked up this plan, I don't know. There are very practical wars, wars for water, wars for territory, whenever you have a situation where there is only a limited amount of water, or land. In fact a lot of Arab wars are sensible wars. There isn't enough water to go around, so one group grabs it.

SL: Judging by the increasing number of "underdeveloping" countries, sensible wars are here to stay.

WB: We've got to realize that we just can't allow the population to increase without any sort of limits. If you cut the population in half, that would simplify a lot of the problems.

SL: How would you achieve that goal: would you impose population control?

WB: You distribute a pill so there would be only males born. You wouldn't have to impose it. Most people, particularly in underdeveloped areas, would perfer male children anyway. It's economical. Only in places like America and Western Europe would they want a balanced family. This plan, if implemented, would upset the whole military balance of the world. In twenty or thirty years, the number of males of military age in the underdeveloped countries, where males are at a premium, would be such that they would overrun Africa, which might be a good thing too. It's an interesting idea. Of course, the reduction of population would not be immediate; it would occur over several generations.

Klein: I spent about nine months in that Palestinian camp. I don't recall taking part in more than one single real political discussion. And in Europe, the only discussions we had concerned our missions. There was always a political basis to it, but they were technical discussions. To me, things like how we're going to strike a bank or kidnap somebody are technical discussions.

JMB: One gets the impression that the actual political situation in West Germany really doesn't interest the different guerrilla groups. Their analyses always come down to the same formula that could be found in their texts years ago.

Klein: The RAF has always said this from the beginning: it's a question of sharpening the contradictions in such a way as to make the situation become more and more openly fascist. They want to bring the latent fascism that reigns in W. Germany out in the open. After that, they'll have the masses — and the left as well, including those who are against them today.

They think the left doesn't understand anything. So the RAF tries to exert moral pressure on the left concerning the prisoners that are really in a terrible position. But once you show solidarity, you've got to do so on the political basis of the guerrilla movement or else you're treated like a charity lady.

These acts have their own dynamics. They become objectified. This trend continued with the attempt against Springer[20] in Hamburg, which I opposed from the very beginning. It's a vicious circle. From one act to the next, it's become more and more rotten, more and more apolitical. Even fascist. As I've said before, to me what happened at Entebbe was fascism.

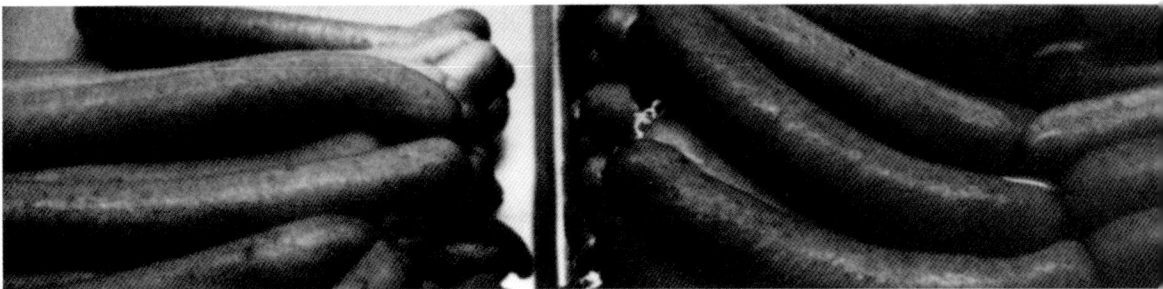

SL: Is this a fairy tale on a world scale or a concrete proposal?

WB: Dr. Postgate is the man who proposed to give this pill that reproduces only male children. When he put forth his theory the technology wasn't there, but it's here now. They can do it. Needless to say, Postgate received hate letters from the women community — and he's not even a homosexual himself, at least he claims he isn't.

SL: You don't think that the confrontation between the two systems, capitalism and socialism, has anything to do with the exhaustion of world resources?

WB: These words mean absolutely nothing anymore. There's no difference between them so far as the basic needs that they have to satisfy. Suppose the communists would take over America tomorrow, or even that the terrorists succeed. They'd have to do much the same things that are being done now. I'm talking about problems like food distribution, fire, police, sanitation, all these services on which city dwellers are absolutely dependent. If those are cut off, there's going to be millions of people starving overnight.

SL: Or they'd have to be shipped out of cities, like in Cambodia.

WB: They couldn't ship them anywhere in the USA. The chaos would be such that there

93

JMB: What role do the mobilization and the emotions aroused by the prisoners' conditions play in people's enlistment in the guerrilla movement?

Klein: Nothing's changed. They still treat the prisoners like so much shit. The best example of this is what happened recently to Sonnenberg.[21] After the shower of gunshots was over, half his brain was blown away — he should've spent a year in the hospital. They operated on him, threw his ass in jail, and gave him a trial he couldn't even follow. That's how you breed new generations of guerrillas. There's no need for scholarly studies on the roots of terrorism.

JMB: I remember a text from the RAF, attributed to Ulrike Meinhof,* who implicitly kept her distance from the action against Springer.

Klein: That's right. But there's more to that. At the Stammheim trial, Gudrun Ensslin* read a statement saying that the bombs used against Springer were not from the RAF, that the RAF had had no control over it. It wasn't true; that's tactics. I can't stand that.

Ulrike Meinhof Committed Suicide

JMB: Are you of the opinion that people like Ulrike Meinhof had a more critical attitude towards all that?

Klein: Yes, I think so. And I also think she wanted to end it all. That's why she killed herself.

JMB: You believe she committed suicide?

Klein: At least, I imagine so. You have to put yourself in her place. When

wouldn't be any possible way of relocating them. They'd swarm out into the country like a horde of locusts and strip everything bare, murdering the farmers, just grabbing what food they could. And in a year or so, they wouldn't know how to manage the farms. You would revert to the city-states like in the Middle Ages. This is what happens in all the disaster novels.

SL: So the future is behind us. Clans will form again, warlords assert their power. The world will become a big Beirut slum.

WB: It could happen, but I doubt it very much. This is a possible scenario, and you could get some approximation of it in a state of chaos, but somehow history doesn't repeat itself word for word. Radicals always assume that the army wants things to be in order. They never think that chaos could come from the institution. But the system itself could induce chaos. You may decide that the political danger comes from the cities. So you switch the generator off. And then you apply a plan of total eradication. A good clean-up. That's what they did in Argentina.

SL: I don't think the German State would ever induce chaos. Even terrorist groups in Germany can't help being organized.

WB: Well, I wonder if it's all that orderly in Germany. They have a terrific crime problem

you're in such a terrible situation as she was in, in Stammheim, after having been in Ossendorf,[22] it's like you're in a vacuum. And when, on top of that, your own partners fuck you over the way they did...

JMB: What do you mean?

Klein: There are letters that were published — which aren't fake, as has sometimes been said — where the others...

JMB: ...The others?

Klein: Gudrun Ensslin, for example, who denounced her "pig mentality." These letters are well-known — you can read them. And there are others that were not published which I was able to read when I was in the Revolutionary Cells.

I think she must have begun to have second thoughts about the political sense of it all.

To say, as some people have claimed, that secret agents came to Stammheim by helicopter to knock her off, is totally absurd.

There comes a time when you've got nothing left. In a situation like that, I'd do the same as she did.

JMB: And as for the deaths of Baader, Ensslin, and Raspe,[23] which was a year ago. You had already left the guerrilla outfit, and you were hiding. What were your feelings then, what did you think?

Klein: As soon as I learned that the GSG9[24] had successfully competed their mission in Mogadishu,* I thought Schleyer would be killed and something

"It's becoming fashionable to know somebody who knew somebody who maybe knew somebody like Ulrike Meinhof. I didn't know who she was."

Annette Humpe

in the big cities. I was just reading a book about the last days of Berlin. The chaos there was un-be-lie-va-ble. There was no water, no food, no electricity, people were dying in the street, the SS were going around hanging anyone whose papers weren't in order, and the Russians were coming in, shooting anyone in uniform, everybody was trying to get out of them as quickly as possible. and that's Germany. Then, I mean, OK, you've got order, but when that order cracks...

SL: In a sense, whatever their political justifications, terrorists already act as warlords. The right to kill has always been the prerogative of the State.

WB: These ideas, many people have them in America who are not terrorists. People are stock-piling automatic weapons, dry food and they've got places, country places that they are prepared to defend. They try to be self-sustaining. So this doesn't necessarily come from the terrorists. These people would be violently anti-terrorists in theory because many of them are right-wing although these words don't mean very much. The terrorists would be hard put to compete with them.

SL: Terrorists don't have a territory. But they're colonizing the media.

WB: Look at the number of people involved: it's really no more than a handful.

would happen in Stammheim. Either a suicide mission, or a single suicide. Not that I can read the future; I knew there were weapons in the prison since 1975.

I know that even back during the Stammheim trial, they wanted to stage a grenade attack on the courtroom the moment the verdict was being read. They asked us to prepare grenades.

On several occasions we tried to get them out. There was the Stockholm mission, then that big thing with Schleyer. After that, we worked something out with Haddad where he would have an airplane hijacked at the right moment.

Put yourself in their place. If all those things won't work, it must mean that nothing will.

JMB: You've had contacts, however limited, with all three German guerrilla movements: The RAF, June 2nd, which is a little less well-known, and the Revolutionary Cells, which, oddly enough, are almost unknown, and which Germany is still only in the process of discovering. We know from reading their texts only that they are more "anarchistic" than the others, more closely linked ideologically to the "Spontaneists" movement. Have you yourself seen any important differences that justify the existence of three separate groups?

Klein: There are, but I couldn't really say. Considering the losses suffered by June 2 and the RAF, logic would have it that the three movements would unite. But logic... The problem that cropped up over and over again was the position the Revolutionary Cells held on being underground. They are not for a systematically underground movement. You only go that way if you're forced to. Whereas the other groups are underground on principle. Whenever they

SL: Isn't that strange, though, that a handful of terrorists can capture people's imagination? It is the combination of old attitudes and modern communication systems that somehow proved effective, at least to a point.

WB: I read a book about Carlos. I heard that somewhere he had been disposed of, like so many of them are by their own, somewhere in the Middle East. There was some disagreement or other, so they knocked him off.

SL: Hans-Joachim Klein, who was closely associated with Carlos for a while, asserts that he was not an ideologist, but a pure technician totally indifferent to the human cost of his actions.

WB: He went to Lumumba University in Moscow and was thrown out because he was resistent to discipline. Then he was approached by the Palestinians, which were much more his sort of people anyway, because he always said the only thing that makes any sense is bullets. He didn't find the Russians good at all in this respect.

SL: Klein couldn't really tell that much about him. Carlos didn't speak German.

WB: Why not? A good terrorist should be a linguist, like an agent.

SL: Can you really put underground fighters and secret agents in the same bag?

had joint discussions they would always attack the Revolutionary Cells for this, accusing them of trying to give themselves an "out."

JMB: Last February, I took part in a debate in Frankfurt with Sybille Haag (the wife of Siegfried Haag, who is now in prison under suspicion of belonging to the RAF), Rudi Dutschke, and Cohn-Bendit. Dutschke found it unrealistic to launch an amnesty campaign. Dany was all for it, and proposed that the left remobilize through this campaign in support of the prisoners. Just what do you think of an amnesty plan?

Klein: I'm for it. I know the kind of reactions I'm going to provoke by saying that. Some people will write me off as a crazy fool — "That bastard hasn't learned anything, he's kissing their ass and begging forgiveness." Others will tell me: "Klein, first go to the police, come have a chat with us, then we'll see..."

I don't give a damn, it doesn't even concern me. Amnesty wouldn't solve my problems. The police aren't the only ones interested in my case: By the time my old friends pardon me, Strauss* will have gone Marxist.

No, I propose amnesty as a political solution. I mean, a partial one. I'm not so naive as to think that'll be enough, as long as Germany is Germany. And I'm sure that the guerrillas will look upon amnesty with the utmost scorn. But I don't believe that everyone will reject it, or that it will be possible to say that the fight can continue as before.

It's the insane reactions of the State that have made a Hydra out of the armed struggle. Every time the State has arrested somebody, it has given birth to five new guerrillas. Telling people to give themselves up will never be a

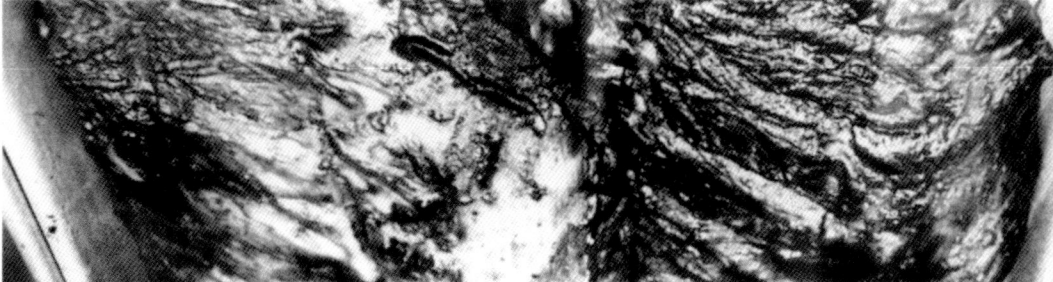

WB: They have to do the same sort of things. They have to get themselves from one country to another, usually with forged papers. They have to have codes and set up tales. It is the same operation in many ways.

SL: So what is the difference between them according to you? Is it that some are professionally trained and some are not?

WB: But the secret service and the terrorists, if they are Palestinians, are protecting, as they think, the interest of their country. There's not much of a difference. An important thing about terrorism is that it is exclusive. They are not going to take everybody who wants to be a terrorist. They have to keep their numbers down, and they have to have people they can trust. Just like the CIA is a very select club. There are a lot of people who want to be CIA agents, but one in a thousand is selected. The CIA have the power of the mask; the power to feel different from what they seem to be. No one knows who they really are: this is a very powerful motivation. And they know that, some day, who they are will be known. Remember this Colonel from the KGB who lived in Brooklyn for ten years? He must have got an incredible kick from it. Not everyone can be a double agent. It takes a special kind of person.

SL: There is something very seductive about any sort of clandestine action.

97

solution. That's why this vicious circle must be broken and a way out must be opened.

If the federal government does not take an initiative in this direction, people will have legitimate cause to think that, since the government doesn't bother, it must need the guerrilla movement.☐

Translated by Harold Chester

1. A sensationalist tabloid published by Springer*.
2. Rudi Dutschke, an early leader of the extra-parliamentary Left.
3. President of West Germany from 1959 to 1969.
4. A leader of the "Revolutionary Cells," killed at Entebbe.
5. District in Frankfurt, site of numerous housing occupations during the late 60's and early 70's.
6. Clandestine group originating in Frankfurt.
7. "Vienna" is a reference to the attack on the OPEC conference (See Chronology), December 21, 1975.
8. A prisoner support organization.
9. Ulrich Schmücker, a police informer in the June 2 Movement, was shot in 1974.
10. Activist in the early APO* and author of *How It all Began* (released in the U.S. as *Terror in Love*), an account of his own turn to armed resistance.
11. Member of the RAF*, died in prison following a hunger strike in 1974.
12. President of the West Berlin supreme court, shot during an attempted kidnapping in 1974.
13. The elusive and politically mysterious "super-terrorist."
14. An anti-fascist, Basque-autonomist underground organization.
15. The "muscle" behind Franco, assassinated by the ETA in 1974.
16. "Special operations" police.
17. Leader of a small splinter group from the PLO.

WB: Oh yes, it gives you something to do, something that's meaningful. Something is meaningful when your survival is at stake.

SL: Going to an office and working everyday isn't quite enough.

WB: No (laughs). Nietzsche said: Men need play and danger, civilization gives them work and safety.

SL: How did you deal with that yourself?

WB: Unfortunately I never had to deal with danger. I volunteered. I went down and saw Bill Donovan, Chief of the OSS in Washington. An uncle of mine had told him: This boy is a natural. He's travelled a lot and so on. That was during the war. I wanted to be something else than a private soldier. He said: Well, I think we could use you. I thought I was in and I wasn't. He told me to see so and so. It was the man who'd been the head of my House at Harvard. He just didn't like me and I didn't like him. This fucking Baxter, that was his name (he later became the President of Williams College), put the skids under me. We don't want this guy. So that was that.

SL: Would you have really liked to be accepted?

98 **WB:** It would have been interesting, yes. I would have enjoyed it. If Donovan would have

18. Terrorist attack on the Israeli team during the 1972 Munich Olympics.

19. Japanese Air Lines.

20. The Springer Press*, a sensationalist newspaper chain that provided much fuel for anti-terrorist hysteria throughout the 70's.

21. Günter Sonnenberg was one of the participants in the assassination of Attorney General Buback (See Chronology).

22. A high-security prison near Cologne.

23. Following Mogadishu*, Baader, Ensslin and Raspe were found dead in their Stammheim maximum security cells.

24. West German anti-terrorist police squad.

"If the East German authorities learn that homosexuals meet in a bar, you can be sure there is a secret service agent sitting among them."

An East German Lesbian

accepted me, I would have been into that whole espionage thing. And I might, and probably would, have turned out to be quite good at it because my whole intricate turn of mind would have lent itself very well to this kind of job. Well, this didn't work out. Which may well be all for the good.

SL: Would you have missed writing?

WB: I don't know. That was considerably later. In anyone's life there's a real point at which you could have gone another way, and that was one such point in my life. God knows what would have happened, I could have wound up head of the CIA and I probably wouldn't have written what I wrote. James Angleton had started as an intellectual and a poet and he became head of the CIA. He was the one who really saved Ezra Pound. He hated Colby, who eventually threw him out. Angleton told Allen that he felt his life had been wasted, it was too late for him as a poet and writer. So you see.

SL: The CIA isn't a good school for the arts.

WB: Not really, because you get yourself into a very limited situation. First, you find you are expected to do things that you don't want to do; and you are not expected to think for yourself at all. They do not want any people who are creative in the CIA. They don't

99

HORST MAHLER

Look Back On Terror

Sylvère Lotringer: Were you ever in favor of urban guerrilla action?

Horst Mahler: Yes.

SL: And you justified this theoretically?

HM: I justified it in a little booklet. I tried to explain what the motives and assumptions of our group were. At the time I believed them to be correct.

SL: Wasn't the group then involved with kidnappings, killings, bank robberies?

HM: Well, such a group needs a lot of money. Carlos Marie Gella in his handbook for the urban guerrilla told us to attack banks. At that time we did not want to wage an abstract warfare against the people of this country as we ended up doing in 1972. We wanted to peacefully 'occupy' satellite cities where conflicts were breaking open, especially in the housing section, and make them the basis for a guerrilla movement. One day this would have become the start-

---

Horst Mahler, a West German lawyer, was one of the founders of what was to become the Red Army Fraction.

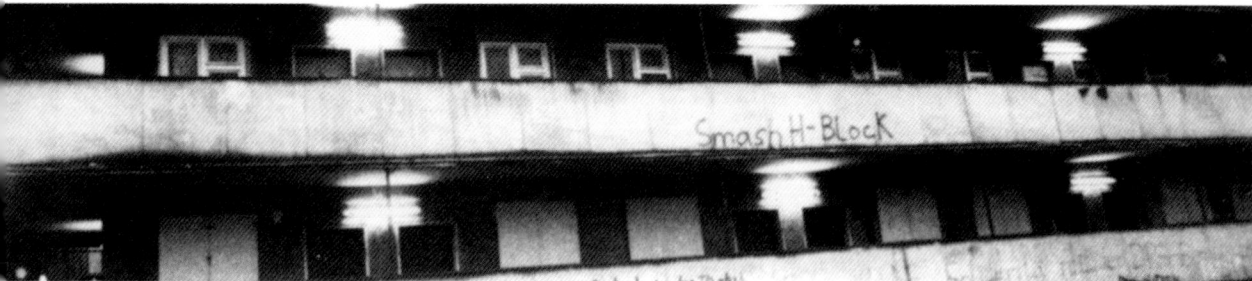

want them in any secret service. They get too many ideas. No, they do not want someone who can see too many sides of a question.

SL: Basically, they want good technicians.

WB: Well, yes. They have to be very resourceful, very clever in some ways.

SL: But they do not want people who think.

WB: People who think? Hell, no.

SL: This certainly doesn't apply to most terrorists, at least not the RAF people. Some, like Ulrike Meinhof, were quite brilliant intellectuals.

WB: They think up to a point, and not beyond that point.

SL: And what is that point?

WB: The point is seeing a number of sides to any questions, even questioning the whole numan endeavor. Where do they think they're going as a species, knowing where other species went—they don't think about things like that at all. It's not too healthy to think such things.

ing point for a social revolution. We wanted to establish a connection with the youth. They in return would trust us, inform us of problems, of enemy activities. However, Andreas Baader was arrested and the group was infiltrated. After he was freed in May 1970 the group abandoned the strategy I have outlined and adopted much more violent and less systematic tactics.

I was personally against the liberation of Baader. I felt nobody could be so important as to justify this kind of revision of our goals. And after this action, the group was no longer able to work in the city. We had to go underground, cut off all the connections with the social scene. From then on the reliance on the squatters was finished. In place of this first strategy came some abstract form of warfare against the United States, begun with the bombing of the Heidelberg headquarters and the officers' canteen in Frankfurt. Nobody here in the German public could understand why they were being bombed. We lost a great deal of the sympathy of the Left as well. The group was isolated.

SL: Were you still involved with the Baader-Meinhof group at that time?

HM: Although I was in jail, I had the opportunity to write letters to the members. There was another important event in 1972. The group bombed a house in Hamburg. Of the six bombs planted, only two exploded, injuring 17 workers in the building. The action was especially criminal since the ideology of the group was that "we are fighting for the liberation of the working class." That was the starting point for my criticism. Baader and Ensslin were aggressively against me. This served to cut off any emotional links I had with these people.

SL: I know very few healthy people then. Many people would deserve to be terrorists on that account. I'm sure Carlos didn't meditate on the future of the species. Although he did his best to expedite a few unhealthy specimens. □

SL: In prison, you must have thought a great deal about the judicial and penal systems. Was your own trial fair?

HM: Not one trial was fair.

SL: Did you expect fairness from the authorities? Did this confirm your idea that there was something right with terrorism?

HM: Excuse me, but I am a lawyer and I've defended many people — not only students — in court. Many trials are not correct here. And this is one point of personal motivation for resistance. But now, I know that even if there are misuses or bad management of justice we cannot renounce these institutions. We must fight to realize the law *by way of* these institutions. The knowledge and the experience of mistreatment by the Judicial apparatus cannot justify the armed struggle against the State as long as we have the possibility of political, parliamentary means — the framework of our constitution — to change it.

SL: Is there any place at all then, today, for a group like the RAF?

HM: Since 1978 we've had a very large discussion to that effect. Even the last hunger strike a couple of weeks ago demonstrated quite clearly that the RAF is not able to set the goals for today's young people who are acting against the authorities by occupying houses. The struggle of the RAF is not their own.

SL: The Squatter's Movement may be cornered into political terrorism. They are young and inexperienced politically.

HM: Yes, this possibility does exist, but not in relation to the RAF. It can only

FELIX GUATTARI

Like the Echo of A Collective Melancholia

In many ways the film *Germany in Autumn* will make its mark in the history of the cinema or, rather, of "engaged" cinema. First because it is a collective work which presents not a juxtaposition of sequences made by different filmmakers but rather the fruit of discussions and elaborations in common. Next, because it was made in the heat of the moment, immediately after the events of Autumn 1977, which allowed for the crea-tion of a remarkably authentic atmosphere. One feels, even when the sequences are

Felix Guattari is a prominent French anti-psychiatrist and political activist, coauthor, with Gilles Deleuze, of *Anti-Oedipus* (Viking) and *On the Line*, (Semiotext(e), "Foreign Agents Series," Spring 1982).

be caused by State repression. And that's what's now on the table.

SL: All the same, the outcome may be a renewal of the underground movement.

HM: Yes, but quite another type — not in the abstract manner of the RAF. You would witness instead an attack on the house owners and on some politicians. Not by killing them, but by frightening them through huge damage in the city as we had it before the election here.

SL: Is there any discussion as to what attitude the Left should adopt toward the Squatters' Movement?

HM: There is a deep feeling of sympathy with the squatters in the so-called Left as a whole. But it is not clear what you mean by Left now. We all realize that this movement, and especially the youth movement, is a very important step, that it marks the beginning of a new political evolution in this country. If you want to have some impression of what the political scene is on the Left, look at the Alternative List.

SL: But the Alternative List is also a new phenomenon. So in a way you have two new leftist alternatives: the young people, who have little political experience, and the Alternative List where most people come, I understand, from the KPD* and from the 60's movement.

HM: It's correct that many people from the 60's movement and former members of the so-called Communist Party are part of the Alternative List.

acted out, that the actors and directors (who sometimes play themselves) are still under the sway of these events in such a way that a truth passes directly, with no visible break between the elements of reporting, fiction, and documentary.

This attempt, call it analytic, to go beyond auteur cinema suggests to me a new possibility for grasping collective emotional elements through film. This kind of "analysis" occurs around two poles.

The first involves the manipulation of events by the mass media. Schleyer's death,* the skyjacking to Mogadishu,* and the deaths of the inmates of Stammheim* prison have been transformed into an emotional charge placed entirely at the disposal of social control and repression. The reference to Sophocles' Antigone becomes a key to the film, the events in Germany that autumn taking on the proportions of ancient drama. In this light, the deaths of Hans-Martin Schleyer and of the RAF* prisoners would function as an outlet or an exorcism in two acts, a double sacrifice meant to internalize a collective guilt that goes back to Nazism and beyond that in a violence supposedly essential to the German mentality.

The other pole of the film consists in the authors' attempts to counteract this collective intoxication by the media, to obstruct the "infernal machine" of guilt inducement — to paraphrase here Jean Cocteau on Oedipus. It is essentially a matter of getting out

However, they are now very harsh critics of orthodox communist ideas. They have learned something.

SL: Are you involved in the Alternative List?

HM: Yes, I'm not a member, but I'm very interested, and I hope that this experiment will have some political results. I'm working together with them in a group which is debating the special problems of Berlin as an isolated city. The Alternative List is favoring a neutral status of Berlin in Germany as a whole without the East-West option.

SL: How do you explain that only four years after such dramatic events as Stammheim, it is not clear anymore what is meant by "Left"?

HM: Our ideological structures were still dependent upon the Marxist interpretation of social development. But these ideas don't really touch upon what is going on now. Workers are not at the core of the conflict anymore. And the youth today is gaining a self-consciousness which is quite different from those of former young generations. We witness now a so-called de-ideologization. This means that all the schemes from the Cold War don't apply. It's very difficult for the authorities now, because they can't say the Alternative List is a subversive communist group under the direction of Moscow.

SL: I have a feeling that the present Alternative scene is a reaction to years of over-ideologization. People still think in some sort of a Left way, but they don't want to be identified with an ideology. That's precisely what interests us in post-Marxist politics. What does it mean to be on the Left today, at a time

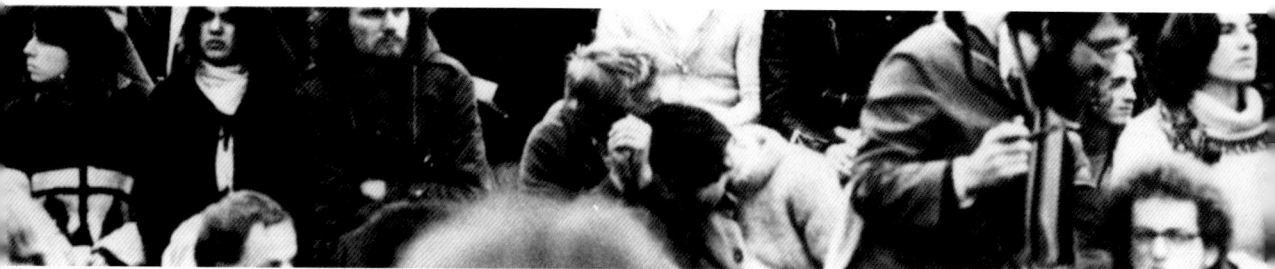

of the RAF-West Germany confrontation, of the repression-reprisals cycle, of the quasi-symmetrical simplification of ideologies in opposition. For the most part, the film-makers manage to keep their own reactions on the most immediate level: on the level of what they felt and what they saw camera in hand; they film their squabbles with their peers, they stage their own fantasies. On such a serious topic, in such a dramatic context, that takes guts! And yet the result is no less serious. And no doubt much more truthful than any other means of inquiry or reporting, or propaganda film. Through each sequence, we are witnessing the proliferation of the escape routes, sometimes minor, laughable, or bizarre, that personally enabled the authors to become disengaged, to a certain extent, from this Manicheaen drama. The very personal behavior which in any event defies current political classifications — Fassbinder embracing a friend, a young woman professor starting out with a shovel over a frozen field, a child watching in astonishment the burial of the Stammheim prisoners, a young man remaining seated near the gravediggers and the police after the procession's departure, a young woman and her little daughter on the road home — constitutes so many elements of life, elements of survival, so many flashes, escapes from the so-called "tragic destiny" of the German people. This in no way implies that the problematic of repressive power is left aside, nor that of social control, of the media's role in daily fascism! In this respect, the

when Marxist ideology has ceased to provide us with ready-made answers?

HM: The old German leftist movements, together with the movements of the Right, do apply to a historical situation which is now disappearing. It's very misleading to mechanically apply this scheme to what's going on now. The new movements include elements traditionally associated with the Right. My estimation is that we must recommence a discussion about fascism and reactionary social movements at the beginning of this century. Why did Hitler gain the support of Germans, with their particular intellectual tradition. It seems that Hitler relied on something in everybody's mind which was ignored by both Marxists and liberals.

SL: What is it in the Alternative scene that you could previously have considered reactionary or conservative?

HM: In the ecology issue, for example, some of the terms used are in contradiction with standard Marxist or socialist schemata. For example, a form of conservative romanticism is now embraced by 'soil ideology' — their mystical attachment to the ground, the cyclical sowing, nurturing, reaping. They also hang on to conservative standards of family life. However, I'm not ready to repudiate or denounce these ideas simply because Hitler also relied on them. We are mistaken if we think that we can stamp every problem of political orientation with "Left" and "Right." It doesn't work anymore.

SL: The type of action you were part of was possibly one of the last attempts to impose Marxist schemes on a society which had diversified and gone "beyond production," as we say in France. Now that the working class has ceased to be

film is quite explicit in its descriptions and denunciations. But its main objective lies elsewhere. On these points, opinions are already crystallized, and one explanation more or less will hardly make a noticeable difference. What is questioned here is the collective emotional context in which these opinions take shape, that is, one of the essential components in the massive foundation of any opinion *that becomes law.*

In this domain, the real consequence of "terrorist" actions of the RAF, Red Brigades type does not at all seem to have been taken into account by the leaders of these movements. Schematically, two positions come face to face on this question of armed struggle, in the heart of the European far left. The first, close to that of the RAF, considering that current social struggles go beyond the national and onto the international scale, and especially those between German-American imperialism and the Third World, deems it appropriate to destabilize the bastions of capitalism *by all available means,* beginning with armed underground warfare, and to reveal the intrinsically fascist nature of their democratic bourgeois regimes, while waiting for the avant-garde of the working classes, together with the oppressed masses of the Third World, once more to grasp hold of the old torch of the struggle for socialist revolution. The second

position, which can be compared to that of the so-called "spontaneist"* tendency, represented in the film by Horst Mahler, former "terrorist" practicing his self-criticism, **105**

the massive reference for any sort of revolutionary change, and revolution itself is in question, we are being confronted with a whole new set of problems. The terrorist temptation is part of a labor of birth for a new political thinking — a very bloody type of birth, but perhaps unavoidably so.

HM: Yes, in my thinking too.

SL: How does it feel being caught in this mechanism? You paid for it with 10 years of your life . . .

HM: But I wasn't "caught." I wasn't a passive object. I don't renounce my responsibility for what was done. I am part of this development. It is perhaps one possible consequence of modern thinking, which starts with Descartes in France and goes through philosophical rationalism to Marx. If you take Sartre and Marx together, you have exactly the RAF ideological grid. Only because we have had the RAF in Germany and Red Brigades in Italy are we able to see the absurd consequences of this kind of thinking.

SL: So it was pedagogical, but not in the way the RAF or the Red Brigades intended.

HM: We were a demonstration object. It shows what is perilous in our fantasies. This statement could be misunderstood, but I see this period as very necessary, both in my personal development and for the leftist movement as a whole. The experience of the RAF realized and then surpassed the ideology of the 60's in a very indirect way. I take this to be our contribution to history. □

consists on the contrary in denouncing, and rightly so, a "politics of the worst" which would only lead away from its initial objectives.

But this second view quickly plunges one into social-democratic, humanist re-appropriation and ends by condemning all violent acts in the name of a morality that accomodates itself to even greater acts of violence perpetrated in its own name! It promotes the idea that the only means of social transformation are those sanctioned by the law.

In its own way, each of these two positions seems to mask the true meaning of the new forms of underground action which are developing all over Europe and which seemingly are becoming one of the specific features of the blocked political situation characteristic of capitalist regimes.

What a film like *Germany in Autumn* brings to light, in an original way, is that the intense emotional charge associated with the "terrorist phenomenon" has become a fundamental given of current political strategies. Like it or not, politics today has become inseparable from the collective affects molded and transmitted by the mass-media, which constitutes a means of subjection crossing over classes and nations, and at the heart of which it is very difficult to separate the manipulated fantasies from socio-economic realities.

All formations of power, at whatever level, are the object and/or agent of this

"*One day, alternatives on both sides will meet. The silent majorities never will.*"

Heiner Müller

manipulation of the mass-media "material." Thus when young men and women rush headlong down the road of "terrorism," they don't do so only because of ideological systems, but also as delegates or sacrificial offerings of a subjective movement that surpasses them on all sides. Their actions, their feelings are "in touch" with those who approve of them, but also with all those layers of militants, of young revolutionaries, who have found no end to the struggles they have led for fifteen years. Furthermore, it is the passivity of the "swine," of the meek who comprise public opinion, which is worked on from within by their spectacular and desperate gestures. They, in return, manipulate the information and images transmitted by the media, and use their prestige to force the hand of those with whom they rub elbows.

In my view, what should be questioned is not the *principle* of armed struggle, nor its methods which are a part of all revolutionary movements, but, at the heart of each specific situation, its real influence on *the totality of anticapitalist struggles.* Clearly, the liquidation of a leader like Schleyer could never derail the functioning of the system. Instead, by providing power with the opportunity to fully deploy its police brigades and its mass-media arsenals, it helped to further ensnare millions among the exploited. In other words, the real drama is not that a man was killed, but that these actions were conducted in a way that simply does not break free of the repressive bourgeois system,

JEAN BAUDRILLARD

Our Theater of Cruelty

I. Mogadishu

In the terrorist act there is a simultaneous power of death and simulation which it is intolerable to see confused with the "morbid taste of death," and with the frenzy of the "morbid" and the "spectacular." Dead or living, it is elsewhere that terrorism wins out. At least by this single fact: it alone makes the event, and thus returns the whole "political" order to its nullity. And the media, all while orchestrating the victory of order, only cause the evidence for the opposite to reverberate: to wit, that terrorism is burying the political order.

The media are terrorists in their own fashion, working continually to produce (good) sense, but, at the same time, violently defeating it by arousing everywhere a fascination without scruples, that is to say, a paralysis of meaning, to the profit of a single scenario.

Terrorism is not violent in itself; only the spectacle it unleashes is truly violent. It is our Theater of Cruelty, the only one that remains to us, perhaps

Jean Baudrillard is an important French sociologist and thinker, author of *Political Economy of the Sign* (Telos) and *In the Shadow of the Silent Majority* (Semiotext(e), "Foreign Agents Series," Spring 1982).

fascist assassinations, or kidnappings carried out by unofficial police gangs, and that in the final account, their only result will have been to echo the collective melancholy that has present-day Germany in its grip. For my own part I know of nothing more sinister or odious than those photos of Schleyer or Moro,[1] with their little placards on their chests. While I refuse to judge whether or not their executions were well-founded — to judge their judges — I cannot stand this type of operation; for it is this sort of image, propelled across the media, which leads to a legitimate feeling of pity for those who are its objects and of disgust and revulsion toward those who are its authors.

Capitalism has only managed to consolidate those very bastions that the RAF and the Red Brigades claim to shake, insofar as it has managed to develop a majority consensus founded on social ultra-conservatism, the protection of acquired advantages and the systematic misinterpretation of anything that falls outside of corporate or national interests. And whatever works toward the isolation of individuals, whatever reinforces their feelings of impotence, whatever makes them feel guilty and dependent on the State, on Collective Agencies and their extensions — which the Unions and traditional leftist parties are fast becoming — feeds this consensus. To claim to lead a revolutionary movement without attacking these phenomena of mass manipulation is an absurdity. While the secret war conducted by the industrial powers along the north-

equal in every respect to that of Artaud or to that of the Renaissance, and extraordinary in that it brings together *the spectacular and the challenge at their highest points*. It is at the same time a model of simulation, a micro-model flashing with a minimally real event and a maximal echo chamber, like a crystal thrown into an unstable solution or an experimental matrix, an insoluble equation which makes all the variables appear suddenly. Not a real event, but a condensed narrative, a flash, a scenario — that is to say, that which opposes to every event said to be real the purest form of the spectacular — and a ritual, or that which, of all possible events, opposes to the political and historical model or order the purest symbolic form of challenge.

A strange mixture of the symbolic and the spectacular, of challenge and simulation. This paradoxical configuration is the only original form of our time, and subversive because insoluble. There is neither victory nor defeat: no sense can be made of an event which is irremediably spectacular, or irremediably symbolic. Everything in terrorism is ambivalent and reversible: death, the media, violence, victory. Who plays into the other's hands? Death itself is undefinable: the death of the terrorists is equivalent to that of the hostages; they are substitutable. In spite of all the efforts to set them into radical opposition, fascination allows no distinction to be made, and rightly so, for power finally does not make any either, but settles its accounts with everyone, and buries Baader and Schleyer together at Stuttgart in its incapacity to unravel the deaths and rediscover the fine dividing line, the distinctive and valid oppositions which are the secret of law and order. Nor is it possible to reclaim a positive use for the media, or a transparence of repression: the repressive act traverses the same unforeseeable spiral as the terrorist act; no

south axis to keep the Third World in tow is indeed the main issue, it should not make us forget that there is another north-south axis, which encircles the globe and along which conflicts of an equally essential nature are played out, involving the powers of the State and oppressed nationalities, immigrant workers, the unemployed, the "marginals," the "non-guaranteed"[2] and the "standardized" wage-earners, the people of the cities and of the barrios, of the favellas, the ghettoes, the shanty-towns, engaging the opposition of races, sexes, classes, age-groups, etc. To conduct this other war, to insure its social and mental control over this whole everyday, desiring world, capitalism mobilizes tremendous forces. To ignore this kind of opposition or to consider it of secondary importance is to condemn all other forms of social struggle led by the traditional Workers' Movement to impotence or reappropriation. Like it or not, in today's world, violence and the media work hand in glove. And when a revolutionary group plays the game of the most reactionary media, the game of collective guilt, then it has been mistaken: mistaken in its target, mistaken in its method, mistaken in its strategy, mistaken in its theory, mistaken in its dreams...

To affirm complete solidarity with the victims of capitalist repression — with all of the victims — in no way implies exonerating the aberrations that led to the unconscionable spectacles of the skyjacking to Mogadishu or the supposed People's Courts

109

one knows where it will stop, nor all the setbacks and reversals that will ensue. There is no distinction possible between the spectacular and the symbolic, no distinction possible between the "crime" and the "repression." *It is this uncontrollable eruption of reversibility that is the true victory of terrorism.*

This victory lies not at all in the fact of imposing a negotiation and forcing a government to capitulate. Besides, the objective — most of the time to liberate imprisoned comrades — is typically a zero sum equation. The stakes are elsewhere. And if power wins out at the level of the objective, it loses at the level of the real stakes. It loses its political definition, and is forced to accept, all the while trying to thwart, this reversibility of all the actors in the same process. Terrorists, killers, hostages, leaders, spectators, public opinion — there is no more innocence in a system which has no meaning. No tragedy either (in spite of the ideology of the Baader group itself, and the pedagogy of the terrorist model on a world-wide scale). The force of the terrorists comes to them precisely from the fact that they have no logic. The others do: it is quick, effective, flawless, without scruples; it is why they "win." If the terrorists had one, they would not make the errors that they do, but they would no longer be terrorists. To demand that they be at the same time illogical, which gives them their power, and logical tacticians, which would make them successful, is absurd — again a fantasy of synthesis, and of defense on our part, which allows us to recuperate ourselves in the fury of defeat.

Hence the stupidity and the obscenity of all that is reported about the terrorists: everywhere the wish to palm off meaning on them, to exterminate them with meaning, which is more effective than the bullets of specialized commandoes (and all the while subjecting them elsewhere, in the prisons, to

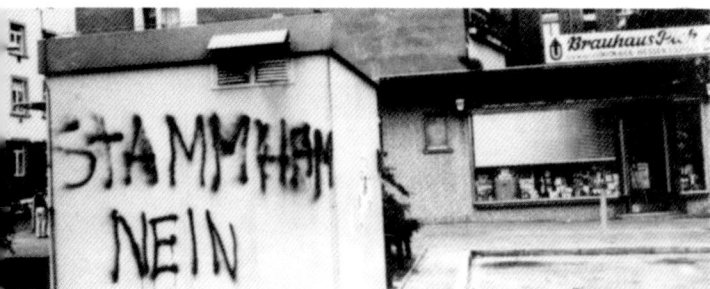

that deliberated in a cellar! The inane reproduction of the State's model of "justice" and repression, the revolting use of the media, the narrow-minded sectarianism, the manipulation of the "fellow travellers" are not questions of secondary importance. The merit of a film like *Germany in Autumn* is that it helps us to see these problems in their entirety. It not only gives us a virulent critique of German society, but also initiates an examination of underground armed struggle on its own terms. In this last matter, its criticisms still remain too timid and unfocused. Again one feels the weight of the event and the fear of reappropriation by the powers that be. But it does touch on the main point, which is the *morbid dramatization* spawned by the altogether absurd confrontation between a monstrous State power and pitiful politico-military machines. The authors of this film are not shooting with a P.38, but with a most singular expression of desire, the right to an unrestrained word, regardless of the pressures, regardless of the dramatic, or rather tragic, character of the situation constitutes today an essential prerequisite of any effective revolutionary advance. □

Translated by Mark Polizzotti

1. Aldo Moro, President of the Christian Democrats, was kidnapped by the Red Brigades and executed in Rome on March 16, 1978.

2. By the term "Guaranteeism" is meant all the victories achieved by traditional proletarian struggles on the level of wages, job security, working conditions, social services. Cf. *Autonomia* issue of *Semiotext(e)*, III, 3, 1980.

sensory deprivation). It is still this rage for meaning which makes us, with the best will in the world, treat them like idiots incapable of going all the way and blowing up the airplane and the passengers, which makes us want them not to have "won."

Not only have they not won, but they have encouraged inordinately the sacred union of all the world forces of repression; they have reinforced the political order, etc. — let's go all the way — they have killed their Stammheim* comrades, since if they had not launched and then botched up this operation, the others would still be living. But all this participates in the same conspiracy of meaning, which amounts to setting an action in contradiction with itself (here to ends that were not desired, or according to a logic which was not its own). Strangulation.

II. Stammheim

The insoluble polemic on the manner in which Baader and his comrades died is itself obscene, and for the same reason: there is an equal obscenity in wanting to forcibly impose meaning on the hijackers' act and in wanting to restore Baader's death to the order of factual reality. Principle of meaning as principle of truth: there you have the real life blood of State terrorism.

It is to believe that the German government's strategy attains perfection in a single blow: not only does it link together in an almost improvised manner the bungled taking of hostages with the immediately subsequent liquidation of the prisoners who disturbed it, but it does so in such a way (coarse, equivocal, incoherent) that it traps everyone in the hysterical search for truth, which is the best way to abolish the symbolic futility of this death.

"What is it about this society that needs to produce for its own security such a threatening military apparatus."

Daniel Cohn-Bendit

Telefon-Fahndung
1166
01166
1162
01162

The hijackers made so many errors at Mogadishu* that one can only think that they were done "on purpose." They have finally attained their objective obliquely, which was the challenge of their own death, the latter summing up the virtual one of all the hostages, and more radically still, that of the power which kills them. For it absolutely must be repeated that the stakes are not to beat power on its own ground, but to oppose another political order of force. One knows nothing about terrorism if one does not see that it is not a question of real violence, nor of opposing one violence to another (which, owing to their disproportion, is absurd, and besides, all *real* violence, like real order in general, is always on the side of power), but to oppose to the *full* violence and to the *full* order a clearly superior model of extermination and virulence operating through emptiness.

The secret is to oppose to the order of the real an absolutely imaginary realm, absolutely ineffectual at the level of reality, but whose implosive energy absorbs everything real and all the violence of real power which founders there. Such a model is no longer of the order of transgression: repression and transgression are of the old order of the law, that is to say, of the order of a real *system* in expansion. In such a system, all that comes into contradiction with it, including the violence of its opposite, only makes the expansion accelerate. Here, the virulence comes from the implosion — and the death of the terrorists (or of the hostages) is of this implosive order: the abolition of value, of meaning, of the real, at a determined point. This point can be infinitesimal, and yet provokes a suction, an absorption, a gigantic convection, as could be seen at Mogadishu. Around this tiny point, the whole system of the real condenses, is tetanized, and launches all its anti-bodies. It becomes so dense that it

ALEXANDER KLUGE

A Trained Conscience Will Bite and Kiss at the Same Time

A. Merkl: Why did I, an official of the government's security forces, shoot him? Because I had a gun.[1]

Question: Seriously now, why did you shoot him?

AM: I'm tired of not being able to deal with certain groups. We are ready and able. I wanted to draw attention to that.

Q: Was there, perhaps, another reason?

Alexander Kluge, one of the founders of the New German Cinema, is a filmmaker and writer.

goes beyond its own laws of equilibrium and involutes in its own over-effectiveness. At bottom, the profound tactic of simulation (for it's very much a matter of simulation in the terrorist model, and not of real death) is to provoke an excess of reality, and *to make the system collapse under an excess of reality.*

The paradoxical sleep is this fringe of sleep where one does not really sleep, but where one dreams. The paradoxical death is the one where the reality of death is suspended, this fringe where it acquires the status of a challenge that is symbolic *before becoming real,* that is to say, residue, the real always being only the residual principle of death's degradation and of what's left over.

If it is possible then to think that the hijackers have acted purposefully in order to meet their death, this kind of paradoxical death which shines intensely for a moment before falling back into the real, it is posssible to think inversely that the German government itself did not commit so many errors in the Baader affair except towards a well defined end (even without desiring it). It was able to stage Baader's death neatly — he did not do it. Far from seeing there a secondary episode, it must be seen as the *key* to the situation. By sowing this doubt, this deliberate ambiguity concerning the facts, it insured that the truth about this death, and not the death itself, became fascinating. Everyone exhausted himself in argument and in attempts at clarification — clarifications reinforced by the theatricality of the event which acts as a gigantic dissuasion of the terrorists' execution — everyone, and above all the revolutionaries who wanted strongly to have it that Baader has been "assassinated." They too were vultures of the truth. What's the bloody difference, anyway — suicides or victims of liquidation? The difference, of

AM: I wanted to show that an assassin could get the honorable minister, despite preventive measures; that the security forces, if they were on the other side, could do it. I regret I hit the minister in the mouth (and it cost me my government job). I had aimed at the wall behind the minister, and the bullet was supposed to zip by his head by half a meter.

Q: Why were you arrested?

AM: There were too many body guards. The officials of the 18th commissariat wouldn't have caught me. But since the men from security in Bonn are younger, have more stamina, and had a good course in anticipating avenues of escape, it's not surprising that they would catch an attempted assassin. They can catch him, but not prevent assassinations. We can prevent assassinations by infiltrating their groups, then getting rid of them. This would require changes in the code of criminal procedure and the judicial organization, as well as the centralizing of all security forces, improving international cooperation, increasing pay, creative training, and finally setting clear goals. It's good that we are supposed to protect the constitution and the officials of the government. That is gratifying. The constitution as it stands and the officials of government in office now make that impossible.

113

course, is that if they were liquidated and it can be proven, then the masses guided by the truth of the facts, would know that the German State is fascist, and would mobilize in order to wreak revenge. What a load of rubbish. A death is romantic or it is not. And in the latter case,there is no need for revenge; it is of the imaginary order. What non-sense to fall back into the reality of a contract of revenge and equivalence! The avengers are worth the moralists: always evaluate the price, and have the just price paid. It matters little that the "reality" of this death (the truth about . . .) is stolen from you, since it is not of the order of the real, and therein lies its force. You are the one who depreciates it by wanting to institute it as a fact, as capital with the value of death, and to exhaust it in death, whereas this death at full price, not liquidated in the equivalence of meaning and vengeance, opens a cycle of vertigo in which the system itself can only come to be implicated in the end, or brutally, through its own death. Against this vertiginous death the system defends itself by setting in place an inverse cycle — a recycling of the truth against the insoluble cycle of death. Such is the inspired manoeuvre of the German government, which consists in delivering through its "calculated" errors an unfinished product, an unrecoverable truth. Thus everyone will exhaust himself finishing the work, and going to the end of the truth. A subtle incitement to self-management. It is content to produce an event involving death; others will put the finishing touches on the job. The truth. Even among the very ones who revolt at Baader's death, no one sees through this trap, and all function with the same automatism in the fringe of open complicity which all intelligent power contrives to spread around its decisions.

Far from harming him, the flaws of Stammheim stem from a strategy of

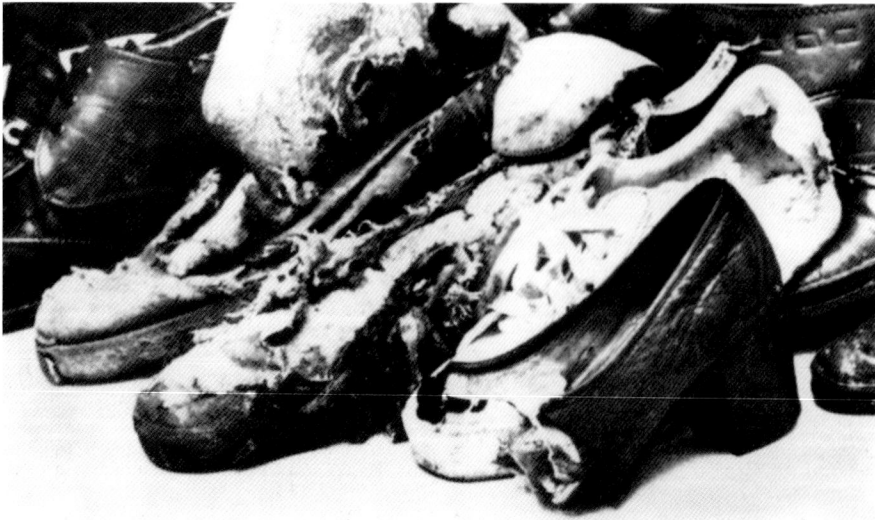

simulation by the German State which alone would merit analysis and denunciation. A strategy of sacred union, and not at all moral, against the terrorist violence, but, much more profoundly, *a sacred union in the production of truth,* of the facts, of the real. Even if this truth explodes (if in fifteen years it is finally established that Baader was coldly liquidated), it will hardly be a scandal. No power will be frightened by it; if necessary, the crew of leaders will be changed. The price of the truth for power is superficial. On the other hand, the benefits of general mobilization, dissuasion, pacification and mental socialization obtained through this crystalization of the truth are immense. A smart operation, under which Baader's death threatens to be buried definitively. □

Translated by John Johnston

"Even when you're dead you're not rid of history. Death itself can be used."

Sylvère Lotringer

FRITZ TEUFEL

On Rudi Dutschke's Death

Preliminary remarks: since the news of Rudi's death, I've made three attempts to write something about him — so many thoughts and memories come to mind, fragments of our common history. I'm just going to type it up, even though I should keep working on it — but it's better than nothing.

First Attempt.

Rudi's statement at Holger Mein's grave,[1] "Holger, the struggle goes on!", wasn't immediately understood by everyone. Reactionaries understood it as the call to terrorism of a professional revolutionary, a spy from the East, horror of the Establishment, and leading ideologist of the Extra-Parliamentary Opposition* (APO): Rudi Dutschke. A few ultimate fighters of the West German urban guerrilla understood the sentence as the attempt of an old, burnt out APO fighter and University assistant turned bourgeois to polish his revolutionary image. In fact, Rudi found it necessary to comment on the meaning of the sentence in a letter to the editor of *Spiegel*[2] magazine, but I

Considered the most "devilish" (*Teufel*, in German) personality of the early anti-authoritarian movement, Fritz Teufel has spent much of the past decade behind bars for "terrorist" allegations that have remained largely unproven. Now a "fun-guerrilla" living in West Berlin.

Q: What kind of change do you see possible?

AM: As a member of the security force, I've given this a lot of thought. First of all, we should be allowed to do what we can do. The opposition calls this "the release of the powers of production." We consider ourselves to be "powers of production." Our goal is the production of constitutional order.

Q: Do you consider the bullet in the minister's head, which destroyed a portion of his chin and teeth, a contribution to change?

AM: As I said, it was a bad shot.

Q: Didn't you exceed your ability to act, if you couldn't aim accurately?

AM: Even the best sharpshooter, at a distance of 400 meters can't guarantee absolute accuracy. And besides, the minister moved.

Q: You should have anticipated that.

AM: I did.

Q: Then you consciously risked a bad shot?

can't remember the wording. However, I think that the statement at the grave was easier to understand than his letter to the editor. If that's the case, then it was characteristic of Rudi. His speeches were easier to understand than his writings. I knew Rudi the way many knew him. We weren't particularly close friends. I loved him anyway. Personal encounters with Rudi were electrifying. His uprightness, his passion, his patience when explaining, his ability to concentrate intently, his bubbling wealth of ideas and his ability to listen to everyone. I don't know how successful he was in restoring all of this after the assassination attempt on his life.

Second Attempt.

On Maundy Thursday '68, the news of THE ASSASSINATION ATTEMPT hit us hard and sent us into a flurry of activity at the same time. Kunzelmann stated [3] what could later have been interpreted as inhuman: "Hopefully he'll die now, and then everyone will be on Springer's back." Rudi was everyone's friend, and Kunzel would have said that even if it were his own life at stake. It was very clear to us that Springer's agitation had hit one of us, and that the movement had now to take the next step from protest to resistance. When pictures of Bachman,[4] the assassin, appeared in the paper, Rainer Langhans[5] remembered that he had given directions (from Stuttgart Square to the SDS Headquarters on Kudamm on the morning before the assassination attempt) to an agitated young man, standing at the front door of the commune, who thought that Rudi lived with us. He would have been content with violence against any one of the people in the commune, but it was

AM: Of course. An action according to our opposition (and we are perfectly ready to be instructed by the enemy!) is a function of the strategy adopted. If we replace the word strategy here with intent, then an element of uncertainty, which invests all our intentions, must necessarily also be a part of our individual actions. This includes the elements of uncertainty, or as you call them: risks. It has become impossible nowadays to manage any kind of business without taking risks.

Q: Could you say this once again, a bit more simply, for our audience?

AM: I shot him in the cheek because life today has no real direction or meaning. Under such circumstances, you can't always hit the mark.

Q: But you could have waited until the minister was closer.

AM: Then I would have been recognised in the shot's flash.

Q: But you were caught anyway.

AM: I didn't know then.

Q: But you realised that was a possibility?

AM: Certainly.

Rudi after all, who, as the leading ideologist of the red APO-Terror, had been dragged through Springer's smear campaign.

Easter 68. On the evening of the assassination attempt — or was it a day later? — a huge train of enraged demonstrators marched from the Technical University in the center of Berlin past the America House — where the first window-panes rattled — over to the Springer Skyscraper on Kochstrasse in Kreuzberg, directly by the wall. RU-DI DUTSCH-KE SPRING-ER MUR-DERER! and "DUTSCHKE LIVES, WHEN SPRINGER BURNS!" Our shouts echoed through the streets, we screamed our lungs out, and a few Springer trucks were actually burning that night, in the parking lot in front of the building. In the following days a blockade was organized spontaneously to stop the delivery of the *Bild* in Berlin and in other places that published the scandal sheet.

Third Attempt

The snail pace of the revolutionary movement after its first anti-authoritarian flourish in 68 and the discrepancy between our great expectations and the difficulty and wearisomeness of the historical process to fulfill these hopes — providing that we are still capable of perceiving this process at all and haven't written off every hope as an illusionary utopia of our younger days — make an hommage to Rudi a very difficult task.

He didn't understand enlightenment as having a few revolutionary leftist high school teachers cramming the truth into the stupid "people"; instead he understood it to mean the collective learning process of unknowing people

Q: Are you satisfied with the results of your action?

AM: Of course not. I lost the position, which I wanted to make meaningful by this action, and am now faced with a trial. My colleagues ignore me, no one wants to take responsibility, even though the action in question was a *bona fide* practice exercise. This was not successful.

Q: Did you really expect a different result?

AM: Of course. But what can one do? Somehow someone has to be able to express himself.

Q: You have an excellent service record.

AM: Yes, of course.

Q: You are a logical thinker — you even have a university degree — and yet your behaviour seems contradictory.

AM: It only seems so. We've learned, studied, practiced, and want now simply to utilize our skills.

118   **Q:** What will you do when you are released from prison?

with a brotherly attitude. Like all great teachers, Rudi always thought of himself as a student.

In fact Rudi was often involved in arguments with Leftists. He was already taking part in quarrels, insults and counter-insults in 68. But Rudi didn't take it personally. He never criticized without being open to dialogue. Solidarity criticism, critical solidarity, self-criticism weren't just cliches for him. Rudi's understanding of the West German Leftists of the old and the new APO was incredibly comprehensive and extensive and had a lot to do with the understanding of himself. As far as Rudi was concerned Jusos* and RAF were both comrades.

If it weren't for the assassination attempt, Erich Fried[6] said, Rudi would have kept Ulrike Meinhoff from taking up an armed struggle. If it weren't for the assassination attempt, I think Rudi may have taken that route himself and he would have given the armed struggle in the metropolitan areas a decisive impulse, like Ulrike did. These are just speculations. But it's not speculation to say that the assassination attempt on Rudi's life had served as such an impulse. And Rudi knew it, when he went to the revolutionary Holger Mein's grave — who was let to die in a hunger strike — and said, "Holger, the struggle goes on." He was serious about it and we should be serious about it too.

The struggle for democracy and socialism and for the enjoyment of life, in all facets of life and in every corner of the globe, continues.

Rudi, the struggle goes on!

Moabit jail, the 8th of Jan. 1980. □

Translated by Barbara Kosta

AM: I intend to start a private detective agency, to take jobs from the business sector, together with a friend who was expelled from the police service when he was exposed by a prostitute (he was supposedly involved with some kind of extortion).

Q: Because business espionage, sabotage, and harassment of employers are on the rise?

AM: That's right. Here is a task the State is not, and cannot, be qualified to do — from which it has to disqualify itself — since it (as we know from the opposition) cannot be regarded as a structure of production or represent relations of production, but must serve a third function: to be a managerial body representing the interests of the ruling class. (It goes without saying that we don't believe in class structures, but use this concept nonetheless, because it provides a clear overview of the relationships we address by our tactics). As such the State cannot regulate details. Our mission is precisely related to these details, which, through intervention, and by using everything at our disposal, can be corrected.

Q: Do you have a negative view of your former job?

AM: This also applies to my future as a detective. We've got to get beyond this.

1. RAF* member, imprisoned in 1972. Died following a hunger strike in 1974.

2. A weekly news magazine, roughly equivalent to *Newsweek*.

3. One of the founding members of *Kommune I* in 1967. Spent several years in prison during the 70's. Now a member of the West Berlin Alternative List.

4. Testifying in court that he had been "inspired" to assassinate Dutschke through the Springer* *Bild-Zeitung,* Bachmann subsequently committed suicide in prison.

5. Founding member of *Komune I,* Langhans later became a Jesus freak.

6. Fried is a poet now living in London.

Q: Do you see anything positive?

AM: Not on our side.

Q: Do you take your task to be negative?

AM: Absolutely.

Q: Why do you continue to accept it then?

AM: We have to, otherwise we will be unable to make use of the skills we have acquired. We are realists.

Q: But you are headed straight for jail with your realism.

AM: But we'll be released again . . .

Q: Are you fighting for a cause you don't believe in?

AM: No one can believe in it.

Q: Then you fight imprecisely and badly.

120   **AM:** We are also paid different salaries and badly.

"*I like to stand with one leg on each side of the wall. No other position seems to me real enough.*"

Heiner Müller

MARLIS KRÜGER

Notes on
Critical Theory in Germany

1

In the early seventies, some influential German periodicals, many Marxist-oriented students, and not a few intellectuals of Marxist or positivist persuasion pronounced the Frankfurt School of Social Theory dead.[1]

A couple of years later, the American Martin Jay attributed this pronouncement to wishful thinking on the part of the School's (political) opponents and pointed to the widespread and growing reception of Critical Theory in the English-speaking countries, especially in America, in order to underscore that the School was well and alive and rapidly expanding — abroad. That it was not defunct in Germany either could be recognized by Jürgen Habermas' prolific output of publications (even in the '70s), which in the eyes of Martin Jay constitute important contributions to epistemology and methodology.

Paul Piccone, a compatriot of Jay's, pondered the fate of the Frankfurt School in 1976.[2] According to his diagnosis, Critical Theory was thriving in

Marlis Krüger is a West German sociologist at the University of Bremen.

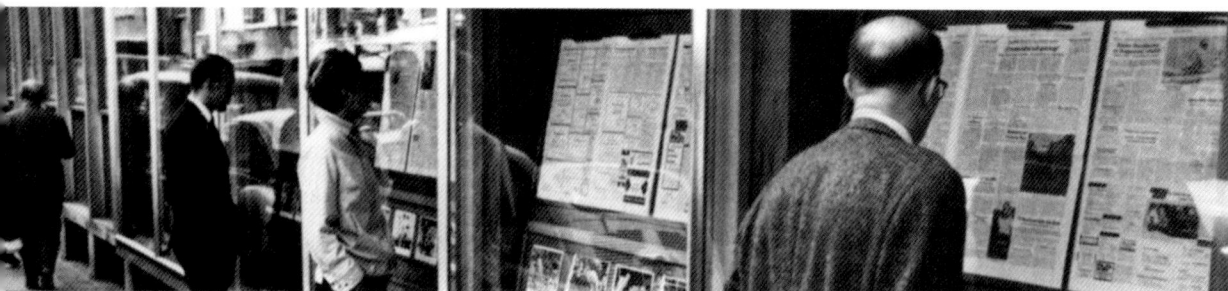

Q: But you've received a regular salary.

AM: That's true. But a man does not live by money alone. We need work we can believe in, and that's the problem. Sometimes I consider the possibility of combining the work of the opposition with our skills. But then I dismiss such ideas, because many of us are too old to be converted. Besides, these groups don't have any power.

Q: But you have power and could use it.

AM: No, that's a mistake. We don't have power. Power is so divided between the various authorities, that everyone is powerless.

Q: Even the minister you wounded is powerless in this sense?

AM: No. He can try to protect himself, but he did not have the power to escape from my shot.

Q: A partnership of the powerless, who together can assert their authority?

AM: Exactly.

Q: The groups you call the opposition, are they powerless?

the English-speaking world, whereas it was dead in its birthplace. Discussing Hegelian Marxism in the 1920's and '30s and, particularly, Adorno's critique of identity theory — Habermas was not mentioned at all — Piccone informed his readers about the reason for these differences in the development of Critical Theory: the U.S., which had come fully under the sway of monopoly capitalism, soon discovered "that it is *too repressive* for its own good" and thus opened itself up to Critical Theory as a much needed systemic corrective.

Germany, on the other hand, was still passing — in 1976 (!), thus Piccone — from entrepreneurial to monopoly capitalism. And Critical Theory, alas, did not provide organizational conceptions against the growing subsumption of all remaining "otherness" under the advancing technocracy — hence its irrelevance in Germany.

German capitalism, it thus seems, entered into its monopolist stage last year: in 1980 Jurgen Habermas, who is, according to Jay, a major protagonist of the Frankfurt School, delivered the major lecture (on Talcott Parsons) at the opening session of the meetings of the German Sociological Association in Bremen, while a special session on the older Frankfurt School (Adorno and Horkheimer) attracted the largest crowds.

Has there been a reversal of trends then? How can this development be accounted for? Certainly not by Piccone's absurd economic explanation, which is not only empirically false but also uses the very same simplistic substructure-superstructure model which critical theorists have always attempted to resist. In order to analyze the existing *mediated* interconnectedness of social reality and thought processes and ideas, one has to look at the *immanent* structure of a theory as well as at its social context in *all* its dimensions

"Sometimes I feel so heavy, so German. I have to go very deep all the time and think and think. I don't know why."

Annette Humpe

AM: Let's say we can learn from them by carefully studying their publications. I would like to organise a division, whose primary task is to watch over such an education and to collect everything we have to know in order to survive.

Q: Will you use your time in prison to begin such a project?

AM: Obviously. □

Translated by Reinhard Mayer

1. Officials of the security forces do not carry weapons when on the job. Mr. Merkl chose to carry a gun.

(socio-economic, political, cultural, etc.). When one wants to focus especially on the reception, further development, modification and cross-cultural transference of a set of ideas, one must take into account both its immanent structure and ambiguities, inconsistencies, or contradictions and the ways in which the theory is dealt with by the "receiving" subjects: whether in terms of an *immanent* reconstruction, appropriation, and critique or in terms of a hermeneutic exploitation, (i.e., from a perspective transcending the theory itself or external to it). The extent to which a critique, even a radical critique, is itself influenced by the axiomatic structure of the theory under scrutiny is in part *also* dependent on whether or not the basic problem of the theory continues to exist.

Before we turn to the "fate" of Critical Theory in West Germany, its life as well as alleged death and resurrection, we would like to deal briefly with the question of why a treatment of this subject matter should be of any intrinsic interest and/or value for American intellectuals. For, certainly, their own interest or disinterest in Critical Theory would not necessarily be influenced by whether or not a set of ideas existed in other countries, its birthplace included. That is, if we accept for a moment the thesis that the Frankfurt School is dead in Germany — why should this "fact" prevent Americans from appropriating, exploring, criticizing, dealing with it? It would do so only if Americans derived their intellectual interests exclusively from other peoples' — an absurd idea — and/or firmly believed in a strict developmental *logic* of intellectual life: that Germany, for instance, had already reached the next and higher stage of theoretical accomplishment while the U.S. was still lagging behind or, vice versa, if one would take Critical Theory as the end point of human intellectual

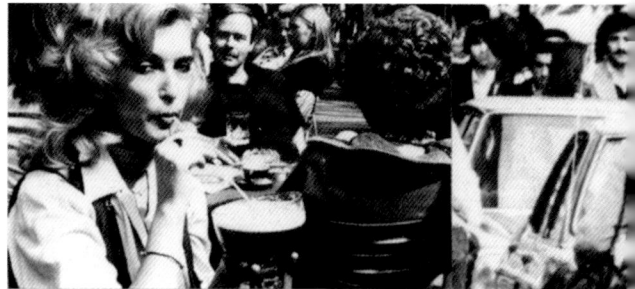

Buback: In Memoriam

My immediate reaction to the gunning down of Buback can be described simply: I didn't want to and couldn't hide my joy. I had often heard this guy incite people; I know that he played a leading role in the pursuit, criminalization, and torture of the left. Someone who recently has looked closely at his face could recognize the traits of our democratic State, and he could recognize as well a few features of those righteous democrats who are now in an uproar. Honestly, I am a little sorry that we can't include this face anymore in the little red and black book containing mug shots, which we will publish after the revolution, of the most wanted and detested representative of the old world whom we will put on public trial. He is no more — *enfant perdu*.

But that's not all that was going through my mind and a lot of other people's minds.

Siegfried Buback, Federal Attorney in West Germany, was assassinated in 1977 by the RAF*. Several university professors endorsed the publication of this text, whose author was never identified. The only professor to maintain his endorsement despite the official ban, Peter Brückner, a political scientist, was subsequently barred from teaching.

development . . .

In contrast to these hypothetical beliefs, we would like to suggest that a fresh look at the "development" of Critical Theory in Germany in the last decade might at best provide Americans with some intellectual stimulation for their critical analyses of their own society and its intellectual and political life.

2

In the authoritarian, conservative and apolitical ambiance of German society of the '50s and '60s, the Frankfurt School represented the last bastion of cultural and social critique in academia. The first post-World War II generation of German students was attracted to this "counterculture" dimension of the Frankfurt scholars because it seemed a weapon suitable to breaking the stranglehold of the traditional pre-bourgeois, anti-democratic political and cultural German traditions which had been totally bankrupted under Nazi totalitarianism. The political impetus of many students, who encountered the teaching and writings of the Frankfurt School in the 50s and 60s, was radical democratic and therefore rather well attuned to the School's theoretical development, which was a far cry from its Marxist inspired beginnings. Only as the self-education and political learning process of the young Germans progressed by going back to the sources of radical political theory and philosophy did it become aparent that the Frankfurt scholars were also a tenuous link of postwar German academia to Marxist intellectual traditions. Because of this linkage, Critical Theory has more lately been interpreted frequently as the most advanced bourgeois product of the decline of Marxist theory. This inter-

The sublime joy evoked by a viewing of Carrero Blanco's *Ascension*[1] wasn't produced. Not that I let myself be tamed by well-orchestrated public outrage and hysteria; sometimes this show is more effective than at other times, and no one believes anymore that a single critical voice will be raised by the political eunuchs who earn their living (a good thing) by manufacturing public opinion.

But I am not so indifferent to this hermetic bloc of one-dimensional media of official announcements and commentary. I don't need to be bothered by it anymore — concerning any kind of action at all. The bugging incident showed that this chorus of righteous people can't whitewash themselves. Cracks appeared in this facade of legitimacy, which we must take advantage of even in respect to Stammheim.* We missed an opportunity there, a public whispering campaign, a public uneasiness about the nonchalance with which the Bubacks, the Maihofers, Schiess and Benda[2] commit the most heinous crimes. The opportunity passed us by. Now, after the attack, isn't every method to destroy the brood of terrorists just?

That may just be my personal impression. I have no desire or power to intervene in this case. But what I'm trying to say may become clearer if we look at the example of the Roth-Otto[3] trial in Cologne. During this trial, it was the strategy of the Bubacks to sentence the leftists who had not fired a shot, as murderers of policemen. Revolutionary

pretation, incidentally, like that of many Frankfurt scholars, tends to paint a rather idyllic picture of the past, however bad in actuality, in order to measure the always much more oppressive and devastating present against it. It becomes obvious here how much the critics of Critical Theory are still entangled in some of its basic tenets.

The social and political influence of the Frankfurt School increased markedly with the rise of the student movement. Contrary to many accounts, the student movement did not start at the instigation of the Frankfurt School or as carrier of its precepts and theoretical prescriptions. The German student movement started with a democratic or radical democratic stance and only in the course of its unfolding dynamics and encounter with administrative and state repression did the relatively small Marxist oriented groups gain larger influence. To most students, Critical Theory — outside of Frankfurt — was known through the Positivist Dispute, a controversial dialogue and discussion about the proper methodology and philosophy of science for the social sciences between Adorno and Habermas, on one hand, and K. Popper and H. Albert on the other. That the critical theorists engaged in this debate adamantly held to the criterion of a succcessful human emancipation as constitutive for a critical theory of society inspired the students in their critiques of the established conceptions and institutionalized practice of science, as well as in their attempts at the conceptualization of new, socially relevant, and politically emancipatory scientific endeavors.

It was, however, Critical Theory's own insistence on the abolition and elevation of the traditional separation of theory and *praxis* which eventually led to the mutual disaffection of the Frankfurt School and the emerging New

leftists are killers. Their attitude, their practice predestine them to become killers, who are not afraid to use any means. Thus they equated the prosecution with the judge.

With arduous efforts our comrades were at least able to initially thwart this strategy and to thwart it in a manner, so that the one-dimensional media were forced to report the mess, inhumane prison restrictions, procedural errors, etc. Little Stammheim in Cologne cast a shadow on the real Stammheim. Last Wednesday, Roth's and Otto's attorneys moved to have the charges dropped because there just wasn't any evidence. The equation of leftists with killers was struck. I'm afraid, as a result of Buback's murder, our comrades will lose their advantage, and the verdict may be influenced negatively.

The blindness of those people who reduce the political world to Stammheim and who carry on the struggle independent of daily political fluctuations could disarm other comrades and could unwittingly contribute to their downfall. Reverse counterinsurgency...

These thoughts were enough to stop my internal handwringing. But it gets worse. For a while (like so many of us) I savored the activities of the armed struggle, a civilian who has never carried a gun, never set off a bomb. I rejoiced a little when something exploded, and the whole capitalist chicanery complete with its cops was injured in the process. Things I would like to do some day in my daydreams, but which I never really dared to do.

Left. Whereas Adorno and Horkheimer reverted to a philosophy-of-history position and tried to insulate their "critical" theory from the newly gathered experiences, Habermas engaged in a harsh public critique of the student movement and denounced it as "left fascist." (Not that he criticized the students, but that and how he went public with his criticisms in a society without even so much as a bourgeois public led to the irreversible break between Habermas and the student movement.)

Not only had Critical Theory failed to live up to its own claim but some of its proponents had also violated the principle of solidarity with the student protesters. The seemingly endless critical reflexions of ideological theories, which the Frankfurt scholars were so expert at, had — in the eyes of more and more of its adherents — turned into an all-absorbing end in itself. Critical Theory became less and less immune to dogmatism, which endangers all social theories that cut themselves off from social reality and practical experiences.

Once Critical Theory had lost much of its appeal and lure for the political dissenters, other of its weaknesses were also dissected: although Critical Theory, as programmatically conceptionalized by Horkheimer in 1937, had aimed at the dialectical appropriation of unclear forms of consciousness and theories, it has never realized the Marxian postulate of the concrete appropriation (and practical elevation) of philosophy. Nor has it ever provided a substantive theory of bourgeois society, which would be the prerequisite of any materialist ideology critique. And its social analysis was reduced to nothing but the occasional use of abstract economic categories. Adorno's negation of negation remained also exclusively negative. Positive judgements or theories, even experimental theories, were no longer possible according to

I just imagined again that I was with the armed soldiers, was being pursued, lived somewhere in a conspiratorial relationship with a few people, had to watch (when I went shopping, emptied the waste basket, saw a film) that I wasn't done in while doing mundane tasks. I asked myself how I — cut off from normal personal and political connections — could make decisions with my people about such an action. How I would prepare myself for months to dispose of Buback, how my whole mind would be determined by logistics and ballistics. How I could be sure that this man and no one else had to die. That someone else there will fall victim, and a third person might become a paraplegic, etc.

I had to shift gears completely: I still believe that the decision to put people to death lies with the ruling power, with judges, policemen, security guards, the military. I would have to be specially educated to be a cold-blooded, ruthless, calculating killer like Al Capone.

How should I decide that Buback is important not just for me and my people, but for others as well. That he is more important that Judge X of Prison Y or his warden. Or that the salesman on the corner, who continually screams, "Off with his head!" is less guilty than Buback. Only because he has less responsibility?

Shouldn't we just concentrate on the cooks?

him. Human action, however, and even human spontaneity cannot occur — thus his critics argued — in totally empty and unimaginable situations.

What Critical Theory seemed to lack in terms of substantive and praxis-oriented theories, Marxism seemed to offer. And the reception of Marx's works, which gained momentum in the late '60s, had an exhilarating effect on may young academics, for Marx seemed to provide the much needed categorical framework for an adequate analysis of societal structures and processes.

So, when the German public read the obituraries of the Frankfurt School in the early 70s, the School had in fact lost out to Marxian theory as well as Marxism in its various political and/or ideological variants. But an intellectual tradition does not die that easily. It may be superseded for a while or become latent or exist only subterraneously. This is especially true of a tradition which has profoundly influenced the professionalization of many young social scientists and philosophers as in the case of Adorno and Horkheimer. Thus, the only prerequisite for the continued, potential relevance of Critical Theory was that its basic problems and questions, albeit not its solutions, persisted. And that they did was becoming apparent the more the student movement, with its partly decentralized and spontaneously organized activities, dissolved into a number of hierarchically structured "parties" — rigid, disciplinarian and each with the claim to total knowledge and the right route to *praxis*. For, in this situation, any questioning of a dogmatic Marxist theory or any search for an alternative to an ossified Marxist *praxis* could find intellectual support in many writings of the Frankfurt School. Yes, it can be safely argued that the early essays and studies of Adorno and Horkheimer from the 1930s became of ever greater significance, the more rigid and isolated the left became (a few

"It's always a military terminology that comes to Marx. He describes the productive collective as an 'army of workers with officers of production.'"

André Gorz

When one of these State-sanctioned killers is shot down in Argentina, or even Spain, I have no problem. I think I feel that the people's hatred for these men is really the hatred of the people. But who, and how many people hated Buback? What criteria could I use, as an armed soldier, to decide matters of life and death?

We've got to get away from despising the oppressors of the people as surrogates for the people, as we had already gotten away from acting on other people's behalf and forming a party. If Buback doesn't become a victim of the people's anger, then the force used will come as little from the people as Buback's face came from the people.

We just need to follow the news reports: liquidation strategy is the strategy of the rulers. Why must we copy them? The people are afraid of it; they've had experience with it, just like with prisons and work camps. We won't liquidate our enemies. We won't shut them up in prisons or work camps, but we won't be gentle with them either.

Our purpose, a society without terror or force (though not without aggression and militancy); a society without forced labor (though not without drudgery); a society without courts, prisons, institutions (though not without rules and regulations — or better, suggestions); the purpose does not justify any means. Our path to socialism (anarchy for me) cannot be paved with corpses.

Why should we liquidate people? Ridicule can also kill in the long run. Our weapons

despaired and turned terrorists and others retreated from active politics into the realm of academic Marxism) while at the same time the State drastically increased its political repression of anybody vaguely suspicious of a critical attitude toward the *status quo* (cf. *Berufsverbote*"*).

3

On the surface, however, Critical Theory was practically non-existent in the mid-seventies, at least among its Marxist-turned former adherents. If judged by the number of publications, commentaries, critiques, public discussions, or even its curricular presence in the universities, Critical Theory fared very badly indeed if compared to the rush of translations of the classical texts of Adorno and Horkheimer and contemporary works of Habermas in America or the numerous articles in such journals as *Telos* and *New German Critique*, which provided an institutional back-up system of Critical Theory American style. Moreover, the "Frankfurt School" of Critical Theory, in the sense of a distinct group of cooperating scholars, had ceased to exist. The precise date is open to debate: while some place it at Adorno's death in 1969, others connect it with the departure of Habermas from Frankfurt University to a Max-Planck Institute in 1971. Be this as it may, the dissolution of the Frankfurt School as an institution did not — thus we would argue — lead to the final demise of Critical Theory. For, not only are there still Frankfurt scholars of the second or third generation — e.g. J. Habermas, O. Negt, A. Schmidt, H. Reichelt — who in one way or another view themselves as continuing the tradition of Horkheimer's original program of Critical Theory, albeit as individuals and no

are not an imitation of military weapons, but rather the kind they can't shoot out of our hands. Therefore our strength doesn't need to rest upon a single phrase, like "Solidarity." Our force cannot be Al Capone's force, a copy of street terror, and constant terror; not authoritarian, but rather anti-authoritarian and therefore more effective. Leftists shouldn't be killers, shouldn't be ruthlessly brutal people, shouldn't be rapists, but also not saints or innocent lambs. Our daily objective is to formulate a concept and *modus operandi* of force and militancy which are fun and have the blessings of the masses, so that the left doesn't acquire the same face as the Bubacks.

A little crude, but honest . . . .

A Mescalero from Göttingen. ☐

Translated by Wynn Gundarson

1. The "muscle" behind Franco, assassinated by the ETA in 1974.
2. Maihofer is a Federal minister of internal affairs. Schiess is a regional Secretary of Justice and Benda a Federal Justice.
3. Otto and Roth were accused and convicted for attempted murder.

longer as members or representatives of a school. But also, Critical Theory has become the subject of a renewed *historical* interest on the part of young university students, as well as a reservoir of ideas or better: questions concerning the possibilities and limitations of an emacipatory theory and experimental historical *praxis* for at least some German intellectuals who have not yet given up on the possibilities of a radical transformation of their society.

Let us pick up the historical thread at this juncture. Most of the leftist critiques of the Frankfurt School had been published by the late 60s/early 70s. In the '70s, the scholarly interest of many left intellectuals focused on a faithful reconstruction of Marx's structural analysis of capitalism. The neglect of political economy by the Frankfurt scholars found here its necessary compensation. However, the reconstruction of Marxian theory on the categorical level proved futile also in terms of a formulation of a viable Marxist *praxis*.

If Critical Theory had been mostly criticized by German students for its failure of providing organizational categories for its theoretical precepts, the same students — some of them now young professors on the march through the institutions — found themselves only a little later similarly helpless *vis-a-vis* the seemingly overpowering repressive administrative apparatus and an apathetic population. The Marxian theory of the revolutionary subject had failed in theory and *praxis*, and Critical Theory's principal question of the possibilities of a social emancipatory *praxis* in the absence of a visible social carrier of a radical transformation of society acquired new importance. Its insistence on a successful emancipation as the major criterion of its own theory seems heuristically fruitful for a reconstruction of the Marxian theory of political economy and historical *praxis* which would take seriously Marx's

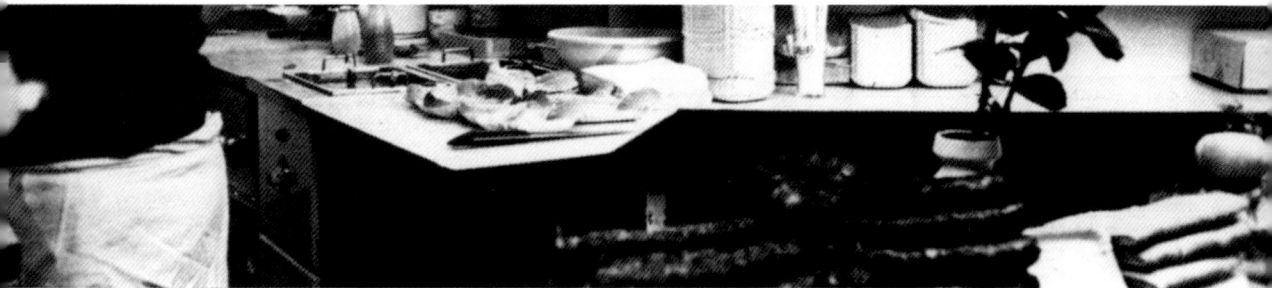

To Have Done with Armed Isolation

With their bombs they had intended to herald armed resistance and have instead disarmed their comrades of their political and other weapons. With their bombs they wanted to give us courage to fight and to put up resistance, but instead they have only frightened most of us and driven us into a powerless rage. And finally they wanted to show us that armed resistance was possible and necessary and instead they showed us the way to self-destruction.

We are serious about our criticism of this self-destruction, very serious indeed. And we don't mean to be derogatory. For many of us, the refusal to give up politically is an essential part of our political identity. In the past it was the jealousy of hungry people which the bourgeoisie suspected of hiding under their lavishly-set table, today it is the insanity of shattered lives, which cannot fit into careers and a consumer-oriented society. Generals and politicians who plan total annihilation are normal. Soldiers, wardens, teachers — all the people who do what is demanded of them — are normal. A worker ap-

11th thesis on Feuerbach.[3]

While Marxist-oriented scholars have attempted to derive *logically* the actual behavior of individuals from their charactermasks, i.e., the objectively existing system requirements, the concrete actions and behavior of individuals as well as the newly emerging social movements of women, ecologists, squatters (*Hausbesetzer*), etc. have demonstrated that subjective actions cannot be conceptualized as individuations of objective situations. Because a revolutionary *praxis* is only possible if it is carried out by the existing individuals — whatever their limitations — it has been argued that the Marxian theory of historical and revolutionary *praxis* should be reformulated in terms of acting individuals rather than objective processes.

On the practical-political level, the short-lived attempts of the so-called "Sponti"-groups* of students (1977/8) to create and practice a new form of politics which was to forge a viable connection between social analysis, theoretical interests, subjective experiences, and individual needs and wishes also challenged a Marxism consisting of abstract logical deductions, as well as a *praxis* without *concrete* individuals.

While the political context of the "Spontis" soon fell apart, their central demand for a undogmatic politics geared to the felt needs and grievances of their own carriers has been adopted by many political and social groups which have emerged, for the most part outside the universities, in recent years. The often locally-centered and issue-oriented movements certainly present a rather diffuse and fragmented scene to those used to traditional party politics of whatever persuasion. Many anti-nuke and ecology groups, feminists, squatters, etc. have not only provoked and challenged traditional political organiza-

proaching his thirtieth year on the assembly line is also normal. And we radicals of the left, who speak of happiness and satisfaction, of other forms of work and lifestyles, we are the crazy ones, the utopians.

Some people think only of their survival and ossify. For them revolution, socialism, liberation, solidarity are theory, a political demand which has little to do with their daily lives. For them they are "limitations of the system" which they as teachers, professors, social workers, and union leaders cannot escape. And these limitations of the system, this "limitation of West German reality," makes them into what the left has always been in this country, into "socialist subjects" of the purest kind. Socialism on paper, of course. But as soon as it's no longer a matter of an abstract criticism of family and socialization, but rather of practical alternative lifestyles, then they give up and point to the "limitations of the system."

And if the question of violence surfaces from below, they quickly distance themselves in horror or, at the most, resort to giving bureaucratic lectures on the senselessness of such violence.

Other people think only of resistance, of combat, and have banished from their minds all other modes of existence. They turn the alienation forced upon them by the limitations of the system, into a physical and mental sacrifice to the cause. Their utopia

tions but Marxist ones as well. Some leftist theoreticians have accepted this challenge and learned to rely now more on *experimental* theories, i.e., on theories formulated in the context of concrete experiences and learning processes of these groups engaged in various forms of *praxis*.[4] It is taken for granted that this cooperation can succeed only if the university, which is no longer the *locus* of any relevant emancipatory *praxis* at the moment, does not act as a theoretical vanguard but rather engages in an open dialogue with the "alternative scene." It is clear that the new protest groups do not hold as universally valid the overly rationalistic ideals of emancipation as articulated by Critical Theory and many Marxists alike. Habermas's ideal of a general and unforced consensus through a discussion free from domination, for example, is certainly not appealing to people struggling for an emancipation of the *whole* individual. It is at this juncture, however, that the theoretically trained intellectuals will have to guard against a possible rejection of all rational analysis in favor of a purely "experiential" approach to politics. More importantly, perhaps, they will have to guard against a beginning trend toward a blind embrace of irrational philosophical trends and a violent anti-Marxism as well as a onesided and radical destruction of Reason as one, if not the only emancipatory principle — a destruction presently pursued by the French New Philosophers.[5]

This is not to say that the dismantling of Critical Theory and Marxism as total theories has not also opened up new theoretical vistas, which might lead, once the French framework of interpretations is left behind, to a fruitful appropriation of the genuinely German philosophical traditions (e.g. idealism,

they now find as soldiers of the world revolution among the oppressed masses of the Third World. Their revolution amounts to making the imperialist enemy's hinterland militarily insecure. They act like technicians, like soldiers, like shock troops in enemy territory cut off from practical reality, from the personal and political experiences of the people among whom they live. They isolate themselves from every form of mass resistance, brand us as mere spectators of their assaults and single-handedly put the knife of military power to the throat of the system — and each time cut their own throats with it.

We cannot simply disassociate ourselves from our urban guerrilla comrades; we would have to disassociate ourselves from ourselves. We painfully vacillate between the same contradiction of hopelessness and blind activism.

But for the same reason we must decisively attack the activities of our urban guerrilla comrades, because we know and feel that their cause means despairing of life, fighting to the death, and to self-destruction. We believe that revolutionaries must maintain at all cost the unity of resistance and life, even under the circumstances in West Germany today. Only in this way can our liberation take on a real form.

If our platform contains only despair, prison and death, then we have finally suc-

phenomenology, Nietzsche, Heidegger, etc.) which have not been seriously discussed in their own right since the Nazi catastrophe. □

1. C.F. Martin Jay, "Some Recent Developments in Critical Theory," in: *Berkeley Journal of Sociology*, 18, 1973/74, pp. 27-44.

2. Paul Piccone, "From Tragedy to Farce: The Return of Critical Theory," in: *New German Critique*, 7, 1976, pp. 91-104.

3. Cf. Gerd-E. Famulla, *Geschichtsbegriff und Politische Oekonomie*, Frankfurt/M: Campus, 1978.

4. Cf. Joachim Hirsch, *Der Sicherheitsstaat*. Frankfurt/M: EVA, 1980.

5. For the German reception of these French intellectual trends, see the journal *Konkursbuch*.

"I'm deeply opposed to playing up fear in order to stir up anti-nuclear feelings among the population. One of the major problems of bourgeois society is fear anyway."

Daniel Cohn-Bendit

cumbed to this society forever. Then it has robbed us of our hopes, our power to achieve utopia and our ability to resist.

On the other hand, we understand only too well comrades who say they just can't go on any more. We are not driven by a hunger for food, but by a hunger for freedom, love, gentleness, for other forms of work and human interaction. And this hunger cannot be postponed by ever-so-clever speeches and analyses, particularly if one still has to live in the present West German conditions. We cannot dismiss them as agents nor insane people, as "*desperados* who don't want to have anything to do with the left," as a leftist professor once formulated it. But we can't accept their political action either because it means disarmament and self-destruction for all of us.

Precisely because we owe our comrades in the underground solidarity, because we are closely tied to them, we challenge them now to stop their death trip, to come out of their self-imposed "armed isolation," to discard their bombs, and to recommit themselves to a resistance for another kind of life. □

Translated by Wynn Gundarson

FRITZ TEUFEL

Terrorism with a Fun Face

Sylvère Lotringer: You're considered the most popular terrorist in Germany. How do you account for that?

Fritz Teufel: I was the first prisoner of the political movement in Germany. There were many demonstrations in my favour.

SL: What were you accused of?

FT: "Breaking the peace of the country." It meant: throwing stones at the police.

SL: Did you break the peace of the police?

FT: I only threw eggs filled with paint at the Shah's car. Horst Mahler, a lawyer of the movement and one of the founders of the Baader-Meinhof group, found witnesses who testified that I was peacefully sitting in front of the German opera house when the stoning occurred.

SL: Now each time the police is stoned at, I bet you have to show up at the Opera. When were you arrested?

FT: On June 2nd, 1967.

FRITZ TEUFEL BEFORE THE COURT

From A-libi to B-libi

I. From A-libi to B-libi
An alibidinous explanation concerning the question of participation in the two bank robberies and the amoral pressure to produce an alibi for a modern inquisition — magically pulled out of a hat in Moabit, 25th of July, 1980.

2. My dear hat,
serve me well!
don't leave me
before this pigheadedly stupid,
highly intelligent court!
134   Help truth come to light!

SL: Was the June 2nd Movement named after you?

FT: No. It was named after Benno Ohnesorg, shot by a policeman, Kurass, during a big demonstration against the Shah of Iran that was held that day.

SL: You eventually became a member of the June 2nd Movement.

FT: It depends on the definition of the Movement.

FT: What's **your** definition?

FT: There are at least two. One is very broad and includes whoever is doing any sort of resistance. Another more restrictive definition says that only people who are part of the armed struggle belong to the June 2nd Movement. Something like the Red Army Fraction.

It's unimportant for me whether or not you are a member of a club or an organization. I don't believe in any organization. Once I belonged to the SDS, the students' radical movement, and I ended up being excluded from it with my fellow comrades from Kommune 1 (the first German commune in Berlin). The June 2nd date is important for me because it was the first time in my life that I went to jail.

SL: When were you released?

FT: After two and a half months. Then I had to report twice a week to the police. I wasn't allowed to leave Berlin, which was pure nonsense. Instead of following the police order, we made a happening. I stood on a cart with ball and chain. People with KKK hoods pushed me to the Moabit jail. We rang the

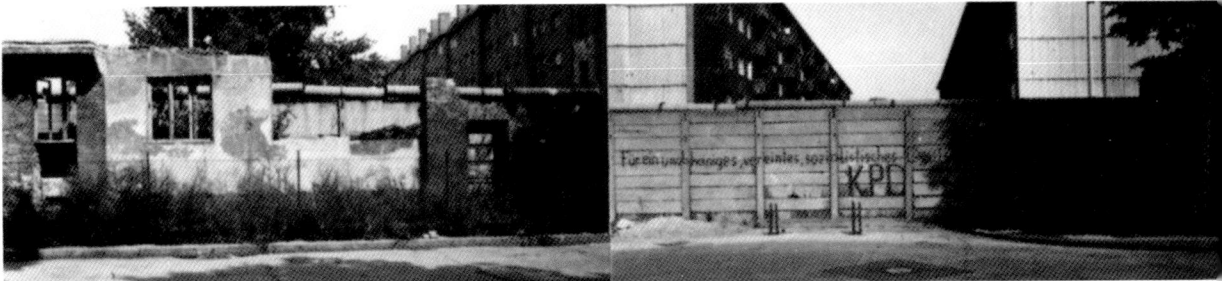

Simsalabim!
Fritz Teufel has an alibi!
But what is a B-libi?
Ladies and Gentlemen, look at this:
Fritz Teufel also has a B-libi!
That's the topic of my lecture today.
The B-libi follows:

3. **The B-libi is no joke.**
The B-libi is a word, that I had to make up to explain the difficulties of my situation, which only someone knows, whose face was once on a wanted poster and lived in the so-called "underground."

4. **An Alibi is irrefutable proof of so-called innocence supported by official documents and the testimony of good citizens. Such proof which the high court (sitting on its throne about six feet above the common people) had to accept, gritting its teeth, I could offer in the case of the Lorenz kidnapping. That caused my mother to remark that perhaps I might be a lucky child after all.**

bell: "Here I am," I said. "Take me back in." The State Prosecutor replied: "It's not as easy to be admitted as Mr. Devil believes."

SL: "Teufel" (**devil**, in German), is that your real name?

FT: It is.

SL: You didn't have much of a choice, did you?

FT: I had to be the Evil One.

SL: You could have become an angel, just out of spite.

FT: I did. I flew to Frankfurt to attend a SDS meeting. They sent the police after me, but they couldn't find me. We all went to the main police station in Frankfurt, a crowd of 200 people shouting "Take us all in, or leave us alone!"

SL: What did the police do?

FT: They left us alone, although they finally booked three people who had a beard like mine. In the meantime I flew from Cologne back to Berlin where I disappeared for a few weeks. It was the first time I went underground.

A hearing on the demonstration was to be held in Berlin and I let it be known that I would be there too. They swore they would catch me. So I shaved my beard and went undetected into the courtroom. But the police had been tipped off and I was arrested as I left.

SL: Who turned you in?

FT: Someone I used to trust as an activist. A good-humoured fellow always up

YOU REJOICED TOO EARLY, LOTTE TEUFEL!

5. The B-libi is no A-libi, but an alibi of lesser quality.

The B-libi is a story, which the accused doesn't prove, and which the court cannot refute.

It is up to the dis-cretion of the court to accept a B-libi or reject it.

Therein lies the secret power of the — according to civil constitutional theory — "independent" judge in this society.

6. **THE REVERSAL OF THE BURDEN OF PROOF**

As much a theory as the "independence of the judge" is the principle of "innocent until proven guilty."

Innocent until proven guilty, the alleged Nazi war criminal.

Innocent until proven guilty, the accused white collar criminal.

Innocent until proven guilty, the rarely prosecuted environment polluter.

Innocent until proven guilty, the corrupt bourgeois politician, who is constantly on the take, like Peter Lorenz or Kurt Neubauer.[1]

Innocent until proven guilty, the long-haired bearded demonstrator?

the communist? the alleged terrorist? the alleged partisans and "sympathizers?"

to anything. In 1968 he was the first to set fire to Springer, the newspaper chain. Years later he appeared to testify against Horst Mahler. He came as a witness for the German CIA. I ended up being locked-in for another 21 months.

SL: Is there another reason for your being so popular in Germany?

FT: The way I handled the trial. When the judge entered the room, they ordered us to stand up. I hesitated a moment, then: "If this can help find the truth," I said. This reply is very often quoted.

SL: Your attitude reminds me somewhat of the American Yippies'.

FT: We hadn't heard of Abbie Hoffman and the Yippies yet. Later on, I translated Jerry Rubin's book, which I liked very much. Then I learned that someone else had already done it.

SL: Jerry Rubin now is a respectable banker.

FT: A banker?

SL: A Wall Street entrepreneur.

FT: My career was somewhat different.

SL: What was your career like?

FT: In 1973 my name mysteriously appeared on the Most Wanted List (**Caution: These Terrorists Are Armed and Dangerous. We Want Them Dead or Alive.**) When my lawyer asked why I had been put on the list, they told him I

Innocent until proven guilty, the confirmed enemy of the State — or, as our prosecutors like to say: "Enemies of our democratic justice"? What does reality really look like?

7. And then another of these ideal principles of justice surfaces, which doesn't have anything to do with the reality of our republic:
The silence of the accused must not be used against him
It musn't? Didn't this happen in my case in the Lorenz kidnapping? Did any judge or prosecutor apologize to me (or to the public) because they allowed injustice to flourish? Even if they had wanted to as human beings, they couldn't because of their political logic.
They were not allowed to use their imagination, to think of possible alternatives to events.
They are not allowed to.
According to all rules of judicial sophistry, they have to find reasons for continuing detention and maximum sentences. Supposedly that's how people like it. The politicians do it, although they are supposed to be independent of them. They get paid for this. If they applied principles of justice in my sensational case, hundreds of thousands of victims of justice would also demand their rights.
THE WITNESSES WOULD BE KEPT IN JAIL LONGER THAN I ENVISION FOR MYSELF.   **137**

had painted slogans on the prison walls...

SL: They didn't appreciate your art. Or maybe it was the wrong kind of wall. You've got quite a choice in Berlin.

FT: I also made graffiti on the Berlin subway.

SL: Was the public moved by them?

FT: Not a bit. There was another reason for the List, but they didn't mention it. A student from Munich was caught after a bank robbery in 1973. He told the police I was the one through whom he'd met the other "robbers." He didn't say I had been involved in the actual robbery, but you can never be sure.

SL: Weren't you accused of that later on?

FT: When they arrested me in September 1975, I had some money on me that came from two bank robberies.

SL: You seem to share Jerry Rubin's banking interests after all, although in a distinctly German fashion. Did you participate in any way to these respectable enterprises?

FT: There was no proof that I had. I was also accused of participating in the kidnapping of Peter Lorenz, a very important political figure in Berlin.

SL: Did you have anything to do with it?

FT: Everyone believed I did, but I was lucky enough to come up with an alibi at the right time.

SL: Is that the alibi that made you so famous in Germany?

FT: Yes. It was a very big surprise for the public. I have to admit that I came very late with the alibi.

SL: Why did you?

FT: I knew that if I had produced it from the start, they would have tried me for something else. They would have found another accusation for which I would have had no alibi. They were all convinced that I had something to do with the kidnapping and the robberies because I had been closely associated with the other conspirators. My fingerprints were found in one of their apartments.

SL: What do you mean by "conspirators"?

FT (laughs): I don't mean anything. This is police language. I was able to prove that at the time Peter Lorenz was kidnapped I was working in a factory in Hessen — a very stupid job too. Some colleagues of mine came to testify during the trial. I was the first defendant to prove that the accusation was unfounded.

SL: How long did you keep your alibi secret?

FT: For 5 years.

SL: Did anyone know about it?

FT: I told my lawyer, and my fellow accused knew it too. My original plan was

"It's better to have millions of little walls than one or two big walls."
Heiner Muller

to allow myself to be sentenced for 15 years or for life, but after Stammheim* I changed my mind.

SL: It was getting too hot.

FT: I was getting pretty scared, so we decided I would come up in the open with the alibi when the Federal prosecutor had done with his pleading — which, by the way, I kept calling **bleating**.

SL: Were you released immediately?

FT: Only after the sentence. I had no alibi for the two bank robberies.

SL: Did you eventually find one?

FT: I developed instead a new theory: the theory of "bilibi."

SL: What's that?

FT: I called "bilibi" a story I couldn't prove because I didn't want the main witnesses to be arrested and spend years in jail. Three of my witnesses had been sent to prison. One woman got 3½ years just because she had found an apartment for me. A math teacher got one year in prison because he gave me his ID card. Trials against these "accomplices" were held before the main trial started. At that time nobody knew that I was innocent and that it constituted a pre-trial against us. Once they were sentenced, however, there was nothing anyone could do about it. The teacher was released merely because he already had done his time.

SL: What about the woman?

8. **Back to the B-libi. I have watched you, Mr. Geus, Mr. Weis, Mr. Bauer and Mr. Weichbrodt² long enough, to know that you don't feel the least bit of sympathy. And that is reciprocally true.**
Who says, my honorable judges, that I wasn't with Putzi von Opel³ in St. Tropez at the time in question?
Perhaps under the alias of Fritzi von Popel?
You don't believe that. Neither do I.
But let's assume: Teufel was at the time of the "Negerküsse" ("niggerkiss," a German candy resembling a Mallomar) in another West German city. Maybe Cologne.
When I pulled an explanation out of my hat the last time, I mentioned my friend Leo. In the official records, he is called Werner Sauber.⁵ Leo's files are closed. His example remains. If Leo hadn't been shot, he could be sitting next to me as an accused, or we both could be somewhere else. Leo needn't substantiate Alibis anymore.

9. **Let's just assume: after Leo's death, after leaving the print shop and the interlude in the Bochum dormitory, I hid in Cologne. In the truest sense of the word. Unemployed. No colleagues, no neighbor who could remember me. There were still only four weeks. Once in a while I met comrades, who helped me. Or with other wanted people. Why**

FT: She stayed 4½ years in prison. So my argument in "bilibi" is that I couldn't possibly name anybody else. The other aspect of the bilibi is that the prosecutor couldn't prove the contrary.

SL: So bilibi worked...

FT: Because alibi was O.K. I promised the court next time I'd come with my alibi one week in advance. The Springer* papers were outraged. They actually believed I would do that.

SL: How did you get involved with politics in the first place?

FT: Through women. It was a woman who took me to the SDS, and then I became seriously interested in politics, at least for a while. Since I am German, my interest also had something to do with Nazi history. When I went to school in South Germany, near Stuttgart, I attended what's known as the "Auschwitz trial." There wasn't much public interest in it at the time, I must say, but I was terrified to realize that these people looked like my own father. They were "biedermeier,' good family people. Later on in Berlin we read a lot of books which we stole because they were too expensive.

SL: Were they spirited writers?

FT: I've always been a great fan of Mark Twain, Erich Kastner or the Dadaist movement. At that time, however, it was Marcuse and Wilhelm Reich. I studied the history of the working class movement as well as Marxism and psychoanalysis at a seminar with Rudi Dutschke.* Together we read Adorno, Horkheimer and the so-called Frankfurt School. We came to the con-

would I give the names of people who, as alleged terrorists, or because they helped me, run the risk of being imprisoned for months and years, like Waltraut Siepert, Eberhard Dreher, Christina Domeland, Erhard Oestereich, and many others.

10. Let's just assume: I also took a side trip to Frankfurt and, in the middle of August, flew from there to Berlin.

11. Who controls the State Police? Who controls eager officers, prosecutors, judges? WHO?
The public.
And what does the public look like? Let's say: "deceived" is not the word.
Public opinion is made by the owner of the means of production. The ruling opinion is the opinion of the rulers. Under such circumstances, telling the truth is an art which borders on magic.

12. I state that I, Fritz Teufel, did NOT take part in the preparation, planning, and execution of the bank robberies of the 30th and 31st of July, 1975.
And now to the complete surprise of all participants in the trial, my confession follows: at the time in question I was addicted to drugs and on a trip. Shit and LSD didn't hurt me, but once in a while, I took the wrong one. Fixers are my unfortunate brothers.

clusion that the authoritarian character had to do with German family life, the way children are brought up, so we tried to change it all. We started living together, a whole bunch of us.

SL: Was that the idea behind Kommune 1?

FT: It started in 1967, and it's still going on strong. It became a broad movement.

SL: Were there other reasons for its success?

FT: There are commercial reasons as well. It's the same now with the occupation of houses. What we already dreamt of in 1967, but couldn't do because we were not strong enough, has gained momentum. Squatters today are as young as we were, even younger. They don't have much theory, but lots of energy.

SL: How did you get young again?

FT: I joined the Squatter's Movement through a woman, of course. I met her in January this year. She's 16. She was in one of the first occupied houses in Kreuzberg, a "kinderfarm" set up right against the wall.

SL: Were you looking for a place, or attracted by the squatters' looks?

FT: When I came out of jail a few months ago I felt like a man from another planet. Everything had changed. Of course I knew it, but I had not really experienced it. I first moved with the woman I had exchanged a lot of love letters with while I was in jail...

SL: Did you know her beforehand?

13. At that time, I wasn't in Berlin.
By the way: the main part of the trial showed that none of the accused was positively identified as a primary participant in these raids and, therefore, justice demands they be released. Also the question arises whether the federal prosecutors and judges can count to three. The testimony shows that the Negerküsse robberies were committed by two men and three women. In spite of this, the federal prosecutors asked in their bleatings [pun on pleadings] for 10-year sentences for three men; Ralf Reinders, Andreas Vogel,[5] and me. If this is logic, then this is one of necessity.
With all due self-criticism, I consider myself a truth-loving man — and when I talk about love, I always also mean erotically — I have an erotic relationship with truth.
I have often been misunderstood.
I err often.
In contrast to politicians, judges, and public prosecutors, I don't need to lie.

14. I am deeply indebted to my comrades who, because they supposedly supported me, served years in jail. Waltraud Siepert was in jail almost five years under terrible conditions, and Erhard Oestereich served more than a half a year of a one-year sentence.

passing his sentence, the judge said I was the most wanted and the most dangerous-

FT: I had never met her, but I always liked writing love letters. I need love, and that was the only way I could get some. Jail life is so boring. They punish you by cutting sex out for years on end. So when you get out, you get a little crazy, at least for a while. But the woman seldom feels that way.

SL: She didn't like your "going crazy" for sex?

FT: It was something like a marriage. She wanted to be with me all the time. There was some sort of a **kampf** (conflict) going on between us. Radicals from the 60's now live a fairly bourgeois life, although I shouldn't say anything since they did a lot to get me out of jail.

SL: So you left her bourgeois apartment and moved in with the young squatters.

FT: And I'm very happy about that.

SL: Some people fear that squatters will bring new blood to the failing underground movement.

FT: Many squatters are getting busted. Some of them are sentenced for up to 2½ years in prison for throwing stones at the police during demonstrations. As long as there is police violence in the street as well as against occupied houses, terrorism will remain a temptation — although going undergound nowadays isn't an easy job.

SL: Are you looking forward to seeing squatters join the armed struggle?

FT: Not in the least. I hope terrorism disappears. I hope the RAF* is finished.

ly violent criminal and the Siepert sentence says I participated in the Lorenz abduction. A legal Moabit State police sentence! I don't know what will happen to Joerg Rasche, Mr. Osterreich has lost his job because of the trial at least once already. I have to assume that comrades of this caliber, called as witness substantiating my alibi, would risk longer jail terms together than I without an alibi. They would be treated as criminals without credibility, opposed to the well-primed State witnesses.
The immoral demand for an alibi I will first reply with the B-libi. To save my own skin, should I misuse others?

15. No thanks, Mr. Franke!

Not with me, Mr. Geus!

No way, Mr. Weiss!

Nothing doing, Dr. Wolldecke !

That's not the game, Mr. Bauer!

You'd like that, Mr. Weichbrodt!

P.S. Kiss my ass, Mr. Volz!

143

It's been a part of our history, but it has proved that we can't get very far that way.

SL: What other way is there?

FT: I hope other ideas will develop along the line of what I call "Spassgerilja" (Fun Guerrilla).

SL: How do you define this kind of guerrilla?

FT: Ridicule. Ridicule kills.

SL: Is that an alternative to actual terrorist killings?

FT: It's a smarter way to win.

SL: Do you think that the RAF people took themselves too seriously?

FT: Some of them, and some of their followers too.

SL: Were they that way from the very beginning?

FT: No. The media painted them as monsters, but a lot of them were very close friends of mine in the Hippie days. Then they developed a kind of isolation and dogmatism. We call that: "The Time of the Sectarians." Marxist-Leninist groups came out of the student movement. They all called themselves "Communist" parties. It is just about that time that the RAF started.

SL: Have you ever had serious discussions with sectarians?

FT: Of course.

As a means for fighting in the metropoles I would still recommend the *Spassgerilja*, no one knows what I mean by *Spassgerilja*. Perhaps I will return to this in the final words of the trial. As a former filosophy [sic] student, I have struggled long against the uncanny desire to bore a larger audience with a pompous exegesis on the theme which I will fail to develop adequately: LIFE AS FUN AND GUERRILLA or WHY THE RIDICULOUS ARMY FICTION (RAF) IS SUBJECTIVELY ANTI-IMPERIALISTIC AND OBJECTIVELY AND IN-VOLUNTARILY PART OF THE FUN GUERRILLA . . .
but that's another story and will be told at another time. ☐

Translated by Cesar Loaiza

1. CDU* politicians in West Berlin.
2. The legal authorities in Teufel's trial.
3. Daughter of an industrialist, arrested in France for drug dealing.
4. Mallomar candy handed to the bank tellers during the bank robbery.
5. Member of the June 2nd Movement.

SL: Did they manage to convince you?

FT: Always (laugh).

SL: But spending 5 years in jail is a serious affair.

FT: Exactly seven, if you count the two years I spent in Bavaria for having placed a few "time bombs" in Munich.

SL: Were they fun bombs?

FT: They were the kind of bomb that doesn't explode, only burns. These ended up not even doing that. I don't think they were made properly.

SL: They could also have exploded inadvertently.

FT: They were meant to ignite at midnight anyway. Now there was no proof I had done it. All they found against me was the lid of a fruit juice can just like this one (I shouldn't drink that stuff anymore) in the apartment I had rented. After a close microscopic analysis, they declared it had been used to make the "bombs." This happened in 1970. The RAF didn't exist yet, but there were other groups like Tupamaros West-Berlin, or Tupamaros Middle-Europa. They used to throw Molotov cocktails at the police.

    I was tried in Munich and sent to a Bavarian jail from 1970 to 1972. Some of the other accused, among my best friends, later joined the RAF. There's always been personal relations between the two streams, the serious stream who was planning terrorist actions and the fun stream of people who were smoking dope and advocating free sex.

SL: Did serious people like Andreas Baader ever smoke dope?

"You don't have a chance, but take it."
Herbert Achternbusch

FT: I believe he did, but he sure didn't want people to know about it. When they found some hash in Stammheim, he claimed the police had planted it in his cell.

SL: How do prisoners manage to get some hash just like this one in jail?

FT: I can't tell you (laughs). Some people who work there aren't as bad as the rest of them. Or they need money. Or the authorities think it will keep you quiet.

SL: How does it feel to spend 7 years in jail?

FT: It depends on which jail. Moabit is an old prison. You can still talk with the other prisoners from window to window. Three women even managed to escape by tying their bedsheets on July 7, 1976. It happened to be Women's Emancipation Day.

The high security department is something else altogether. I spent 9½ months there. When most people get out of it, they're broken.

SL: You seem pretty much in one piece.

FT: I kept busy writing. I like writing. I wrote thousands of letters while I was in jail. But as a prisoner you always have to keep in mind this fucking judge who reads every word you write. Thoughts have to be formulated in very odd ways to beat censorship. You have to become a writer if you want to write in jail. Or stop writing altogether.

SL: You've got to write like a dream.

"People in the East know what is going on between the words."

Heiner Müller

Violent Women

In our opinion, life is in a state of vertiginous decadence and no new philosophy is required to experience this decay.

(A revolutionary poet, an accomplice)

We all heard the shots which struck Ponto. And despite that, it seems we were all deaf. Deaf out of fear. Stockholm, Drenckmann, Buback, Ponto:[1] an unbroken chain of screams. Screams of women.

Since Ponto it can no longer be kept quiet: a relatively large number of women are active in the so-called terrorist movement. Never before have bombings, liquidations, bank robberies, etc. caused so much irritation, in which it is clear that women have given up their silence. And actually everywhere else as well. What's the difference between a woman who leaves her husband after thirty years of a "happy" marriage and a woman who arms herself? Turning one's back on normality, leaving bourgeois life behind is a move which everyone can make. The way in which this is achieved depends on their

146

FT: When you are held in solitary confinement, every room is like a submarine — no window, very high ceiling, you feel as if you were one mile under water, it's horrible. And every word you say is monitored electronically, so they get to know everybody in the most intimate way. There was a great fear among the RAF people of being used psychologically.

SL: How did you deal with such a situation?

FT: Either you become an actor, or you're dead. You've got to stop showing anything on your face. But you can't be an actor twenty-four hours a day, so it's an unbearable situation. You can't retain any sense of dignity. You are a clown or a monkey.

SL: You learn to become a con-artist.

FT: You have to. Occasionally we had fights with the wardens. I prefer kissing them. They go away and cry.

SL: Horst Mahler told me that the RAF was considering playing up the prison conditions in order to mobilize the movement behind them. Do you think Ulrike Meinhof exaggerated her ordeal for tactical reasons?

FT: She spent one year in some of the most brutal conditions. She was held in total confinement and total isolation. On the other hand, the RAF exaggerated somewhat these conditions to prove that they were the revolutionary avant-garde. It didn't work: there are a lot of avant-gardes in the leftist movement and repression doesn't prove that you're right in every account.

history, the present circumstances, and their particular personality. Trying to decide which form is the right one — as the fearful left does in respect to their armed brothers and sisters — is arrogance by frightened people; people who never bear arms, but embody in their paranoid reactions a permanent bomb arsenal which never explodes.

"Other people," blacksheep, as the Spiegel calls them, are supposed to embody violence — and despite that it is the legal left which talks as if it had done everything and begs forgiveness. The West German left has become just a legitimation. The left is its own neurosis. It is totally consumed by fear. It stopped short at the threshold of a sure death. Not just the armed left is on a death trip, but all of society. To demand that they come down from their death trip means asking them to come down to *what*?

At a time when the neutron bomb is being developed not to destroy buildings, only millions of people caught in the gruesome pangs of death, is the death of one person a greater terror than the annihilation of a large portion of mankind? At a time when the systematic annihilation of mankind is being legally planned by unleashing atomic energy on the earth, is the disappearance of a single responsible of this death a crime? When a leading Fascist's return, Kappler, who murdered 336 Italians and had more than a thousand Jews deported, is greeted in the Federal Republic of Germany as an act of liberation, is an act of liberation (Stockholm, Lorenz kidnapping) which preserves the

SL: Do you feel that some of the killings by the RAF were justified?

FT: I don't like bloody actions, although most people forget that our comrades were killed first. Killing has always been a **reaction** on the part of the movement. When the police sets up a huge manhunt against the RAF, when every cop has your picture and is ready to shoot you down without warning, maybe it's not a bad idea to shoot first.

SL: I understand you're involved in a campaign to free prisoners or to grant a general amnesty.

FT: To free prisoners from the Squatters' Movement. Some liberals are thinking about a general amnesty, but I believe amnesty can only result from a strong pressure from below, from the street.

SL: Don't you think the violence of the Squatters' Movement is going to delay the prospect of an amnesty?

FT: On the contrary. In 1970 an amnesty was granted because there had been thousands of trials. The authorities simply were overwhelmed. If the Squatters' Movement spreads all over Germany, maybe they'll find it easier to grant an amnesty.

I really hope Berlin will be the first city in the world to abolish jails. Prisons are a relic of the Middle Ages. There must be other ways of dealing with crime, especially since it's never the big criminals who end up in jail, but mainly social prisoners.

captive from death to be called terror? Today when, without being able to prevent it, we must witness the collapse of life, is a bomb which hits the power plant of death something other than a sign of revulsion from mankind?

How blind have we become? Too many eyeglasses, too much education, too much analysis, too dead to be true: the West German left. You have forgotten that we are crazy. Your feelings are nothing more than a murderous regurgitation. Near total asphyxiation, your minds keep working for nothing. Before something explodes, you will be dead. Never before had I confronted so blatantly the intellectuals' sheer fear: one simply can't be any dumber.

In contrast, the bourgeois newspapers write about patricide, the education of terrorists, particularly by women.

Of course, in this total confusion of interpretations of the terrorist phenomenon, the truth shines through more than the left's inability to mourn — not for Buback, not for Ponto, but rather for our own fear.

After more than a thousand years of domination by the father, isn't it time to topple him? The consciousness of patriarchal society prevails everywhere. And then suddenly it breaks down. It's perfectly clear why women are attacking. As always. There are many kinds of self-defense.

SL: Do you mean "political" prisoners?

FT: I don't like that expression. The official term is: "Terrorists with political motivations." I myself call that: "Socks thiefs with political motivations," a reference to my first criminal act. I got busted in a supermarket.

SL: For stealing socks?

FT: Yes, as well as half-a-pound of butter and some spray for leather shoes. □

The State, this super-father, who sends with a deafening roar his glistening penises into the skies, erects his petrified penises so that we can't see our neighbors, not to mention the sky.

This father who can only disseminate his artificial energy in lethal doses, the dumb huffing and puffing of his nuclear reactors. This father who owns everything and destroys everything which isn't his. Who considers himself God and wants to decide matters of life and death. This is the pimp against whom every liberated woman fights. Be it a prohibition on abortion, censorship, rape, punishment, terror, not one of these fathers will deceive us. We've seen through everything. We see mankind where it is supposed to be denied. We are insane because we defend life in a world bent on death: with shouting, with guns, with petitions, with boycotts, with letters and articles, with everything we have. We didn't invent war. Not the bombs, not the guns. Not concentration camps, not prisons, not mental hospitals and other kinds of confinement in which the father locks us up. Not the science which invents the destruction of mankind. We will abandon everything which belongs to him.

Shall we despair?

We have learned from our mothers not to. That is an ability of a fatherless upbringing, which is most odious to you: there is someone for whom life means more than war,

HELKE SANDER

Who Still Believes in Revolution?

Vera: Helke, did you ever really believe in revolution?

Helke Sander: Some time ago, I realized that the society we live in is made by man. This really blew my mind. On the other hand, if that situation does not result from natural laws, then utopia is possible. The student movement suddenly became the societal space in which fantasies could be realized.

I met a bunch of people in the SDS who were about to break down traditional thought patterns. That fascinated me. I wanted to belong to them, but there are still barriers. I was afraid of the word revolution because it is linked to the word victim. At that time, I was unable to articulate the feeling which caused my uneasiness. I thought that there must be a way to help society that could also enrich my own life. In any case, I looked at change as a long-term process. That also applied to me. I was very shy. I knew how many years it

Helke Sander, filmmaker, mother, member of the SDS*, active in the alternative school movement, co-founder of the Action Council for Women's Liberation, and the group "Bread and Roses" (the first women's groups in the Federal Republic of Germany) is co-publisher of the magazine *Women and Film.* She's just finished a movie, which deals with questions similar to those discussed in this interview for the "taz."*

death, competition, achievement, and work.

We are not afraid of work; we are simply lazy. We are not violent; we are aggressive and gentle. We don't kill anyone. We are just getting rid of people and things that kill. We don't lock up. We open up everything which you closed. We don't give speeches. We keep our mouths shut when there is nothing to say. We look when you give blind orders. We live because you have died once and for all. You: the eternal rulers, the fathers, the grown-ups, you who always know everything better, you managers of death, you with your bombs which are better than any created before. You: with your rockets, wars, diseases, assembly lines. You: with your extreme lack of feeling. You: who are incapable of love. Beware, we'll get you if you disturb us. We who are hated, who are betrayed, the new youth: women, sons, children, the elderly, the insane, criminals, terrorists, anarchists, gays, radical leftists — in a word, social outcasts. *We,* the partisans of life, the swamp of your dreams, which you have tried to dredge in vain. *We,* your crazy people.

Get out of our way, otherwise fur will fly!

viva medusa. □

Translated by Wynn Gundarson

1. Targets of the armed underground. See Chronology, 1975.

had taken me to open my mouth. (That was my standard for measuring time.) I valued slowness and that led to many conflicts with my comrades.

V: Are ten years a long time for change?

HS: Yes and no. I've changed little, and none of my convictions. Basically, I'm following up on what I learned from the students' movement. It's very precious to me. There I met people who took themselves seriously. To take myself seriously as a person must have been the most important step in my development. That meant that I had dealt with my own situation, intellectually as well as emotionally. I saw myself as a woman: an artist, a mother, a European, a white, a worker, etc. That is, I got down to the basics. What was new about the student movement was that it enabled me not only to think about my relationship toward the SDS, but also toward the revolution, as well as about my relationship to the universe. This new exchange led to exciting initiatives, for example, the women's movement and the anti-authoritarian daycare centers. I contributed something to these new developments. That couldn't be considered revolutionary then, but tens of thousands of people were able to reorganize their lives, and I find that important. The practical consequence was that I started to take myself seriously. To quote Socrates: "Your knowledge will increase about the things you don't know only to the extent of how much you know." My relative optimism sprang from a relative naivete. Because I knew so little, I could do so much.

V: What about your optimism today?

HS: I'm more disillusioned, but I'm not resigned, either. I'm fighting like crazy

"Murder
begins with self-defense."
Reto Hanny

to live in dignity. Here is an example: I read the now famous Gailer article in the "taz" and laughed my head off. I thought, there's finally somebody with the courage to talk about himself. It didn't matter whether I could identify with it; whether I liked those fantasies. I was glad that he had had a chance to express himself, because I believe it is a basic human right. It's very important for me to fight for such a right, and, when it is denied me, I get very angry. It didn't occur to me that this article would provoke such a scandal. I assumed that the women working for "taz" would be glad that a man dared to write about his contradictory feelings. I figured they'd immediately interview Peter Schneider and Thomas Brasch, because the article referred to a rumor that both were going to go to a brothel. Perhaps we might find out some more about the secret paths of sexuality, brute force, and fear, I thought. I had hoped for a reaction that would have something to do with real emotional upheaval. But, instead, I was disturbed by the consequences. I couldn't imagine the fight for women's liberation being subordinated to censorship. I find it extremely hard to deal with any such attempts to prevent the publishing of similar articles, because that would suppress existing emotions which in turn will inhibit people form telling the truth.

V: What moves you?

HS: I have a tremendous thirst for knowledge, and my life moves me without bounds. By trying to get at the root of things that hurt me, I also discover other things. The famous sentence, "The personal is political," appropriated by the women's movement, has never been understood. I detect a connection between the treatment of the Gailer article and the observation that people who

ULRIKE MARIE MEINHOF

Revolt

1

The number of young people living in State-run homes isn't very large. According to official statistics, a little over 30,000; others estimate 50,000. These are the figures for youngsters who are in the State's care because the courts have decreed that their parents must relinquish their right to raise their own children or the parents have agreed to let the State care for their children. The latter parents may withdraw their offspring at any time. But that doesn't make any difference to the youngsters, since they are all

---

Ulrike Meinhof, a founding member of the RAF, * was a journalist and writer throughout the 60's. She was found dead in her high security cell at Stammheim in 1976 under circumstances that remain unclear.

work in a group don't like to act alone or take sole responsibility for things they do. In fact, despite our love for peace, fears of arms build-up and militarization, we all dutifully pay taxes to subsidize war. And then, where do you find a serious discussion about the fact that unhappy people are interested neither in politics nor in the possibility of an atomic holocaust? Maybe someone who expresses his sexual fantasies will be so relieved and acquire enough courage as to refuse to serve in the army. People who are frightened will only learn from the debate to shut up and keep a low profile.

V: What could be done then?

HS: It is important to think about a problem publicly. I cannot reconcile my concept of personal dignity with the fact that Mr. Reagan possesses the power to determine my life and death. That's what I would like to be able to think about publicly. But this is also inhibited by such concepts as military-industrial complex or the military-bureaucratic complex. These concepts don't take the individual into account. We stare helplessly at the power of others while forgetting our own. I now return to what I said earlier: we have to cut the automatic link between revolution and sacrifice.

V: Can you fight without sacrifice?

HS: "Fighting" is probably the wrong word. I don't fight, I just try to live according to my principles. I'm striving for integrity. I don't want to be destructive to myself. I don't want to weigh people against each other. I believe that one thousand people killed in South America is as bad as one person killed by violence in this country. Let me put it another way: I read a statement in "taz"

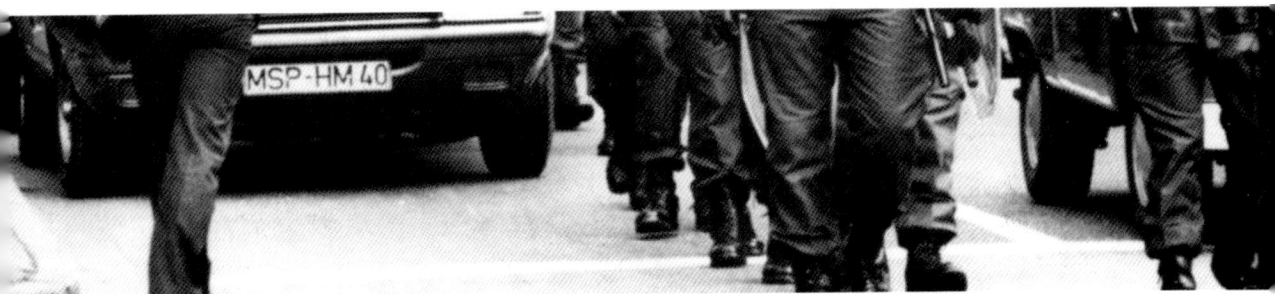

treated the same.

The youths the court sends to these homes come from proletarian families. Middle-class families usually don't come into contact with the juvenile courts, family welfare agencies don't deal with the middle-class. Not enough money, too many children, not enough space are catastrophic for proletarian families. Such conditions do not cause as much stress in middle-class families, since they can always turn to helpful neighbors, relatives, a savings account, can get loans; they aren't suffocated by bills when the fathers get sick, don't collapse immediately when the mothers collapse.

State care and training of children has two functions for proletarian families: to ease the burden on the family, to discipline the youngsters. State care does not essentially change the conditions which led to the child's transgression. The juvenile courts don't care that an apprenticeship was intolerable, but rather focus on the fact that the young people have left it. They don't care that an apartment was too small and the number of siblings too large for the youngsters to do their homework, but focus instead on the child's absence from school. They don't care that their allowances aren't large enough, but focus instead on their thefts. They don't care that girls don't have any clothes to wear, as the commercials dictate, but focus instead on the fact that they became prostitutes.

153

about El Salvador, calling their "brothers" to support them with weapons. I must rely on media reports. I believe I know enough to say that the conditions there are unbearable for any human being and that the people have the right of resistance. But, because I don't really know what's going on, I can't give any advice on what should be done. I can only say that I dislike these kinds of statements. I don't know a single example of a manifesto where the brothers praise each other and the ideology of sacrifice is prevalent, which establishes any links with their sisters. As an editor of "taz," I would find some way out of the dilemma and preserve my integrity. Sometimes this can take a long time. But we don't have to rely on automatic solutions for resolving conflicts.

About three weeks ago, there was a report about a rape trial. The "taz" article condemned the trial procedure and at the end it said that it approved of the women present who wore t-shirts saying "Cut his dick off." Not only do I find the reporting illogical, but I also find it dehumanizing. (If the trial had been conducted in a different way, wouldn't the t-shirts still be there?) But above all, I have to fight the claim that these women speak in the name of all women. Moreover, I find in this example a germ of the mechanism of force and counterforce.

V: You once said that it is possible to fight side by side with men if they are willing to follow the women's lead. Are women the avant-garde?

HS: When women have worked out something for themselves — I mean, really worked on something — when something confronts us in a new way, like the law against abortion, then I believe we have to challenge those in power to see the problem differently and find a solution which doesn't oppress us any

"Suicide chambers agglutinated into public housing."

Reto Hänny

When they want to cope creatively with their deprivation, proletarian youngsters are threatened with State care. When they try to improve their miserable lot, the State punishes them.

The State does nothing to improve the proletarian youth's miserable life, but rather forces him to accept it. If the parents can't coerce their child into accepting his miserable lot, then the State takes over, exerting the necessary pressure with its homes.

Since State care disciplines the young person, they can be threatened with it. "If you don't behave, you'll end up in a home." "If your daughter keeps skipping school, we'll have to send her to a home." These are idle threats for the middle-class. Proletarian families must take them seriously.

These homes are used to convince proletarian youths that it is senseless to resist their lot in life, to want something more than manning an assembly line, working at a menial job, always taking orders and never getting promoted, keeping your mouth shut.

These homes offer a public education. Parents have no say in their children's education. The State does what it thinks is best. In this respect, State care mirrors well existing educational philosophy.

The external pressure exerted upon these children in the homes is supposed to bring about good behavior. The authorities believe if external pressure is applied long

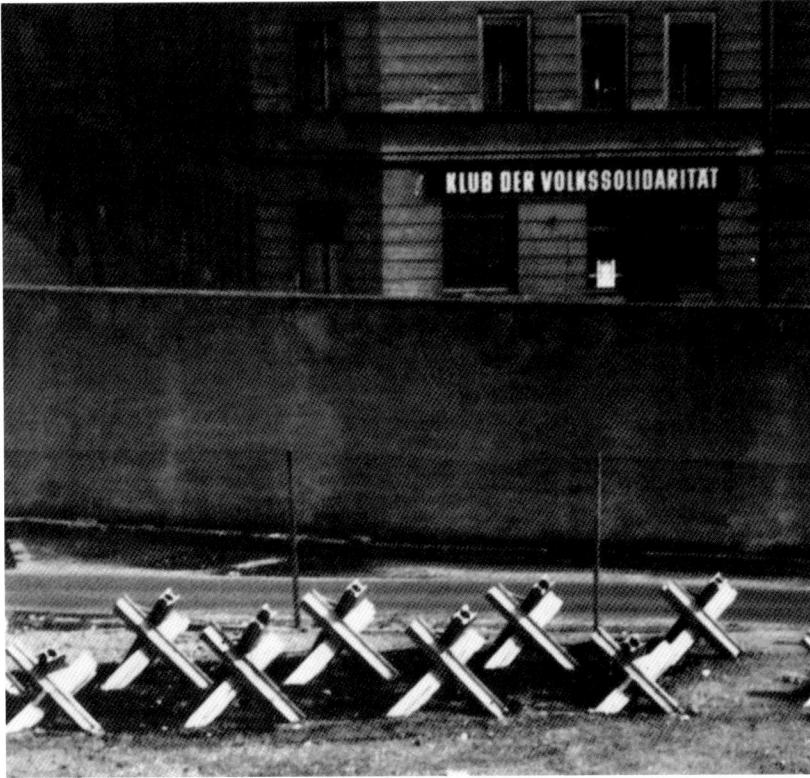

enough the child will eventually internalize good behavior and this mode of deportment will become a habit. Ways of exerting pressure are detention, lock-up, withholding allowances, denial of smoking privileges.

2

Life in a home doesn't change a girl's subsequent life. When she came, she had no one and nothing and didn't want to accept her lot. The home doesn't change these facts.

Not having anyone means there's no food in the house when you come home from work if you haven't bought it yourself. Not having anyone means there's no one to ask you about work when you get home. Not having anyone means you're out on the street if you're evicted. If you're penniless, you can't borrow money from anyone. When you're in a bind, no one will help you out. In other words, not having anyone means you have to hang around in bars if you want to meet someone, which means you have to spend money, which means you have to stay up all night, which means you don't know what's the sense of it all.

At a time when other girls are just leaving home, finding friends, establishing contacts, these girls are in homes. Lasting relationships between other girls and teachers are impossible in these homes. Being in the system means changing homes, leaving old

more. Only because women took themselves seriously, were they able to establish the link between abortion, sexuality, contraception and the claim for a pension. They created a new concept to oppose the one of the existing power structure. This is the way to handle all questions.

V: Do you feel that you belong to a group?

HS: I worked with many groups and founded all sorts of things, and I like working with other people. Let me put it this way: I prefer to work with co-operative individuals, and, if they want, they can call themselves a group, but I find most groups which primarily consider themselves groups horrible. I appreciate it most when a group leaves enough room for the individual.

V: Didn't you belong to various women's groups for a long time?

HS: For a while, yes. I have this special relationship with the women's movement, because at the beginning I contributed so decisively to its rise. I sometimes feel like a mother with wayward children. Especially when I read t-shirts saying, "Cut his dick off."

This is, of course, an overreaction. It is arrogant and reveals something of my own neurosis. But I see how women repeat structures which we once tried to destroy, for example dogmatism, substituting the part for the whole, knowing-it-better, "cliquish" behaviour, etc. I probably expected too much from the women, which was unrealistic. My critique does not reflect badly on them, rather on my illusions.

Often I feel that the means we use to fight fear and all these horrible and suppressed things are wrong. I can't say anything definitive, but I feel what we

friends, new friends, leaving new friends, leaving, friends, leaving. Waywardness is, according to psychologists, among other things, an inability to enter into lasting relationships.

Girls in homes don't receive an education. They earn ten cents an hour working in the laundry, in the kitchen, in the garden, in the sewing room. Factory work consists of gluing paper bags together, assembling lamp shades, lining silverware boxes with satin, dressing dolls — idiotic, unskilled labor. They aren't even trained to run a household. They don't learn budgeting, marketing, cooking but sewing sheets and brewery aprons, and sweeping the courtyard.

When they're taken from school, their schooling ends. They get no job training. They practice reading — how God gave the animals their names — they learn about the Versailles Treaty and the poverty of the starving Indian children. They learn nothing about child labor laws, the equality of women, and the actual discrimination against them on the job

Part of the discrimination against these children is the fact that no one believes them. This doesn't just affect them, but also their parents and friends. Poverty is a disgrace, is close to criminality, in a society with classes. Poor people cannot be believed, while professionals and bureaucrats manipulate the truth in their files.

156

just discussed is essentially linked to our survival.

V: What do you think about the women's peace movement?

HS: Of course, I approve of it and I approve of getting people to demonstrate and sign petitions. But at the same time, I also sense a great deal of resignation about it all. Many women quietly ask themselves why they're still doing something, if they shouldn't take a trip south to enjoy themselves for a couple of months, since everything is going to fall apart soon anyway. Women are thinking about their relationship to the tremendous development of technology and destruction and at the same time are developing an uneasy feeling about their own capabilities. Whether this feeling of inadequacy is realistic, I don't know. As I said before, I have the definite feeling that we are doing something wrong. We are still being fooled by something which can be traced to a deeply rooted political pattern.

V: What gives you courage?

HS: I'm not embarrassed as often as I used to be. I find that most important. I have less and less inhibitions to talk about myself. There are so many lies in this world. Our closest friends have the biggest secrets but the BKA[2] knows already everything anyway. When you admit to yourself that your development is a series of complications and it's the same for other people, then you don't need to have any secrets.

Why then, I ask myself, are we so afraid of computers? Computers scare you because you presume that there have to be secrets. I don't want to play down these things, I just want to say that there's also a good aspect to it which

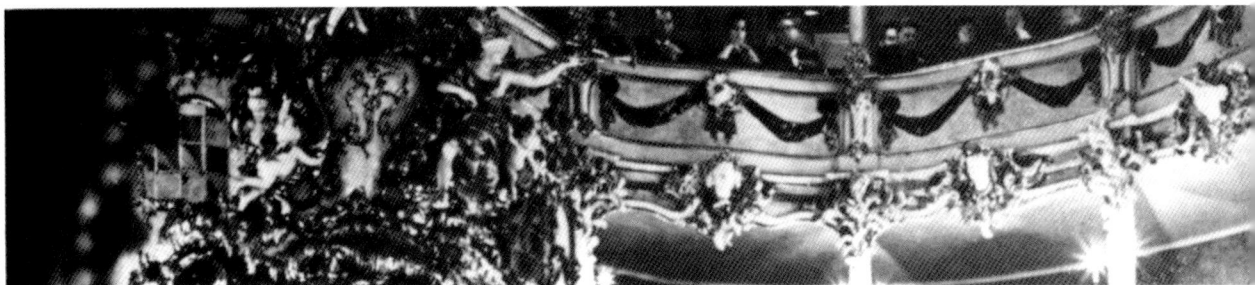

Their records say sexually decadent, vagrant, prostitute, changes jobs. Or: associates with foreigners, wears miniskirts. Or: obstinate, rebellious, lies. Their records contain everything which is unflattering to the girls, at least in the eyes of those who keep them. They are called stupid because the schools have failed them. Failing to get a job because of bad grades is seen as shirking. Girls with children who have been abandoned by the father are called foolish for getting involved. Leaving intolerable, exploitative jobs is seen as personal failure. They are blamed for sexual decadence if they sleep with their employers. Their parents' homes, which can't help them, become burdens for them.

Middle-class children learn discipline through their professional training. By failing to train them professionally, proletarian youths are disciplined and punished.

3

Force produces counterforce; pressure, counterpressure. The resistance which arises in these homes always develops spontaneously and without a set plan of action, unorganized, as an uproar, a riot, resistance, an uprising, as a revolt. □

Translated by Dagmar Stern   157

we really haven't talked about that much. If I stand totally behind my actions, then everybody who wants to may know about them. I would be a very unsuitable confidant, primarily because I do not recognize anything as a secret. Therefore, I am in a certain sense not that easily black-mailed. Secrets are perhaps *thought traps*, too. Do you feel threatened that somebody unknown to you knows some intimate detail about your life or does it threaten you that people whom you know will learn these details? If you really stand by your own convictions, it shouldn't matter whether Mr. Herold gets a kick out of the information he has about you. ☐

Translated by Barbara Helfferich

1. This controversial article aggressively asserted that even the most emancipated male leftist is filled with sexual fantasies.
2. BKA, the West German FBI.

WALTER ABISH

Wie Deutsch Ist Es

Sylvère Lotringer: The title of your most recent novel, *How German Is It*, is phrased like a question. But I wonder if it really calls for an answer. For one, this question has no question mark.

Walter Abish: To me the title is not primarily a question. Essentially it functions as a sign, the most effective sign I could find to describe the text.

SL: So the text itself doesn't raise any questions, or shouldn't have to provide any answer, especially in regard to Germany. As a matter of fact, I don't find the book that German.

WA: The title calls attention to a preoccupation, in this case, Germany. It's a highly charged issue. Most of us have set responses to Germany, as we do to so much else. In general, readers compliantly accept what they are offered. Their chief concern is, "how readable is the text?" For the most part, novels about Germany, or those simply located in Germany, without having to raise the question of, "How German is it?" resolve the unspoken question by explaining Germany. In one way or another, they explain Germany away and thereby

Walter Abish is an American writer whose works include *Alphabetical Africa, In the Future Perfect* and, in 1980, *How German Is It* (New *Directions*).

HANS MAGNUS ENZENSBERGER

The End Of Being Consistent

"Puree," said the little man with the blond mustache and the old-fashioned horn-rimmed glasses. He made a dismissing gesture with his hand, indicating that this applied to more than the huge studio and the multicolored props which had been used to construct an old-German tavern, just for this broadcast.

"All Puree."

I had run into one of those notorious performances in our country which are called "discussions," in obvious ignorance of the meaning of this word. I had forgotten the title of the broadcast: The Culture Trap, The Idea Disco? Also, I do not remember any more what it was all about, that evening. I am certain only that it dealt with one of those ANXIOUS QUESTIONS which burn the soul of every moderator between Kiel and

H.M. Enzenburger is a well-known West German editor, poet and essayist.

provide satisfaction. I have avoided an explanation. I have introduced German signs to create and to authenticate a "German" novel.

SL: Would you have written it if it had meant actually writing about Germany?

WA: I don't know to what degree a novel can be said to be about a country. Is Musil's, *The Man Without Qualities*, a book about Austria? I think certain books including mine permit a glimpse of a society. I've been asked by reporters, why I picked Germany. Well, *Alphabetical Africa* was set in Africa; an unpublished earlier book was located in Tel Aviv. I deliberately chose and continue to prefer a foreign surface because it gives me much greater freedom as a writer.

SL: A more familiar surface — an American surface — wouldn't give you as much leeway?

WA: Here I *know* what is familiar, and I don't feel as free to break away from it. On the other hand, I tend to establish or reestablish the familiar in what is foreign, allowing the familiar to determine the subsequent defamiliarization. The result is a tension, a sense of *unbehagen*, a discomfort.

SL: In your novel, Ulrich Hargenau, a German writer formerly involved with a terrorist group, is being interviewed about his forthcoming book, "The Idea of Switzerland" (which gives its title to one of your chapters.) Why Switzerland? the journalist also asks. And Ulrich answers: "Oh, Switzerland is simply a catchword." You obviously use foreign countries as catchwords, or catchworlds. You make them so "familiar" to the reader that any manipulation on your part will catch him off guard.

Konstanz. Is our nation a late-comer? Is a new youth rebellion in store for us? Do we need more (or less) government? Can our universities be saved? Have the rebels given up?

Generally, anxious questions don't allow binding answers. Therein lies their great value: they encourage mutiplicity of opinions.

The little man with the horn-rimmed glasses had pushed me into a corner.

"All nonsense!" he said. "I cannot understand — much as I would like to — how you could have gotten into this: a man like you!"

I had little to offer for my defense. "After all, I didn't open my mouth once."

"That is just it," he cried. "Just from you I would have expected an unequivocal position. One clear word would have been sufficient to end this ridiculous blabbering. I must say, I am disappointed."

I humbly inquired what had caused him, the man with the blond mustache, to participate in the performance.

"That I shall tell you, I never miss it. I am an expert on the subject, so to speak. For me only one thing counts: one's viewpoint on spiritual life. I also will gladly tell you what spiritual life consists of, namely, puree."

I found myself unable to contradict him.

His tirade did not leave my mind. The man was right, no doubt. Actually, the usual

WA: The presentation of the "familiar world" is not an innocent one. To me, the familiar details are also *signs* of a familiar world. In projecting these *signs* I am aware of my own preoccupation with the "familiar" and the presentation of it. Essentially, I am questioning how we see and write about something. Lévi-Strauss, wherever he went in Brazil, embodied Western culture. How could he avoid that? He reduced everything to *signs* in order to comprehend it. At the same time his own cultural as well as personal history may distort the *signs* he uses by attaching a particular Western significance to them. Perhaps that is why I feel that the text I write lies between me and the experience.

SL: Lévi-Strauss reduces the "savage" culture to a savage "mind," and the savage mind to his own. So minds do meet, and brilliantly so, but at the expense of the foreign culture. How could there be anything "savage" about minds that reflect Lévi-Strauss own preoccupation with understanding? The signs of a "savage" culture have little to do with our own. They function symbolically, from the depths of their own culture, and not semiotically on the surface of our own. Lévi-Strauss doesn't intend to write fiction, as you do. He assumes that his viewing is accurate. The paradox is that he ends up fictionalizing his own mind by painting it with "savage" colors. Between his writing and yours, his is by far the most innocent.

WA: Possibly because he has to refrain from "inventing." He must, whether he likes the word or not, focus on the "real" as opposed to the "possible" or "probable." I sense that what I invent will become "real"...that writing can and frequently does construct what is imminently about to take place. The question is, how free are we to invent? To embrace the "real" events is to remain in-

jabbering that substitutes here for democracy is difficult to tolerate. Flunkies, card-carrying party members, Mafiosi, dumb and aggressive smart-alecks set the tone in such a setting. Militant mediocrity reigns and reproduces whatever opinions on whatever subjects. On the whole, neither qualitative distinctions nor critical judgment cloud my discussions.

On these points I could easily agree with my expert, Mr. G. (that was his name). It was only remarkable that he seemed genuinely to suffer because of the situation.

I understood his longing for a kind of blizzard that might dispel overnight everything that bothered him: amorphous confusion, opportunism, the sheer adjustment to the puree. Nevertheless, his biting voice shocked me when he stated his demands. He requested — it was not clear from whom, but presumably he addressed the intelligentsia of the country — adherence to principles, radicalism, incorruptibility, clarity without compromise, unrelenting consistency. Yes, consistency was his special concern. He pronounced the word in a painful way, as if it meant a holy need.

The devastating humor of Mr. G's situation — of which he was totally unaware — lay in the fact that his existence was a denial of every one of the numerous syllables which he had expounded in his moist, excited staccato. The embodiment of an opportunist raged against accomodation. The versatile twaddler protested against twaddle.

nocent. For it is to embrace the answers. That is, essentially, what the institutions in Western society churn out. A great many answers that authenticate the "real" and "familiar" world.

SL: You're a writer and not a semiotician; a sophisticated mind, not a "savage" anthropologist. You are not writing about Germany in order to "understand" another culture; you are using the signs of a foreign culture to establish another attitude toward our own. Your truth is not a hard truth, like Lévi-Strauss', it is a soft truth, "sweet truth" (which is the title of the longest chapter of *How German Is It*.) Yours is a familiar truth to be played with, not believed in, at least in terms of understanding. I was very sensitive to the playfulness of your writing.

WA: I'm glad you are aware of it. So far, the critics who have reviewed the book in Germany have failed to understand it. They cannot see the element of play in the book. The "history" is too close.

SL: They are too German.

WA: Yes. Maybe they *become* too German. It may be an inevitable response, a Pavlovian response. Their distress or discomfort with German *signs*, by that I mean signs we have come to identify with Germany, brings about a critical response that is focused on the sign itself. The question whether or not all Germans eat knackwurst becomes an important issue. It's reduced to that level.

SL: On what level was the American response?

WA: I received a considerable amount of mail from readers who strongly iden-

"In my films Americans laughed at scenes and lines that caused the Germans to pretend to think."

Herbert Achternbusch

At this point we can forego further deepening our acquaintance with Mr. G. because his personal characteristics are of no importance and the humor of his situation is not unique. There are hundreds of thousands, if not millions, of his kind in our land. His type is characteristic for the state of this peculiar republic.

The American black revolutionary, Eldridge Cleaver, who has since suffered bankruptcy as a pants manufacturer, coined a phrase in the 'sixties which became a familiar quotation: "Baby," the Black Panther said then, "you are either part of the problem, or you are part of the solution." It subsequently became apparent that this is not correct. The less a "solution" is in sight, the clearer becomes the fact that there is nobody who is not part of the problem. It is worth noticing how vehemently the intelligentsia in our country refuses to accept this simple insight. Thus, repression becomes the main task of critical criticism.

Everybody who takes the trouble to observe the carnival of consciousness for a while can easily convince himself of the validity of the following rules of thumb:

The more insecure one's own identity, the more urgent the demand for clarity. The more servile the dependency on fashion, the louder the call for fundamental convictions. The more frenetic the chase after expense-accounts, the more heroic the struggle for integrity. The more stylish the ambiance, the more ardent the trend toward "subver-

tified with Ulrich. Then there was a response to the German element. And then the questions. Why that particular ending. And had Helmuth, the architect, become homosexual? And why did I fail to write about it in greater detail. And what about Paula and Daphne. Essentially, the inquiries focused on details and explanations I failed to provide. I don't think they are very important. Helmuth, for instance, is open to great many experiences. That much should be clear. But despite his sexual experimentation, he is an extremely ambitious albeit not very innovative architect. One is left with the feeling that he will succeed. But it is not spelled out.

SL: So that's the Pavlovian response here. The individual response. How American is it. Are your really interested in the characters as individuals? Can you talk about them that way?

WA: If I am asked about them. Why not? It means that I invest in them a reality they do not have outside the text. But I am not asked to provide additional text. I am asked for what amounts to gossip. What happened to so and so. In a number of interviews I have been questioned about the characters and managed to describe them quite vividly.

SL: It's like asking a chessplayer what the Queen feels in a chess game.

WA: The characters are not remote. They're not two dimensional. They are more than just signifiers. But they are not characters I really would wish to explore. They are not terribly attractive. They just happened. They emerged when I started to write.

SL: I feel that you deliberately refrain from exploring anything in depth.

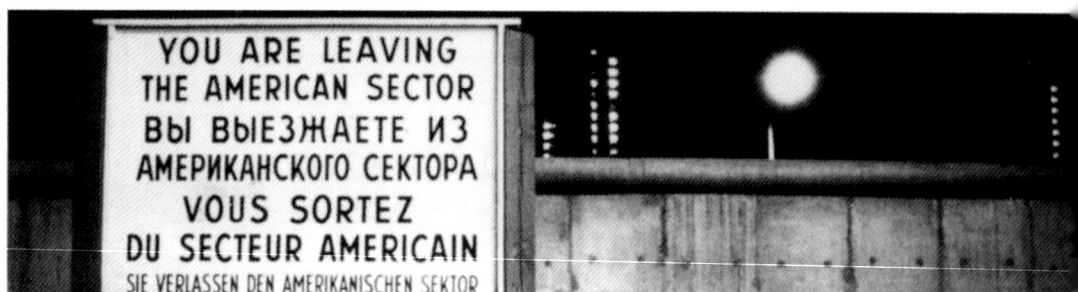

sion." The greater the corruptibility, the stronger the fear of becoming "integrated." The softer the mush, the firmer the principles, and the more helpless the floundering, the greater the love of consistency.

Of course, relief appears at the same time, according to the law of supply and demand. The longing for no compromise produces the cultural heroes. One feels no longer capable of fulfilling one's demands, so one delegates them to a multistriped crowd of philosophers, therapists, artists, mystics, ideologues, terrorists, sectarians, and criminals. What is lacking in oneself is attributed to them: integrity beyond any doubt. Thus a curious no-compromise Walhalla comes into existence where one can admire Sid Vicious and Mother Teresa, Castaneda and Einstein, Samuel Beckett and Joseph Stalin, Charles Manson and Erich Fromm, John Cage and Ulrike Meinhof, Jiang Quing and Arno Schmidt, Reverend Moon and Professor Beuys. The unhappy love for consistency seems to be a German obsession; at least, our neighbors do not share it readily.

I don't know the historic roots for this bizarre predilection. Has it something to do with Protestantism, with the Reformation? Does it have to do with a sad remnant of a long dead philosophical tradition? Was it not the ablest politician in German history who announced with pride: "To be German means to do something for its own sake?" The distant echo of this phrase can still be heard today in Germany's retail trade when the

WA: I try not to conceal anything. I feel that everything is on the surface. Our preoccupation with depth — and the title of the book signifies depth — is a desire for resolution, for explanation. Depth is analogous to wisdom and understanding. Which is terribly misleading. In German the word *Tiefe* has greater cultural weight than our word "depth." One could say that the word *Tiefe* and *depth* are celebrated in Hesse's *Das Glassperlenspiel*, and Maugham's *The Razor's Edge*, two books that in their time have probably inspired thousands of "innocent" readers to undertake the arduous journey in search of "self-recognition" and "depth." Quite an accomplishment for a popular book.

SL: Well, there's nothing more seductive than the surface. Nothing produces more meaning than touching it lightly, playfully. Your text is definitely perverse.

WA: You are the first person to refer to it as perverse. I believe the word has a different meaning in Europe than it does here. In Europe it can mean to defy or fly in the face of a certain order or a certain expectation.

SL: I was struck with the fact that you describe in minute details endless sequences of actions, daily occurences, weather, menu, clothes, but major events are kept in the backgroud. The discovery of the mass grave in the middle of Brumholdstein, on the former site of a concentration camp, is hardly commented upon. You well know that this is a sensitive area and you walk around very quietly as if there was nothing to it.

WA: They are the details of the reassuring familiar world. What is more familiar than the preoccupation with weather, menu, clothes? As for the event

saleslady makes the customer understand with a certain satisfaction: "We carry no mass-produced goods *on principle*." Here, in this specialty store, does one not hear the ridiculously diluted echo of authoritarian decisiveness which the well-read knows from the writings of Carl Schmitt, Ernst Jünger, and Martin Heidegger? It's only a question. And I really don't want to insist that Germans have monopolized dogmatism and the rhetoric of inflexibility. Italian Utopians, Spanish theologians, and French Jacobins understood bloody consistency only too well, even though they lacked the *mot juste*.

The jargon of consistency roars from the rostrums in every continent and poisons all channels of public discourse; the 'iron' laws of history, 'irrevocable' decisions, 'fanatical' conviction, 'iron-clad,' 'unerring,' and so on and always so on. People in dire need of consistency allow themselves readily to be organized. The consistency's name is usually: School, Group, Church, Army Barracks, or Party. The student of the pathos of decisiveness makes a mistake if he thinks that it brings individuality into play, that it involves self-realization. Nothing is more systematic and controlled than the unerring ones running amok. Something regulated, yes bureaucratic, is part of all radicalism which refers to nothing more than dogma. Whoever speaks of loyalty to principles has forgotten already that one can betray only people, not ideas.

Against such insidious and conniving tricks, Adorno once objected — polite as he

that is hardly commented upon. The grave is unearthed. The skeletons are shipped away during the night. The characters in the book are understandably disinclined to discuss the episode. It makes them uncomfortable. They just want to get it over with. It's the reader who seems, for obvious reasons, to read into this material much more than I say.

SL: The less you say, the more irrepressible it is for the reader to come up with an interpretation. Especially with this kind of material. So you keep it at a low key. You present the mass burial as you would any other incident. Your equanimity is also, you realize, an open invitation for a misreading.

WA: To think is to interpret. A reviewer in *Der Spiegel* referred to the opaqueness of the text. However, he went on to say, when I focused on what he chose to call the "bad years" everything became all too clear. So you see, it is relative. What you consider low key was all too evident for the German reviewer. Actually, I thought I was being opaque there. To begin with, it is not certain that the skeletal remains in the mass grave were Jews. They might have been Germans. At least I toy with the idea. Or permit the characters in the book to toy with the thought.

SL: You toy with everything.

WA: In life we are forever, it seems, confronted by situations that defy explanation. We simply do not have sufficient information about them. Yet we interpret and explain. Anything. Everything. Puzzles and mysteries, if used well, energize the text.

SL: Puzzles are questions that are meant to be toyed with. Questions without

"It was not a model for Germany but for the world."
Ona Zukumpft

was — that the separation of theory and practice was a great step forward for civilization. This was held against him. Thus he experienced the sadistic rage that can flow from the consistency commandment. One is reminded of the call of the mob to the potential suicide crouched on top of the roof: jump already!

Dear Countrymen! In consideration of these historical preconditions and situations, I want to inform you about the advantages, or shall I say joys, of inconsistency. I know that you don't like to hear this, and I count on your harsh retaliation for this good deed. One does not like to part with a cherished toy, even if it consists of a butcher's knife with which one runs the risk of hurting oneself as well as others.

First of all, I ask you to realize that you owe your life to vacillation, indecision, compromise. Think about it, it does not cost you anything, whether you would still be able to get angry at my modest sentences if Nikita Khrushchev, this unprincipled opportunist, had not retreated with his rockets at the time, in 1962 — you know what I mean. Nothing but wavering, foot-dragging, faint-hearted procrastination at the decisive moment.

Yet, we know how far we can get with acting consistently: when executed ruthlessly, each economic doctrine brings about the breakdown of the economic system that it was meant to cure.

question marks, like the title of your novel. Whether or not the novel is "German" is obviously besides the point. The signs you use are meant to *present* Germany, to give it a strong presence in the novel — not to represent it. They treat Germany as a fiction, not a reality.

WA: Presentation can, in one year's time, become representation. "The English Garden," a story in my collection *In the Future Perfect*, is a good introduction to *How German Is It*. The story describes an American who has come to Germany to interview a German writer. On his arrival the American buys a coloring book, really a children's coloring book, at the airport. During his brief stay he keeps questioning the signs in the coloring book and comparing them to other signs in Germany. That immediately reduces the landscape, everything I describe, to a set of signs and images and also introduces, not the interpretation itself, but the need for interpretation as well as the level on which the interpretation as well as the speculation is to be conducted. A level of seriousness is implied and suggested.

SL: This is the "English Garden" effect John Ashbery wrote about. The signs you play with don't refer directly to anything external, like Germany. They do it obliquely, to give the "required air of naturalness." They call attention to themselves.

WA: This mirrors my own involvement with writing, my awareness of the limitations of writing as well as a certain ambivalence with respect to the role of the writer. The reason I introduced Heidegger in the novel is because of his questionable political role in the thirties, as well as his extraordinary preoc-

Consistent capitalism brings about fascist dictatorship.

Consistent political struggle with the use of any means leads to terrorism, just as consistent defense of national security does.

The pure theory of ecology does not protect men from environment but environment from men; it returns us logically to simple huts.

Building communism without ifs and buts ends in the aptly named "socialist camp."

Industrial growth, continued without compromise, results in the destruction of the biosphere.

The consequence of the arms race is atomic war.

Etcetera.

It can't be helped; we find ourselves in a new situation which seems quite dangerous to me. The risks involved will be hard to overcome, will test our courage. Perhaps we should try the following maxim: a good thing, any good thing, becomes false as soon as we think it through to the end. "In times of danger and great need, consistency means death."

There are a good number of politicians who understand this, not only in the West. These are bad times for charismatic hero-types and leader-types. Fortunately, VERY

cupation with language. Here was a man who had to shape language in order to address himself to the questions he found to be of overriding importance. His history, as I see it, was always a universal history that he somehow managed to locate in his own beloved forest. But was his history not shaped by specific historical events? When Heidegger, a most remarkable thinker, touches on German history he verges on the banal. That is perplexing.

SL: Brumhold's metaphysical quest in your book is also defined by the title: How German Is It. It is a question Brumhold, who is really Heidegger, asks of language, but his question has a question mark. So the philosopher formulates questions for which solutions can be found; whereas the writer sets up questions like a trap.

WA: Incidentally, there are a number of references to language in the book. It is made clear throughout that language at best is unreliable. But the language to which I refer is German. The book suggests that all communication is in German. Yet it is written in English, which creates an interesting tension — a form of estrangement, really.

SL: The tension is already established in the title — since it is given in two languages. The two titles answer to each other, although neither of them is a question. This tension, however, is for the English reader only. The Germans will feel that the book was written by a foreigner.

WA: That would be a defensive reaction. They might say that in order not to feel foreign themselves. For to examine something is to establish a distance between your "self" and what is being examined. In examining Germany, Ger-

GREAT MEN are nowhere in sight. Increasingly, world politics resembles repair shops where worried mechanics are bent over stuttering motors and scratch their heads pondering how to make their jalopies work again. (Correspondingly, the bills turn out high.)

This environment of mediocrity, this artificially propped up politics of muddling through does not exist only in our immediate surroundings. Is there one single society on earth that does not stumble toward the future on crutches. Many have been misled to believe that a well-aimed kick was sufficient to overthrow "conditions" so that nothing would stand in the way of building a beautiful New World. Experience teaches that this is a wrong conclusion, unfortunately.

During the late 'fifties and early 'sixties, a man by the name of Samir Amin taught sociology and political economy at one of the universities in Paris, the Sorbonne, I believe. The professor was a young man, barely thirty years old, born in Cairo, i.e., an Egyptian. His special field was the economy of the so-called developing countries. He had worked for various international organizations and was just named planning consultant to the Sahel country, Mali. Therefore, many stipend holders from the former French colonies were seen in his seminars: Senegalese and Madagascans, Algerians and Somalis, Vietnamese and Moroccans.

169

mans are thrust into a German role. They are forever compelled to explain and re-explain history.

SL: The German reader loses the estrangement of the two languages. But he also gets more than he bargained for. Its humor addresses the reader personally. I wonder what happens when it is confronted by a collective reading. A reading by German culture.

WA: That was not my intention. A collective reading is a reading I find very menacing. I should add that I didn't have the German reader in mind when I wrote the novel.

SL: That makes the German reaction all the more interesting.

WA: I did not rule out the possibility of the book appearing in Germany. In fact, there is a reference to foreign authors coming to Germany to publicize their books which have appeared there in translation. Now, I have just finished reading the German translation of *How German Is It*. The translator, Renate Herms-Hampke, did a very good job. She caught the flow of my writing, yet, in German, the book is less playful, less humorous.

SL: The epigraph of your novel is a sentence by Jean-Luc Godard: "What is really at stake is one's image of oneself." What image of themselves do you think the Germans are going to read in the mirror of their own language? How German are they going to make it?

WA: A number of Germans I know have read the book in English. Some ad-

On the basis of his theoretical and empirical analyses Amin had concluded that the liberation movements in poor countries could cope with their economic misery only by plowing over, so to speak, the colonial societies which had been deformed by foreign domination. The expulsion of imperialists and the takeover of political power would be of no use if one left untouched the existing social structures. Indeed, one would have to overturn them completely with radical means. In detail, Samir Amin proposed three fundamental interventions:

First, the relationship between city and country had to be changed. Urbanization in poor countries would be disastrous; it would have to be reversed by all means. Industrial projects would be postponed; they would only create new dependency on foreign capital. Agriculture deserved absolute preference.

Secondly, the poor countries would have to detach themselves from the world market, where, by its very nature, the capitalist law of the stronger prevails, they would have to put up with a long period of isolation from the rest of the world. Self-sufficiency would have to be the first economic goal. Of course, some deprivation would be the consequence of autarchy in a subsistence level economy, but this would hit mainly the privileged.

Thirdly, it would be necessary to break the cultural influence of the West. The native

mire it greatly. Some say it expresses what they cannot bring themselves to express. Only one person I know said that I had established too strong a link between that horrific period of annihilation and the Germany of today. He implied that 1940 to 1945 were only five years of a long, long German history. Well, that may be so, but they happen to be very crucial years.

SL: And they are also crucial for the type of effect you intended to produce. Is this setting comparable to any other foreign surface you could have played with? Is there anything specific in your choice of Germany?

WA: To mention Germany is to refer to the specific. The specific in turn is hierarchized. We have set responses for the German specific, whether it be Bach, Goethe, Kleist, Nietzsche, Heidegger or the methodical extermination of twelve million, of which six million were Jews. As a Jew, born in Austria, with a knowledge of the language, the culture, it was not all that difficult to construct a Germany.

SL: How does one enter German culture today when one is Jewish? How can one remain on the surface when so much of the horrific episode still lies buried in the German consciousness?

WA: I am not interested in trying to determine a German guilt, or to establish a link between the German past and the present.

SL: Even in the form of terrorism?

WA: Even in that form.

SL: The two episodes are closely related in your novel.

elite, merchants and civil servants, teachers and physicians, were all infested with the values and ideologies of the metropolis. These were corrupt, parasitic groups posing a constant threat of contamination, and they were determined to prevent any truly independent national development. Therefore, their influence would have to be liquidated, once and for all, and their power broken.

Among the diligent quiet students in Amin's seminar were also some Cambodians; one was named Khieu Samphan, another Jeng Sary, a third Saloth Sar — better known under his *nom de guerre* POL POT. Fifteen years after they all had passed their exam with high honors, these people carried out the advice of their teacher with consistency. Anyone who can read or owns a TV knows about the result; the historians disagree only about whether the experiment of the Khmer Rouge cost the lives of one-half or two-and-one-half million Cambodians. What happened to Samir Amin and what he thinks of his pupils, I do not know.

I don't want my dear friends to misunderstand me. Nobody insists that it would be a crime to think something through to the end. We are, indeed, curious people who are dying to know where this hypothesis or that sudden idea is going to land. But as the fable teaches, the lovers of consistency think very little of the difference between theory and practice. Just when there is no going any further, they want to turn their ideas into ac-

WA: They are also neutralized. The comparison they invite is the easy comparison much of history seems to invite.

SL: The first episode involves the abortive plot against Hitler by Ulrich's father, the second Ulrich's own participation in a terrorist group. The relationship between the two actions remains unclear, as does Ulrich's actual birth. Both are open for interpretation.

WA: Yes, but I am not willing to interpret. I try to give meaning to what is left unsaid, if that is possible. I want what is left unsaid to remain a strong presence. As strong as what is stated specifically. Certain things in the book continue to intrigue me: the painting, the cleaning of the interiors. The house-painters don't have a clear symbolic function. Painting is just another sign in the book, but it is a powerful sign. At one point the assistant painter Obbie is listening to a couple make love while he, in order to listen to them, keeps painting the door to their room over and over again. That scene is given a physical intensity.

SL: This is a primal scene as Freud would have dreamt it. The oedipal resonance of the situation is visible, but you carefully refrain from any comment. This is what I would call, on your part, a "perverse" attitude. I'll try to clarify this point now. For Freud, perversion is the sunny side of neurosis. Neurosis has depth and meaning; it involves anguish and repression. "Perversion," on the contrary, is a way of dancing around the deadly seriousness of neurosis. The neurotic symptoms are still present, but they are dealt with playfully at a safe distance: from the other side of the door. The scene keeps crying for interpretation.

tion. That can have murderous consequences, as the fable teaches. Where consistency can be accomplished only at the cost of barbarism and self-emulation, I look at it as an abominable anachronism.

Yet the alternative is quite near at hand. Dear colleagues, when your thinking reaches those limits, why not simply turn around and try out the next unresearched path? It won't hurt as much as you think.

If you want to call that opportunism or accommodation, blessed be the accomodation! In case of doubt, I prefer Paul Feyerabend's statement: "It is not the elimination of opportunism which turns us into good people — it makes us stupid, at most — but it is the elimination of a tendency to objectivize immediately our selfish dreams about a good or 'rational' or 'responsible' life, and to force it on others as objective values."

Who knows, some useful and surprising stuff could be found among the forbidden suppressed thoughts which would surface after the removal of self-censorship; and how pleasant it would be if the whole apparatus of painstaking repression, of political bigotry and of self-indulgent dogmatism would disappear on the garbage heap!

And the puree? Right, we almost lost sight of it! But it still exists, a fact of our times, ever present like hamburgers and credit cards, a world historical continuum. The puree remains. I know that it is part of the cost of democratic civilization, the only one

WA: I think the ideal text is one that cries for interpretation. Obbie's action, in this case, it self-evident, but it merges and gives greater sexual emphasis to other descriptions of house painting. The smell of turpentine in the first section of the book is an anticipation of this.

SL: The mass grave also cries for interpretation, but it may be too strong to elude it altogether. The exhumation of the corpses is a perfect metaphor for repression, as much as the painting scene is a metaphor for the alleged primal scene. Here the traumatic event is painted over, there it is brought to the open. Freud was very fond of the archeological metaphor to represent the working of the unconscious. The chance discovery and hasty dismissal of the human remains right in the middle of a new German community, on the previous site of a concentration camp, obviously testify for the uneasy return of a German past whose existence is still being denied. As you said earlier, nothing proves that the corpses are Jews. The repressed doesn't reappear as such. By an ingenious shift of scenery, the symptom of the crime surfaces as an "English Garden." The stench of the ruptured sewage pipe, however, is a blunt reminder that there is something rotten in the Republic of Germany. Your deliberate detachment in relation to the horrific episode is much more powerful than any interpretation. I noticed that from "The English Garden" to *How German Is It*, the reference to Jews and to the concentration camp has been drastically played down. How do you account for that disappearance?

WA: All the same, their presence is felt. But everything for which there exists a strong explanation has been played down. Hence, Jews, Nazis, concentration camps, terrorists are the components of a German explanation. To introduce

we have. Like the huge garbage piles towering around our cities, it stinks to high heaven; but violent it is not.

Since I can't find anything else especially worth glorifying, I am in a mood to end with a tribute to wilfulness. Naturally, there will be no lack of fools — I actually hear their heckling — who throw wilfulness and consistency into the same sack, and who believe that when one comes to an end the other must let go, too. That is wrong. Wilfulness is a question of attitude, not a question of principle.

For example — we can do without models but not without examples — an inconspicuous man sits in the train from Munich to Konstanz. He is quiet, friendly, but not talkative. A dreary November afternoon is seen through the windows of his third-class compartment; it gets dark early. The man with grey eyes is in his middle thirties, neatly but poorly clad, like a small craftsman; his dialect is somewhat Swabian; and his delicately boned hands look skillful. What trade did he learn: cabinet-making, perhaps or fine mechanics? After work he plays the zither, or he goes dancing if he has enough money. No, he does not read newspapers. Sometimes he goes to church, but he does not have any distinct religious or ideological convictions; and he does not think much about politics.

them in a certain context is to introduce the interpretation. The narrator in "The English Garden" fails to provide an explanation for his odd behaviour. The reader cannot be certain why, for instance, this man refuses to take off his shirt while making love. Could he possibly be trying to conceal a number tatooed on his forearm, or does he merely wish to leave the woman with that impression. When he claims that his missing wife was Jewish, is he saying that in order to agitate the librarian with whom he is having an affair?

SL: So we don't know the truth about him or his wife, but we assume there should be one somewhere.

WA: He thrusts the woman into a specific role, compelling her — for the moment — to surrender her personal identity and become a prisoner of a collective identity, a German identity. The absence of Jews in the book enables the German characters to retain their personal identity. In the book the collective German role — inasmuch as it exists — is identified as a formula. By that I mean, formula as explanation. But the formula provides only a frame of reference, it is not the substance of the book.

SL: Could you have made the concentration camp as formula the substance of the novel?

WA: I wouldn't dream of doing it.

SL: It's been done, mostly unwillingly though. We've had the "Holocaust." In a sense the production of the "Holocaust" is the right answer to the German problem.

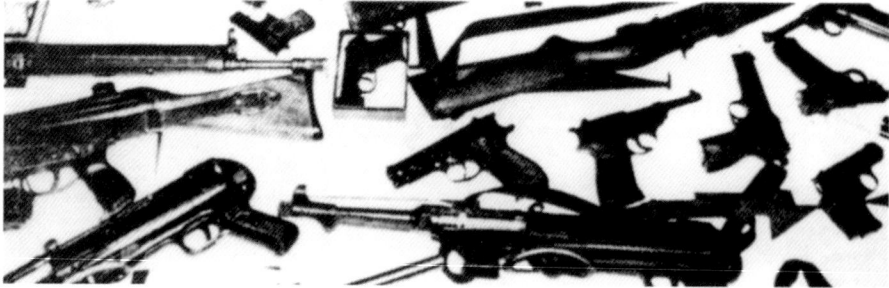

Finally, the train stops in Konstanz. He gets off, walks without haste but resolutely through the darkness, passing small plots and barns. It is now a quarter to nine; soon he will reach the Swiss border. Two customs officials bar the road, ask for his passport which has expired, and demand that he empty his pockets. He has no contraband, only a few slips of paper in his pocket, and an old button from the Red-Front Fighters ("an old souvenir"), a few screws, nuts and bolts, and a picture postcard from a beer hall in Munich, the Bürgerbräukeller. The customs officials demand that he accompany them to the border police. It is only a routine control.

While he is waiting there in the office — the calendar on the wall indicates November 8, 1939 — a bomb explodes at exactly 9:10 in Munich three minutes after Hitler has left the hall, earlier than foreseen. Georg Elser had produced it in four months of hard work and built it into a support post of the beer hall.

Georg Elser, born on January 4, 1903, in Hermaringen and murdered on April 9, 1945, in the concentration camp of Dachau, Hitler's most dangerous enemy, did not belong to a group of conspirators and did not obey the orders of a party. He planned, prepared, and executed the assassination attempt all by himself. His story does not appear in the textbooks of German students. German historians mention it in a footnote, if at all. It does not lend itself to discussions. It cannot be generalized. □

Translated by Lieselotte Wolff and Rick Wolff

WA: It's the popular answer. The Walt Disney answer. It's the only answer possible. Walt Disney is our truth.

SL: History returns, not as a comedy or tragedy: a cartoon.

WA: The Germans had Wagner to designate their space in the world. We have Walt Disney. Where is the grave of all this. In Hollywood?

SL: And Hollywood somewhere in Germany, if one follows Syberberg's projections of Nazi cosmology.

WA: There is a marvelous link in Syberberg's film between the Hitler period and cinema. A merging of the cinematic formula with the Wagnerian formula of the Nazis.

SL: *Our Hitler* is the German answer to the "Holocaust." Syberberg's enterprise though may be too much of a Grand Opera, and not enough of a Grand Guignol to achieve any catharsis. Your novel is successful in this respect. There's so very little humor in Syberberg's film.

WA: But he, on the other hand, deals with Hitler and Nazism. A subject I barely touch. In the interview of Hitler's valet and projectionist in the film we are provided with a great deal of information that is tantalizing because, on the face of it, it is so innocuous. It's not very meaningful. But it is personal and as such seems to demand a special response. The private Hitler as opposed to the public Hitler. It's intriguing.

SL: Probably as much as your own novel is. It is at this point, I feel, that you're

"As for the Holocaust, *I can only agree with Joseph Strauss. That wasn't for real."*

Hitler's bodyguard

175

the closest to Syberberg's film. Both your novel and Syberberg's film keep referring to their own medium while talking about Germany, yet they stand as far apart as could be. *Our Hitler* is so serious, so inflated, so self-indulgent. It doesn't maintain, as you do, any distance in relation to its model. It represents representation, it doesn't really play with it.

WA: I was much more taken by Joseph Beuys' show at the Guggenheim. To me, the entire body of work was made to represent an overwhelming German undertaking. The sled piece embodied a basic German energy and determination. Mind you, nothing in the exhibition conveyed anything but this German drive. Of course, everything in the show reflected the past. But still, a Germany free of Nazi signs. It was interesting to listen to Beuys on tape explaining the work, because one could detect a duplicity in what he was saying.

SL: A total duplicity, as far as I am concerned. Beuy's work is very strong, but I couldn't stand his explanations. There was too much repression in his humanistic stand, too much guilt in his heavy Christian symbolization. To me, it was the worst type of resurgence of the German past.

WA: Beuys was less than candid because he was addressing an American audience. He tried to make the work appear as harmless, to view it only as art in an art context. To what degree a viewer would accept Beuy's highly dubious explanations and fail to associate the "Fat" sculpture with the fat of Jews made into soap is hard to say.

SL: When I first read *How German Is It*, I felt somewhat confused. I didn't understand what you were getting at. It was the wrong approach to

JOSEPH BEUYS

The Ecology
of the Social Body

Q: How do you relate your political activity to your creative activity?

JB: For a long time I've had nothing to do with the ideology of so-called "modern art." My attitude, which I would call anthropological, consists in connecting my work to the work of all those who at the same time transform, recast, and radically regenerate society in one way or another. I thus pose the problem of relating a particular capability, mine for example, to the capabilities existing elsewhere in society. How can we all cooperate to find a strategy that used different media in order to present our ideas and persuade

Joseph Beuys, influential German Art professor, active as artist and ecologist.

your novel, which uses understanding like a decoy. I was walking beside the text, each time creating anew my own labyrinth. To take the familiar images seriously, at face value, is to be left with one's image of oneself. An individual image for the American, as suggested by the question whether Helmuth is gay; a cultural image for the Germans (Are we a nation of knackwursts?) Your novel is like a machine made of broken pieces of mirror that flash elements of meaning to attract the birds. Do you actually mean to trap the reader?

WA: I wouldn't write in order to trap or to fool the reader. To elicit a false response deliberately or intentionally mislead would be to reduce the meaning this book has for me as a literary accomplishment.

SL: I recently talked with Vito Acconci. He has these pieces which are machines. People machines. Decoy for birds and people. Machines that are meant to trap people. You sit on them and the flaps fold back upon you. Only then do the other viewers notice the American flag or the German flag painted outside the flaps that imprison that one person who is made to look like a fool, a puppet. But this is Vito's game, his own brand of perversion. Your approach is more urbane. You'd rather invite an intelligent response on the reader's part; a pleasure to be shared.

WA: Acconci invests his anger in everything he does. In a sense, he is attacking himself and that attack is necessary. It generates a kind of energy he needs. It permits him to continue. It enables him to carry on. I don't have that necessity. I am able to generate energy when I fall back on certain recognizable cultural signs.

"I have an erotic relationship to truth."
Fritz Teufel

the greatest majority in the shortest time to either change something or at least exert pressure on certain structural tendencies? For me this is the question continuously raised by the destruction and disruption naturally spawned by capitalism, its structural chaos that daily grows worse.

Q: You often refer to phenomenology...

JB: For me it is the only way to seek after the axiomatic truths. The principal axioms at the base of the capitalist system no longer obtain once the real is looked at as phenomenon. Phenomenology also deals with the notion of possibility. We must ask ourselves what is truly possible, what can be accomplished, and then cease discussing, day after day, what is *not* possible.

Q: Germany then remains the country in which philosophy and politics are intimately connected?

JB: Yes. The German tradition is to dig into philosophy for the foundations and basis of political thought. I think it's necessary to develop the tool which phenomenology represents, by re-examining Novalis, Schelling, Goethe and of course Hegel. These ideas have begun to penetrate the Green movement.

SL: Would you be disappointed in any way if people read your book right? If they read it on level with your writing?

WA: I hardly think that likely, except for a small group of readers. Most of the reviews I have received dealt strictly with the book as a novel that focuses on Germany, Germany today, the new Germany in relation to the old. I haven't discussed the book at great length. I found there was no need to discuss it. I have been congratulated for this book in America by people who have misread it. The only reason they like it is because they misread it. And I have accepted their accolades without pointing out that they have misinterpreted the book.

SL: They haven't misinterpreted the book. They have *interpreted* it, and this is enough.

WA: Okay, they have interpreted it.

SL: Misreading is no accident. It is not external to your writing. It is an integral part of it.

WA: If a book is strong enough, powerful enough to invite a misreading — does this not say something about the book and about writing in general?

SL: It may help turn your novel into a powerful instrument of investigation. Your book keeps flashing elements of meaning, but they are somehow disconnected, like a puzzle. The way the Germans will put them together will be very revealing of their culture. □

Q: A number of your pieces are built on dualities of almost identical elements.

JB: All my work attempts to destroy statistical equilibrium. I use identical elements, such as a pair of hospital beds, which at the outset are rigidly related to each other, frozen in static symmetry. This symmetry seems to exclude any possibility of directing one of the elements onto a radical different path, of creating a moving alternate. Then along comes the idea of disaggregation, as I see it, advancing, already active. Acting through the social body wherein one group takes a route radically different from those which support the status quo . . . Outside the muffled din of the social body conserving itself. This is a kind of x-ray of the social body that only reflects the process of disaggregation of identity, of sameness, of symmetry. Perhaps it is the equality of life which shines through this mortal melancholy, when even this melancholy takes the appearance of beauty, hiding itself under a cosmetic surface. □

Translated by Michael Lazarin

HANS JÜRGEN SYBERBERG

Our Syberberg

Let's put an end to art serving as the handmaiden of politics. Art should be Divine inspiration. Art should be a yearning for the hereafter, the eternal, and the sublime. It should be the way to the truth, wisdom, immortality, and what we call love. Politics as an organizing principle for mediocre compromises needs the assistance of art, which always seeks justice and uses dreams to overcome death. Art is the reason for living, to-day as in the past. Since Hitler no one in Germany speaks of official government art anymore. The Third Reich was guilty of the highest perversion when it turned the State and society into the ultimate *Gesamtkunstwerk* (Total work of art). For years we heard of the politicization of art. Now you shall have it. Art as the only true and total opposition.

Syberberg is a West German filmmaker, producer and director of *Our Hitler*, which created a furor in Germany.

STEVE KATZ

"The Forest Continues
to Beckon Us...":

*...everyone is passionately in love with the outdoors, in love with
what they refer to as* Natur, *and the splendid weather is an added
inducement to put on their* Lederhosen *and spend several hours
serenely tramping through the woods, studiously looking at birds
and trees, haphazardly selecting one path, then another, without
knowing where the path might lead.*

Walter Abish, *How German Is It*

It is not splendid weather when M. and I park the car and walk out into
the woods near Mörfelden-Walldorf, a small town near Frankfurt, but cloudy
and gray, autumn in the Rhine-Main region. We pass the barricades erected by
the police, concrete blocks pushed onto the roadway where the asphalt gives
way to dirt.

It is a good hour's walk to the site of today's demonstration and to the
Hüttendorf (or "hut village") standing squarely in the path of Startbahn West,
the runway which the West German State and the Frankfurt Airport Authority
are trying to construct. On a map, Startbahn West moves at a right angle from

If film is the child of the twentieth century, the democratic century, and if it is true
that film is not just a product of individuals designed for individuals, but rather a large
mass happening, then film must give us in its old age interesting information about our
time, the spirit of a country in this world. And that just does not apply to Hitler's time.
We can find out a lot about ourselves if we make an effort to thoroughly investigate film.
And it is connected to everything we value today.

The general case could become a special case for *Our Hitler*, and from that special
case generalizations can be drawn. Not only for Germany. The Hitler film can be seen as
an exemplary case of a Germany thirty-five years after Hitler. The need to understand art
as a necessity, as a release from guilt, beauty as an accomplishment, work, challenge,
an agent of truth, a victor over evil and terror, not as a fascination, but as its opposite,
the reverse image of terror, a new rationally-tested beauty, the freedom of truth in a
society conscious of itself with spiritual pride and an identity out of grief, from the grief
of art as an examination with possibilities for release; to negate political mistakes,
monstrosities of political power through total artistic means, to portray tragedy with
aesthetic rituals of new possibilities of our technology, to banish the demons, to create
a myth appropriate to this analytical time, with the intention to try everything,
everything. An art of projection, a meditative "heroism, crossing borders," questioning

the existing airport, neatly cutting the woods near Mörfelden-Walldorf in half. The runway would be four kilometers long, 800 meters wide, and would clear an estimated three million trees. While M. and I are at the demonstration and the Hüttendorf, the police attack the demonstrators with water cannon filled with CN gas, and with plastic shields and long, dark clubs.

In its aftermath, I wake up from a dream without characters, a dream of destructive power. I experience a fear of total loss, a loss of M. I think of the woods near Mörfelden-Walldorf, near the Frankfurt Airport, near the United States Rhine-Main military airbase.

I. From the Opera House to Gateway Gardens

Apparently, the military viewpoint is the critical one in understanding Startbahn West. From this, it follows directly who is interested in Startbahn West — and why, in this confrontation, we need the greatest clarity.

Umwelt Express, September 1981

It takes about twenty minutes by autobahn to get from Frankfurt to the demonstration against Startbahn West. We pass two or three massive office tower complexes, efficiently planned concentrations of international service activity. The Rhine-Main countryside is filled with new apartments and houses, offices, stores and shops, and occasionally small gardens and horse stables squeezed into the leftover spaces near the autobahn. We get off at the exit marked "Gateway Gardens/U.S. Airbase," and head for Mörfelden-Walldorf.

"Out of the North Sea surfaces a nuclear bunker — or is that a high security prison?"

Ona Zukumpft

everything else without the intent to entertain or moralize, of course understood as opposition and antithesis for rescuing us from our present misery. With inquiries to those who make politics about their honesty. Not a political film, not film politics, but rather the total challenge to the powerful people of democracy and the organizers of freedom and the media establishment. Questions that art has to pose as much as the political and artistic totality of its topic, to challenge our democracy and culture.

Projection, in the psychological sense, is the primary structural principle of *Our Hitler*. The film activates the audience to produce its own projections. It animates them like the director animates the film. That explains the similarity of Hitler's tricks and techniques to those of filmmaking. Hitler's *Blitzkrieg*, the whole temperament of his political appearance become obvious in the intoxicated, moving camera of the Leni Riefenstahl films. This is the perverted form of Dionysian intoxication according to the principle of *panta rhei*, everything flows, everything is in motion.

Film is a seismograph of cultural and power politics. □

Translated by Gaby Moritz

Model Deutschland appears as ordered, sleek and efficient; West Germany's economic survival seems to depend upon it. Most German traditions — at least those which are considered appropriate for official memory, those which do not refer to the War — are by now packaged, commodified and available for consumption on weekends or after work. Nevertheless, there is solace and meaning to be found in a walk in the woods, where for instance, this massive new runway is planned.

The German problem of memory often comes uncomfortably to the surface. This year, the haute bourgeoisie of Frankfurt rededicated their Opera House, a mammoth Baroque building that had stood as an empty wreck since the War. The Frankfurt Airport Authority takes great pride in its support for the reopening of the Opera House.

Even during the period of Prussian political and military dominance, I am told, Frankfurters prided themselves on their cultural tradition. However, it is left this time to Frankfurt's "Alternative Scene" to point out that this renewal of a tradition is nothing of the sort, at least until the citizens and sponsors are willing to come to terms with the fact that during a few years back in the 1930's, half of the Frankfurt orchestra and opera company quietly disappeared: Jews, sent to the concentration camps. Memory "takes place." As a disintegrating Modell Deutschland attempts to brace itself, both opera houses and airports become reorganized in accordance with the demands of security space.

"Gateway Gardens" is the deceptively suburban name for the United States Rhine-Main military airbase, the largest U.S. military airbase outside of the United States. Rhine-Main employs some ten thousand people, and has

MICHEL FOUCAULT

19th Century Imaginations

The "Ring" of the century, conducted by Pierre Boulez and directed by Patrice Chereau, ended in its fifth and last year. One and a half hours of applause, as once again Walhalla went down in flames. Again and again the artists are called back on the stage. The boos of the first year, the outraged musicians, the unwillingness of the orchestra and of some singers are forgotten; forgotten are the Action Committee for the Preservation of Richard Wagner's Work, the leaflets and the anonymous letters calling for the head of the conductor and director. To be honest, there are still some unsuccessfully conspiring ghosts left on the green hill. This unexpected "Ring", produced by

Michel Foucault, leading historian and philosopher, is the author of *The Order of Things* and *Power/Knowledge* (Pantheon).

183

been a key transport and command center since the end of World War II. Recently set up to serve as a stopping point for any military movement into the Middle East, the airbase is capable of handling massive shifts of personnel and materiel. Under the code name of "Reforger I — Celested Cap 1980," some 17,000 troops were airlifted into NATO war games last year via Rhine-Main in two days. The military airbase butts up against the civilian airport; NATO planes regularly use the civilian runways.

Rhine-Main is also at the center of NATO planning for "theater war" in Europe. Figuring that Central Europe will be the region in which the two superpowers will fight it out and that such a war would be limited in scope, NATO planners assume that they will have enough time — measured in days — to ship new weaponry and manpower into the Rhine-Main region. A European theater war would, in the words of a 1978 NATO report on its "Long Term Deployment Program," "demand the transfer of more than a million men and a million tons of materiel and equipment by sea and land in the shortest possible time."

However, the report notes, "NATO's ability to reinforce its strike capacity through fast transport is, in both its conception and its practice, unproven." Nor could its "ability" be proven, at least before the onset of a real war crisis, be it "conventional" or nuclear. NATO planners can never know if they have sufficiently expanded their capacity until it is too late: until the missiles have been fired.

As a result, military strategy dictates that *all* European transportation systems — and especially the Frankfurt Airport — be expanded to fit the future crisis, be they military or civilian. Moreover, should NATO and the

"And America? If America is a dog, I said, then we have the dog shit."

Herbert Achternbusch

foreigners, probably upset them. But they were pale enough, just like the fallen gods. In the bookstore windows of Bayreuth there is, among hundreds of works about, for or against Wagner (it seems that after Jesus Christ, Wagner has the most extensive list of annual bibliographies) a thin volume whose cover bears a curious photograph: Winifried, Wagner's granddaughter, raising her hand above a small man, who is bowing his head to give her a respectful kiss. One can only see his back, but even though his face is turned away, the little moustache is clearly recognizable. Who is doing whom the honor: is the heiress-directress honoring the painter-dictator or is he honoring her? I had the impression that very few were interested in such problems.

The times have changed. Don't they want to know what those who had sent the race of blond warriors, the massacred slaughterers, into the slaughterhouse, have made out of Wagner? Instead, they want to know what to make out of the unavoidable Wagner today.

Most of all, what to do with this *"tetralogy"* which dominates and is the "most sullied" of Wagner's entire work. If it weren't for the "Ring" the life of the directors would be simpler. Simpler, too, would be our relation to the culture which is nearest to us.

There was an elegant solution immediately after the war: Wieland Wagner's symbolic purge, the motionless forms of ageless and outcast myths. There was Joachim Herz's parsimonious, political solution for East Germany: he anchored the "Ring" to the

Schmidt* regime overcome domestic opposition, 112 Cruise and Pershing II missiles will be stationed in and around West German airbases. "Gateway Gardens" would be the arrival and distribution point for the new weapons, as well as a key command center. A few thousand trees cannot be allowed to stand in the way of these security needs.

II. Good citizens in revolt

We are not some wild bunch of looters, but people who want to continue to live well.
Speaker at a rally against Startbahn West.

We get out of the car in Mörfelden-Walldorf and walk through the town to the beginning of the woods. Mörfelden-Walldorf is a small suburban community, providing workers for the Frankfurt financial and service economy. We walk past small bungalows, the pride of West Germany's postwar working class, as well as more elaborate apartment complexes. The town is new, clean and orderly. The soccer team, sponsored by Ford Motor Company, jogs past us on their way to the well-manicured playing field near the woods.

A survey conducted by faculty and students from the Johann Wolfgang Goethe University at Frankfurt found that over 86% of the residents of Mörfelden-Walldorf were opposed to the Startbahn West expansion, and that 80% had engaged in some form of opposition. National church councils and municipal governments have passed resolutions against it. The project has also widened cracks within the ruling Social Democratic Party. In an open letter to the central government, a local SPD official wrote that the construction of the

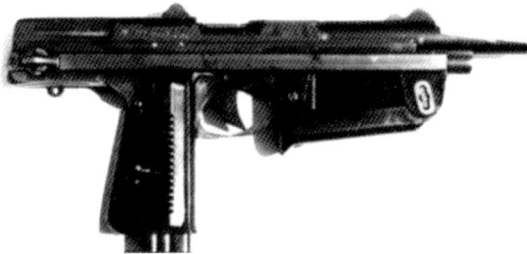

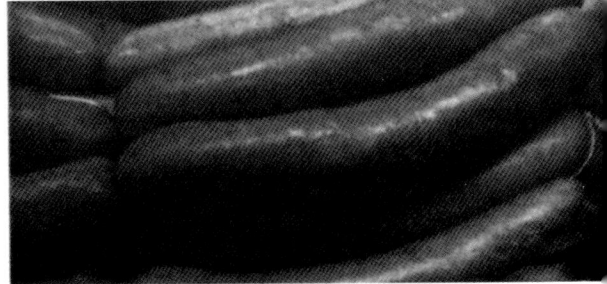

historic shores of the 1848 Revolution. And finally there was Peter Stein's "ingenious" solution,[1] discovering the enigma Wagner in the theater of the nineteenth century: his Walhalla was revealed as the center of dance of the Paris opera. In all of these solutions a direct encounter with Wagner's mythology, this inflammable, dangerous, and also somewhat ridiculous content, is avoided.

Boulez, Chereau and the scenic designer Peduzzi took a more daring approach. They wanted, quite correctly, to revive this mythology. Against all expectations the old guard of Bayreuth screamed of treason, whereas in reality it was a return to Wagner, the Wagner of the "music-drama," something that has to be clearly differentiated from opera. Back to the Wagner who wanted to give the nineteenth century a world of fantasy, who did not want a commemoration festival, but a celebration where every time the ritual was meant to be a new event.

Boulez is the strictest and most creative heir of the Vienna School, one of the most important representatives of that strong current which permeated and renewed all the art (and not only the music) of the nineteenth century; and there he stands conducting the "*tetralogy*" as if it were a matter of "accompanying" a scene full of noises, horrors and images. Some wondered about so much passion for musical structures devoted to such an iconography . . .

runway was based on a "false economics, strategically unnecessary, and ecologically catastrophic." Public opposition by party members has spread from the local level to regional and federal domains; expulsion proceedings against party dissidents have been initiated by the national leadership. Startbahn West has become a core test for the Social Democratic ruling coalition. Meanwhile, following the police attack in late October, demonstrations were held throughout West Germany pulling thousands of demonstrators into the streets — an opposition that is situated largely outside of the political parties.

The current popular movement or "Bürgerinitiative" (citizens' initiative) and its predecessors have already succeeded in delaying the project. First proposed in 1964, the project was tabled in 1968 after some 4,000 people signed a petition against it. Three years later, in 1971, the plan was publicized again; this time, 9,000 people signed a petition against it. Between 1971 and 1978, a period of "critical dialogue" was instituted in the hope that the authorities and the opposition could negotiate a settlement. However, in 1979 the dialogue was canceled and the Airport Authority announced its intention to begin construction on Startbahn West. On Easter Day, 1979, 3,000 people marched onto the Startbahn site to protest the decision. In October, 1980, fearing that construction was about to begin, a small group of activists occupied a space in the forest directly in the path of construction, establishing the Hüttendorf.

III. Responding obstacles

"The Hüttendorf is no longer the central point of the protest over Startbahn West. It has become more and more isolated."
Hessian Minister of the Interior Griese

And yet Boulez rediscovered the meaning of Wagner's "music-drama" by looking through the eyes of the music of the entire nineteenth century.

Accompaniment? Naturally, says Boulez, that is precisely what Wagner wanted. Of course, one has to know what kind of accompaniment. He conducts more clearly, brightly, more intelligently and more intelligibly than others. He did not bring the orchestra to this dimension merely to assign a supporting role to the music. On the contrary, the music wasn't meant to only underline, emphasize or announce what happens on the stage. Boulez took seriously Wagner's idea of a "drama" in which music and text do not repeat each other, do not both restate the same thing in their own way. Here the orchestra, the singing, the recitation, the rhythms of the music, the movements on the stage and the decor must come together as the basic elements in order to first constitute the time of the production, a unified form, a single moment.

Boulez thus acted on the simple fact that spectators aren't deaf and listeners aren't blind. When he attempts to let "everything" be sensed, he does so not to suggest to the ear what the eye can clearly see but because the dramatic development of the music is interwoven with that of the text. Boulez does not consider Wagner's leitmotiv to be a tonal doubling of the figure, a mere costume made out of notes. It is itself an *individuum*, albeit a musical one. Rather than a coined, repeatedly stamped out figure it is

186

As M. and I head into the woods, the terrain is flat and the entire forest is pine with a thick underbrush. The dirt roads stretch on for miles, crisscrossed every so often by other roads. Now, the two maps I had seen this morning begin to make sense.

The first map is the one reproduced in the four-color flyer deposited in every Frankfurt mailbox this weekend by the Airport Authority. The map shows an enormous area, from Frankfort in the north, to Rüsselsheim in the west, to Darmstadt in the south, to Dietzenbach in the east. The urban centers are shown in white. The spaces between the towns and cities — at least 80% of this map — are shown as green and empty. In the middle of this sea of green sits the Frankfurt Airport, colored baby blue like a lake in a natural wilderness.

The map and the articles in the flyer suggest that the Frankfurt Airport is a perfectly efficient machine, representing the best that West Germany can offer. It is a totally functional space, harmoniously embedded in the greater Rhine-Main region. The airport sits in the middle of the green map; its disruption would reverberate throughout the entire region's seemingly organic calm.

Startbahn West and its opponents are not mentioned, except to imply that that opposition represents a dangerous undercurrent to the stability of German society. Front page center is a letter from a spokesperson for the Airport Authority, Herr Theo Preis. With great concern he notes that the police have seen "molotov cocktails" being made, that they fear "hand to hand combat," and have seen demonstrators "building barricades and ditches," — "and this," he writes, as if standing cross-armed before the concerned good citizen with proof positive in hand, "this is called non-violent resistance." He warns

a flexible, ambiguous, extravagant structure, a developmental principle of a tonal world.

If the drama has to work itself out in the music, and if the music may not be reduced to a repetition of the drama, a conductor like Boulez is absolutely necessary: a conductor who analyzes, who dissects every moment with a scalpel — Nietzsche spoke about Wagner's "miniatures" — and who in every instant unfolds the increasingly complex dynamic of the work.

One has to have heard Boulez' interpretation on the last evening. One was reminded of what he once said about the "tetralogy": "Wagner's gigantic construction," his "intimate diary". Right up to the last pause, he constructs with extraordinary precision the enormous musical forest; it was as if Boulez had once again invoked his own way. It is also the whole movement of a century of modern music, which beginning with Wagner, found its way through the great adventure of the formal, and arrived at the intensity and movement of drama. The entirely deciphered form wove itself into the image.

One can again find in the "Ring" that tension characteristic of Chereau: an infallible logic in the relations between the characters, the perspicuity of all the elements of the text, a particular sensibility for every single movement and gesture, in brief, the absence of anything cheap linked with a desired uncertainty as far as time and place are concerned, an extreme diffusion of the elements of reality. The daughters of the Rhine are pro·

that "the political goals of these elements are very suspect" and implants the keyword for fear: "Could not," he asks, "these actions be described as terrorist, at least in the widest sense?" What conclusion is a good citizen to draw?

The second map, actually an aerial photograph, is reproduced in the citizens' initiative newspaper, *Umwelt Express.* Super-imposed upon the map, which includes the area from Frankfurt to Mörfelden-Walldorf, is the outline of the Startbahn West expansion with a black dot indicating the location of the Hüttendorf. On this map, Startbahn West looks like a blunt intrusion into nature, rather than an organic, functional ornament. The space which the Airport Authority showed as green and empty looks on this one to be filled with urban and industrial concrete, not a sea of tranquility in the landscape of Modell Deutschland.

As we walk out to the Hüttendorf, we are surrounded by others heading the same way. Most of them are university and high school students but there is a solid representation of middle strata German families with young children in bright slickers and boots together with a number of older couples dressed in gray and green, knickers and long socks. It takes over an hour to get to the demonstration site.

Actually, this is the second rally of the day; earlier in Mörfelden-Walldorf 20,000 people had gathered to protest the latest efforts to build Startbahn West. A few days before, police and construction crews had been sent out to begin work on a road which had to be diverted in preparation for the runway. Before construction could begin, 3,000 "obstacles" — children, old folks, students, unionists, ministers, leftists — had to be removed.

stitutes who hang their clothes on a nail. The old bespectacled Jew Mime digs in his trunks to find the holy sword wrapped in newspaper. The gods pace back and forth like exiled princes of a melancholy eighteenth century or like members of the family of a bankrupt company. The Valkyrie has a helmet whereas Siegfried dares to wear tails. The same goes for Peduzzi's scenery: big, immobile architectures collapsed like eternal ruins, gigantic wheels that nothing could set in motion again. But the wheels stand in the heart of a forest, two busts of angels on the hills, and an imperturbable Dorian capital on the walls of Walhalla over the Valkyrie's fire bed, or in the Nibelungen palace, which sometimes resembles a small harbor painted by Claude Lorrain, other times the neoclassicist palaces of the Wilhelminian bourgeoisie.

Not that Chereau and Peduzzi, like Brecht, might have wanted to play with various time references (the epoch to which the work refers, in which it was written, in which it was produced). They, too, took Wagner seriously, even at the cost of having to show the opposite of what Wagner wanted to show. Wagner wanted to give the nineteenth century a mythology? Very well. Did he choose to assemble it from Indo-European legends? Fine. Did he thus want to give his epoch the world of images which it lacked? It is precisely at this point that Chereau's "realization" intervenes.

The nineteenth century was full of images which were the true reason for those

There was no fighting, no violence; the demonstrators went limp when the police approached. The removal took on an almost festive atmosphere as the police spent the entire day removing the squatters. When the police finished their business, police civil engineers supervised the construction of a concrete wall several hundred meters long topped with barbed wire. The rallies today are to protest the wall. We all expect that the rally at the wall will simply be a continuation of this morning's affair.

As we approach the site, it is clear that the atmosphere has changed dramatically. First we see three police with automatic weapons standing atop a mound of dirt, surveying all who approach. Overhead, a helicopter persistently buzzes the area. We cross over a couple of ditches constructed by the Hüttendorf squatters and walk around barricades of logs and brush. We walk past dozens of tents put up within the past few days, a kind of suburban addition to the Hüttendorf proper. Finally, past the tents are the thousands of demonstrators and the wall. Spraypainted on the wall are slogans: "Wall of Shame," "the second German wall," and "Here is the boundary of German democracy." While the helmeted police stand at attention behind the wall, the water cannon begins spraying the crowd with CN gas.

IV. Hüttendorf

We walk back into the woods along with hundreds of others moving away from the water cannon and gas. A steady stream of people is headed up to the wall with logs for the barricades, dry clothing, and water to rinse gas from the eyes. We come into the village and walk towards the central gathering place.

great mythological reconstructions, which they changed and concealed. Chereau did not want to elevate the bazaar of Wagnerian mythology into the sky of eternal myths, nor did he want to reduce it to concrete historical reality. He wanted to unearth those true images which lent power to the invented ones.

Thus Chereau dug out the images buried under Wagner's text. Desperate images: utopian fragments, machine parts, social types, the waste of luxury towns, children dragons, Strindberg scenes, the profile of a ghetto Jew. But his successful "tour de force" lies in the perfect integration of all these elements into the tense dramatics of personal relations and the embodiment of the broad, picturesque visions suggested by Peduzzi. Chereau's production is always humorous, never malevolent. He does not say, "Wagner's mythology was nothing more than a narcotic for the successful bourgeoisie." He subjects all this material to a metamorphosis of beauty and to the power of dramatic tension. In a certain sense he thus descends from Wagner's mythology to the bustling images which populated it and recreates for us a new myth out of them, while simultaneously showing their paradoxical splendor and disagreeable logic.

On the stage of Bayreuth, where Wagner wanted to create a mythology for the nineteenth century, Chereau and Peduzzi again resurrected the world of images of that cen- **189**

It is a remarkable site, no "tent village'" as the Associated Press later described it. There are sixty wooden buildings in the village, made of logs from the forest. There are three tree huts in addition to a tower which has full view of the village and demonstration.

Around the central "square" are the church, library, community center, information center, medical clinic, daycare center, printing press room, and broadcast hut for the contraband radio of the resistance, "Radio Luftikus." There are huts constructed by members of the citizens' initiatives, by the Young Socialists, by faculty and students of both the university and high school, even one from the Youth Union of the Christian Democrats. The Hüttendorf is a meeting space for people who have never been involved in an oppositional movement before, as well as for veterans of the last fifteen years. A survey in nearby communities found that 70% of those responding approved of the Hüttendorf occupation.

After it had become clear that the police would not immediately take action to clear the site, the squatters were confronted with the problem of how to deal with long stretches of inactivity and the resulting resignation and apathy. The Hüttendorf was then transformed into a living space with a history and a meaning, rather than simply a base from which to confront the State.

"Live alternatively," a slogan for the Hüttendorf, differs from the call to resistance put forth by the citizens' initiatives, the desire to "continue to live well." As in the Berlin squatters' struggle, the demand put out by the Hüttendorf squatters is for a particular kind of space: social space, collective space, magic space, space which allows for the integration of alternative living and alternative working. Moreover, behind the living space of the Hüttendorf is

tury which Bakunin probably shared with Marx, Dickens, Jules Verne, Boecklin, the architects of bourgeois factories and villas, with the illustrators of childrens books, and the agents of anti-semitism. These images appear to them as mythology, closely related to the one dominating us today. Thus they give the fantasy of the nineteenth century, whose mark we still bear in our wounds, the terrifying magnitude of a mythology. From Wagner up to today Boulez spanned the thread of contemporary musical development. Simultaneously, Chereau and Peduzzi let the Wagnerian *universa* ascend into the firmament of a mythology, which we must recognize as ours. Thanks to the rediscovered contemporaneity of his music, Wagner's mythology doesn't first have to be painfully translated for us, for it is part of our own.

Wolfgang Wagner asked himself on the last evening of this "Ring" what other "Ring" may still be possible. If that cannot be known, it is because Bayreuth is no longer that conservatorium of a mythically ever identical Wagner — the tradition, as we know, is nothing but "neglect." Bayreuth will finally be the place where Wagner himself will be treated as one of our contemporary myths. □

Translated by Alex Susteric

1. Peter Stein is theater director at the "Schaubühne" in West Berlin.

the Frankfurt "Alternative Scene." Criticized for its theoreticism by the new squatters' movement, the Frankfurt "Scene" offers a variety of clubs, cafes, meeting places, journals, newspapers, collectives producing goods and services, communes providing a variety of living spaces. Capable of mobilizing a few thousand people onto the streets in a matter of hours, it provides a social context in which experimentation, aging, working and politics can occur.

Despite potential sources of shear and tension between the alternative movements and the citizens' initiatives, the insistent intransigence of the German State has created conditions under which an alliance can be sustained, while the Hüttendorf has come to represent something more than mere opposition to the State. It is a gathering space for a new combination of social forces. As a positive statement of *how* to live, the Hüttendorf has made it that much more difficult for the State to dissipate the power of Startbahn West opposition by labeling one group as legal and the other as criminal.

V. "Kriminelle, Chaoten, und Asoziale."

Since I've been here, I've learned what 'Chaoten' really means: nothing. I am also a 'Chaoten.'
Woman living with her daughter and grandson at the Hüttendorf

As the police begin their attack in earnest at the wall, two or three thousand people have gathered in the village. Every few minutes a report comes over the loudspeaker reporting on the latest moves by the police or requesting dry clothes, food, or water for the demonstrators. The police apparently intend to clear the space near the wall and to knock the tower down. They do not intend to seize the village, at least not today.

"The wall of history is totally visible here. I'd rather see it that way than hidden in people's minds."

Sylvère Lotringer

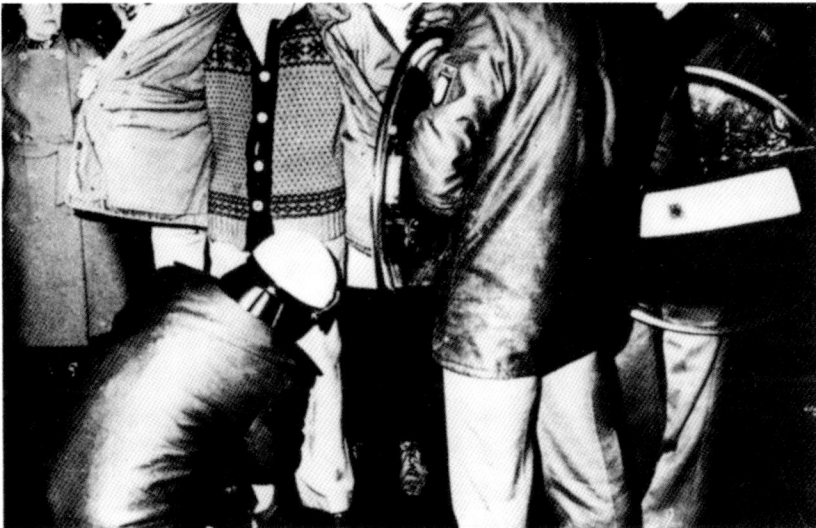

Most of the people now in the village are young, but there are hundreds of children and older people. A man in traditional gray and green dress takes photographs while a cluster of gray-haired couples quietly discuss what is happening around them. The authorities would have us believe that these people are "Kriminelle, Chaoten und Asoziale." "Certainly," Minister Gries had been quoted earlier, "the peaceful demonstrators of the citizens' initiatives want nothing to do with these elements."

Unfortunately for Gries, among the forty to fifty civilian injuries in the afternoon a sixty-five year-old man suffered massive internal bleeding, a seventy-year old man sustained a serious concusssion, and one report, never officially corroborated, stated that a fourteen year-old girl died two weeks later from injuries received at the Startbahn. At a rally in Frankfurt the following weekend, one speaker flatly stated: "The police action on last Sunday constituted an open ecological civil war against an entire region."

VI. "Grünes Licht."

"If they try to clear this, there's going to be a four year war until the runway gets built."   Resident of Mörfelden-Walldorf

On October 23rd, 1981 *Frankfurter Rundschau* reported that the Hessian Minister of Finance, Klaus Jürgen Hoffie, had given the "green light" for Startbahn West. Construction was to be completed in 1984. In response, the mayor of Mörfelden-Walldorf, Bernhard Brehl, stated that the decision was a "perversion of justice, and a total disregard of the parliamentary process at the local level."

HERBERT RÖTTGEN

Mythology In Revolution?

Q: Your press's program has changed. To what extent does that reflect personal changes in you?

HR: We make the assumption now that consciousness determines being, rather than the reverse. We have taken seriously something that's been a flourishing part of our literature for a long time: what gypsies, shamans, Indians say, and what was also

This piece is part of a series of articles and interviews published in 1981 by *die tageszeitung* (or "TAZ"), the leftist daily newspaper from Berlin. It exemplifies what has become of the idea of revolution one decade after the anti-authoritarian movement peaked in Germany.

On November 2nd, orders were given to the police to begin the elimination of the Hüttendorf. Within two days, the site had been cleared. For five nights running, thousands of people filled the streets of Frankfurt, shutting down the railway station, blocking traffic on the autobahn, and disrupting services at the Airport. In mid-November, 125,000 people gathered in the Hessian capital city of Wiesbaden as representatives of the citizens' initiatives formally presented their petition calling for a popular referendum on Startbahn West. Willy Brandt,* representing the national leadership of the Social Democratic Party, arrived in Wiesbaden to ensure that the Hessian branch did not delay the Startbahn West project. The petitions were rejected — the runway, SPD leaders said, was a matter of overriding national importance.

Green light to steam shovel the obstacles; the obstacles sit tight. □

discussed by the Left, for example in *Dreamtime* by Hans-Peter Dürr[1]. We believe that an altered consciousness initiates significant changes in point of view and political ideas.

Q: What you write in the *Dances on the Volcano*,[2] for instance, shows a queasiness about the path the Left has taken: psychologizing, too much self-criticism, too much energy spent in the discussion about relationships and communes.

HR: That was probably the decisive point. In philosophical terms, you can call it the spread of negative thinking. I'll give two examples: Buddha says there are people who always talk about sickness, and so they'll never be healthy. And in the *Dialectics of the Enlightenment*, Adorno says that it's not only material interests and psychological power which bind people to the system; it's also overpowering psychic suggestion. I think one becomes a monster oneself if one constantly stares at a monster. In the Left, people no longer know what they're fighting for, they only know what they're fighting against: against nuclear power plants, against problems in relating, etc. It's also a basic law of magical thinking that one develops ideas one can see, feel, smell and touch. Magic for me doesn't mean leaving the social network, but developing the five senses. If we don't succeed now in finding a connection with something — images, myths, traditions — then we are left with the same old miserable complaints: that we've made mistakes, that we live under repression.

193

HUGO BÜTRER

From The Pleasure Principle
to the Wolves' Philosophy

"We want everything!"
Herbert Röttgen

Surely people who assert that the violent rebellion of 1980 was the expression of a "speechless" young generation are missing the essence of the new "movement." It may be true that quite a few camp followers are speechless and politically ignorant, that they lack social consciousness. These young ones are easy to recruit for kicking up a row or antagonizing the police; but they would never on their own stage a tough revolution, let alone carry it out the way it was carried out in Zurich and elsewhere (Bremen, Amsterdam, Freiburg, etc.). Even if a search for explanations could give us some small satisfaction, it would apply only to camp followers, to those who as an afterthought get on board "events" set in motion by others; it merely lists the eternal returns of historical youth phenomena and relies on the old maxim: young people have a right to be boisterous and crazy.

Hugo Bütrer is a journalist for the *Neue Zuricher Zeitung*, an influential conservative Swiss daily paper. This article is an intelligent analysis of the roots of the youth revolt written by a partisan of law and order.

Meanwhile, the discourse between the sexes has become very destructive. The definition and perception of oppositions was necessary in order to dismantle the structure of repression in relationships, but the time has come when people could get together again because women have now reached positions, also in terms of their consciousness, which make a balance between the sexes possible. That's one meaning of the Dianus head on our program: it means a state beyond patriarchal, but also beyond matriarchal, forms of consciousness.

This hang up on oppression, the constant concentration on what's doing us in, robs us of the possibility of living fully. In his book *Only the Tribes Will Survive*, Vine Deloria blamed the failure of the hippie movement on its inability to find a link with a tradition. It couldn't integrate similar historical or mythical movements of rebellion into itself, it didn't take up its historical connection with heretics, gypsies, and Albigensians. They reasoned, discussed, and psychologized about it, but no vital connection was established. The history of witches has suffered a similar fate. I always read about the history of the oppression of witches and rarely that they were also a very positive counter-force.

Q: Your current program includes many non-European texts; why this exoticism? Is it hard for instance to find German texts?

HR: Yes, it always is. But it's also been a principle since the Middle Ages that you have

In fact, we cannot dismiss all these events as a mere youth phenomenon. You can see and hear too many things that point to a provocation and subversion not at all specifically youth-related. In a certain kind of left-wing literature there are plenty of premises, explanations, parallels, theories and suggestions, preludes and examples for the present confrontation. I will discuss the mentalities which in the recent disturbances can be grasped and seen behind the active core's commissions and omissions.

One Strand of the Alternative Movement

Claudia Mast, in her *Departure for Paradise*, offers a useful survey of the "alternative movement's" motley colors and many faces into which after 1970 the energies of the 1968 anti-authoritarian departure have flown and branched out. No matter how different the names, the themes, the lifestyles of the blessed islands searched for, how contradictory and antagonistic the views and their basic individual and social motivations: they all meet somewhere in a longing to get out of a "model society," to try life in a "counter-society," to live in a "counterculture" or "alternative culture." This, by the way, reflects the theoretical parlance which originated in Italy around 1977 when the Italian Communist Party was steering for the "historic compromise" and the autonomous opposition felt abandoned; later, after the autonomous Left's "Tunix" Congress in Berlin in 1978, these terms became the rage in German-speaking countries.

Seeking to build their own happiness, to find a "different life," has always been the dream of imaginative people, whether their name was Robinson Crusoe or Thoreau. The liberal postulate, ever-present since the Enlighten-

to go abroad to learn that there are other ways of living. Craftsmen, mystics, knights and travelling scholars did that. So the path to the Indians, to the East Indians, to the Africans, and to the archaic cultures is a necessary one. We have to use the distance we gain to reanimate our experiences.

Q: Do you have any comments on the ecology movement?

HR: We're very concerned with ecology. Shamanism gives us a very close connection with nature. But we don't see that in terms of party politics; small jumping-off points are more important to us than long articles about it. We also published Stan Steiner's book *The Decline of the White Man*, about the Hopis. It's a hardhitting political book about the debate in the U.S. Congress over nuclear power plants, the destruction of nature, but its starting point is prophecies, myths, and the continuity of life. The political ecology movement doesn't develop these connections, it can't give us back myth.

Q: You talk about the authority of myth. Isn't it a matter of pursuing politics in a personal, voluntary way?

HR: Yes, that too. I don't believe there is such a thing as the ego. We are also the space and the world of ideas and images we live in, and everything that surrounds us. Myth is certainly a part of our soul and is something in us, as Jung pointed out, but it's also the

ment, of achieving your own, free living space, is not necessarily tied to rejecting society; the "alternative man," whether he breeds sheep in the mountains or lives in an urban collective of small artisans, always remains in a kind of exchange relationship with his social environment.

Unmistakably, however, many have found shelter in the alternative movement's winding and crooked lanes who consider "getting off" a political breakaway, who repudiate an achievement-oriented, capitalistically organized society, a liberally organized State, in fact any State, and who wish to totally restructure the State. This is obviously what the "autonomous" groups which here and elsewhere inspired the 1980 revolt keep busy with.

Taking Leave from Fixations and Pure Dogma

One of the characteristics of the new "movement" is, of course, their absolute refusal to get fixated on anything — on either external or internal structures. So, to begin with, a temporary assessment suggests itself: locating the movement where it finds political sympathies. This plainly means that it belongs in the general area of the extreme Left. There have been numerous expressions of assent and support coming from the neo-Left wing of the Socialist Party, from the Trotskyists, from the "Vörwarts" Communists, from "independent" neo-Marxists of diverse shadings, all of whom apparently feel an affinity with the events triggered by the "movement," even if at first, now and then, there was a certain feeling of surprise and something like connection difficulties. Among other reasons, for organized Marxists these difficulties result from the fact that the "movement" acts just as autonomously facing those established left extremists as facing bourgeois ways of life and political ways of

world we see, or rather the world we want to see. One key idea is that myth doesn't separate the subjective and the objective, but places them in relation to each other. I encounter myth in the outer world too, in a tree and so on, it blends with my subjectivity. For us, the spiritual path that leads inward is not the only correct one; that's why we have trouble with spiritual movements. We don't want to evade the world, or our sensuality, or even conflict; that's why we're misunderstood by the spiritual and leftist movements. The spiritual movement says you have to withdraw from the world into yourself, and I even know some people who read our press's books and have no connection with the world whatsoever. We want to take up the world, in all its fullness. In leftist jargon on the other hand, we're withdrawing to inwardness. Historically, also, that's not the case at all. Except for the short phase of rationalism which we're in now, there were numerous revolutionary movements which were matrixed in a cosmic consciousness. Whether they succeeded or not, what matters is that the people weren't done in, they still felt pride and strength. I'm not opposed to the struggle, but I want to give it back the epic dimension that the samurai or the bandit chief had. But even a warrior has the right to withdraw.

Q: Myth also has a strongly emotional character that makes it hard to grasp rationally. Fascism too used mythologies. How can you avoid the danger of fascism?

organizing, even though it shares the claim of doing revolutionary work with organized way-out-left groups (and, like them, likes to revile the Social Democrats as the historical party of treason).

Antipsychiatry and Revolution of Desire

What does that total autonomy amount to? Although today both the historical and the recent literature of anarchism are having a boom in the neo-Left crowd and carry considerable fascination, what we have here is not just a resurrection of the old antagonism between Marx and Bakunin, between totalitarian and libertarian socialists. The core of the "movement" derives a vigorous consciousness of itself and of its autonomy from two recent developments: from a negative experience, the self-barricading of Western-European organized Marxism, and from recent trends in a left-wing psychiatry that has been politicized — you might say an "antipsychiatry."

The most pointed criticism of "really existing communism," of the Gulags produced by it, and of Marxism as a "State science" (André Glucksman) was of course offered by the autonomous neo-Left in France and Italy. As Félix Guattari's pamphlet, *Desire and Revolution*, justly observed, their denunciation used the background of the Left's own May 1968 experiences "and the way the desires and fantasies produced at the time had subsequently hardened into party programs and sectarian ideologies." On the other hand, antipsychiatrists like Guattari and Deleuze, like Laing and Cooper, have contributed to this autonomous movement a wealth of concepts and notions which in turn are bent on dissolving hierarchic societal organizations, tradi-

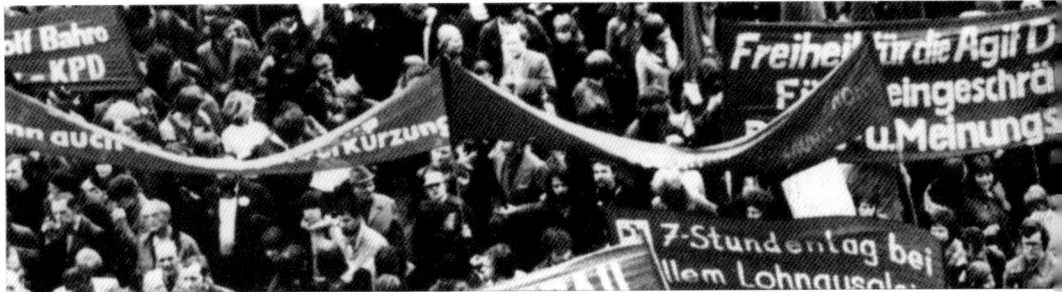

HR: The myth of fascism doesn't present any danger to us. What's dangerous is a leftist movement that doesn't take up a myth and thus ousts emotionally from the movement. Fascism was a union of myth and technocracy, centralism and military apparatus, whose content was not exactly individuality and the destruction of central structures. We talk about folk myth in the sense that we want mythological thinking to bear fruit again in a local sense, in relation to a landscape, in the relations I have with other people, and that's as far from fascism as it could be.

Q: In *Dances on the Volcano* you write: "Myth is a form of emotional thinking . . . it is the only means revolutionary politics has to evoke enthusiasm in the masses again . . ."

HR: I wrote that four years ago. Today I no longer count on the masses. For me it's just an historical insight that myth was a driving force in mass movements, whether communist or fascist. I don't like the concept "masses" any more either, those were remnants of my old political thinking. Basically I am more interested in individuals.

Q: Myth refers back to a past which isn't present to people; that makes your ideas hard to transmit.

HR: The movement also makes its own myths, but they don't stay in our awareness like Till Eulenspiegel.[3] There are Fritz Teufel and Jerry Rubin, but there are so few images, no

tional family structures, bourgeois attitudes, bourgeois ways of thinking, and, last but not least, of speaking.

The New Subjectivism

Desire and Revolution: in the new movement the combination of these two terms in a way replaces the old twin pair of Capitalism and Revolution. Instead of a rational, theoretical analysis of the "class enemy" in which they used to get stuck and locked in, we now have speaking-out and, wherever possible, immediate abreaction of the subjective desire directed against the hated "system" — those very desires which are susceptible to assail (*unterlaufen*, to rush the enemy from below, a favorite action verb of the "movement") and destroy the behavior norms set by the liberal achievement society.

The Paris psychiatrist Guattari, for a long time active in the communist Left opposition, is the main author of the idea, meant to be subversive, that by skillfully and collectively linking the libidinous desires of many individuals into a "revolution machine," you can gradually topple the capitalist achievement society, which allegedly is built on the suppression of desire.

This crowd, then, considers the Russian-October-type revolution a failure, and does not count on the "long march through the institutions." Rather than thinking up great Marxist-rational revolutionary strategies, they now endeavor — taking up the fashionable *rhizome* metaphor — to "build networks, dig multiple canals, to create an environment, to occupy nooks and crannies, to assail the State, to crumble it . . ." Such a concern gets condensed into vivid images and slogans like the one that says: let's make the State into cucumber salad.

legends, hardly any anecdotes, just hard political discourse. Reality is seen with such seriousness that one is overpowered and disoriented and adopts its structures. The monsters which are approaching us are more ridiculous than we think. There are new attempts to revive the tradition of the jokesters like Till Eulenspiegel, irony, laughter. Till lived in a much more brutal society, all the members of his family were tortured, and still he brought irony and a positive attitude into society. □

Translated by Ruth Crowley

1. Hans-Peter Duerr, *Dreamtime*, published in 1979, focuses on the borderline between civilization and savagery.
2. Herbert Röttgen, *Dances on the Volcano* (Vulkantänze), published in 1978, examines the new perspectives of the Left at the end of the 70's.
3. Till Eulenspiegel, popular rascal of 15th century Germany.

Looking Toward Italy

Resembling the Zurich events, but as early as 1976, norm-destroying behavior (such as the collective clearing out, on a hot summer day, of a wine shop or hotel bar, evidently responding to the "desire" for a free-of-charge thirst quencher) had been practiced after the "autonomia's" failed assault on La Scala and the subsequent traffic chaoticization in Milan; euphemistically, the originators called their own vandalism *"spesa proletaria,"* proletarian shopping. The latest *Stilett*, in a reflection on revolutionary counter-violence, flatly justifies looting and "swipe-ins" as "collective, spontaneous expropriations of the exploiters; you take what is yours and fulfill your childhood dreams."

To be sure, we should not overstrain parallels nor disregard certain genuine, expressive features of the Zurich rebellion. But in many ways it is instructive to compare Zurich with Italy: with the Italian autonomists and "urban Indians," with their dirty language, with Radio Alice in Bologna ("sense-negating" and subversive in the way it practiced communication, eventually picked off by the police), with their nihilistic and heavy-profound motto samplers on the wall and their confrontation with the State.

A Seeming Refusal to Organize

When a psychiatrist (and socialist politician), right in the midst of the Zurich debates, publishes a defense speech for the Pleasure Principle and against the Rationality Principle, there is an objective and positive relation to the "revolution of desire" discussed above. The "movement's" structurelessness and leaderlessness, asserted with an astonishing obstinacy, is

related to the sujectivity of the pleasure principle, which allegedly leaves any "action" to the will of individual members of the movement. No chief ideologist, no Party Central Committee is supposed to say: Thou shalt. Rather, the "movement" is supposed to appear as an expression of individuals, standing side by side, having equal rights; none of them can, or ought to, direct the other one, let alone represent him in face of the outside world. Hence the mania for plenary meetings — which actually are the power instrument of the "autonomous" core — and hence the refusal to designate any proper spokesmen or delegations assigned to negotiate. Hence, too, the term "movement," which deliberately is meant to suggest that there is nothing rigid or committed to any course of action, that everything is in flux.

The concept of a free-and-easy movement, without a structure, without a central point, without the exact ideological boundary line that distinguishes all Marxist revolutionary parties, serves to enable everyone freely to join the "revolution of desire." No one has to enlist in, let alone submit to, a "revolutionary party." The person who asks for an alternative is presented with a freedom of nothingness, a nihilist freedom. (Certainly the revolutionaries who are tightly organized would, if the occasion arose, know at once how to make use of this freedom. In fact, Marxist discussion is already striving to appropriate and incorporate into its cause individual subjectivity, the human "emotions" which it used to neglect.)

"Prisoners" liberating themselves.

Abolishing boundaries, melting the "pack ice," having the "streams of desire flowing freely": these concepts throw additional light on the new

"The real enemy today is less external than internal: our own armaments, our own scientific power, which promote the end of our society."

Paul Virilio

HANS PETER DUERR

Savage Ethnology

Helmut Krauch: You want to readmit savagery. But we already have that as waves of gluttony, intoxication and sex. We also already have ways of seeing another reality. Mind-altering drugs are ingested regularly by a large number of people, and then anything goes. Isn't the desire to cast off restraints innate in men?

Hans Peter Duerr: In my latest book, *Traumzeit* (Dream Time), I described a ritual of the Bokweri of Cameroon mountain in which the women, representing the entire society, go wild by changing into mermaids. Because they consciously go wild, they are not helpless victims of the "OUTSIDE." When an ethnologist asked Nyakusa why she per-

---

200 Hans Peter Duerr, a political anthropologist popular within the Movement, is the German counterpart of Pierre Clastres in France.

formed such violent rituals, she answered, "If we don't do that, we'll all go crazy."

K: What do you mean by that?

D: That it's not enough to simply go wild. It's much more a matter of establishing a rational relationship with the "OTHER SIDE," your own savagery, not by repressing it but by looking it squarely in the face. Our culture has not understood the dialectic between civilization and savagery. More precisely it has sacrificed the dialectic for a dualism. Someone who rationalizes and civilizes without limit must create a destructive savagery in himself or others. I know Positivists and Marxists who, for years, dilligently tried to structure the convulsions of their brains properly, and then suddenly they short-circuited. They fled to the local brothel and got themselves fucked physically and intellectually. If savagery is restrained, then it bursts forth as soon as the restraints are removed.

K: What's your opinion on the idea that this society markets every change of consciousness and co-opts every form of "alternative," from Shamanism to revolution?

D: Perhaps you should not overstrain the concept of society as an all-devouring Moloch. That's typical of intellectuals. I do think that there are changes in the Western world, if only subtle ones.

201

rebellion's self-comprehension. Their theoreticians start out from a supposition which is totally self-indulgent and wrong both in terms of social psychology and individual psychology and which says that, all things considered, every tie, every structure, every hierarchy, and every situation of order implies limitation, loss of freedom, compulsion. The English anti-psychiatrist David Cooper, for one, goes as far as to maintain that there is a fitting symbol of our social situation and of the powers that rule it: the most appalling instances of mental institutions with their straitjackets are such a symbol; so is the Soviet Gulag, which in more sophisticated form reappears in the mental institutions of the capitalist societies and their "dissidents." The "ruling powers" are denounced as originators of the inmates' insanity; in fact they themselves are said to suffer from repressive insanity — an example of the reverse-mirror-image argument, so popular in the "movement" crowd, used as foremost weapon in the campaign to "suggestively deprive the counterpowers of their power." This outlook ends up characterizing the powers of our society as the "lock-up system" (Michel Foucault) which day after day "chains up" the individuals' world of desires, and flatly putting down "existantial reality" as "societal pokey."

Breaking out of this "prison" is said to be the "movement's" meaning; you could hear it from many a Zurich teen-ager. In an easy next step, this revolution is called an outright war of liberation — *"distruzione e liberazione,"* they said in Italy.

The Hard Kernel and the Good Soil

In one of the essays, *The Iridescent Revolt*, it is stated that there is a breaking-up of "the rigid social structures" in the groups "which make

K: Your book seems to proclaim something: how you can achieve greater happiness.

D: Nietzsche said, "You ran too fast for happiness. Now that you're exhausted, happiness can catch up with you." It's obvious that most of us run much too fast and I don't just mean the people who rush to the store and the TV, I also include the people who chase wildly after liberating ideas and ideal modes of existence, with their attending gurus. It is not a matter of getting something or striving for it, but rather losing something. Until recently we were all victims of an ideology which convinced us that the evolution of civilization since the New Stone Age brought us closer to happiness, well-being and truth. I'm convinced that's not true. Look at us in our concrete shafts, "by the sweat of our brows," with hassle and coldness, or our scientists who level a colourful, multifaceted reality to a gray, lifeless slush, to presumptuous theories and boring books. And then read *Kalahari Hunters and Gatherers,* a recent collection of essays describing the lives of bush people. No, our trip into today's civilization wasn't worth it for mankind.

K: If we abolish our constraints, then we must also abolish many institutions, like insurance which reduces fear and uncertainty.

D: Hunters gather firewood without getting a hernia. They only work a few hours per day

themselves into carriers of their own desire;" that in the groups "we have to create the preconditions for an analysis of desire, which at the same time will be the analysis of the desire of the masses;" that the "movement of March 22" exemplifies "the prototype of a subject group" which was "the center of all activities" without laying claim to a closed totalization which would carry the germ of division.

The book on "Indians and P.38" in Italy deals most interestingly with the role of the "small group" which, in a sort of intangible, slovenly rascals' autonomy, organizes the "crystallization of desire" of those youngsters, unemployed, students, and women who later on were to be the "good soil" of the movement. Of course "malcontents" of all kinds are the most suitable to be the "good soil" from which the "kernel" is to sprout: the ones with unfulfilled desires, flipped-out apprentices, harassed students, drug-haunted teen-agers, the unemployed, those suffering from civilization and its anxieties, frustrated minorities, homosexuals, all sorts of drop-outs or potential drop-outs, in short people who are in trouble with the ethical norms established in private and in public and who share a latent readiness to assail them.

There is no need to emphasize that the vicissitudes suffered by these followers of the "movement" reflect an entire spectrum of more or less weighty problems of our society, difficulties that, at least in spots, indisputably exist; the public at large should pay attention to them for their own sake and also in order to deprive the "kernel" of its "good soil."

Where the revolutionary "movement" renounces giving clear reasons for its activities, it has to expect all sorts of inner contradictions. So their inspirators see them as an ideological potpourri, as an "iridescent revolt," where

and are much healthier than farmers who look down on them as savages. And when they sit around the camp fire in the evening, they don't write about Dream Time, they tell about it, and sometimes they surrender themselves to it, like the Australians. The fear and insecurity we know today in such large quantities are the result of our settling down. Then you had your back to the wall from harvest to harvest, planting to planting, people became warriors, they separated into classes, etc. You know the rest.

K: What are you for? Should we ask the police to turn their service caps into little boats for playing games? Should the security people pick the buttercups? Should federal judges practice levitation?

D: I don't believe in a return to the hunter's lifestyle — for most of us, such a regression would be catastrophic because we need the products of civilization, rulers, subordinates. The path to ever-increasing complexity, consumerism, blind rationality, subordinating nature, etc. was the wrong path — and still is. The lifestyles of hunters and gatherers illustrate the point that it wasn't always that way and didn't need to be that way.

K: What good does that do us?

D: It shows us where we should stop, if possible get out. I think many people today find

from Freud to Nietzsche, from the anarcho-syndicalist theoretician Georges Sorel to Jean Genet's or Charles Bukowski's poesies of dirt and off-scourings, there is room for anything, anything goes, not excluding — in fact deliberately including — fascistoid impulses.

Celebrating the Irrational

The ideologists of the new non-spirit go back to these elements, from which in his time Mussolini the anarcho-socialist drew sustenance, even when they reject the old Führer-and-follower myths and instead advocate a merry polytheism, which in its practical application results in a motley phenomenon of subversive guerrillas operating with violence exactly as with fun and comedy. In this context Herbert Röttgen and Florian Rabe's *Dances on the Volcano*,[1] offers an informative self-comprehension about the mentalities behind the new rebellion. The myth of the Dionysian, of a wild life, of an uprising against all barriers of reason, and of State and society has been resurrected; myths, images, emotions, the animal in us, in short the irrational, are ruthlessly played off not just against a cold rationality but against intelligent experiences gathered in life. Of course, intelligent people would not suppress their feelings and emotions; but using their personal and political experience, they keep them under a certain control. Here, however, consciousness and intelligence are debased outright into "transportation vehicles to unleash drive."

Unleasing the drives means, among other things, unleashing aggression and violence. A theoretician of the iridescent revolt asserts that in our practice we have to assail the Christian-humanistic antithesis of spirit and violence;

"Habermas engaged in a harsh public critique of the student movement and denounced it as "left fascist."

Marlis Krüger

the chatter about freedom from the powers of production, about socialistic atomic reactors for the good of the working class, etc. unbearable. And therefore, you shouldn't underestimate the roles other lifestyles can play. Every revolt needs its myths.

K: Most journalists like your new book — many are very enthusiastic about it. Specialists have been reticent so far, while some freaks are unexpectedly unhappy with you. Could it be that the journalists are attracted by the humor you use to criticize the scholars, and the freaks are disappointed because you combine, too often, weighty scholarship with recipes for witches' brews and herbal cures?

D: I only want to comment on the freaks. You know that I don't have much sympathy for the Positivists (Marxist and non-Marxist) or for the chicanery found in Hegel seminars. I'm particularly unsympathetic toward the irrationality of those who, without changing, venerate Don Juan today as they venerated Marx just five or six years ago. I know people who were in favor in 1969 who turned their noses up at me and gave each other knowing looks, because I carried a black flag instead of a red one. These people accuse me today of being a university type, because I like to sit in libraries reading old books. They say I'm not radical enough. Well, that's true. I'm not a radical. So what! If people imagine I am and am not, that's their problem, not mine.

others refer to "the wall-eyed Frenchman" (Sartre) or to Jean Genet, who pits violence and life, almost as synonyms, against the power of the State which operates, sometimes overtly but mostly as a "secret omnipotence which reaches all the way into man's soul." Thoroughly assimilating this absurd-destructive antithesis, the local movement's core has integrated violence and militancy into its self-comprehension.

By now the "discretionary philosophy" ("nothing is true, anything goes") is shifting into what the ethnological promoter of the new anarchist way of thinking, Hans Peter Duerr, lately has called "the wolves' favorite philosophy." The issue of the Right of the Strongest, of protecting the weaker, of protecting the sheep from the wolves, sneaks in through the back door.

The Need to Have a Police

The Zurich philosopher of science, P.K. Feyerabend in plain terms named the problem and the solution which no society has ever gotten around: "The problem now is: How does one prevent one group from entrenching upon the desires of others? For, after all, the desires have to be circumscribed. Not everything can be permitted. War lovers, for instance, must not be allowed to force peace-loving people into their war games." Since Feyerabend does not see much of a chance of educating people to pure humaneness without paying the price, too bitter, of spiritual self-chastisement, he endorses the following solution: "I therefore am for the police from the outside, a police which limits freedom of physical movement but not the flight of thought. For physical limitation, I insist, is far less limiting than spiritual limitation. The one curtails

But getting back to the freaks: many of them, like their Christian forefathers, are going diagonally through the vale of tears in search of the most pure light of salvation. And then they turn you into some kind of divine master, and when they discover you have a gray halo, they feel betrayed and deceived.

K: I wonder how seriously we should take Paul Feyerabend's gentle advice of liberalism and pluralism.

D: Feyerabend believes that the desires and interests of people are very different from each other and they have a right to be different because there doesn't seem to be a Super-reason to use as a yardstick. Therefore there should be a police force to keep order among the various groups. That's not unreasonable, is it? His error, in my opinion, occurs when he believes this police force can be free of any ideology and be completely tolerant, that it is not based on an humanitarian ethic. Feyerabend is an extreme liberal. The State, as he conceives it, presupposes that the various interests must be protected. Therefore the State interferes in people's lives and restricts them considerably. Feyerabend says that people have a right to live the way they want to even if their lifestyle seems barbaric or irrational to others. But what would Feyerabend say if a fascist or Stalinist faction would suddenly arise? And they believed they knew the ultimate truth

man's liberty to move, the other man himself. One can abolish freedom to move but not freedom to think." The spiritual originators, too, of the 1980 rebellion will have to comprehend that even in a society of freedom, among free men, we cannot do and probably will never be able to do, without a protective and equal right for all, without certain institutions to provide order, without people empowered to maintain order. They might come to comprehend it of their own free will, in a progress of enlightenment — or else through the hard experiences of societal reality. The flight of the kite, undertaken in narcissistic hubris by the unchained ego, cannot but meet with a sobering end. □

Translated by Hedwig Pächter

1. *Dance on the Volcano* (1978) traces the change of perspective within the Left in the 70's.

and therefore could force it on the rest of us. According to Feyerabend the State would have to curtail their activity. Why? Because it is against Feyerabend's morality to force one's will on others. This demonstrates that a humanitarian ethic is not just a morality like all others, but rather the fundamental morality of the State, as he sees it. I believe Feyerabend, like so many before him, cannot avoid the dilemma of relativity, whether in philosophy or his political vision. If you want to be so tolerant that you tolerate every lifestyle and opinion, then you have to assume that you'll get kicked out of bed at the first possible opportunity by someone who isn't a relativist.

K: You put great store on sensuality, emotions, passions, etc. There are people who consider you part of the "new inwardness."

D: Many people suffer from the delusion of categorization. They don't feel comfortable until they can put you into a box with the proper label on it. Presently, reviewers of my latest book are vacillating between irrationalist and romantic.

K: But it's not too far-fetched to call you a romantic.

D: Of course not. The world in which we live desperately demands that we become romantic, by which I mean a person who is not satisfied with a life castrated by science and technology.

STEFAN SCHÜTZ

Stasch

Office

Stasch: (sitting on a stretcher) Ladies and gentlemen, I can't hide my joy. I'm going to be branded today. A brand, recognizing my seven years of drudgery, will be emblazoned on my bare stomach.

(Walli and Krömlich talk quietly in a corner of the room.)

Walli: Comrade Krömlich, your brand!

Krömlich: Walli, Walli. Resist temptation. Keep your hands off Stasch.

Walli: He needs to be guided. He can be guided.

Krömlich: If I brand him, I'm not doing it as an experiment.

Walli: He can still be changed. He's not gone wild yet.

Krömlich: A smooth white skin isn't enough for my brand. Anyone has that, if he isn't black. Here we fold the skin back before we brand. Nobody deceives us. We're experienced! Comrade, my experience keeps me from making mistakes. I think that this body is infested with leprosy. Its stomach, liver, gallbladder and brain don't work our way.

Stefan Schütz is a young dramatist working as an actor and director in East Berlin.

K: Do you believe that this new world that we could create would produce much more than the archaic cultures of the past?

D: I believe that something less would be more. We live in a "hot" culture, as Levi-Strauss calls it. We are moving too fast, too brutally, too pointed, too metallic. That also applies to our science in its limitless desire to kill everything which speaks in a soft voice and which recoils from laboratory illumination and ossified questions. In my book, I quoted a Voodoo priest who said, "When the ethnologists arrive, the spirits will leave the islands." I repeated it to Hans Albert, a philosopher of science, who replied immediately, "Aha, a strategy to avoid scientific scrutiny!" What does it mean if Hans Albert doesn't see any clues. Just that he doesn't see any.

K: You mean you can't just catch any fish with just any net?

D: Yes, that's exactly what I mean. Werner Müeller, an old ethnologist in Tübingen — incidentally one of the few folklorists whose publications live and breathe — described how the passive attitudes of the Sioux Indians allow them to hear the voices of nature, which we can no longer hear with our homo faber activity. We trample everything down and see nothing anymore. That's also true of many ethnologists who miserably screw up the chance to learn about foreign peoples. I'm thinking of two publications which ap-

Walli: I wouldn't have made the request, if that were true.

Krömlich: What's the hurry, dear lady. Let sleeping dogs lie. Everything will take care of itself.

Krömlich makes several phone calls and then resigned he takes an outsized brand and presses it forcefully on Stasch's stomach. Stasch screams.

Stasch: (looking at himself in the mirror) Look at that! What a brand! Isn't that something? After being a dog who was ridiculed and spit upon, I've become a human being. From now on, I'll walk tall: "Hello, good sir," I'll say. "You dare greet me, you nothing." I'll reply, "Sir, I don't like your looks and when I get a chance, I'll push your face in." And the gentleman, the swine, the pig, the liar, the motherfucker, the bigwig, will try to kick me. And I, the personification of composure, will pull up my shirt and show him my brand. I'll say nothing and just leave! I'll be so happy that I'll want to masturbate. My God! — hey, you monsters, you ghosts, full moons and my conscience come on out. I'm not afraid anymore. My brand has driven away fear.

Anteroom

Zwuller: (enters) Ah, Stasch is already here. You're too early. An artist is always too late. You'll just never amount to anything.

Stasch: We'll see.

Zwuller: Already getting high-handed and haven't done a thing yet. (Exits)

"Most people in East Germany know that it's easier to live on the east side."

Heiner Müller

peared in the last two years: *Systematic Anthropology* by Tschol and *Methodological Problems of Intercultural Comparisons* by Schweizer. These scholars descend upon a flourishing landscape and leave a desert. There are still many ethnologists who have an intellectual General Custer attitude, who will soon experience their Little Big Horn. This isn't too far-fetched, because there are a sufficient number of disguised Cheyennes on the warpath. □

Translated by Wynn Gundarson

Stasch: (dreamily and pompously) The moon, skinny animal, was once ruler of the earth. Wait until we become a moon for a new star.

Walli: (enters) That's it, Stasch. Now I hope you'll write something about contemporary man as well.

Stasch: Oh, sure.

Walli: How nice, my dear little writer. With your new book, we're on our way to success.

Stasch: Sitting on the john and shitting is the only way to think.

Walli: Just keep on writing.

Street

Stasch: Don't start again with your life. I don't give a shit about it. You're not going to pacify me with your promises for the future. I'm thirty years old and know the score. I've been raised to be a supplicant who begs forgiveness for the things I didn't do, you cripples. Look at me, the monster. Once I possessed numerous skins and twenty-three souls for touching the essence of the things I loved, but the State greedily devours people, devours souls, turns skin into leather. You're the State. You're devouring yourselves. You incestuous pustules. A pox on you! Take me and choke to death on me.

Apartment

Stascha: I don't drink much, but once in a while I need to get roaring drunk.

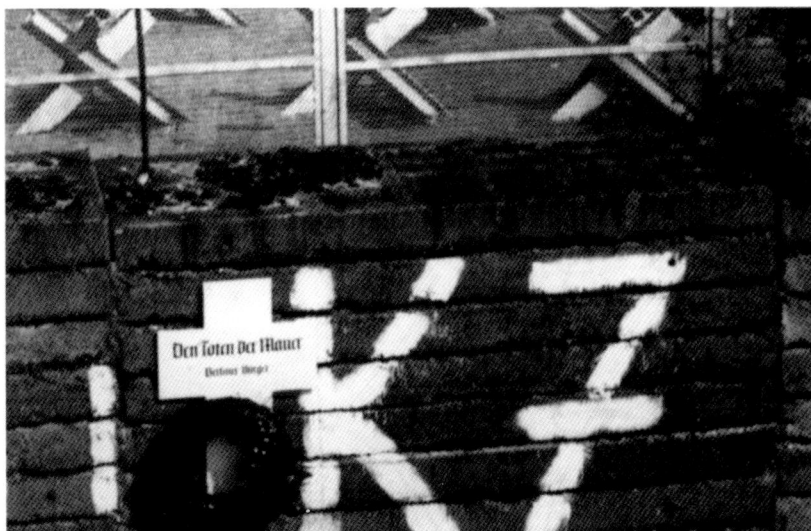

Stasch: Don't bother me.

Stascha: My husband is a coward! I'll get so pie-eyed that I won't see you pigs anymore. And you too.

Stasch: Shut up!

Stascha: Nobody's going to tell me to shut up today. Who is the whore?

Stasch: I'm tired. Leave me alone.

Stascha: You're always tired. I should have known. You turn women into dish-rags. You pig. (Stasch doesn't say anything) Just sits there like an idiot. Why? Cat got your tongue? When you're with your whore, you've got plenty to say.

Stasch: Yes.

Stascha: Get out of here. Right now. Go pack your bags.

Stasch: I don't need anything.

Stascha: I'm sick of you.

Stasch: Don't drink so much.

Stascha: I'll drink myself to death if I want to.

Stasch: I want to go to sleep.

Stascha: Not in my bed you don't.

Stasch: On the floor.

"At the beginning you think you're going to master the gun, and after a while the gun takes over."

Hans-Joachim Klein

PETER KATTENBERG

Snapshot Painting

Not since the Pop Art of the 60s has there been an art sweep comparable to the Young Savages' assault on the art world. After a purist interlude of Minimalism and Conceptual Art in the 70's, Luciano Castelli, Rainer Fetting, Karl Horst Hödicke, Bernd Koberling, Markus Lüpertz, Helmut Middendorf, A.R. Penck, and Salome and Bernd Zimmer have created the New Beginning of Painting. Vehement Painting, Violent Painting, Wild Painting, Bad Painting, and Apathetic Painting are successfully challenging the preceding art's striving for anonymity. These new movements violate yesterday's ascetic concentration on the formal aspects of painting. With a single bold brushstroke, four years ago primarily in New York, the New Savages took on Post Abstractionism and Fundamental Painting.

The sudden shift from the artist's neutrality in painting to nomadic subjectivity

emerged from West Germany, where it continues to thrive. The new movements seemed to suddenly burst upon the art scene, but the seeds for an art with dithyrambic pretentions had been germinating for two decades. Anselm Kiefer and George Baselitz — headstrongly defying the Minimalist hegemony — quietly kept painting their nightmares. Their humorless works portrayed painfully introverted imagery, occasionally presented upside down.

Vaingloryving the collapse of teleological optimism, the death shriek of their art is too carefully studied. With their heavy colors and predominance of black, Kiefer's paintings display moroseness and gloom. They invite associations of wounded *Weltschmerz*. George Baselitz, whose works are close to those of the Young Savages in physical appearance, is misleadingly regarded as their patriarch. He differs from them in intention by still researching the very limits of painting. Fundamentally, he is not a painter of explosive sentiment, but a philosopher reflecting on the process of painting in transcendental terms.

Paintings by the Savages were ignored until recently by the arbiters of art. Today the galleries are dressed to thrill with two generations of Savage Masters. In fact, once on display, Nuclear Expressionism, exemplified by Jiri Dokoupil's Provocation of Atomic Power, with its tactility and untamed appearance, shook the art world.

211

Stascha: Your body is bloodless and opaque. Nothing stirs in you anymore. You're burned out. And dumb cow that I am, I fell for it. Can't you even defend yourself? You piece of garbage!

Stasch: I'm supposd to leave! Well. I'll leave!

Stascha: Get out!

Stasch: I hate you.

Stascha: There's nothing left to say.

Stasch: How are we going to go on living? I'm living on your money. For the children? We'll choke each other to death. There's no hope at all. Except death. We've got to separate.

Stascha: (smiles) Life isn't made to be lived. I've had enough of you. I know how it goes. It's macho to kick someone in the ass. (She cries. Stasch remains silent.) Everyone scratches the earth with his fingernails and gleefully digs a grave for others. (She continues drinking.) The louts aren't worth crying for.

Stasch: You just don't want to understand. I don't give a shit which woman it is. I can't stand the confinement anymore. The fodder. This State which kicks my head until it's as soft as a football. The art of the whore. And newspapers. All of them pigs. They destroy everything.

Stascha: What you write will endure. But it hangs on to me like rats. What I do won't endure. You pessimist!

Stasch: You don't understand a thing. I'm finished. I don't want to piss half-

The catalyst for international dissemination of this kind of rustic painting was the Texas-trained Julian Schnabel. He assimilated the German Savages' artistic attitude and accentuated the centrality of the artist's ego. A Promethean painter, Schnabel stole the German Savages' fire and thunder. Metaphorically as close to blasphemy as Michelangelo's figures, his paintings anticipated the rupture in the art scene in the U.S.

As a result of Schnabel's and his admirers' influence, the popularity of Savage Art grew to the point of holding center stage in New York under the rubric Neo-Expressionism. Now two generations of Neo-expressionists are in the spotlight. Members of the first generation, Young Savages approaching their fifties, are Karl Horst Hödicke, Bernd Koberling, and Markus Lupertz. A.R. Penck acts as a mediator between the old guard and the second generation. These young turks, almost thirty, approach their work with vigor and self-consciousness. In West Berlin members of this group, the Moritz Boys, include Luciano Castelli, Rainer Fetting, Helmut Middendorf, as well as Salome and Bernd Zimmer. The Young Savages are indistinguishable from each other in color, execution, intention, motif, and style. Underneath their feigned naiveté, resonances of the Expressionistic tradition betray a common longing for a Deutschland still untouched by schizo-culture. Although each painter claims to be unique, they legitimize each other by collaborating like tag-team wrestlers on collective pieces:

words unto paper anymore. I don't want to be servile to an artistic brat of a country with the gout. To the old men who run it. I want to fuck everything so that I don't get fucked.

Stascha: I don't understand you anymore, Stasch!

Stasch: If I stay, I'll strangle the children. I'd beat you like a dog. (Exits)

Stascha: Stasch!

Street

Stasch: In these time, you've got to defend yourself against love. Love lowers your defenses and lets everyone's arrows slay you. You have to become hard so that you can survive. I want to be horny, but not vulnerable.

Big Shot's Apartment

Kolbe: That's Stasch, he's almost famous already.

Böcklin: Does he have a brand?

Kolbe: When is your next book coming out — in these lousy times?

Stasch: Very soon.

Kolbe: How senseless.

Stasch: Isn't anybody else here?

Kolbe: The Big Shot's in the john. He's been in there thinking for a half hour.

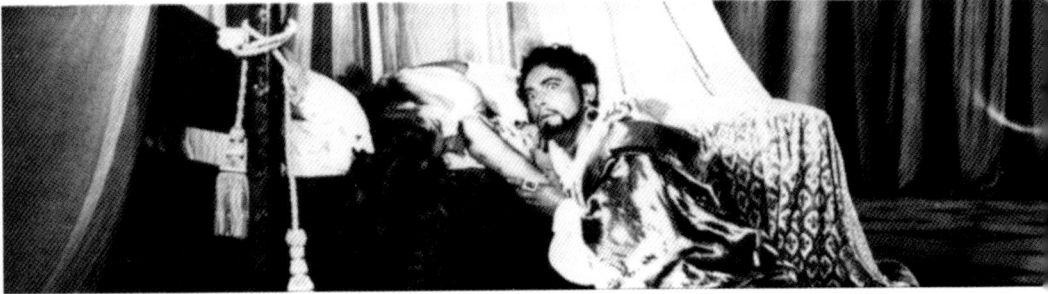

Castelli-Salome, Dokoupil-Dahn, and Penck-Immendorf.

Newcomers — or the New Savages — are already on the horizon for a third generation. Among these, Hans Peter Adamski, Peter Bömmels, Walter Dahn, Jiri Georg Dokoupil, Gerard Kever, and Gerhard Naschberger, members of the Mülheimer Freiheit, show particular promise.

Most of these New Savages come out of the New Wave. They have no credo or manifesto, but an overwhelming desire for popular recognition. Most notorious for the attitude that "everything is a rehash of something else," espoused by Mick Jagger, is the Mülheimer Freiheit, which strongly reveals an affiliation with Punk music. In fact, Bommels, who depicts wild city night life and atomic fear, is the editor of the Punk magazine *Spex*.

Individualistic to the point of solipsism, the New Savages are attached to chaos. Their dictum is "Because we can't paint, we paint." Despite their emphasis on originality and singularity, a few common characteristics emerge within the group's diversity:
- awkwardly painted figures as the new image.
- nervous articulation of extreme individual feelings.
- autistic, rather than artistic.
- rough color for texture, not for emotion.

213

Böcklin: Only his wife looks restively in on us every once in a while (Stasch takes a drink.)

Kolbe: You've got to survive.

Böcklin: To go along, but always sitting on the horse backwards. That causes unrest.

Kolbe: Mister, you can't turn philosophy upside down like that so easily. Who wants to be dumped in full-tilt into the muck.

Böcklin: Let's ask the Big Shot what he thinks.

Stasch: A bomb should be shoved up the horse's ass. (Silence)

Kolbe: Have you read his new book?

Böcklin: He's a poet.

Inka: (enters) Still on the john. How intemperate. (Exits)

Kolbe: He doesn't deserve to have his bowel habits watched.

Bocklin: A chained rooster usually gets constipation. (Laughs)

Kolbe: I'd be afraid of her, except in a brothel. (Laughs)

Stasch: She is the poetry; he's only the tool.

Inka: (enters) I'm the one who's going to commit suicide someday to free my body from myself. The one who will fight against what is left over from it and

- colors not an icon of the object.
- no notion of composition, perspective and proportion.

Though the incipient generation also tries to play innocent, their work does not look child-like, but rather childish. It does not display a sense of simple spontaneous line. Their simplicity is always affected. No longer is painting the expression of a feeling as it was in Expressionism. The feelings are *impuissant* and as such they become inexpressible. The emotion lies in the mere act of painting. The New Savages' paintings embody an unidentifiable mood — mood as manifestation. Living by the fine art books' pictures, these New Savages do not draw from their own experiences, but from art history's arsenal of forms. Although . . .

The New Savages want to look young and slick. They want to fast-paint. Good or bad art, who cares? They believe the art world is in a hilarious, totalitarian state. Distinct categories have disappeared.

Even the established art world welcomed the Savages' invasion, assuming they possessed the hermeneutic implements to understand art's magnetic romanticism. They enthusiastically embraced the new expression of feeling and like them concluded that everything is "fine art" as long as it is mindless and unpolished.

214   Imagination is discontent and rightly so. Every attempt to step outside culture ends

constantly wants to return to me. But in the meantime, I'm the one who erects a deceptive world in this age of transition.

Kolbe: The poet has to create where he lives and breathes.

Böcklin: Yes, he's captured our present mood exactly. (Inka cries.)

Kolbe: She's upset.

Böcklin: Who could leave him. (Inka exit.)

Inka: (enters again) He's dead. A corpse. He's hanged himself. It's all over. The waiting paid off. In the john, shit. Go eat shit all of you. (All exit.)

Kolbe: We've cut him down. And put him in the tub. It's too late to save him.

Böcklin: A great talent has been extinguished. We have become poorer, but he remains with us in his works.

Stasch: My brand aches like a wound.

Anteroom

Stasch: I've gone from one bench to the other, but can't find any peace. Pursued myself the way others hunt animals. And finally these are four walls that I recognize. (Sits down.)

Walli: Mr. Stasch. How good to see you.

Stasch: I want to get rid of my brand. It aches and itches like crazy. All at the same time. I can't stand it anymore.

up confirming it. Therefore, it is possible that today's retreat toward subjectivity and ego art legitimize bad painting as an authentic response to cultural integration. Emotionality and refuge in extreme individuality may anticipate an art of the ego in its own right. It could be the only possible response, since everything out-of-order ends up museum material.

Several international artists, inspired by the recent German outburst, but going their own ways, may suggest a fresh prospective — among them, Ernst Caramelle, Martin Disler, Hans-Felix Müller, Martin Sjardijn, and Rolf Winnewisser. At the moment though, it is questionable whether the new painting from West Gemany is a sign of mutation or mutilation. □

Walli: I don't understand. You fought seven years to get it. Not to mention my intervention. You must be kidding.

Stasch: Yes.

Bar

Schmittke: (drunk) I don't agree with socialism, including the Party, and I see no future for myself in this country. That's why I asked to be allowed to leave this land. (Applause) Because I find the dictatorship of the proletariat, like the social order which I oppose, unbearable for me.

Ranko: And you mailed that?

Schmittke: Word for word. (Applause)

Elmis: A beer for the idiot.

Ranko: They're going to come and take you away.

Schmittke: You have to irritate the officials. Then they can't rest and they'll let you leave. Cheers!

Stasch: (gets up, is completely drunk) The Big Shot is dead!

Elmis: Who?

Ranko: Someone from the government?

Stasch: Oh, shit!

HERBERT ACHTERNBUSCH

Animadversions of a Bavarian Anarchist

This man is dangerous: he wishes harm to our Bavarian vacationland, to the mountain pastures surveyed by leatherclad shepherds and the charming domes of baroque chapels, to Louis the Second and Franz-Joseph Strauss. This unreasonable man wants the impossible — to swim across the Atlantic, for example. "You don't have a chance," he says, "but grab it!"

Jacques Le Rider: The Exotic seems to play a major role in your films. In "Bye-Bye Bavaria," you show Greenland. Elsewhere the Canary Islands and Bali...

Achternbusch: They are more accessible to us than the North of Germany. When I say that Bavaria is "trapped in ice," I mean that life there has disappeared. The State has

Elmis: To Schmittke and freedom!

Schmittke: Let me out of here!

Street

Stasch: You've got to survive. And live. We need a new method for fighting, to get us out of these strictures. I'll find it. Plagued with impotence since birth, I'll get rid of my impotence, if I have to — even if I harm my body. Otherwise, I'll go crazy, but still go on living. I have to scream. (Hits himself in the stomach. Turns around.)

Square

Stasch: (wearing Dionysos' mask) Say, where are you going?

People: To the morning.

Stasch: Not that, not to your destruction. (Laughing people pass by.) Stop, I challenge you, you gnawers. Just come closer!

People: Show us your wares. We don't have much time.

Stasch: Your senses have been corrupted. Mine too. We don't see anymore, only shadows which they concede to us. Only caricatures, silhouette of an invisible body. You're deceiving yourselves. Our ears are frayed by their noise. When you make noise, you're even deafer than they are. Your noses smell nothing but your own shit. Their phrases, the ones they want to hear, resound

been so oppressive for so long that Bavaria hasn't been able to blossom. Reform has been repressed here in the most savage way.

Today one celebrates the Wittelsbach bastards. All they wanted was to annihilate Bavaria, to sell it so that they could settle on the Rhine. Like Franz-Joseph Strauss, a monster of stupidity. Greenland is an island the size of Bavaria, itself an island in Germany and in Europe. I propose to surround it with a large body of water and separate it from it all.

LR: Are you an anarchist?

A: According to the *Frankfurter Rundschau*, our best newspaper, ten years ago I was a stupid individualist. But in the meantime Germany has gone so far to the right that suddenly I'm on the left. Frankly, I can't conceive of art coming from the right; yet one cannot be apolitical either. One has to understand that revolution starts with the individual. There is more order in the individual than in all of the State.

LR: Is provocation for you an aesthetic principle?

A: I disturb the Bavarians by showing them parts of their familiar decor: folk music, baroque churches, beerfests. But in a radically different context, one opposed to Franz-

217

from your mouths. New lies. Your heads have been degraded to machines which cannot be turned on and off! — I've got a brand. Not everyone has a brand which itches and aches. Cut your brands out of your flesh. (Takes the knife.) I'll show you. I'll cut out my own brand!

People: Take the knife away from him! (Stasch shows his brand.) Such a nice brand. Too bad!

Stasch: Can't even blood help me! Are we no longer people? Perhaps, if I cut myself, I won't bleed and the apparatus will rattle like a defective machine?

People: Come on. Do it! He's a robot!

Stasch: No! I can't!

People: First, he makes a big noise and then he chickens out. Come on. Do it!

Stasch: I'm rehearsing a play!

People: The cops. (The people continue on their way.)

Police: Name, number, and address. Identification papers.

Office

Walli: What you did was senseless. I stuck out my neck for you and that's all the thanks I get.

Stasch: I'm sick.

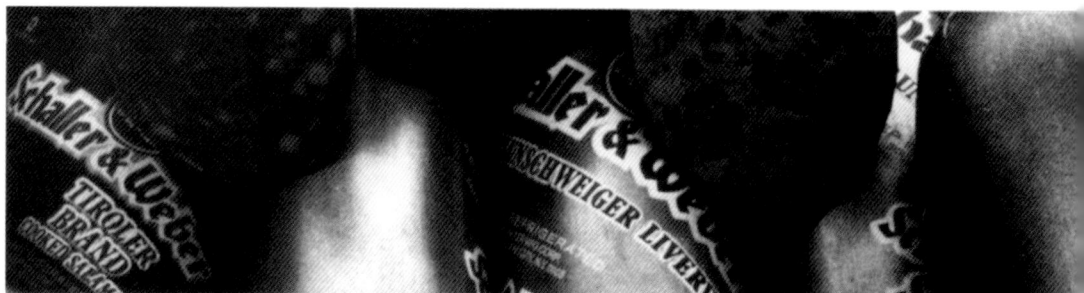

Joseph Strauss. He's number one on my shit list. To those who tell me: "These Alpine countrysides are fascist cliches," I respond: "Bunch of idiots, there are partisans and poachers hiding in the mountains!"

LR: "Beer Battle" is a film rife with violence: murders, rapes, tortures...

A: The State kills, not art. I am confronted with a disgusting German reality. This violence you mention is everywhere in our society — and behind it, Hitler. Art will never equal that kind of violence. Brutality can be released in art, but not all in life. Imagine if Hitler had painted six million tortured Jews on icons.

LR: Apart from Franz-Joseph Strauss, what do you hate most?

A: Fascism. Not only as an historical fact, but as a potentiality in all individuals. I hate the school I had to attend. But what I hate most is the perfect continuity between the Federal Republic and the Third Reich. Germany is so hopeless, so depressing. It's a diabolic bureaucratic invention. The Germans work so hard they don't see that their hands are drenched in blood.

But I refuse to moan. As a pacifist, I yell "To Arms!" Today people prefer to boil with indignation because some comic-strip terrorists slaughter twenty people. And the

Walli: Don't play games with me. We failed to make a real poet out of you, despite our wanting to. People have doubts about you.

Stasch: I'm drowning in too much saliva.

Walli: Didn't we concern ourselves with everything. Didn't you accept our confidence gladly? In whose territory did you end up?

Stasch: I can't pull a rabbit out of my hat.

Walli: Then obey our helping hands.

Stasch: I obey where I can, but I can't.

Walli: Once in my life I decided to really do something. To bring your talent into the spotlight — out from the gutter. But you want to get back into the gutter.

Stasch: I can swim better in shit than in the spotlight.

Walli: You're demoralized. A terrible end sticks in your head.

Stasch: The end is a beginning!

Night

Stascha: There aren't any more tears. My soul is cold. Cold enough to die. Life was a war and I had hoped not to fall alone at the front. He and I defended ourselves in the trenches, which this room was. Often numb, our bodies fought each other, pressed together and survived all wounds. But love is only a seeming peace in the middle of war. I'm tired. I'll have to hang myself on the

hullabaloo resounds throughout the State. But ultimately it is the State that's guilty. Take a look at the biographies of the fathers of all these terrorists: they were National-Socialists just like our beloved President Carstens. □

*Translated by Marc Parent and
Nick Chance*

window bars to sleep. Because it's easier to die alone than to have to live alone. I hear voices! Stasch!

(Two Party members enter as ghosts.)

First Party Member: Hang yourself, Stascha. It's time!

Second Party Member: Hurry up, woman. We, the Party, have come to accompany you on your death march.

Stascha: You, flesh without heads. You won't find any mourning. I'll fly past you with my death.

First Party Member: Comrade, we won't miss you.

Second Party Member: We'll forget your crimes like we forget weeds. Arrogant woman.

Stascha: You'll win battles, but the final victory will elude you. Because the exhausted filth you call your bodies will be dumped into the toilet, like bad smelling soap. Comrades. Men.

First Party Member: Hit her. A comrade should hit women often.

(Second Party Member hits Stascha. She laughs. The laughing drives the Party members away.)

Street

Stasch: Now I'm crazy. I'm in treatment. I'm a creature who can't scream. What am I afraid of? I'm afraid to pick up a pencil so that I have to write. But

KRAFT WETZEL

New German Cinema: Economics Without Miracle

The contemporary West German film is not a cohesive movement. The only thing which today's films have in common with each other is the way they are produced. They are not funded by profits from previous productions, as in the U.S., France and Italy. While a few producers still bankroll an occasional film with their own capital, the vast majority of cinematic features are government-supported. Government subvention takes on several forms: extensions of credit, prizes, grants and contracts for co-productions with the State-owned television stations. Since the films made in the Federal Republic of Germany usually don't even gross enough to cover distribution

Kraft Wetzel is a Berliner journalist and film critic.

the pills calm me down. Yesterday, I saw two eyes which will not forget me. I dived into them, but they didn't answer. As if they were the only eyes in which I could find mself again. I couldn't recognize anything else. Only this light. □

Translated by Dagmar Stern

cost—not to mention production expenditures—there is no possibility of establishing a fund for financing other films. Therefore, West German filmmakers can only produce as many films as the government can afford to subsidize. Consequently, the history of West German film is the history of a struggle to convince the government to create subsidies, to gain access to these funds, and then to persuade the State to increase the amount of money available. The following sketch delineates the most important steps of this struggle and its most significant consequences.

In Oberhausen on February 28, 1962, twenty-six filmmakers issued the Oberhausen Manifesto. In it, they speak of the collapse of the conventional German film and their commitment to the creation of a new German film. Although long on conviction, only two of the signatories had made their film debut—with works that had never even played in legitimate theaters—and access for the group to film production remained impossible for some years.

The old-boy producers' network resisted their challenge vehemently partly because of a crisis, which was rapidly getting worse, that they had created themselves. After 1956, as television became more popular, movie attendance shrank from 817,000,000 in 1956 to 115,100,000 in 1976. Of course the Federal Republic film industry felt the effects of this contraction. The industry reacted by clinging tenaciously to their eroding

OSWALD WIENER
Austria Go Home!

Shortly after World War II, a group of artists, writers and musicians banded together to form the *artclub*. After seven years in an artistic and literary vacuum, young intellectuals felt the need to rejuvenate the arts and to educate themselves with regard to movements which for Austria had not existed: Constructivism, Dadaism, Expressionism and Surrealism. In 1951 the *hundsgruppe* (literally "hound's group"), one of the numerous splinters of the *artclub*, succeeded in raising Austria's petrified eyebrows with its decidely left and radically aggressive exhibit *cave canem*. Staid audiences were hard pressed, for example, to understand Hans Kann and Gerhard Rühm's sound symphonies — a recorded montage of noises — to which they were exposed. Influenced by Pierre Schaeffer and Pierre Henry and their *musique concrete*, Rühm went on to create his *ein-ton-musik* for the piano in 1952. In the same year he met fellow Austrian H.C. Artmann who had recently returned from Paris. Together they read and discussed the Expressionists, Arp, Behrens, Schwitters, Gertude Stein's *last operas and plays*, and Alain Bosquet's anthology *Surrealismus*. There were readings and concerts, particularly by Uzi Forster's Jazz combo, until the early morning hours. In April of 1953 Artmann made public his *eight-point-proclamation of the poetic art* and organized the first "poetic demonstration." Costumes, make-up, route and accoutrements

economic position and obsolete concepts of filmmaking. Impetus for such a reactionary response came in part from the structure of the sclerotic CDU* State under the patriarchal protection of the elderly Adenauer. Adenauer's economic policy in the 1950's and early 1960's was based on a tacit agreement to repress the recent Third Reich past, war guilt, and the murder of Jews in favor of strong support for federal reconstruction and the Economic Miracle. Since the West German film industry could portray the recent past and present social reality, it was part of this repression. Seismographic for this phenomenon was the unusual number of films which took place in no particular geographical location. Moreover, as late as 1967, the film critic Urs Jenny could still maintain that the Berlin Wall has only appeared in Hollywood films, but not in a single West German film. Instead, West German producers prefer to depict a pseudo-Italy, a pseudo-London, a pseudo-America, a pseudo-Hong Kong, or a pseudo-Istanbul—if at all German, then a pseudo-Bavaria.

The more alert viewers saw through this facade, this anti-reality. They opposed the conspiracy of silence about the past and the problems of the present, which they encountered in schools, universities, and cultural markets. Against their parents' and teachers' wishes they developed a historical conscience and then offered them opposition. Not only could they, like every generation, express the wish that the old men step

were specified. Passages from Baudelaire, Nerval, Poe and de la Serna were loudly declaimed amid incense and macabre ceremony. The success of this venture lead to the formation of the *franciscan catacombes club,* an Artmann-run clique which found refuge in a labyrinthian basement. At a further event in honor of the French Revolution, Artmann and Ruhm met a young musician by the name of Oswald Wiener, a member of Walter Terharen's *jazzband jesus christbaum* (jazzband jesus christmastree).

The *cafe glory* became the new meeting place. Here Wiener wrote his first poems. It soon became clear that a progressively radical approach to art bound the three young men together. The seed of the *Wiener Gruppe* (Viennese Group) had been planted. In the late 1950's, together with Konrad Bayer and Friedrich Achleitner, the three men staged happenings of the most radical nature, presented randy chansons (such as Rühm's "o come again and piss on me my dear my dear my dear" and the Ruhm/Wiener collaboration "marina, present me with a sausage") and performed in the *Literarische Cabaret.* Two performances sufficed to ensure a place in literary almanachs. In the mid-60-'s the *Wiener Gruppe* made its last appearance in the nightclub Chattanooga in Vienna. In October of 1964, Konrad Bayer committed suicide. The remaining four members went their separate ways. Achleitner is no longer involved with the arts. Artmann and Ruhm continue to publish. Only Wiener has taken a different road.

Together with Otto Muhl he initiated the organization ZOCK. Like the Dutch Provos, the members of ZOCK accepted clownery, blasphemy and ridicule as a means to an end: change in the establishment. Their guiding light: "dear God, we are all epileptic." Although he had "moved" to Berlin in 1967,

aside, but they could condemn them as morally corrupt men who proved their guilt by suppressing the horrors of the Third Reich.

Blocked from traditional production paths, Alexander Kluge and Rolf Strobel,[1] spokesmen and champions of the Oberhausen Manifesto, tried to establish a new source for financing their projects: the government coffers. They got ammunition for their battle from the established film critics, who had denounced the commercially, aesthetically, and ideologically bankrupt German film which could not compete with the international market. After three years of arduous lobbying, the two succeeded in dislodging money from the Ministry of Internal Affairs, MIA, for new German films. In 1965, three young directors received subsidies for scripts from the MIA: Volker Schlöndorff for *Young Torless*, Peter Fleischamm for *The Hunters are Hunted,* and Alexander Kluge for *Yesterday Girl.* The Committee for New German Film supported the first feature films with loans. It got its funding until 1968 from the MIA and thereafter from the individual federal states, which are primarily responsible for promoting the arts. Since 1966, the lion's share of funds have gone to the new German film.

The first new German films were shown in theaters in 1966 and 1967. Ulrich Schamoni's *It* and Schlöndorff's *Young Torless* were lauded not only by critics but by the paying public as well. Kluge's *Yesterday Girl* won a prize at the Venice Film Festival   **223**

Wiener, the recognized leader of the loosely knit organization, returned to Vienna in the summer of 1968. On June 7, 1968, Wiener was lecturing at the University of Vienna about his theories of writing and *Sprache* (language). Standing at the blackboard in Lecture Hall 1, Wiener observed the following: derision of Robert Kennedy, Günther Brus' self-inflicted wound, his urination and defecation display, a singing of the national anthem, Mühl's whipping of a masochist and his urination contest with five nude young men. Wiener provided the piece of wood which, jammed between doorknob and floor, prevented a quick rear exit. Needless to say, everyone was arrested, jailed and brought to trial in August. During his time in prison, Wiener completed the manuscript of his first novel *the bettering of middle europe.*

Once again in Berlin, Wiener, who once termed himself a student of a new anarchy, set up a mock "Austrian Exil Government" along with fellow dissident Günther Brus. The initiator and organizer opened a restaurant/bar not unlike the various literary clubs which flourished in Vienna during the 1950's. From this establishment, a place where the literati assembled, Wiener and Brus issued a literary magazine *Die Schastrommel* (*Schas:* onomotopoetic rendering of *Jazz;* hence, *Jazzdrum*). After the magazine folded in 1976, Wiener continued to issue various diatribes against his Mother Country. An unwelcome guest in his native land, he has sought refuge in the political hotbed and cadaver West Berlin. Ossi Wiener: dandy, iconoclast, joiner, organizer, leader, writer, critic. Christian-Albrecht Gollub

Friedrich Geyrhofer: How did you become involved in the restaurant business? After all, you were a pioneer. After you, it almost became fashionable for in-

and brought him international recognition.

When some of the newcomers achieved commercial success, the old-boy producers started to pay attention to them. A few dared to try these modern themes, but some were even bolder. Constantin-Film financed Kluge's second film *Artists in the Circus Tent: Perplexed.* It won the Golden Lion at the Venice Film Festival in 1968.

The Filmförderungsgesetz (Law to Promote Film, LPF), enacted in 1968, negated the new German film's success because it failed to consider it almost completely. The law established a commission in Berlin to collect a certain percentage of every ticket sold and to distribute the money among FRG's film producers, according to their box-office success. All films which grossed 500,000 DM in distribution receipts in two years became eligible for funds to finance new productions. Films which were cited for excellence by a commission established by each state or won a major prize at an important film festival needed to earn only 300,000 DM.

People who profited from this system were Franz Seitz with his Lümmel and Panker films,[2] Luggi Waldleitner with his filming of a bestseller, and Wolf Hartwig with his *School Girl Reports*—a commercially successful schema which he varied endlessly—as well as the large distribution firms.

The new German filmmakers survived with the help of television. In addition the

tellectuals to open restaurants.

Oswald Wiener: At that time there were only 2 restaurants in Vienna where one could go. The Cafe Sport and the Cafe Savoy — both no longer exist. But you only went there to get drunk. People who really wanted to talk to each other came to our apartment in the Judengasse. It was a very stimulating atmosphere. There were countless records and the newest papers. I also had a billiard table. People felt they were in a cafe-house. Whatever they drank, they brought with them. But in 1968 it had gotten to the point where my remaining in Austria was no longer possible.

FG: Because of the happening in Lecture Hall 1?

OW: I really was the initiator of the Action in Lecture Hall 1, but it was mere chance. Another time it could have been Muhl or somebody else. During the discussion some idiot said, What we're doing at the university is nothing. We should go into Stephan's Cathedral and crap — then he takes his hat off in front of us. I could never have said that. The Church never was my enemy. For me the Church is totally finished. I always laughed about Nitsch[1] and his religious fits. I am very interested in religious ways of experience as they appear in mysticism or in early Christianity, but as a state of consciousness. It doesn't have anything to do with religion. In Lecture Hall 1, one of the witnesses volunteered the information that I was the one who made the suggestion on Stephan's Cathedral. On this basis I was arrested without ceremony, in good Austrian style. I can only explain this whole sequence of events by saying that the prosecutor already knew that he would not be able to convict us.

Film Verlag der Autoren, a distributor founded by the new German filmmakers as a self-help organization, managed to place some of their films into alternative theaters, where they developed an audience for Kluge and Company.

In 1974 when the LPF was revised, Kluge and Co. succeeded in getting a broader financial base because the revision included the promotion of new film projects. Elections too helped the new German filmmakers. The SPD/FDP Coalition* was victorious in the Bundestag in Fall 1969. Now Willy Brandt* became Chancellor and Social Democrats attained key positions in the executive body. The SPD's cultural platform was very similar to the programmatic intentions and declarations of the young turks.

Also in their favor was the continued decline in German film, despite LPF support. Kluge and Co. managed to free the Federal organization of movie owners from the old-boy lobby. It contained the Federal organization of the movie industry and got them to support the young turks' revisionist concepts.

The main innovation of the LPF revision of March 1974 was the provision for funding new film projects. From then on, one-quarter of the percentage collected from theater box offices—an amount which had increased substantially because the percentage from each ticket had been raised—was used for new film productions. Candidates for the money were picked by a commission which included representatives from the

Clearly, he wasn't in any position to do so. The gentlemen of justice wanted to his us over the head with a sledge hammer. All they could do is stick me with two months imprisonment.

In my second week in jail, my friends found out who the fellow was who had made that statement about Stephan's Cathedral. He made a deposition with the investigatory judge. How can you talk such rubbish, the lawyers retorted, and they let him go home. I remained locked up. The last doubts about my guilt had not yet been eliminated. The menace of it being repeated existed. I had already announced that something would happen at Stephan's Cathedral...I didn't get out until after the trial.

FG: And soon after you emigrated to West Berlin.

OW: We were all ostracized after my release. There were all sorts of events...

FG: I read it in the newspapers.

OW: Not only in the papers. In the public, on the street, in restaurants. Close friends and not so close acquaintances looked away. In a restaurant someone tapped me on the shoulder: Mr. Wiener? Let's go over here. I don't know who he is. I follow him, and he says: watch it, Mr. Wiener, I'm Inspector so and so. There's still an irregularity in your case. These smart alecs. You always felt watched and noticed. You are public enemy #1, a very flattering situation. But it got really heavy. Then as a result of a certain event, I had to make myself invisible.

FG: What kind of event?

new German film. Also, an agreement was struck to promote joint ventures between film and television. The stations would invest considerable amounts with the provision that they could show the films after a two-year theater run. Thus, the "amphibious film," appropriate for the movie screen as well as the TV screen, was born.

The amount of money available to the new German filmmakers was doubled by these innovations. Not only could they afford more productions but also more expensive and spectacular ones to attract the large American distributors who controlled the West German film market. And indeed, some of the American distributors picked up a few of them, such as *The Lost Honor of Katharina Blum*, a Paramount co-production which was a box office hit like no German distributor could have realized at the time.

Since few of the old-boy producers could accomodate themselves to the new condition, their share of the market decreased greatly. This was to the advantage of the young turks. From the young German film with a handful of outsider productions it grew in the second half of the 70's into a force to be reckoned with.

With the introduction of funding for new films by the federal states, which started in Berlin in 1978, the financial possibilities for the New German Cinema increased enormously. Including film and television co-productions, federal support for film was now 60,000,000 DM per year and the lion's share of this amount went to the New German

OW: I won't deny that time and again I got into disputes with the law. I am a great hater of the police. Even today, I wouldn't let any opportunity go by. I even owned pistols. There were countless brawls. I was a drunk rowdy, a disturber of the public order. I always have skirmishes with the police.

There was a party at the Viennese Secession. The organizers were good friends of mine. We wanted to get in free, of course. I asked the bouncers at the door to get my friend Mikl. Suddenly the secret police show up. They grab me and take me to the back. After my experience in court I naturally went along with them. They bring Dominik Steiger in. He too had been released after the trial. Kurti Kalb came after me. Some guy goes up to him and gives him a punch in the face. When Dominik Steiger sees that, in a sudden rage he grabs this guy, lifts him up and throws him down. The guy falls and breaks his leg — as it turned out he belongs to the secret police...

In the following spring my novel *the bettering of middle europe* came out. I go to Germany and I find out that I'd better not return to Austria. Dominik Steiger has been indicted, his lawyer saw a warrant of arrest for Oswald Wiener! A warrant for having violated a minor! I was very amused. I was falsely accused of child molesting and when I heard the trial would not come up for months, and I would have to spend them in jail, I said, "So long Austria!"

FG: And how did you get your bearings here in Berlin?

OW: Through a ridiculously lucky coincidence after a reading in Berlin. A representative of the Senate offered me a stipend for 6 months. I had never

"In the 70's the Germans began to reinvent National-Socialism. The Hitler period became an extraordinary creative resource for a whole generation of filmmakers and writers."

Christo

received a stipend in my life. It would have been disgraceful to accept even one penny from the Austrian government.

FG: And how did you get into the restaurant business?

OW: At first, for quite a while, it looked as though I would become a famous writer. I was swamped by offers to write radio plays. I don't believe in radio plays. They are a degeneration of experimental literature. I needed some money all the same. While I was working as a waiter, my friend Mischell said that in the restaurant where he worked the leaseholder wanted to break his lease and that he, Mischell, would immediately take over the place if my wife and I would join in. Well, why not? We decided to work in the restaurant for 9 months. That was 1970, a really neat mood, everybody who was libertaire in Berlin, from the left to the liberals, all the students, the artists, intellectuals, came. I was somewhat surprised how that went. Suddenly, zip, zip, our problems were solved. Except for one, the warrant of arrest in Austria because of the violation of a minor. And because of that my Austrian passport was not renewed.

FG: Amazing that no writ of delivery was issued.

OW: I was amazed about that as well. They said I should surrender, the old tune. A year later I received the message that the warrant no longer existed. A moral perpetrator who fondled young girls had been sentenced. The *Exil*, our restaurant, offered the best in bourgeois entertainment. Bourgeois cooking from Vienna. People came from far and wide to spend an evening with us. Of

Cinema.

The changing of the guard from the old generation to the new, so arduously opposed by the old-boy producers, had taken place. In toto, the young turks could now claim 80% of all film productions. The old-boys who had survived had opted to cooperate with the younger generation: Luggi Waldleitner produced Geissendorfer's *The Glass Cell* and hired Fassbinder for *Lili Marleen* and Franz Seitz, an educated bourgeois and producer of early Jean-Marie Straub and Schlöndorff films, created the first international box office and critical success with the *Tin Drum*. Schlöndorff's film won the Golden Palm at Cannes and the Oscar in L.A.

As the guard changed, a fundamental change in the structure of film production occurred. Essentially only government funded cinema remains in the Federal Republic. It is a system which allows the filmmakers to pocket their profits and lets the government absorb their losses. Kluge wittily referred to the arrangement as "capitalism without money." In this set-up only government money circulates.

This kind of financial support affects the most intimate concept of the socially liberal government film. With the government's help, the New German Cinema has freed itself from the paying customer. Moreover, the box office does not determine who survives, but rather television editors, government appointed committees, and film festival

"I am for a form of Communism where everybody can have his lobster if they want to."

Annette Humpe

judges. The New German Cinema reacts to the cultural values of these groups, not to the real public. Therefore, like the State-supported concert and opera industry which serves the politically conservative cultural bourgeoisie of the reconstruction generation, the socially liberal government film reflects the taste of the new socially liberal 30 to 50-year-old cultural bourgeoisie. The latter values narrative substance, realistic dramatic technique, aesthetic solidity, and moderately progressive ideas. This social class, only a small part of the film-going public, recognizes itself again in these films and gets reinforcement from the praise in the art sections of newspapers and from awards at film festivals, the majority of the film-going public, the 15 to 25-year-old students, workers, and white-collar employees, prefers Hollywood productions. They like action-packed thrillers, science fiction, fantasy, and horror movies. Therefore the New German Cinema's share of the market remains at 10% and even the lion's share falls to a handful of highly successful films, which are usually tailored to traditional commercial film standards. □

Translated by Dagmar Stern

1. German filmmakers.
2. Prank movies.

course, now Kreuzberg is the big attraction, especially for the homesteadlike Berliner Punk. I see a dandyism here which corresponds to a historical dandyism. I experimented with dandyism as a mental attitude. For me dandyism is somehow a mentally historical parallel to behaviorism. Dandyism expresses itself within the psychological science in behaviorism, or in the philosophy of behaviorism. I mean the sincere effort to do without content and only observe the movements of signals. That for me is a dandy-attitude par excellence.

A dandy doesn't want to change his fellow man, influence him through the movement of the contents of the other. The dandy is satisfied by saying that the other guy has absolutely no contents. And the dandy prefers to say that he also has no contents.

FG: Did the historical dandyism influence the Wiener Gruppe? Were the famous dandies of history, Beau Brummel or Baudelaire, "saints" for you and your friends?

OW: No, they weren't "saints," but rather people who appeared literarily much earlier. If you read the *Liaisons Dangereuses* by Choderlos de Laclos, dandyism is completely evident there. Before that there was already Lord Byron with his "Cain." Camus traced dandyism back to the first post-Christian centuries. Time and again they found the figure of Lucifer in literature, but that isn't Satanism in a personalistic sense, rather the attempt to build up the figure of Lucifer into a formalistic rebel against a creativity full of content. But it is true that the Wiener Gruppe experienced dandyism to a large degree, for example in Konrad Bayer.

The Wiener Gruppe is at its best in Gerhard Rühm, in Konrad Bayer,

Heidi/Peter

MONTE VERITA: A Mountain For Minorities

Excavation on a hill near a small Swiss town where Nietzsche, in 1871, finished his *Birth of Tragedy*, brought to light a scene which is not unrelated to the present-day Berlin scene. Actually, at the beginning of the century, it was known as the "Berlin Suburb."

We are speaking of Ascona on Lago Maggiore. This "Bermuda Triangle of the Mind" was made by Harald Szeemann into an exhibition which, after its premiere in Ascona, toured Zurich, West Berlin (the Akademie der Künste), Vienna, and Munich. For, as

Heidi and Peter, anarcho-artists of the Berlin off-off scene, run the *Merve* publishing collective.

more or less consciously also in H.C. Artmann — where the Wiener Gruppe tried to clear up this mechanism of being touched, of understanding, of being shaken emotionally. Whereas pop culture tries to procede as if this process of understanding didn't have to be understood, because that is experience. The mechanisms which give meaning are ignored, by punk, by behaviorism, by dandyism.

FG: What would you say to a connection between the Wiener Gruppe and Pop or Punk? I mean the youthful protest against the fossilized world of adults, the flaring up against gerontocratics?

OW: Generally, that is true.

There is a connection between the Wiener Gruppe and Punk. Pop people were pretty much the first to move symbols without worrying about contents. That is so strong in Punk that the people completely miss the contents. When they take, let's say Marilyn Monroe or a car or just a suit or a hair color, they won't ask what it refers to, what is meant by it, they're only interested in the signs. They move about in a world of scenery, of symbols which can be moved toward one another. They don't only think that this is the world, they simply want it to be the world. This dandyism also exists in behaviorism, which is a science of movement of signs and manipulation of signs.

I always wanted to become a behaviorist, because I consider it a heroic thing to dissolve content completely into formal signs. For me that is an act of self-denial which seems to be the ultimate achievement. But in the meantime I am convinced that it won't work, that it is simply a mistake, that it would be folly to cultivate this heroicism as a leading image.

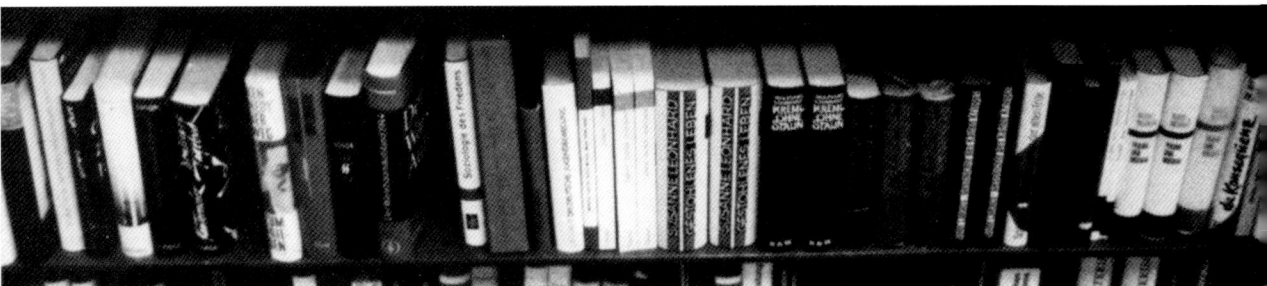

Szeemann said, "Ascona around 1900 was the southernmost outpost of a far-reaching Nordic lifestyle-reform, that is, alternative movement."

Anarchists and Life Reformers

Bakunin could not possibly foresee all the things he was setting in motion when he moved to Ascona. After ten years, spent in Russian prisons and exile, he had returned via Japan and the U.S.A. to Europe, where indefatigably he contrived new uprisings and became Marx's antagonist in the First International. Always fleeing his persecutors and dependent on the help of friends, he settled in 1869 on Lago Maggiore, around the corner from Nietzsche, because he feared the evil gossip of prudish Marxists. (His girlfriend, whom he later married, was pregnant at the time.)

Later on, other anarchists came to gather material on Bakunin, among them Max Nettlau, Peter Kropotkin, and Fritz Brupbacher.[1] And there they met strange people like the theosophes, who had been drawn to the place in 1895 because Alfredo Pioda had intended to found his laymen's monastery, "Fraternitas," on La Monescia Hill. Pioda never lifted one stone to build the monastery, but he founded a joint-stock company — whose shares nobody wanted.

The anarchists also met in Ascona, especially between 1900 and 1920, life style

For us in the Wiener Gruppe it was somewhat different. You were to experience the content during the time you underwent the process of understanding. Even though the content was relevant for the Wiener Gruppe, we didn't ignore examining simple movements of symbols. It was even very important. The content is delivered through this act of understanding, it is produced. Or if it is already present, the content is taken out and coordinated with the sign. For me content is inner movement, movement of myself, movement of this algebraic structure which I think to be, and which can't be reproduced in signs. Signs can only be the starting point for developing contents, but everyone who is such an algebraic structure has to work at it himself. For this reason I feel that there is no tradition of ideas, but rather only a tradition of forms which, time and again, are filled with new content. □

Translated by Christian-Albrecht Gollub

1. Herman Nitsch, one of the original performance artists using the body as a canvas. His work involves physical actions using blood, entrails and a neo-Romantic mythology.

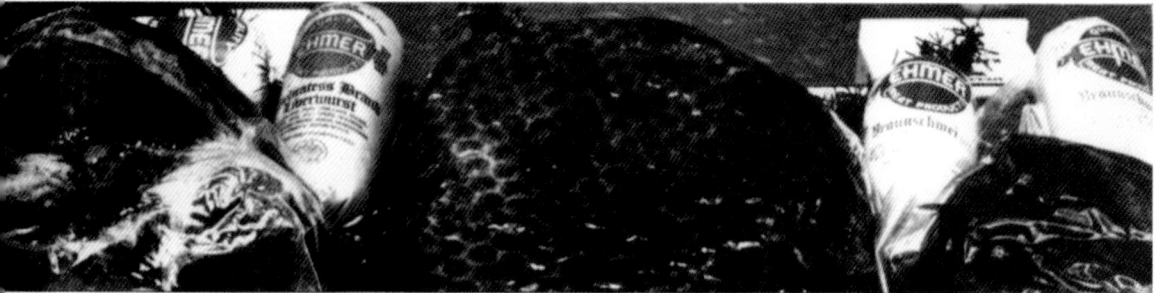

reformers and nature freaks. In 1900 Ascona had been christened Monte Verita (Mount Truth) by Henri Oedenkoven, son of a Belgian industrialist; Ida Hofmann a piano teacher; Gusto Gräser, a former Austrian army officer "who, being an unassuming man, sometimes called himself Gras instead of Gräser (grasses) because one being should not be named in the plural, and who left leaves of grass as his visiting card," (J. Frecot), as well as his brother Karl; Lotte Hattemer the daughter of a Mayor of Berlin and F. Grüne, a theosophist landowner from Graz, Austria.

This group, searching for paradise and hence without much luggage, had come to live on the hill. They were looking for an alternative, a Third Way without or beyond Capitalism and Communism, both of which even back then were getting more and more powerful. Thus Monte Verita came into being as a settlement, sanatorium, and later a school of life.

Then as now "alternative" meant: different styles of production and of life, hence abolition of the sexual division of labor (men vs. women) and the social division of labor (brain vs. brawn); it meant communal property and the beginnings of straight barter. Even so, life reformers did not consider themselves a collective but an individual

cooperative, which complicated their working together. In technical matters Gusto
Gräser advocated the puristic variant: neither running water nor electricity, hibernation

instead of heating. A friend of Hermann Hesse's, he became a model for many of the novelist's guru characters.

Dancers such as Rudolf Laban, Charlotte Bara and Mary Wigman, who founded the new school of expressive dancing, were welcome on Mount Verita: they helped give rhythm to meal-cooking and vegetable-preserving. Debates about technology led to the first factionalizing: on the one hand the nature people (Vester, Gräser, etc.), on the other the vegetarian reformers who, after the "Nature *and* Comfort" slogan, were to move over into the sanatorium and hotel business, complete with promotion prospectuses, their speciality: withdrawal cures for intellectuals, poets, and artists.

In 1904 a lung specialist exhausted by political battles, Dr. Friedeberg, underwent a cure on Monte Verita. While fighting in labor-movement organizations for the General Strike (he was eventually expelled from SPD* in 1907), he hung out his doctor's shingle in Ascona. His first patient was Hermann Hesse, whom he treated for alcoholism; Kropotkin, Brupbacher and Nettlau; Otto Braun and Karl Kautsky of the SPD; Mühsam and Otto Gross met at his place. Dr. Friedeberg tried to enlarge Historical Materialism with Historical Psychism, which led him to reject treatment by medication in favour of a natural therapy that emphasized raising fruits and vegetables and sawing wood.

WOLFGANG HAGEN

"Germany, It's All Over"
A true little story of German rock

Unlike Dylan or Country Joe in the States, the German "protest movement" brought forth no singer, let alone a rock band. The German SDS* was unmusical; and the godfathers of its ideology, the critical theorists Adorno, Horkheimer and Marcuse were enraged by "jazz" and even more by "pop." The revolt had no singers, but of course songs and chants (mostly from the 20's); and, like rock, a huge lack of tradition.

Everything else was 'autochorie': self-growth. The short life of the German rockbands began: the *Rattles* (1961-1967); *Amon Düül* (1967-1971); *City Preachers* (1965-1969); *Frumpy* (1969-1972); *Atlantis* (1972-1976); *Birth Control* (1968-?); *Can* (1968-?); *Kraan* (1971-?); *Kin Ping Meh* (1971-1976); *Randy Pie* (1972-1977); *Scorpions* (1965-...), etc. This is my small selection of "Krautrock" until 1976. Let's forget the revolt of 67-71; its actors have looked in vain for its historical roots in the subsequent years. In multiple costumes (anarchistic, syndicalistic, "råtekommunistisch," Stalinistic, Trotskyistic, etc.) it repeated and re-staged in only five years half of a century of history of the

Wolfgang Hagen is the ultimate disc jockey and music critic for Radio Free Berlin.

Crazy or Anti?

Among the most interesting characters of the early Ascona scene is the psychiatrist and psychoanalyst Otto Gross.

As early as 1908 Freud referred him to his colleague C.G. Jung for an opium and cocaine withdrawal cure at Burgholzli. The analysis with Jung was very intensive, with sessions of up to twenty-four hours. After two weeks, Otto fled from Jung, who certified him as suffering from *dementia praecox*. Freud announced triumphantly to Jung: "I intend to appoint you to continue and finish my work; you are to apply to *psychoses* what I have begun with *neuroses*."

Otto's father, the famous Graz criminologist Dr. Hans Gross, as well as his psychoanalyst colleagues declared him crazy. The reasons are all too apparent. Dr. Hans Gross liked to use psychoanalysis to prove why criminals, vagabonds, revolutionaries, and homosexuals should be deported. Always on the move, living in open relationships, consuming all kinds of drugs, his son, on the other hand, made it clear that he wanted to "turn people into sexual immoralists." In his writings, Otto kept expounding antipatriarchal arguments, questioning the doctor-patient relationship in analysis, rejecting transference. Sure enough, this kind of psychoanalysis and antipsychiatry did not

Workers' Movement. That found its end in the dead of Stammheim* and the dead of the R.A.F.*

Rock found a market in Germany due to the cultural gap left by Fascism. Everything which the masses liked until 1945 was a remnant of the decimated German "Schlager" of the 20's, as well as songs about soldiers and love songs. The delayed influence of rock after 1955 was a welcome "import" as was Big Band Jazz till 1955 which now as before dominates the musical programs of the broadcasting systems. To the present day only German rock must forego every official institutional support (which is perhaps for the best anyway) that is obtained plentifully and overplentifully by all other segments of the popular entertainment genres.

The secret of German rock (if there is one) lies on this intricate economic basis. Now as before sales figures make the "Schlager." Rock culture in Germany is a hybrid between a folk culture seeking social recognition/support and a matter of callous business. What's called "Deutsche Innerlichkeit" (German inwardness) is a by-product of this hybrid.

Curiously, the first groups to become popular in Germany were the ones which refused to enter the market at first and succeeded then as re-imports from other markets. *Kraftwerk* was discovered in 1975 in America. *Tangerine Dream* in England in 1974. Both groups are the innocent children of Mr. Moog; the lack of a tradition of rock was downright elementary for them. Their teachers are Cage, Kagel and the "classical" experimentalists of the 60's including in the case of *Kraftwerk* the Futurists of 1913: minimalists and deconstructors of serial order on both sides of tonality. The titles of the first *Kraftwerk* tracks already gave evidence of this elementary impact: "Strom"

enrapture Freud and Jung, who were attempting to establish psychoanalysis academically. Gross came to Ascona early and returned to it again and again, establishing contacts with Muhsam, Friedeberg, Max Weber, the Richthofen sisters, and through them with D.H. Lawrence.

In 1909 the police started preliminary proceedings against Otto for the death of an anarchist woman, "Lotte." It turned out that Lotte Hattemer, a co-founder of Monte Verita, had committed suicide using morphine she had gotten from Otto. In 1911 another suicide occurred in Ascona in which Gross seemed involved: a young anarchist woman, a painter, had taken a cocaine overdose. Arrest warrants were issued for him in Germany and Switzerland. Eventually, at the request of his father, proceedings against him were stopped. In the following years, Otto lived in Vienna, Florence, and in Berlin, where he collaborated with Franz Jung and the *Aktion* group.[2] Returning to Berlin in 1913, he was arrested as an "anarchist of unsound mind," deported to Austria, put in an insane asylum and declared incompetent. His father had supplied the expert opinion needed for the commitment. A press campaign in which Franz Jung, Blaise Cendrars, Erich Mühsam and others took part forced his release after a year's confinement.

Starting in 1933 one of Otto's friends, Olga Frobe-Kapteyn, ran the Eranos Circle in Ascona, a round table which tried to overcome the East-West, spirit-nature, science-

(electric current), "Spule" (reel), "Megahertz," "Tanzmusik" (dance music), "Heimatklänge" (sounds from the homelands), "Ruck/Zuck" (their first big hit and an idiomatic expression for a quick move). Later they recall more object-like myths: "Autobahn," "Radio," "Roboter," "Trans-Europe Express," "Computer World." Unlike *Tangerine Dream*, who never outgrew their psychedelic sound-painting (and today enjoy a cold glory like that of official jazz), *Kraftwerk* writes texts. Short, minimalist texts, like the elements of their music. But they were and are German.

With this another sore point of "Deutsch-Rock" comes up: can one sing in German? The unanimous answer from the German rock crowd: no, except, perhaps, for Udo Lindenberg (a quarter talent, a coarse German version of Tom Waits, singing in the lingo of the Hamburg youth "scene" accompanied by the best German R&B musicians). Slang is unusual in Germany, since almost all milieus have been destroyed by fascism and war. Hardly a city is really older than 36 years. Young people may speak in dialects, but not in the lingo of a milieu.

Some say German can't be sung because there are too many unsingable consonants and unmelodious vowels. The whole dispute has been going on for twenty years. The very true rock fan in Germany speaks perfect English, reads English or American rock-magazines and fanzines, bids at auctions from Dallas to Brighton, collects transnationally and is the alpha-link in a ponderous multiplying chain of a dogma: rock'n & roll is English, Americans and whoever is 'really into it' would rather be "there" right now than here. To this day, rock'n roll is for many German musicians the music of the Allies and so the feeling towards English music on German soil is one of resistance.

myth antagonisms. Meetings dealt with Yoga and Meditation, redemption and rebirth, symbolism of light and mysteries, or "the Great Mother — the Archetype of the Great Feminine." Among those who attended were Karl Kerenyi, Mircea Eliade, Gershom Scholem, Martin Buber, and Adolf Portmann.[3] The esoteric parties were headed by, of all people, C.G. Jung.

"Next to Capri and Taormina in Italy, Ascona has become a place for the rediscovered cults of the Young Man, of the Woman and Great Mother, of the Wise Old Man, of Elements and Constellations; it has become a focus for the projections and desires of Nordic peoples" (Szeemann).

This finds its architectonic expression in ideas of liberated living space, theosophic building projects, nature-healing facilities, light-and-air huts, solar villas, and temple designs. Fidus[4] wanted to build for the Monte Veritans a "Temple of the Earth" whose model can be seen in the exhibition. The Baltic nobleman Elisar von Kupfer actually built near Ascona his Temple of Clarity, called Sanctuarium Artis Eliasarion, which he dedicated to his hermaphroditic ideals. Even more beautiful is his cyclorama, "Dance of the Blest," with a multitude of transsexual saints in Arcadian realms.

What with so much free love, alternative lifestyle, meditation, antipsychiatry, and Esoterica, the chic of wealth and the golden aristocracy were bound to get curious. In

Resistance in one's own country against the dominating order with the help of foreign subculture: for the majority of German musicians, that's the keynote for their music. The danger is that this feeling of resistance remains mere legitimation instead of providing the basis for a real subculture.

Mountains Explode

Thus far to 1976; a year — better two short summers — which enforced a long hoped-for change in Rock-history similar only to the R&B explosion of Black America in the 40's, the turn to Rock 'n' Roll of White America in the 50's, and the English R&B Revival of the 60's. The Punk Revolution was vigorous enough to hop relatively quickly over to the continent. Its maxims were refusal of any alienating professionalism; restoration of direct contact between public and musician; understanding at a glance; bodily extasis instead of ritual identification; accusations instead of introverted protest; alcohol instead of drugs.

As hard as steel. I am strong. I love metal. Aluminum. Brass. Lead.
(Radierer, a Limburg group — from the so-called "Non Dom Casette")

Many German underground groups have recently released songs of LP-length, although on cassettes. Their music thus bypasses the commercial market. Cassettes tend to be closed systems and forego the logic of hits. Whoever hears it and buys it enters, as it were, an imaginary membership. Hence the freedom and relish to experiment, the impartiality and intensity of most cassette productions. Cassettes enforce their own temporality, be it con-

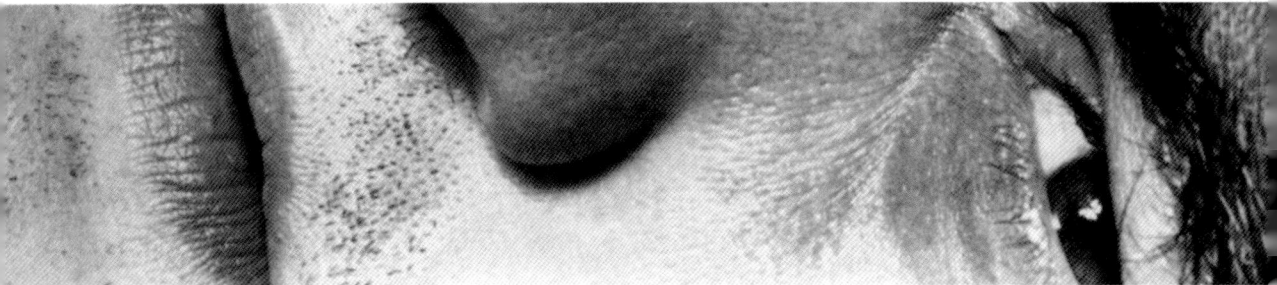

1923 Max Emden, owner of a Hamburg department store, bought the Brissago islands, along with their botanical garden, from Baroness Antonietta von Saint-Leger, who, says Richard Ellman, "had buried seven husbands without a tear" before she invited James Joyce to the islands and inspired the Siren and Circe episodes of *Ulysses*. (She eventually died in the poorhouse in 1948.) Meanwhile, rich Max had naked beauties hop and skip around — for "life too is an art" — in the island garden. The sanitorium closed. Artists were squatting in the Semiramis Hotel, built in 1910. The terrain was for sale. The Kaiser's banker, Eduard Freiherr von der Heydt, without much ceremony, bought the entire Monte Verita, across the water from the islands, which long since had been left by the lifestyle reformers. He built there a de luxe hotel in Bauhaus style.

A Patchwork of Minorities

There is nothing to understand about this dunghill, this mountain of truth; neither didactics nor structure of meaning; at best, there is plenty that can spur the imagination. Ascona has shown how revolutionaries, crazies, hippies, psychoanalysts, theosophists, and artists can "become parts and wheelworks of each other."

Everywhere in this exhibition we meet unpleasant company: next to the anarchist the religious freak, next to the revolutionary the petty-bourgeois gone wild, next to the

237

women's libber the cute little baby doll, next to the "alternative" people the ascetic whole-wheat faddist. If a search for identity drew a sharp line between elements that are in such close touch, it would rest on an ego cult and a personality cult, and we all would be right back in old Berlin's Cafe Megalomania. Instead, the exhibition visualizes a transversal symphony of "a thousand small dissolved egos" (Foucault). As Elisar von Kupfer's temple of transsexual saints has it: a roundelay of most variegated poses of the same person. □

Translated by Hedwig Pachter

1. Max Nettlau is a leading historian of the European anarchist movement. Peter Kropotkin was a Russian anarchist and theorist of mutual aid. Fritz Brupbacher was a writer and "People's Doctor" in Zurich, Switzerland.

2. *Aktion* was a revolutionary anarchist magazine published in 1911 in Berlin by Franz Pfemfert.

3. Karl Kerenyi (1897-1973) was an influential mythologist. Mircea Eliade is Professor in the History of Religions at the University of Chicago. Gershom Scholem is a philosopher (1897-1982). Buber (1878-1965) a philosopher and theologian and Adolf Portmann a biologist.

4. Fidus was the pseudonym for Hugo Hoeppner (1868-1948), a painter, illustrator and concrete utopian.

Berlin Alternative Guide

Hydra — A Meeting Place For Prostitutes

Hydra, the legendary serpent. When one head is chopped off, two new heads are generated. We, a team of four women, want to offer prostitutes a chance to get to know each other. The fun includes numerous group activities, like group trips, group theater visits, photography group, conversation group, and self-defense group. Primarily we want them to abandon hostility toward each other and learn to support each other. We want to recognize as strengths the many fine qualities and abilities which are part of the prostitutes' daily work — actress, animator, clergyman, business woman, marriage counselor, housewife, and mother — that can be used for their own good or the good of other women. □

centrated or empty as a bare background. One can switch it off, but not, like the needle on horizontal vinyl, simply lift it up.

> *We're a happy family. We don't talk about feelings. Incest. I love my mother. Incest. I love my mother. Incest. I make it with my mother. Incest. I murder my father. Incest. With my little sister. With my big sister. Incest.*
> (Radierer, "Nom Dom Cassette")

"Herdentum" (herd-being) and individuality. That is the theme. What the herd ought to be it did not and does not know. The herd has no consciousness of itself. Its characteristics hide themselves in exteriorities; uniformity and fashions; in changing herd tastes and its edges; the "Angesagte" (what's "in") and the "Daneben" ("out-of-it").

Herds feel themselves driven like nomads. They are anti-State and anti-institutional. They renounce the ciphers of educated language and high culture; they develop political experiences on a non-conceptual level, which can seldom be turned into political solidarity. Therefore "punks" and "skins" and all other "tribes" of the underground are not part of the militant sections of the current "alternative" and "squatter" movements.

Herds are nomadic and parasitic. They take what they can get. Mooching. Borrowing money.

> *I and you. We should be. I and he. Like the fire department. We and You. How do you do. Everybody does it with everybody. All fuck each other. Everybody's in it. All screw each other. No one excepted. Every one will get it. No one is left out. Each gets his desserts. Everyone is next.*

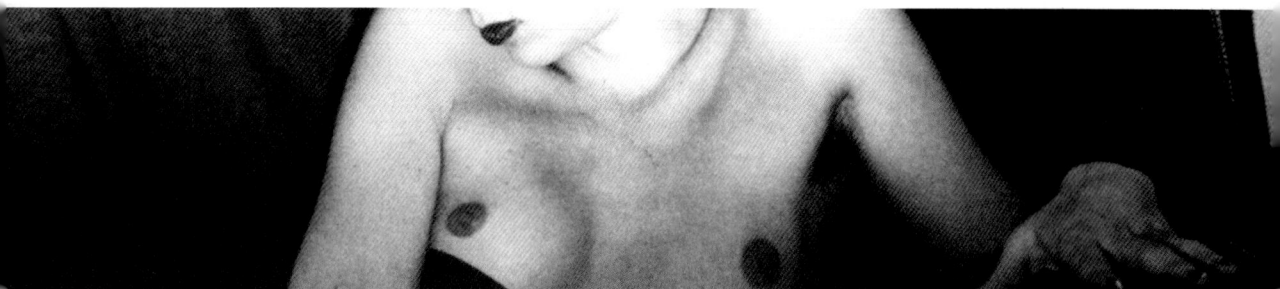

Charlotte

Sitting at a table in a room of a factory, Charlotte is drinking, eating, and conversing with the people around her. A party is going on. Charlotte is the only elderly gentleman and we realize immediately who she is.

Sexuality plays the dominant role in Charlotte's life. She is receptive to all forms of sexuality, but the heterosexual side clearly predominates in her daily life.

Charlotte: Tits, cunt, asshole, I really screwed her with marvelous depravity. But when I wear women's clothes, I'm another person; I don't look at women any more; sex is in the background. You must see my outfits and fourteen wigs. I really have nice things, I really do. I don't understand how women can wear pants, it's awful. Nothing is nicer than being a woman, really. I'm much more familiar and comfortable with female anatomy. I've always had a feminine body.

Charlotte hides her women's clothes in the cellar, gets dressed down there or puts them in plastic bags and takes them with her. She's lived in her building for twenty

Everything vibrates without emotion.
("Alle sind mal dran" [Everyone will get it) — Tumorboys)

Observations. Berlin at the Yorkbrücken.[1] There, where the "Blocksberg" woman's bar once stood, now one finds another bar: RISIKO. The large window pane is covered by a sheetmetal full of holes; the exterior white-washed. The first impression: an artificial garbage-heap. Squeezing scrawny sounds from two boxes on the ceiling. Graffiti all over the wall. *Diving from the clouds.* A poster from a punk festival in the Ruhr. Comments scrawled nearby. *Corrosive junk.* Written over the doorway: *Men also bleed.*

Some people find themselves at home here. They hang around. Short haircuts, spiky and dyed, adventurous, decked-up jackets, faded trousers, worn shoes. Black red glitter shocking leather velvet linen brocade rubber. "Dazzling," less for shock than for difference, among each other (and, naturally, against all outsiders), and to break up the daily monotony. The gear one wears, and not the position of the sun functions as calendar here.

I'm afraid. I'm afraid. Of life. I'm afraid. I'm full of dread.
("I'm afraid," WC = Westdeutsche Christen)

The john, anxiety and blood. The pissoir in this joint is, at first sight, frightening. Here somebody has so splattered the urinal with deceitfully real theater-blood, from here on down to the bottom, that it looks just like someone had slashed an artery in his thigh. Good precaution. On the wall: *New: Deadly Doris* (a Dada/Underground group hereabouts) *now also pseudomusical.* An implicit quotation of the sex ads in the big tabloids: *New: Thai model, 18, now also dominatrix.* Dominating, jerked off, and many times a recurrent theme in graffiti — anxiety. Not anxiety towards, but anxiety as.

years. The neighbors know she is a transvestite. She has no inhibitions. People tell her, "You look your best in drag, sweetie." Charlotte often visits sex film clubs, brothels, and bars. Everyone likes her. She uses her homosexual side to earn money.

A Dialogue with Charlotte

C: I was fifteen when I was initiated. We already fucked each other in the school's toilet. Just the way they do today. When I was sixteen, I wore women's clothes for the first time. We did that just among ourselves in homosexual bars. After 1922, the Spruce, an athletic and nudist club, was founded. I joined then and was a member until Hitler came to power. Then everything was disbanded.

Q: During those years, did you fuck boys and girls?

C: Of course. One after the other.

Q: Did you have any difficulties in those days?

C: No, of course not. Even before then, after World War I, there were communes where five or six couples lived together. I met my first wife in Berlin in a women's bar frequented only by women. I met her there with a girlfriend.

241

Anxiety as, to quote Nietzsche, "cement" of the "monstrous instinctive conspiracy of the herd...against everything that is shepherd, carnivore, hermit,
and Caesar, in favor of the preservation and nurture of everything weak, oppressed, badly turned out, mediocre, half-miscarried, like a slave revolt drawn
out, first secretly, then always more self-consciously, against every kind of
master..." (Nietzsche, Fall 1885)

> *I want to die so no one'll hear me. A little blood in my mouth. A*
> *Black spot on my skin, I breathe deeply and then sound hollow.*
> *Carbolic acid smell doesn't bother me; my head was empty*
> *anyhow. I'm lying still warm under the white sheet.*
> *Someone cuts my toes off, my whole length won't fit in the grave.*

The whole time I'm astonished by some guy sitting on the pinball
machine, legs drawn up to his chest, motionless staring at the wall. His wide,
thick jacket of heavy black rubber buttoned up to his neck, as if it were bitterly
cold in the joint (it was sticky hot). Black rubber pants, heavy work-boots.
Under his seaman's cap, visor down low, piercing, blackened eyes. Next to
him stands a woman I know. Adelere, barely twenty. She is from Fulda, has
been a year in Berlin, thrown out of school, off with her last bit of money,
works as coat-check girl and waitress. She lost her last job at a "scene" cafe;
the owner didn't want to put up with the swastika on her shirt; he forgot that
she usually wore the Star of David. Now she lives off the proceeds of a single
good coke deal. Says she. "Who's the guy?" I ask someone next to me. "Blixa."
I remember. Blixa Bargeld ("Blixa in cash") is the founder of the *Einsturzende
Neubauten* ("collapsing New-Buildings"), Berlin's undergound band most full
of ideas. Blixa gave the group its name *before* Berlin's most famous new

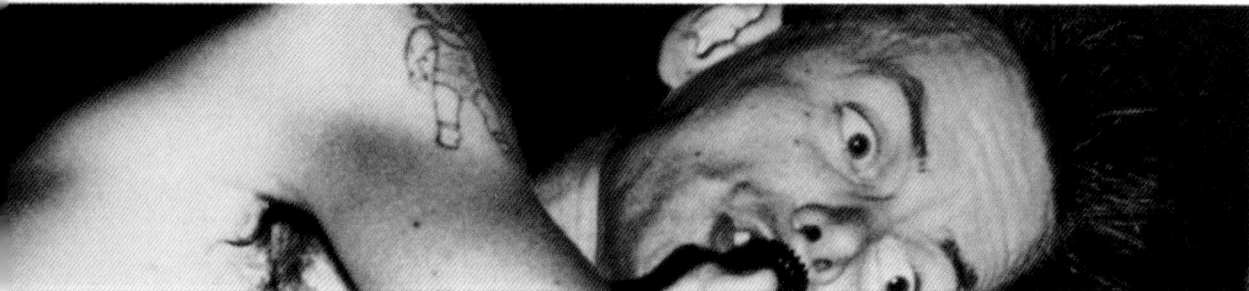

Q: What did your wife think of your women's clothing?

C: She thought it was great. She had a girlfriend who had also married and all four of us
went out together as sisters.

Q: Did it bother you when your wife slept with another man?

C: Boy, are you behind the times. We did everything as a foursome. My wife was tolerant
and so was I. I also fucked her. I had a daughter with her.

Q: Did your wife want a child?

C: What do you mean want. It was just there. What else can you do?

Charlotte's first wife died in Silesia in 1944. Her daughter was sent to a youth camp
in Poland, from which Charlotte rescued her in 1949 with the help of the Red Cross.
Charlotte still keeps in touch with her daughter, who is married and has a daughter.

Q: Were there bars for transvestites and homosexuals before World War II?

C: Not under Hitler. So we did it secretly; under Hitler it was against the law. Homos
were sent to concentration camps. No doctor would give you shots. Right after World

242

building in fact collapsed: the Congress Hall, built with American occupation force money.

Nietzsche again, in a note of 24th Nov. 1887 from Nizza: "One ought not to will of oneself what one is not able to. One asks oneself: *Do you want to go first?* Or do you want to go *on your own?* In the first case you will be, at best, shepherd: which means, the herd's indispensible need. In the other case, you must be capable of something else: from being *able* to go on your own, to being *capable* of something else, and of going elsewhere. In either case you must be capable of it, and you should not want the other."

The strength (perhaps also the reservoir) of the so-called, "New German Wave" (NDW) lies in its underground. Where the NDW encounters incipient commercial success — breaking into the German Schlager and Popmusic markets (as *Abwärts, Fehlfarben, Hans-a-plast, Ideal* are about to do) — this anticommercial, experimental humus is also present in Hamburg, around Düsseldorf, Hanover and West-Berlin. Though small and including only a couple thousand fans altogether, a social reaction is at work in it. These people who find themselves torn apart by this society, existentially and biographically, had lost the language to express themselves. That was the time of Stammheim: the mid-70's, when the traditional codes of protest, the discourse of the New Left decade, had fallen apart; when the moralists of the ecological apocalypse began to diffuse an Apollonian trance; when the women's movement went lame by rediscovering the phallus and becoming in turn an establishment; and finally, English, proletarian Punk offered new subversive levels of expression, which assault even language and speech itself.

I'm all alone. I'm all alone. I'm all alone. Today. Today. Today. Na

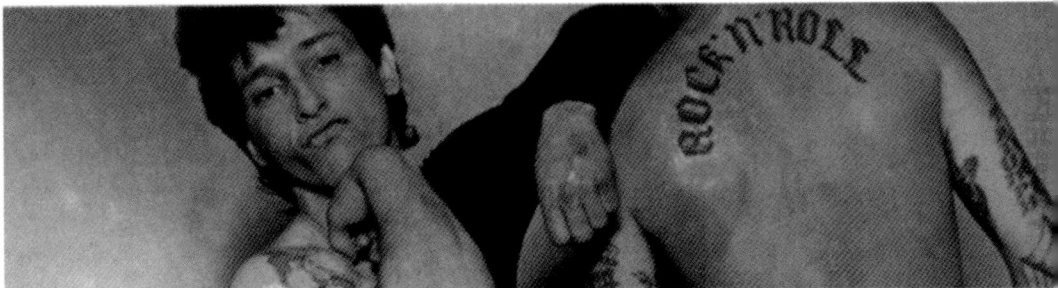

War I was the best time. It was really nice. Then shitty Hitler came to power. That should never have happened. In 1939, I was drafted and sent to France.

Q: Where were you in France?

C: I was with Rommel, Africa Corps. I was everywhere, in Crete. I've seen the world.

Q: Did you get along with military men?

C: Of course, no problem.

Q: Did you earn a little something on the side?

C: I only supplemented my soldier's pay.

Q: What was the War like for you? It must have been terrible.

C: Oh, no! I liked it a lot! Man, I went AWOL after two years. I didn't like it anymore. I wasn't for the War. In 1941, I went AWOL. To France, to Lyon, in a brothel.

Q: Weren't you afraid you'd be discovered?

C: I simply disappeared. Until 1949, I was in a brothel. In those days, I had breasts. As soon as I got to France, I had shots.

243

na na na na na na na. So alone. So alone. So alone. Today. Today.
Today. No No No No.

For the first time, a protest movement of the young generation seems to have almost completely bypassed the intellectuals. The sole frame of clarification which gives at least a few clues to explain the new phenomena was not brought up by them but by a politician (Peter Glotz, now General Secretary of the Social Democratic Party), the so-called "Two Culture-Theory." Did anyone notice that this paradigm included a quote from Lenin?

Glotz' argument rests on an analogy. As in the 90's in tsarist Russia an opposition understanding itself as "narodniki" and partly-Marxistic developed against the francophile Grande Bourgeoisie, so today an "Alternative and Underground Culture" has formed against the language and politics of the media and "high culture." It would be simple if everything resolved itself in this dualistic logic. In fact, the gaps are yawning open in multiple ways, certainly between the "alternatives" and the "underground," as well as between each of these and "high culture." And the formation of these contradictory processes are still going on silently and without any open front-lines and strategies.

The only characteristic of the undergound new German Wave, its only living part, a fragile herd-tendency. Seen historically this undergound has its origin in the English "year of punk" (76-77), which showed its effects half a year later in Hamburg, Berlin, Düsseldorf: the delight in the destruction of rock as an event and its elemental recomposition. Already concerts in Hamburg showed that clearly. No matter who played on stage they were neither applauded nor cheered. The traditional, ritual figure of an identifying relation-

Q: Were you in contact with your wife?

C: I wrote her everything. She was great. She replied, Papa, amuse yourself. It doesn't matter for a soldier. What matters is that you are alive. She was great. Of course my wife knew that I had a French girl. The girl was seventeen. That was great.

Q: Did your girlfriend like your breasts?

C: She didn't think anything of it. After all, it was in a brothel.

Charlotte returned to Berlin with a forged discharge.

Q: Were you a wreck when you got back to Berlin?

C: Oh, no. I felt better then than I do now.

When I returned in 1949, I found work in a hospital. I worked for sixteen years in the Hermsdorf Dominican Hospital, always with nuns. I liked that. Of course, the nuns were always domineering.

Charlotte retired in 1966. From 1967 to 1971, she worked in a transvestite bar, the Lützower Lamp in Berlin.

ship between the group and the audience was extinguished. In place of this appeared what one could call a "Sid Vicious Syndrome," the symbolic and even real violation of the body. The audience down below squeeze and jostle one another, pushing, jumping around, and elbowing each other to the point of fighting (the "Pogo" as a dance preserves all these punching movements). At the same time the vehement attempt to reach the stage, and to grab the musicians. As far as Sid Vicious was concerned, no concert was finished without his leaving the stage with bleeding lips, scratched and cut skin and visible wounds.

The Destruction of the Mirror

Rock as a violation of body. Before the advent of Punk and underground the reaction of an audience to a gig consisted at the most of the production of as much noise as pounded on them from the P.A. system. Now this mirror-reflection is destroyed. What was formerly the symbolic bond of the mirroring of self in the rock-idol (the hard-rock-fans would mime the guitarist), now falls apart into components of its own imaginary energy. A good rock concert always proved itself in the real power of the audience (and the band) to cross the borders of the symbolic order over to the imaginary: The shrieks of teenage Beatle fans louder than the music, the hour-long shaking heads of Zappa and Grateful Dead fans, etc. The early punks kept as an object to be destroyed the symbolic order of the rock-event as such.

"Energy in general seems to be an important theme to you?" "If I can radiate, release, the greatest amount of energy in three or four

Q: Did you earn a lot as a woman in the Lützower Lamp?

Q: Of course. I still do today. After all, I'm not bad looking. [Charlotte worked as a topless dancer.] When my wife was in Wittenau, I got shots. But today young male transvestites don't want shots. They want to be flat, boyish. Many girls are like that too. In Neufert Street there's a young woman who has no tits at all. The girls don't want to have such cannonballs.

Q: And the men?

C: Many still want tits, but it's different today. Of course a man is aroused by a woman with tits. No, I'm not going to do it anymore either. A shot costs thirty marks and lasts for about three weeks, but you've got to get shots at least three to four times for three weeks before that.

Charlotte asks us to accompany her to a film club.

C: Nothing will happen to you. Don't get offended by anything, particularly the film. Don't get offended when horny men walk around naked, when they sit there masturbating. Let's be honest. It's only human. There are also rooms where you can fuck all you want with a threesome or foursome. Whatever you want. In the Hollido Club everyone can take part.

years, of what I believe is put in me — then I will have surpassed
my father that far."
(Interview with Mufti from Abwärts in "Spex," Sept. 1981)

But the destruction of the mirror dissolves all the limits of the body, and with that displaces its imaginary/real violation.

Hamburg 1979:

A Man has met a woman in a market, and she fell in love with him
completely, plain and simple. After he went with her, he went with
her plain and simple and stupidly into the forest; where else should
one go?
However, the experiment was to find out whether this woman in-
deed loves him. Do you know that? How can one find that out? Do
you know Romeo and Juliet? That is a proof of love and not the
shit you are giving me here. (The kids yelled during the narration,
spit and belched, in an air of indifferent tension W.H.) Thus: he
went with her into the forest and took off one after another the
parts of his body, till he was only just a head, just a brain. And
then he asked: do you still love me forever? And that is all.
(Markthalle, Hamburg, 24th Feb. 1979, the leadsinger of "Male.")

One can also read this as an allegory of the rock-event. Next, the aura is taken away; it's like being in the flea-market. By chance. Completely plain and simple and stupid. One just goes. Someone is playing. A feeling of *Mittagspause* (lunchbreak). Thus the name of one band at that time (branched out in the meantime to *D.A.F.* and *Fehlfarben*, the most successful bands of the

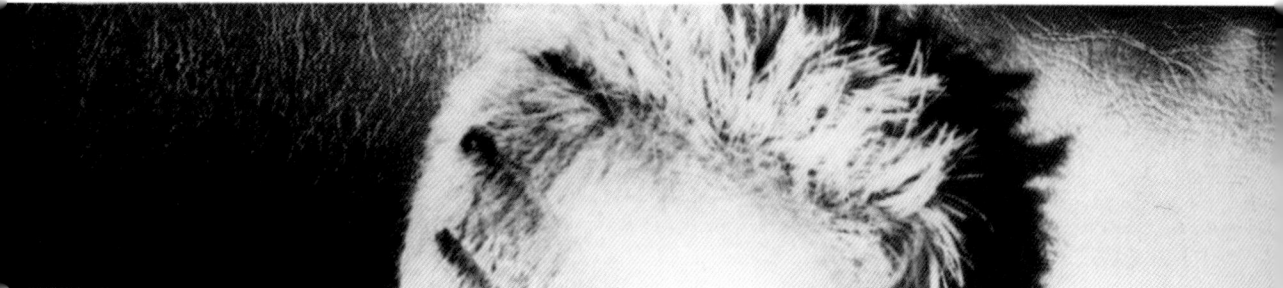

According to Charlotte, the film clubs are well attended even during the day. Charlotte doesn't pay to get in. She belongs to the family. In the clubs she earns something from the sale of her porno magazines, and of herself.

Q: Do you wear only women's clothes to the film clubs?

C: Yes, but not during the day. I can't do it because of the people. But I feel better as a woman. I put everything on under wide trousers when I'm alone. When I hang out in the neighborhood, I go out late in the evening.

Q: Does your wife ask you where you're going?

C: Of course not. That's none of her business.

Q: Doesn't your wife complain when you come home late at night?

C: Oh, no. She's asleep by then. I do what I want. Nobody tells me what to do. When she's away recuperating, I receive guests at home. Then they bring money into the house.

Q: Are they all men?

NDW). What happens is not said or planned. A man falls in love. A woman falls in love.

But what does "falling in love" mean? The chance moment turns into the moment of decision. Yet only the forest preserves the ambiguous mood of ritual secrecy. But for the punks "forest" is also the metaphor of boredom. The grammatical tense becomes stiff. Romeo and Juliet. Love or death. It is not *like* a decision, but Decision itself. Dis-junction, either ... or. To decide the "falling in love," to take off the parts of the body. Self-anatomy. Till he was only a head, only a brain; an idea falls apart to become real.

But it was only an "experiment." And besides, it was not sung, but narrated. A fable, which moreover contains the symptom of an experience. An experience which made its way through this text as a shifting trace, reporting about the great moment of the herd, the tragedies of incest, repeating the murder of the father which the goatherds celebrated dismembering him in their brains.

But it was only an "experiment." The great times of the herd are gone. And belching, spitting and yelling were, finally and initially, not even the worst answer to this priestly apocalyptic narration. It also belongs to the good memories from these early punk concerts, which hardly once left me the feeling of being a lamb herded by mass- or group ecstasy.

The Restoration of the rock-event through its destruction/dismemberment is like walking a tightrope. It presupposes that a linking order arises neither on stage nor in the audience's gestures. This may have the consequence that nothing happens anymore. Only laughter at a group which doesn't play or at a concert which doesn't take place. The experiences which are collected in

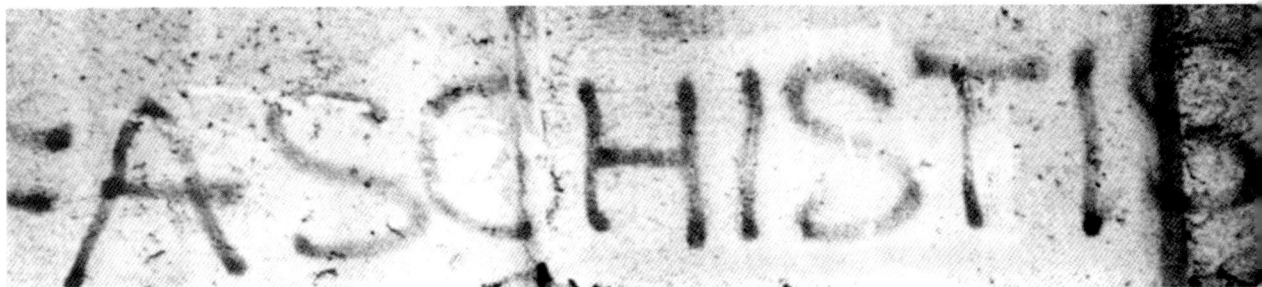

C: Only men, regular customers.

In A Bar With Charlotte

During our trip to Wedding[1] to pick up Charlotte, we decide to go with her to the Small World Lantern. "Well, you little assholes, you" is Charlotte's greeting at her door. It sets the tone for the evening. Charlotte and Thaddäus get horny recalling their years in Kreuzberg. They used to dance naked on the bar. Charlotte often appeared in drag. After numerous thrusts, Charlotte is ours. When we want to pay her, she roguishly taps our fingers. It would threaten her masculinity. □

Translated by Wynn Gundarson

1. Workers' district in West Berlin.

the body of the unfettered herd produce a nice ability for criticism. This ability is not based on individual criteria. To it belongs the presence of the herd, an uncompromising anti-professionalism, the deconstruction and dissolution of borders of relationships between group and audience, the elementarity of the music whether this side of or beyond tonality, the brevity of the songs and the collection of all these elements in the texts. This is only present in small group of musicians and fans. They call themselves the "Genial Dilettants."

> Death is a scandal. Death is a scandal. Rituals of Expiation. Door
> handles. Ventilation grates. Radiators. Death is a scandal. Rituals
> of expiation. The machine works. We are all hostages. Give. Take.
> (Die tödliche Doris)

But let us not forget rock has a traditional dynamic of development, based on the logic of marketing and capitalism. At some point, every musician is faced with the alternative: dropping out or making money. The destruction of the rock-event, the failure of every economy, the lack of ideas of continuity, deferment and accumulation — in a word, the *unreliability* of the herd stands in the way of this need.

> I and I in the real life. I and I in reality. I and I in the true world. I
> and I in reality.
> (Mittagspause)

Another kind of experiment began. It contained a dialectic as old as capitalistic rock-culture: how much of the transgressive element at the beginning, how much of the subversion of this "I," lost in reality; how much of the cracked mirror of the audience/group-relation; how much of all this could stand fast before the masses' taste? A question which once again answered

ANNETTE HUMPE

ROCK LOBSTER

SYLVÈRE LOTRINGER: When did you start writing lyrics?

ANNETTE HUMPE: I started when I was 15, but I never published anything. Writing was self-therapy.

SL: Did you need therapy?

AH: Sure, every German needs therapy.

SL: To get cured of history?

AH: History is one point. Even though I wasn't born at the time.

Annette Humpe is a West Berlin rock star. She belongs to the "No Future" generation.

*"We have reason enough
to cry
even without your tear gas."*
Reto Hanny

SL: That's no reason.

AH: That's no reason, but I don't feel guilty. I have difficulties with national feeling. Germans can't be proud of Germany; there's nothing to be proud of. But I have to like it, because it's in me. Sometimes I feel I'm so heavy, so German. I have to go very deep all the time and think and think. I don't know why. Sometimes I like this heaviness, but I have no choice. It doesn't go away. Before I hate it, I have to love it.

SL: Writing lyrics frees you from this heaviness?

AH: Writing about depression brings more life. I love my depressions. They are not depressions because someone was unkind to me; they are depressions over the whole world.

SL: Do you feel that being German is a problem?

AH: I remember moments in a foreign country when I thought I had a different nationality. I said I was Swedish or French. I wondered about it. It happened in Italy. It happened in Greece too. I said that in a village where the Nazis had been, and I didn't want to discuss it. I didn't want to feel the hate of the people; I just didn't want it.

itself in the logic of hits. And even while the group *Mittagspause*, for instance, still experimented extensively on the stage, there was, for instance, at least one song, which worked, despite everything and every time it was played, as a collective hymn. A hit. This one:

> *Kebab dreams in the walled city. Turk-kultur behind barbed wire. New/Izmir in the GDR.* Ataturk the new master. Kyrie for the Soviet Union. In every snackbar a spy. In the Central Committee: an agent from Turkey. Germany, Germany, it's all over. We are the Turks of tomorrow. We are the Turks of tomorrow.*

A hit which became a relatively big-seller as a single (*Mittagspause* and *D.A.F.*) and an LP (*Fehlfarben*). In the logic of rock-history, the multiplication of songs on the record market plays a co-determinative role alongside the subversive force of the rock event itself. Only from its role does the further existence or break-up of the group derive as a pure question of money, money the "Genial Dilettants" entirely rejected by releasing their productions up to now mostly through cassettes and by not claiming to make a living from their music.

> *No pause for breathing history is made it moves on. Spacelabs fall on islands forgetting is widespread it moves on. Mountains explode the President is guilty it moves on. Gray b-movie heroes govern the world it moves on.*
> ("A year" — Fehlfarben)

The language of both these songs reflects quite well the presuppositions of their genesis. "Kebab-dreams" is a fantasmatic mixture of impressions of Berlin. The Turks in the ghetto of Kreuzberg; the wall with barbed wire;

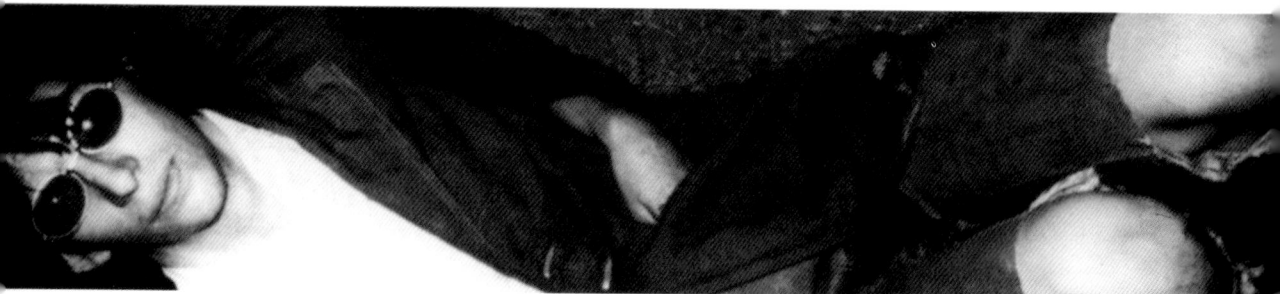

SL: You thought it wasn't fair to inherit that?

AH: Why should I feel guilty? It's bullshit. Even the older generation doesn't feel guilty. The world won't change if sixty milion people feel guilty. My parents don't feel guilty. Before I went to the university, I had many fights with them. In many families the children try to make their parents feel guilty. But without success; they just don't feel guilty.

SL: Why did you leave your parents?

AH: I left home when I was sixteen. It was the first time I was away from my parents. My mother wanted to have a daughter who was a good classical pianist.

SL: Was your mother a musician?

AH: She played organ in church. So I studied in Cologne. I was still obsessed with the idea of becoming a classical pianist, but I didn't have the energy to rehearse ten hours a day. I wanted my life to be different, and I didn't know how, so I came to Berlin. I've been in Berlin for six years now.

250   My parents were very puritanical. When I left home, I had never been drunk before, I had

military guard; the feeling of being caught and yet of remaining undiscovered in the streets of this decaying district; the end-of-time-feeling in face of this No-man's-land before and beyond the wall, *Kyrie eleison*. Thus, it is an extremely political text; it certainly does not stop at the wall of sense, or this side of the barricade of signification. It flattens the wall, jumps back and forth, lets the Turks wander to the other side, into the Central Committee of the East German "Socialist Unity Party" and back again, *in every snackbar* of the free West; the city of the wall, which should denote through its borders the borders of sense, being cut down to a pure signifier, to the indifference of "it's all over." The wall functions only as a simple slash, as the bar in a sign (S/s) that finally negates the hierarchic dualism of its structure (thought/phoneme etc.) in so far as it becomes visible as the wall encircles it.

The herd, left alone at last, and not led around by a shepherd, celebrates a festival. It scans its secret chants in demonstrations: *No pause for breath history is made it moves on.* No ideology, no politically mediated theory, no leader or shepherd has provided these chants. These pithy sounds echo from the walls of houses like laughter. It's laughter, not humor or subversive satire. *We are the Turks of tomorrow.* Not a "negative caricature," as "68ers" might misconstrue it.

But misconstruing is, in general, an epidemic poison of unregulated discourse. Next: the authors of the quoted chants hastened to "deny responsibility" for such political use of their words and music. Because: *Deutsch Amerikanische Freundschaft"* (D.A.F.), *Fehlfarben* and nearly a dozen other bands are on the way to finding a mass audience via TV and the record market. And, lastly, the "Genial Dilettants" themselves are on the way, as last

never smoked marijuana before, I had never slept with a man before; I knew nothing about life. Everything I didn't do before, I did in Berlin.

SL: How did you switch from classical to pop?

AH: I had to earn a living, so I played in bars. I played for transvestites.

SL: How did this happen?

AH: They wanted a special male pianist: a very beautiful one. Either they were not beautiful enough, or they couldn't do it. It was my chance. At first, they didn't like the idea of a real woman in the group, then they realized that I had a neutral face, and it was okay; I was neutral.

SL: Were you in drag yourself?

AH: I had to wear a suit and look like a man in order to play. I learned a lot with them.

SL: Did you learn about men?

AH: No. They were so feminine.

preservers of the genuine experience of Punk and New German Wave, to, at best, restore the old order of shepherd and shepherded. Blixa Bargeld, the already mentioned "spiritus rector" and Ernst Busch[2] of the Dilettants, presents himself recently as propagandist of an obscure dogma of decline, which West Germany has already bitterly experienced.

> The RAF (Red Army Fraction) did their thing: not to overthrow the government. They did not do Schleyer in because he was chairman of the Employers' Association, but so that the CDU* would come to power, so that fascism would triumph sooner in the BRD. – They wanted to drive the process forward; they wanted to rush the decline, which would take place anyway — I don't want anything else.
> (Blixa in "Spex," 9, 1981).

Kyrie eleison. □

Translated by Cesar Loaiza

1. A whole bunch of bridges in the Kreuzberg district.
2. Ernst Busch was the most famous singer of Brecht/Weill songs.

"I never was in the Nazi party, and I still don't belong to any party now. I mind my own business."

Hitler's bodyguard

SL: First time you saw real women?

AH: I thought they were much more women than I am. I was watching them all the time.

SL: What did you do after you left them?

AH: I formed a band called *Expectors* together with my sister. It lasted for half a year. My sister is still in the band, but I left them to play with *Ideal*. They had better musicians. For this kind of music, they are ideal, therefore the name.

SL: Groups form and disappear very fast in Germany. How do you explain that?

AH: It's a punk thing. It comes from this new music scene. Groups split up quickly, and they die, they just die.

SL: Pop music is usually sung in English. Did you ever sing in English?

AH: No, a few German singers did. I cannot express myself in English like I can in German.

SL: Do you feel your lyrics have changed now that you are widely recognized?

MARTIN HEIDEGGER

On My Relation to National Socialism

Regarding the charges made by Mr. E. Hanfstaengel in the Munich city council that in 1933 I pressured students to join the Party, I declare the following: I never pressured a student or anyone else at all to join the Party. I myself unfortunately allowed myself in early summer 1933, as rector of the University of Freiburg elected by the Plenum, to be pressured into joining the Party, to be sure only on the condition (which I also always strictly held to) that I would never work in any way for the Party and certainly not accept an office in it or in one of its organizations. In 1933 I committed the political error, as was the case with many even among those of the highest spiritual and worldly distinction, of seeing constructive strengths for our people in Hitler and his movement and embracing it. I recognized this error already in the first months of the year 1934 and I resigned my office as rector under protest against demands of the National Socialist Minister of Culture of Baden. Since then, i.e. during the last ten years of my academic teaching activity up to fall 1944, I engaged in an

Heidegger's 1950 response, apparently unpublished, to an attack on himself reported in the article "Hanfstaengel contra Heidegger" (the *Münchner Süddeutschen Zeitung*, June 14, 1950).

AH: Something changed. I didn't want to be so direct before. I like to describe special moods, like in the song: "I am a Spy:" I am a spy and I am gifted./ I have many antennas . . . I am a *spy*. I have intuitions about people, about myself, about the things in between. I am in between everything. I'm not a punk, I'm not a student; that's my fate. Sometimes I hate it because you are alone all the time. Sometimes I wish I had a group; a group of people who felt like me, thought like me; where I can hide.

SL: Do you ever think about death?

AH: I don't want to die in bed of old age. I want to die very conscious. I want to see the moment when I am dying. For me, death is totally unsad. No big despair, nothing tragic, something quiet and cool. No spectacle, for me alone. Recently, a friend of mine jumped in front of a subway. I didn't keep him from doing it. I couldn't live for him. He was simply an animalistically sensitive person who no longer wanted to live. He didn't play games with suicide. He died completely untragically.

SL: Did you write a song about death?

AH: I tried to, but it's too heavy. One song is "I'm in the Mood for being Shot." The song is an invitation to someone to die with me, just for fun.

ever more pointed spiritual argument or criticism of the unspiritual foundations of the "National Socialist world view."

This conduct was understood very precisely by thousands of students
whom I educated for responsibility for the West as well as by Party officials
and their press. The many years of informants and surveillance by the S.D.
(Security Service), the continuous attacks on my works in Party journals, later
the publication ban, and finally being drafted into the Volkssturm,[1] unusual
for one of my age and my position, and from which many far younger colleagues remained exempted, prove this unequivocally.

My error of 1933 was established by the Political Cleansing Committee of
the university as the only "taint," and they simultaneously emphasized that I
could no longer be counted as a National Socialist after 1934. A teaching ban
was declared by the French occupation authority in the year 1947, which was
rescinded again in the year 1949. In the German denazification proceedings I
was classified as a fellow-traveler without atonement measures (being required).

Where crimes have occurred, they must be atoned for. But how long does
one want to continue to defame publicly over and over those who erred
politically for a short or even a longer time, and this in a state according to
whose constitution anyone can be a member of and fighter for the communist
party. A strange blindness pushes forward in this way the wearing away and
inner dissolution of the last substantial strengths of our people.□

1. Emergency draft affecting young and old Germans during the last days of the Third Reich.

I love the Wall. There's the possibility to get shot from both sides.

SL: How do you feel in relation to the punks?

AH: I am different. I'm not Punk. I am privileged somehow. The punks I know, they're
really from the working class. They are punks because they have to be punks; they have
no choice. They haven't finished school; they have no possibility to work. They have no
money; they have no place. So I can understand them. I can use my head to see the
reason why they are this way. I like them like a stranger. At the time that I was in the
Russian Communist Party, I never knew what work meant either.

SL: Why Russian?

AH: Just because I met the Russian Communist Party before I met the Maoists'.

SL: I guess you were bound to meet one of the fifteen Communist parties that existed
then?

AH: I didn't know so much. I was 19 at the time. I just knew that something new was a
good idea.

HERE LIE BURIED
1000 BODIES

HIER RUHEN
1000 TOTE

24.4.45

SL: Did you ever envisage living on the other side of the Wall?

AH: That's what my father always says: "Go there." I knew that I didn't want to live in East Berlin.

SL: Did you consider East Germany a communist country?

AH: No, but I still think Communism is winning and has to win. Is what they're doing in East Berlin right? is the wrong question.

SL: Do you have any contact with the squatters?

AH: Contact is too much. I know some squatters. We did a benefit concert for them. But I can't live in an unoccupied house with a piano. You can't run that quickly.

SL: How do you feel in relation to the Squatters' Movement?

AH: Sympathy I have. I know they had to occupy houses because they can't pay the rent. If that's what they want to do, if they like it, they should do it.

SL: What was your reaction when the police started hitting at them?

ANNETTE HUMPE

Red Love

Red as fire, glowing hot
Young, juicy, already tamed
Beauty 1980, red as blood the Playboy goes out
Red Lips are to be kissed
A vulcano turns you on
Sex and money, sex and money
gimme, gimme, gimme, gimme, gimme, gimme,
I am a red mirror
on a red Carousel
Everything spins, everything spins
I, I, I, I, I, I, I, I, I, I,
think about
    Red Love
Wanna be like new
    Red Love
Don't wanna be faithful no more
    Red Love
Be sometimes woman, sometimes man,
    Red Love

Were you affected by the violence?

AH: I am terribly scared of physical force. I could never participate when physical confrontations began with the cops. I couldn't see any gain in it for myself. I just panicked.

SL: What about the terrorists?

AH: I didn't know them. I knew people who did. It's becoming very fashionable to know somebody who knew somebody who maybe knew somebody like Ulrike Meinhof. I didn't know who she was. They were heroes. They're still heroes because they're dead now. It's over; they're not an issue anymore.

SL: Do you think things have gotten more individualistic now?

AH: Yeah. I am not into politics anymore. I have changed; I am just interested in myself, in my universe.

SL: You address a wider audience than most groups in Germany. One of your records sold 150,000 copies. Do you feel any responsibility to your public?

AH: I was in Frankfurt when I realised for the first time the responsibility I refused to

Be naive and clever

Groovy jeans and little glitter
Sweet as red jiggle jello
Cosmo 1980, from the B.O. spray drips blood
Red moon over Tahiti
A poster turns you on
Sex and money, sex and money
gimme, gimme, gimme, gimme, gimme, gimme,
I am a red Sputnik
In a dead outer space
Everything spins, everything spins
I, I, I, I, I, I, I, I, I,
think about
repeat chorus□

Translated by John Mernit and Wolfgang Hagen

have before. We have this song "Berlin," which got very popular in West Germany. When we played it in Frankfurt, for a thousand punks or so, I had a feeling they expected me to say: "Go in the streets, break it down." And I didn't want to say it, because I wouldn't do it, I wouldn't go with them. So they became aggressive, and we had to leave early; it was becoming too dangerous.

SL: Do you think that punks and squatters are connected?

AH: Yes, they're connected, because they don't have places. They don't have money.

SL: Is money important for you?

AH: Very important. It's for my freedom. I want to have a studio, I want to travel, therefore I need money.

SL: Were people shocked when you declared publicly that you wanted money?

AH: I sing a song about luxury. After every concert there is someone from this Alternative Scene asking, "Do you really need this luxury?" I am for a form of Communism where everybody can have his lobster if they want to.
No future, Champagne and lobster now. □

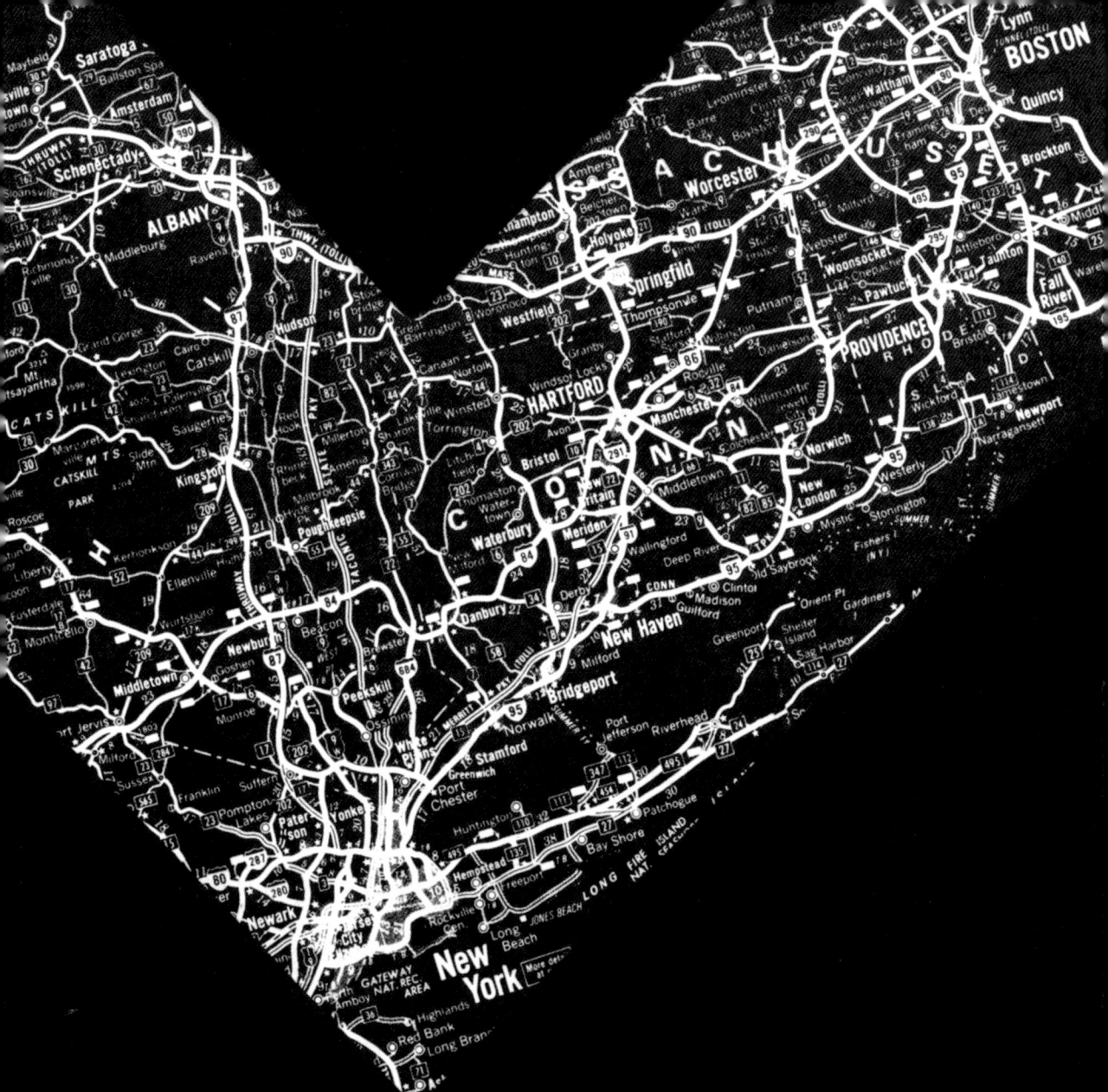

IV

ONA ZUKUMPFT

Modell Deutschland: A Good Future For Us?

In 1976, the West German Social Democratic Party (SPD) displayed a particularly telling election poster. Two healthy, smiling white youths — the perfectly symmetrical young couple — are seated on a motorbike. The male is planted firmly in the driver's seat and appears ready to speed off momentarily. But for the time being he's turned towards the voting public, one arm draped protectively over a young woman. Is this a signal that we are not just looking at carefree youth but at a happy family-in-formation? Whatever he's up to, the motorbike (Made in Germany but undoubtedly assembled in Yugoslavia) is stopped on an otherwise deserted beach framed in the background by an unusually calm North Sea. The slogan turns out to be doubling as an invitation: "Modell Deutschland, A Good Future For Us." No beaming portraits of Helmut Schmidt,* nor of the eternally photogenic Willi Brandt*? And what about the stock iconography of the Social Good, of the Worker's Party? No sign. Both work and politics are conspicuously absent. Instead we are faced by an elegant graphic of a "Good Future," the sunny skies and ample rewards of something called a "Modell Deutschland," a clean-cut picture of the clean-cut promise of prosperity, vacations, free time and a secure tomorrow.

ANDRÉ GORZ

Farewell to the Proletariat

Q: In 1958, in your book *The Traitor* you said the ultimate objective for any intellectual was to join the Communist Party, and now you've issued your *Farewell to the Proletariat*. So who changed, you, the Communist Party or the proletariat?

André Gorz: Everything's changed: the structure of the economy, society, the working class, the means of production and therefore the future. And it's no surprise that the labor movement, formed by the historical past, is weakened rather than radicalized by this crisis. If we are searching for a non-capitalist outcome to this crisis, and even more crucially what potential it holds for the construction of a different kind of society, the

André Gorz, writer, journalist and militant is best known in English for his *Politics of Ecology.*

For the Modern Administrator, a model is an indispensable entry into the political inventory. A model always works; any shortcomings in application have nothing to do with the model itself (or with the modellers) but with incalculable "externalities" such as misbehaving labor unions, greedy and seditious youth with bloated expectations, wild speculation on international money markets and so on. Despite its fail safe features, a model still contains one hidden danger. As is conspicuously true with the Modell Deutschland, a model prefigures the Real Thing, floats a promise of what is to come, makes a pitch for what is in it "For Us." Candidly displaying one's model thereby runs the risk of exposing a ruling regime's most basic and private parts — claims on the future.

What happens if people don't "buy" what the model has in store? What happens if the picture of the future projected by a New Beginning or a Modell Deutschland is widely held to imply *no* future at all?

Made in Germany

The Modell Deutschland represents the final SPD packaging for the often applauded West German "miracle" of post-war reconstruction. At last the SPD could boast a progam that was no longer rhetorically restricted to recovery from an embarassing past. "Make Germany Strong Again" was supplanted by "A Good Future For Us." Through much of the past decade, Modell social policies and political economic architecture were impressive enough to generate worldwide interest, impressive enough even to be classified as suitable for export by the most authoritative consortium of social engineers, the International Monetary Fund. Throughout the 70's the U.S. business press

labor movement, with its parties and its unions, has little to offer. Obviously nothing can happen without it, but it is no longer the inner sanctum for the elaboration of post-capitalist ideas, practice and values.

Q: Nevertheless there seems to have been an important rupture in your thinking.

AG: I think that it's less a rupture than a constant preoccupation in front of a changing reality. Concerning the proletariat, I haven't changed that much. Thirty years ago, when I first wondered why communist thought and the working class exercised such a guilty fascination for young intellectuals, myself included, I had to admit that it was a kind of religious temptation. Marxism, in its successive forms, always brought its own religion of the proletariat. Crucifixion, resurrection, salvation through faith, we had them all. The religious character of the faith in the working class is quite clear in the young Marx.

When you discover the religious character of a supposedly scientific theory, you can no longer be a believer in "good faith"; you are bound to question it. In my first pieces, and especially in *Foundations for a Morality*, I objected that it didn't help much to learn that the proletariat bore within it the meaning of history — if that meaning wasn't proven to be the best, the most valuable, and thus most deserving of adherence — in short, that

has frequently praised the Modell's elegant machinery of guaranteed abundance, praise made with all the enthusiasm of colleagues anxiously longing to be appointed partners. As one example, the much discussed *Business Week* Master Plan for the "Reindustrialization of America" might easily have been translated from the assembly brochures of the Modell Deutschland. Although the U.S. version has been temporarily tabled in favor of a more socially streamlined design, the comparison is striking. In both master plans the key term, the political centerpiece, is the same: the establishment of a "new social contract" among capital, labor and government.

At least until 1976, the picture of the future offered by the Modell Deutschland was one of unabashed material prosperity, a picture of being quite literally at the beach. With the rest of the Western block left to slog along through the swamp, how could such firm assurances of guaranteed well-being be at all plausible, let along "pay cash"? The official pronouncements of Modell management, together with the flattering commentaries of the international business press, made frequent allusion to the prestige enjoyed on world markets by West German commodities ranging from microcomputer software to Leopard Tank hardware. "Prestige" was then identified as the key precipitate for a "favorable investment climate," a climate that could in turn nourish the delicate flora of business confidence. In the New Science of capital-meteorology, the science of the investment climate, West German commodities acquired near metaphysical qualities, floating effortlessly through one world recession after another.

But this particular metaphysics doesn't take us very far, no further than the poster-perfect beach. How to explain so privileged a position within highly

in the working class necessity coincided with freedom and morality wih history. But this demonstration is lacking.

Q: Unlike Sartre, who around 1960 transferred all his revolutionary aspirations to the Third World, you have remained committed to the problems of revolution within the industrialized societies.

AG: I have never been interested in the Third World. I don't see how a revolution in the Third World could topple capitalism and incite revolutions in the Western metropolis. And since no one can make a revolution for us, I've asked myself, since 1960, why people in industrialized countries would want a revolution. What could be the motive for such a desire? At this point I attempted to discover the potentially revolutionary "radical needs" which neo-capitalist developments had created but could not satisfy.

In my opinion, these radical needs essentially derived from the radical alienation of individuals in their work as well as in consumption and relationships to others and to nature. Especially important was the increasing divergence between the stupidity of unskilled labor and the level of information and social competence and therefore aspirations for autonomy among the young. I thought that when an increasing mass of workers possessed abilities far beyond those required or allowed by their restrictive

competitive world markets? Obviously, the spell of Made in Germany could only be cast through the assemblies of the Modell Deutschland. What were its key parts? And how was it all to be pasted together?

According to the official format, the most visible feature of the Modell was the quick and politically "cost effective" internationalization of the assembly line, a process that not only reflected the endless search for cheap labor but served at the same time to release West German capital from a large chunk of social reproduction costs. In itself, such a tendency should come as no surprise. But within the Modell Deutschland internationalization assumed a number of distinct forms, permitting a great deal of managerial flexibility in retaining control over production. Location in Free Trade Zones, the construction of world market factories in Asia, Africa and Latin America, contract processing agreements with the Eastern bloc and "guest" workers were (and continue to be) used separately or in combination to piece together an optimal labor process free from the encumbrance of having too many incalculables in the same place. A comparatively liberal foreign policy and the incomparable stickiness of the Deutschmark both contributed to the speed and efficiency of the Modell line.

Made in Germany meant more than Made Elsewhere; what of those jobs that *did* remain geographically national? Here the procedure was neo-Taylorism as usual, grafting automation and rationalization to elaborate schemes of worker compensation, relocation and training. Moreover, unlike elsewhere in Western Europe, this part of the Modell provoked few political battles, becoming just another clause in the social contract negotiated by management and the German Trade Union Federation (DGB).

forms of employment, then sooner or later the whole system of domination would be called into question, followed by the very system of values upon which capitalist development is based. That's exactly what happened, except that this radical interrogation has yet to be translated into political terms.

Q: Your title, *Farewell to the Proletariat*, rings out as a provocation to the left, as if it were the working class itself that you dismiss from the historical scene...

AG: One of the things I have tried to show is that the working class has become structurally incapable of taking control of production and society. The astonishing thing is that it has taken so long to see this. The demonstration is already in *Capital*. Marx showed with a great wealth of detail, and by citing the first capitalist theoreticians (notably Ferguson and Ure's admirable *Philosophy of Manufacturers*), that techniques, besides being means of producing, are always means of dominating, of disciplining, and of militarizing the worker. It's always a military terminology that comes very naturally to Marx, as to Engels, when he describes the "productive worker collective" as an "army of workers" with its "officers and subordinates of production" on one side and its "soldiers" on the other, whom the owners prefer to be "half-wits" easily marshalled with "the regularity of a huge automaton." At bottom nothing has changed, except that the

"Prestige," then, turns out to be a self-congratulatory euphemism for structurally enforced productivity. Clamping domestic rationalization to internationalization formed one crucially productive pivot, but there is more to prestigious productivity than output per worker. The second dimension to Made in Germany socially materialized the modernizer's most dog-eared axiom: one cannot bring the world up to date unless one's own house is immaculately in order. After all, well-integrated commodities come from well-integrated societies. If the strength of the Modell Deutschland was to be measured by the performance of its products on the world market, then it was not a model merely for Germany but for the world.

Buying German meant buying into that "Good Future For Us." A decollage of the sunny mid-seventies pictures of prosperity reveals detailed blueprints for turning West Germany into a magnificently efficient demonstration project, a scientifically whipped social pudding that was to exist as its own best proof. The physical obliteration of housing, transportation and physical plant during World War II is only a problem if you're Conrad Adenauer feverishly working the miracle of reconstruction; in the more futuristic SPD dimensions of the Modell Deutschland, being able to start from scratch becomes a virtue in itself. What were the new ingredients? High breeder reactors, the treasured network of autobahns, Frankfurt International Airport, the video-prison, sleek and standardized public housing, the electronic kitchen, cruise missiles, the integrated university and other social automata.

It is impossible to grasp what was so graphically ambitious about the storyboards of the Modell Deutschland without understanding that the importance of a "good business climate" is not restricted to the assurance of

"army of workers" have become technicians and the "half-wittedness" demanded of the workers is no longer that of the beast of burden but that of the limited specialist (of the *Fach-idiot*, as the Germans would say).

A structured and militarily hierarchic working class is no more capable of seizing power than the army; the superior officers always monopolize power while the foot-soldiers end up as oppressed as before. To ask the working class to appropriate and direct the means of production *as they exist* today is to ask them to appropriate and direct their own chains. It's no accident that the structure of power within production is precisely the same in Eastern bloc countries as in our own, that the power barons of the East have the same mentality and encounter the same worker resistance as their counterparts in the West. Power in the hands of producers presupposes a radical technical reorganization, a redefinition of the means, units, and ends of production. Though technically this redefinition could be greatly facilitated by the new micro-information processing, worker control of the great systems and of society as a whole strikes me as a utopian fantasy.

Q: Within the distinction that you propose between the sphere of heteronomy, or alienated labor, and the sphere of autonomy, or free activity, isn't there a possible

favorable political forecasts and sound economic forecasts. Moreover, what is good about the "good climate" is nothing so formulaic as tamed unions plus industrial discipline plus functional institutions of social reproduction. Much of the allure of the West German model had to do not with the packaged parts but with their rules of assembly. Shortly after assuming control in 1969, the forward looking Social Democratic regime set out to elaborate a well-illustrated, cogently laid out assembly brochure detailing the rules of political struggle around and about the parts. Writing good rules; what better way for the Social Democratic Party to distinguish itself from the blunt bulldozing of Conrad Adenauer and his fellow caretakers of the post-war miracle?

The rules for the assembly of the model were centered around a peculiar kind of consensus that was to express itself as "responsibility." Just as prestige stood for structurally enforced productivity, responsibility stood for the inclusion within the State of all existing or potential opposition. The proper place for politics was the macro-courthouse. The word spread quickly — don't come in and you can't go speeding along the North Sea.

Responsible rules for moderate and balanced negotiation were certainly most adhesive in the case of "codetermination," defining the relationship between West German business associations and the DGB. Management agreed to "codetermine" by granting the unions formal consultant status in exchange for making agreements on output fully contractual, hence legally binding. Participation by the DGB in some limited spheres of managerial decision making was the price for acquiring predictability over the "factor of production" always most difficult to calculate: living labor power. When labor courts passed rulings in 1979 placing strikes and lock-outs on the same legal footing,

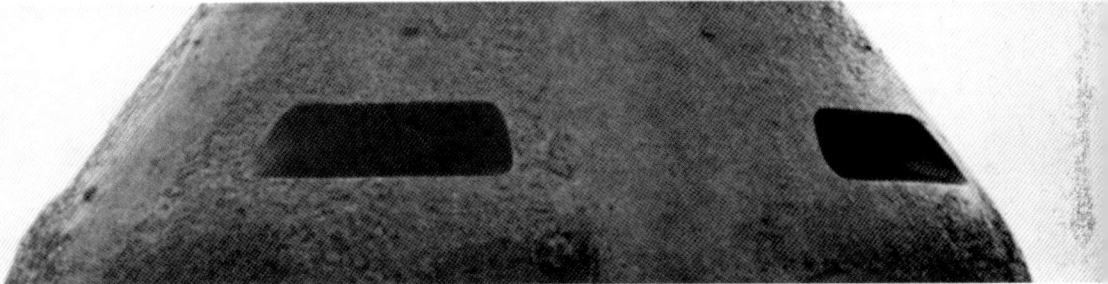

justification for accepting the present productive machinery, a simple quietist appeal to "cultivate one's garden," one's "hobby"?

AG: That's not my idea at all. I claim that within any complex society, some part of social labor is necessarily heteronomous activity: that is, an activity of which neither the nature, nor the rules, nor the object is defined by the individual or his community. At present that sphere of heteronomy embraces all forms of salaried employment. Laborers, bureaucrats and technicians do not pursue their own ends; instead they are employed to operate a complex machine which surpasses the understanding of any single individual, and in which they perform pre-determined duties. The competence which these duties demand is generally useless for the pursuit of autonomous ends. This alienation, then, is not only inherent within the relations of capitalist production but also within the division of labor at all levels of society. It lies within Marx's socialization of the production processes.

Today it is technically and economically possible to reduce the sphere of heteronomy and the importance of heteronomous labor within the life of each person. But without returning to a village or domestic economy which entails other kinds of alienation, it is impossible to completely eliminate heteronomous labor and its social divisions. Moreover, heteronomous labor is not all bad, for it does allow each worker to employ an

the preemptive institutionalization of class struggles exemplified in this relationship reached new heights. At least in the records of the macro-courthouse, unions were classified as just another interest group.

The legal proprieties and interest-etiquette of the macro-courthouse were not restricted to relations between management and union. A "critical dialogue" was established (literally by decree) among State agencies, the pro-nuclear lobby and the anti-nuclear movement around the construction of Brokdorf, Kalkar, Gorleben and other key parts of the model. Public moratoriums on weapons deployment and militarism were frequently organized and officially supervised. Most recently, special state commissions, "disinterested" liaisons and squads of "concerned social scientists" have been appointed to open "exploratory negotiations" with squatters and with the broader Alternative Movement. In the Modell Deutschland, the guidelines for a successful political life were well-charted and unmistakable: the model citizen was to diligently prepare all protest as a legal brief.

Of course, none of these institutions or strategies is especially novel. What kept the Modell Deutschland from looking like another Old Hat was not something new but the exceptional conditions, and timing, within which the familiar was pieced together. While the U.S., Britain and France experimented with their own meteorologics, the West German model was already standing fully erect in the world market. Here at last was a Welfare State that worked, its shape a fluid Bauhaus circle conjoining the prestige of being Made in Germany to the responsibilities of inhabiting the macro-courthouse. The circle even turned in both directions! Prosperity was the banker for social peace that in turn reinforced the conditions for more bankers.

enormous amount of material know-how through devices which draw on a variety of equipment of which each worker can understand but a fraction. For example, a micro-processor cannot be built at the community level, but it allows that community to determine and manage a great variety of productive operations.

The banality and triviality of heteronomous labor is the ransom extorted for the socialization and gigantic productive profits it permits. Socialization is incompatible with autonomy, with integrated worker-management. It prohibits the kind of craftmanship which allows to realize a task, from start to finish, with one's own hands. Integrated autonomy can exist only outside of socially determined, salaried labor. Socialist worker-management is no panacea for it does not overcome the alienation inherent in salaried work. That alienation can only be overcome outside of heteronomous labor and its social divisions.

Q: Doesn't that mean leaving labor to capitalist control while reclaiming the relatively ineffectual control of leisure time?

AG: The error consist in believing that labor, by which I mean heteronomous, salaried labor, can and must remain the essential matter. It's just not so. According to American projections, within twenty years labor time will be less than half that of leisure time. I

"They didn't say that assembly lines eat people and shit cars for nothing."

Gueney Dal

Hold on a second — is that *all* there was to the decade of the Modell Deutschland? Isn't there more (or less) to the fable of 70's prosperity? There does appear to be something else at the bottom of the package, underneath the assembly brochure. It comes in a long white tube and the label reads "Modell Guarantee — Apply Liberally." The application, at least, is obvious. Already in 1976 wide cracks are opening up in the poster pictures of sunny prosperity. The crisp images of well-being become swollen, then explode. All species of incalculables start to dig their way up through the sand and onto the beach, a new wave of poppers chasing our happy couple into the water. The motorbike is quickly reassambled (still in Yugoslavia) as a water cannon and out of the North Sea surfaces a nuclear bunker — or is that a high security prison?

Strong Men can't remain aloof from this skewed incoherence any longer. The newly tooled No Nonsense Schmidt (among others) comes marching boldly back onto what's left of the beach. Within seconds, the warm invitation to the Good Future is replaced by a bald neon warning sign, flashing first "No Future" and then "More Glue."

No Future, More Glue

Writing in *Fortune* magazine (April 20, 1981), a certain David B. Tinnin speculates "Schmidt must also be discouraged by certain aspects of his country's social climate. It would be an exaggeration to call West Germany a sick society or say that the strong German work ethic has weakened dangerously. But the country, much like the U.S. during the anti-war demonstrations of the late 60's, is bombarded — and demoralized — by riots and demonstrations."

see the task of the left as directing and promoting this process of the abolition of labor in a way that will not result in a mass of unemployed on one side, an aristocracy of labor on the other and between them a proletariat which carries out the most distasteful jobs for forty-five hours a week. Instead, let everyone work much less for his salary and thus be free to act in a much more autonomous manner. This means replacing heteronomous, salaried labor with the independent work of freely associated individuals in extended families and neighborhood cooperatives so that autonomous activity based on voluntary cooperation would prevail and market relationships, including the sale of labor time, would waste away.

It is ironic that so-called Marxists brand me a reactionary when I talk like this, since this double society in which the autonomous sphere develops at the expense of the heteronomous sphere is precisely the "communism" envisioned by Marx. Today "communism" is a real possibility and even a realistic proposition for the abolition of salaried labor through automation saps both capitalist logic and the market economy. Nonmarket-bound production processes and the right to a social income independent of one's salaried occupation have become necessities that are avoided only through the economy of war, or through war itself.

Q: Then this "beyond socialism" will be realized not by the classical labor movement

Restricting himself to the housing and anti-nuclear movements, Tinnin goes on to spell out who these "aspects" are: "hordes of squatters, mostly young unemployed Germans and foreign workers" thoroughly infiltrated by "militant agitators" and "dedicated troublemakers," dedicated to "dart from the crowd to fire high-powered slingshots at police." Tinnin's all-bells alarm ends with a lament. "It is a dismaying spectacle that small groups of organized militants can thwart West Germany's public policy."

The article is entitled "The Miracle Economy Hits the Skids." It would appear that the Modell Deutschland has fallen out of fortune as the blue-skies prototype for the international business community. But Tinnin's remarks are instructive for another reason as his choice of phrasing quite accurately reflects the official analysis of the new social movements. Tinnin has listened well to his undoubtedly high-ranking informants. Schmidt *is* discouraged by these "aspects" and joins Tinnin in his dismay over their thwarting capabilities. Beginning with the explosion of the Berlin squatter movement in December of 1980, Schmidt has found his delicate political gears sabotaged by an entire inventory of defect parts, short circuits and social spanners: greens, squatters, eco-freaks, poppers, punkers, lesbo-hexen, alternatives, gays, rockers, anars and pacifists. Speaking with an impeccable responsibility, he complains that even the inner circles of the SPD itself appear to have been thoroughly infiltrated by "chaoten."

Wearing their "dismay" on their sleeves, the administrators of the cracking Modell have spent much of the past year on the stump lecturing the new movements and their parliamentary sympathizers about the hard economics of a world recession. Following each demonstration or "riot," participants are

which continues to defend salaried workers but rather by those whom you call the "non-class of non-workers." Do you really believe that the margins can ever seize power?

AG: It's not a question of the margins nor of seizing power. By the "non-class of non-workers" I don't mean those excluded from production but those who can no longer identify themselves with their salaried labor and, instead of a better job, demand a life wherein self-determined activities displace heterodeterminate labor, regardless of its pay scale. These are realistic necessities.

I've already demonstrated the inanity of the problems of seizing power. The post-industrial neo-proletariat is obviously incapable of seizing power and the same goes for the traditional working class. No strategy nor tactic for seizing power can resist the current repressive, counter-revolutionary capabilities of the modern State. That's why power cannot be directly grasped at the level of the State. The only possibility is to divert the power of the State, to exclude it from those growing areas of non-power.

Q: And you think State-power will tolerate the existence of such regions?

AG: It's not a question of tolerance but of its inability to do anything about them. The civil disobedience of American youths defeated the American Army long before the Vietnamese did. As a paralyzed West watched, a people armed only with roses defeated the

chastised for having "unduly high expectations" to the accompaniment of a re-sounding call to order. But not only a *call*. Where the hard facts of the business climate have not proved persuasive enough, it has become almost routine to deploy the harder facts of riot police and the national guard. What has happened to the smooth protocols of critical dialogue? The miracle of working welfare hits the skids.

Finally, the last part in the Modell box comes out of the tube: *Sicherheitstaat*, or the Security State. The instructions say it is to be nested within the macro-courthouse and that it has the feature of remaining invisible so long as the circle between prosperity and social peace is rotating fluidly. But despite some promising early indicators, the Modell circle was blocked from the beginning in both directions. As early as 1972-1973, the bank of Made in Germany was next to depleted by rising fuel costs, a weakened D-mark and stiffening consensual competition from Japan. In the other direction, the circle was blocked by the refusal of a broad range of movements to enter into the rules and responsibilities of the macro-courthouse.

The Modell Deutschland was caught in the false equations of its own blueprints. Space is as "productive" as labor power, but a squatters movement is *not* a trade union bureaucracy. Whether or not to build a nuclear plant at Brokdorf, or at Gorleben; whether or not to expand the runway system at Frankfurt International Airport; whether or not to provide public funding to women's shelters or abortions; whether or not to sell Leopard tanks to Pinochet; none of these decisions can be negotiated as if it were a wage scale or a productivity level. Although there have been frequent challenges from a

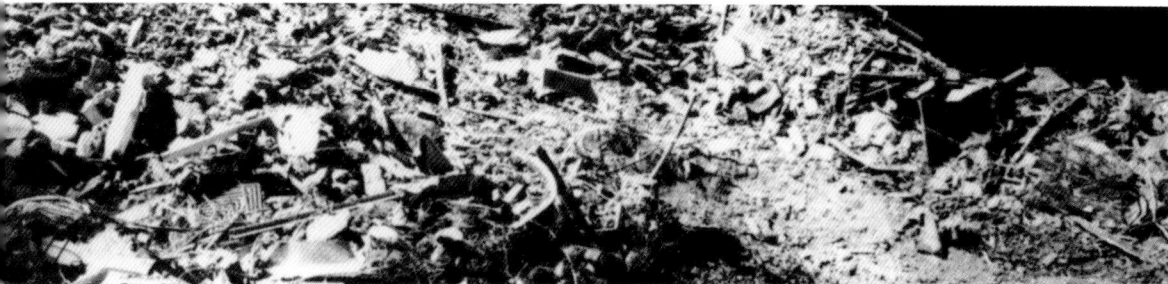

Shah's army and police. I think the "weapon," if it can be so called, of total non-compliance with the established powers will assume a capital importance with regard to the mounting barbarianism □

Translated by Michael Lazarin

"misbehaving" rank and file to the bureaucratic disciplines of codetermination, the social partner State has in each case been able to arbitrate a way out, however temporary the solution. Such has not always been the case with demands and obstructions made by the housing, women's anti-nuclear, anti-war and multi-issue "alternative" movements. Here struggles with Modell management are not over the size or shape of the parts, but over the parts themselves. In this sense they are non-negotiable. The macro-courthouse can no longer continue its sessions.

A recent cover of the *Economist* (October 17, 1981) frames two un-pragmatically painted faces among the 300,000 Bonn marchers against the bold type question "Can European Youth be Wrong about the Bomb?" Open to first page. Answer: "They are Wrong." In strategic detail, the editors of the *Economist* proceed to remind us why a neutral Europe would mean a "neutered" Europe. They complain that "most of the anxious but self-disciplined (!) and non-violent young people" do not fully comprehend the "arithmetic" of nuclear power in Europe. It's all a matter of facing facts — if only the kids would study the issue and stay on the beach! Central to the problem of non-negotiability is the dilemma of being faced by movements that do not speak arithmetic, that lack the well-grooved tongues of responsible politics. An echo from Tinnin: "Schmidt must also be discouraged by certain aspects of his country's social climate."

Although massive demonstrations such as the Bonn march are the events that most easily conform to the optics of the international press, the living spaces of the extra-Modell movements are not as centered, "self-disciplined" or

PETER GLOTZ
Between Revolution and Resignation

In 1961 Jürgen Habermas, Ludwig von Friedeburg, Christoph Oehler and Friedrich Weltz stated in their now-famous study *Student and Politics*: "Compared to the industrial working class, students have not inherited a firmly-rooted image of society, the consciousness of a stable position in society. In connection with that, they lack a reliable identification as a group as well as a clear policy based on their interest and experiences, which could be extended to social conditions in general." In a poll of 171 students conducted in Frankfurt in 1957, the researchers determined that only 10% of

---

Peter Glotz, national director of the Social Democratic Party, is a former "Regent" for the West Berlin universities. He initiated the "dialogue with the Youth" meant to neutralize the tension between the establishement and the young generation.

meticulously mapped as a national capitol. The open spaces staked out by squatted houses or by hut communities founded at the building sites of nuclear plants and NATO runways are significant not only because they have successfully blocked State priorities. The spaces of obstruction are at the same time a kind of counter-territory for the sustenance of new forms of social relations and of everyday life far from the lethal pragmatisms of the Modell Deutschland. Such a direct orientation to living space, space that has not been planned, space where little goes according to plan, space that goes against the plan, is bound to be "thwarting" for the master builders of West German prosperity. As the spaces of the new movements proliferated, the once safely administered margins were all of a sudden very close to home. With nothing to negotiate and with no way to talk, Schmidt ordered the distribution of "No Trespassing" signs. Meanwhile, the macro-courthouse made a fluid shift from "soft" legalization to "hard" criminalization.

Of course, the Modell Deutschland had promised security from the beginning. Model security, far from a jaunt by the North Sea, was built from computerized political surveillance, the infiltration and harassment of movement spaces, anti-"terrorist" legislation, *Berufsverbot** and a polished network of maximum security prisons, reprocessing centers for the most defective Modell parts. Within the politics of criminalization, this familiar apparatus has been mechanically applied to the new movements. Squatter houses are classified as breeding grounds for a "new terrorism," the anti-nuclear movement is accused of threatening "civil war," the whole generation of West German youth who see no future on a moped with their spouse are designated as "chaoten."

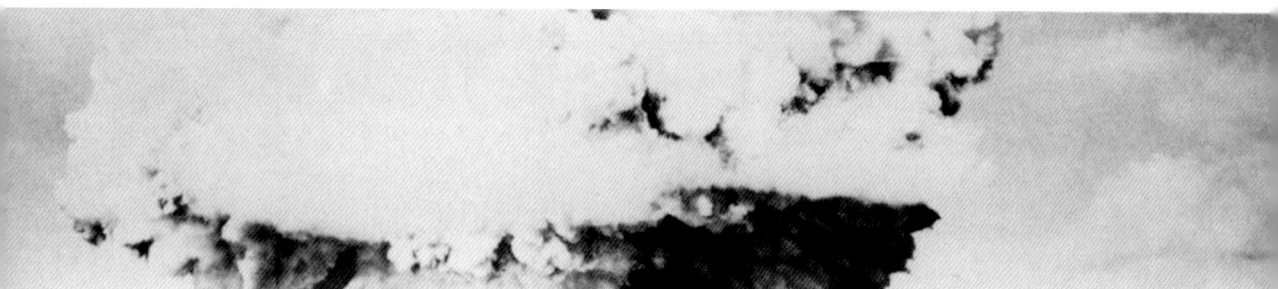

the students possessed "an innate perception of the societal structure." They identified 22% as "authoritarians" who had little sympathy for a parliamentary democracy or the multi-party state, 9% who were "indifferent," and 39% as "nominal democrats" who indeed knew and accepted the ground rules of democracy, but were by no means permeated with its underlying values. They found only 30% who were "genuine democrats." From the results the sociologists conjectured that it would be difficult for this elite to successfully build a democratic state in Germany.

The study, now published by the Friedrich Ebert Stiftung, shows how dramatically the situation has changed. The opportunities for studying at university level now extend far beyond the circle of a self-reproducing upper class or upper-middle class. The decisive point is, however, that in this process it is not the conservative college institution which has recruited new classes in addition to a more or less unchanged ruling class, but rather that the institution itself — in any case the people who are educated by this institution — have undergone a basic change. According to the investigation by Lehnert, Scherer and Krause, 84% of the students support the equal participation of workers in company decision-making. Almost 44% expressed their support for the solution of the unemployment problem by shortening of working hours and by welfare-state measures. Over 43% criticize the concentration of "wealth and power in very few hands." If the

But even in the dispensation of its more glue guarantee, the integrated design of the Modell Deutschland turns back against its administrators. Since housing, airports, nuclear plants, happy couples, shopping centers and autobahns were all part of the same Good Citizen blueprint, the counter-territories of the new movements are naturally linked. The ecology movement is at once an anti-war movement that in turn converges with the housing movement. The "tiny radical minority" won't go away, is suddenly everywhere. The old security apparatus threatens to devour itself.

They Are Wrong

Once again: the key political shape of the early Modell Deutschland was a circle linking prosperity to social peace. Moreover, the circle was expected to be equally as fluid in either direction. The Welfare State had to *work*. Politics entered into the design only as cost-benefit evaluations of the relative productivity of any given rotation. But the working welfare circle was blocked almost before it began to turn. Political demands from groups marginal to the reason of the Modell could not simply be bought for the price of a social concession. The attempt to legally reconcile opposing interests within the State— negotiated compromise— turned out to open spaces that were not only costly, but highly unpredictable.

Instead of turning with well-engineered precision, the circle began to spin off rights (the right to adequate housing, the right to control one's own body, the right to a livable environment) that could not be accomodated within the Modell's closed calculus of prestige and responsibility. From the no-nonsense

negligible minority of republican college teachers during the Weimar Republic could see how greatly times have changed, perhaps they would see some sense in their sacrifice back then.

Now of course one may be rather skeptical about the representativeness of these results. A large representative study by Infratest, however, whose poll was conducted at almost the same time, registers a political potential for the SPD* and FDP* of 48% (Lehnert/Scherer/Krause: 50.5%), for the CDU/CSU* of 17% (as opposed to 12.9%). Infratest's figures for the potential of the "Green"* are even higher. Lehnert, Scherer and Krause register 31.4% whereas Infratest ascertained 57% for the "Green" and "Alternative Lists"* altogether. On the whole then, the results of the present work have been confirmed by more than 3000 interviews. Taking the entire student population into consideration, one will indeed have to count on a higher percentage of conservatives, but there is no need to register a basic revision of the final results.

These results are all the more noteworthy, since the Allensbacher[1] hypothesis about the precariousness of the democratic potential in reference to communism has not been proven. The potential number of those who could be classified as left-wing extremists comes to just under 10%. Even this is a considerable figure, and should give a democrat pause for thought; however, it is certainly not worrisome in the sense of being

prespective of Modell pragmatism, women's self-help collectives, squatted houses, blocked runways, free schools and other institutions of the new movements were all becoming dangerously autonomous, Modell cracks widening into spaces too formless — and pleasurable — to be dryly and efficiently accounted for. The politics of contesting rights was transformed into a politics of defending and extending the social space necessary for the reproduction of a different way of life, a "second society." Given that the sustenance of a different way of life is the most fundamental threat to the one-dimensional disciplines of a restored capitalist competitiveness and of the Good Citizen Everyday, the security state quickly hardened against the misbehaving margins. The circle was braced by a circumscribing pentagon. But what was there left to protect?

The old circle did not fully disappear; it became smaller. The Modell Deutschland was now effectively split into a highly productive, responsible core and outer bounds that, failing integration, could only be contained. A kind of good citizen capitalism of the core came to peacefully coexist and interpenetrate with its Security State guarantee. So long as all was in order at the core, the inner security imperatives of the good citizen garrison could be directed towards disciplining the open spaces, the "autonomous ghetto" of the new movements. The distinction between neo-corporatist liberalism and right populism lost its meaning in a bear hug: Helmut Schmidt, meet Franz Josef Strauss.*

As the inhabitants of extra-Modell counter-territories refuse to "listen to reason" and begin instead to multiply, can the circle harden further still or will it dissolve, consuming itself? It is always a simple task to draw up a laundry

dangerous to the State. This carries even more weight, since the rejection of terrorism and urban guerrilla warfare is an indisputable fact and almost uniformly agreed to. Established dogmatic communism also has no chance at all with German students. A mere 0.9% of the students regard the GDR as having a viable exemplary function. Taking also into account the fact that parliamentarism is only criticized by 1.7% of students on the right, one can state that a good 90% majority uphold the values of a democracy.

Without a doubt this is only a small consolation for the larger parties. The CDU/CSU, which receive the votes of more than 45% of the electorate, will have to ask themselves why less than 20% of the students gave them their vote. The parties of the liberal-socialistic coalition, especially the SPD, will also have to examine carefully why they have lost considerably in recent years to new movements like the "Green." Anyone who has not completely forgotten how to think historically may notice with satisfaction that the second German democracy has managed to instill democratic values in its "upcoming generation of leaders" (suspect and fuzzy as such terminology must be in a democracy). Taking into account the anti-republican "upcoming leaders" of the Weimar Republic and the high percentage of passive-authoritarian personality traits among the students of the "skeptical generation,"[2] one must consider that things have turned out quite happily.

274

list of ominous signs, and as the strategy of criminalization is extended in all directions it becomes difficult not to float a comparison with Italy following the April days of 1977.

The deployment of 10,000 riot police and a squadron of army helicopters to defend the Brokdorf construction site, the search and seizure tactics employed to punish squatters and clear all spacial obstructions to hard facts, drumming the handful of dissidents within the SPD either out of the party or back into step, the near religious glorification of New Productivity and high-tech automation, the insertion of more high security prisons into the innermost framings of the Modell, the constant displays of commitment to NATO and the co-fostering of a "new generation" of nuclear weapons all reveal a thin-lipped determination to brace the fiction of a working circle, at any cost. Ten years after the first proto-sketches of the Modell Deutschland, the neat circle rolling prosperity into social peace turns a double edge. One side faces inward, within the core: what, or who, will replace the exhausted monologues of the old administrators of the Good Future. The other side faces against the extra-Modell polytongue, probing for a place to cut.

Nevertheless, the decentered, erratic, irresponsible, disorganized, speechless, unplanned, lustful and counter-cutting auto-motions of the "second society" remain intractable, can still sustain laughter, difference and a curious inattention to the "indisputable" facts of the matter, to the "elementary arithmetic" of what is, of what "must be done." The verdict passed down by the *Economist* carries an unintended source of hope, a hope that is itself full of ambiguity. At least within the bulldozing logics traditionally deployed to break political ground, They Are Wrong. □

In spite of this fact, it would be a mistake to rest on the laurels plaited from the above data. The political developments uncovered by this political-science study already give rise to enough questions. If almost 50% of all university students demand an immediate shut-down of all atomic plants (which in plain English means that almost half of the German students support a completely unrealistic energy policy), then the federal and all the state governments should see the handwriting on the wall. One hopes that such data will crumble the arrogance of those who think that the ecological movement is only the latest fad of the upper middle class. Still more decisive and far-reaching are the psychological questions which lie beyond this study.

This question doesn't only concern academic new blood, but rather the conditions of socialization under which the post-war generation is growing up. Does this considerable potential for an "alternative " mixture of values which can be discerned in this generation point to a change in the aggregate of our culture? In what way will our society evolve, once these new "gentle cohorts" will come into leadership positions in the economy, in politics, education and social policies, and the bureaucracy?

At the moment the elder generation, insofar as they are still in positions of power, are putting off these questions. My generation, the "skeptical generation," which ought to have been called the "conformed generation" instead, is relating to today's youth in the

"OK, you've got order, but when that order cracks..."
William Burroughs

same way their fathers related to them just after the Second World War: they criticize the young and measure them against the pattern of their own experience. After 1945, members of the (left and right wing) youth movements of the twenties chided the young people for showing absolutely no interest in establishing their own youth culture. Today, those who belong to the skeptical generation criticize the upcoming "cohorts" for not being skeptical enough and for once again establishing a separate youth culture. *Tempora mutantur et nos mutamur in illis?*[3]

The present study is a good basis for fresh reconsideration of all these patterns. □

Translated by Karin Benthin

1. Allensbacher is a well-known West German polling institute.
2. The "skeptical generation" refers to the 50's youth.
3. "Times change and we change with them." Harrison, *Description of Britain.*

DANIEL COHN-BENDIT

The Anti-Nuclear Movement Smashing the German Consensus

Sylvère Lotringer: After being extradited from France in 1968, you became active in the anti-authoritarian movement. How do you see what happened to the German Left in the 70's and how the Red Army Fraction came about?

Daniel Cohn-Bendit: With the end of the anti-authoritarian movement — faced with its failure, with our failure to prolong and regenerate it in a positive way — several distinct political initiatives occurred. One was the creation of political parties of a Marxist-Leninist type that held lesser or greater sway, such as the KPD* or the KBW.

SL: When did this happen?

CB: Towards the beginning of the 70's. This is one line. A second line brought together non-dogmatic groups which never meant to form a party, but were involved in factory work and the like. Our group, "Revolutionary Struggles in

---

"Danny the Red" was a leader of the May 68 events in France. Since then a Frankfurt-based APO* activist and writer.

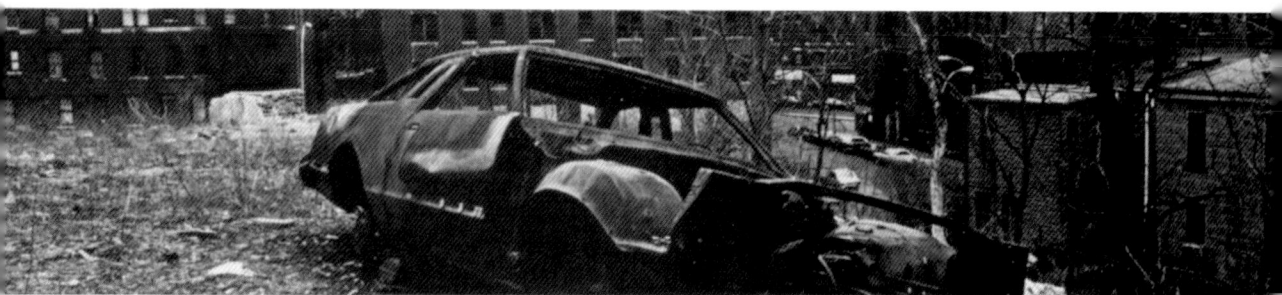

AMOS GRÜNEBAUM

German and Jewish

Amos Grünebaum: I was born in Israel. I arrived in Germany when I was three years old, in 1953. My father is German, my mother Rumanian. Before the war, from 1935 to 1938, my father was one of the first and youngest political inmates at Dachau. He was imprisoned for being a socialist and Jew, then released with instructions to be out of the country within 48 hours. The only country that would accept him was Palestine, which is today Israel.

Atina Grossmann: Was your father in any way religious?

Amos: No, socialist and German. And he is still German. In Palestine, he was a thief and a vagabond. He worked for the English army and later for the Haganah underground. He met my mother in the army. She also came to Israel by way of Germany. She had lived in

Frankfurt" (which was then tied up with the Italian groups of *Lotta Continua* and *Potere Operaio*) came from this line. The third line involved a series of anti-imperialist action groups generally known as urban guerrilla or "terrorist" groups. These are the three outcomes of the anti-authoritarian movement.

The terrorist groups gambled on violent struggle. They acted as if the "people" were actually opposed to the German State and only needed a few well-placed bombs and shoot-outs to be awakened. As far as I'm concerned, they failed not only as regards the German State but even more as regards the unwillingness of people, and even of the political opposition, to become involved in this kind of politics. The deaths at Stammheim are at once a symbol of what can happen within the German State and a symbol of the impossibility of a certain political project.

SL: The situation in Italy is fairly different in this respect. From the start, terrorism there received strong support from the factory workers of the North. The Red Brigades sustained reversals, but they suffered no Stammheims.

CB: It is true that a few thousand people identified with the BR thanks to the breakdown of Italian society. And a few thousand people can form pretty effective terrorist groups. Politically speaking, however, they only worsened an already tense situation, and ended up reinforcing the Italian State.[1] It is the strength of the movement which, in Germany, enables one to evade both the logic of the State and that of the urban guerrilla.

SL: The deaths at Stammheim seem to have provoked a kind of stupor in the Left. For months people literally stopped talking.

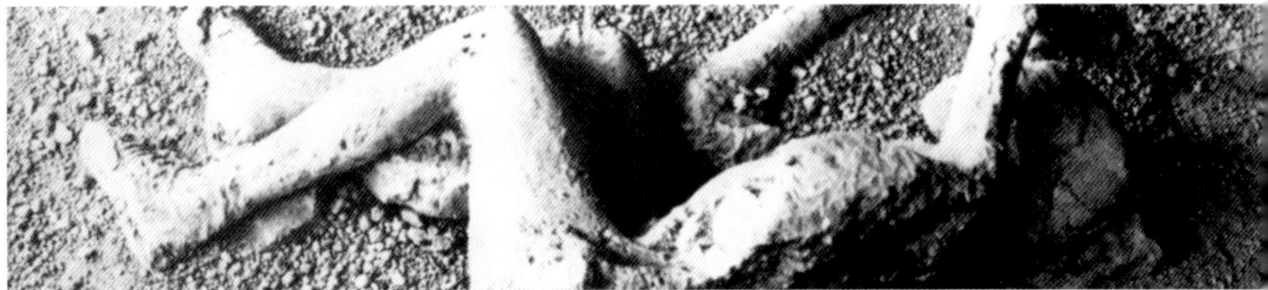

Rumania, then her whole family, about 20 people, were taken to Auschwitz. She was the only one who survived. She was sent to Bergen Belsen and then in a forced labor gang at Krupp in Essen. The works. She was liberated from Bergen Belsen by the English and taken back to Rumania. She was 21. She didn't really know who she was anymore.

My mother came from a very religious family. My father, who was neither religious nor Zionist, kept wanting to go back to Germany. At the first opportunity, he took us to Cologne.

Atina: Was your mother opposed to returning to Germany?

Amos: Absolutely, and still is. She only stays there because of my father. My father was compensated in Germany.

Atina: How was school in Cologne?

Amos: At first, I went to Catholic school. I was the little Jewish boy. I had to learn German because we spoke Hebrew most of the time at home.

Atina: Were you aware that you were a foreign child?

Amos: Yes, but I didn't grasp the full extent of it. When I was 6, I went to the Protestant school.

CB: The repression instilled not only a fear of the State as an institution, but above all of the state of German society, its uniformity and refusal to investigate what had really happened. That of course was right after Stammheim. Since then there's been an attempt at response dubbed "the dialogue with the youth."

SL: You mean Peter Glotz's conception of the "two cultures," so reminiscent of Astor Rosa's in Italy?[2]

CB: Yes. But then everyone is trying to renew the dialogue with the young. The greatest fear of German society is that its youth might drop out altogether. This is also a great opportunity that the alternative movement could take advantage of. Not that the movement is exclusively defined by the young, but it draws a great deal of its strength from their presence in its midst. Whether they're No Future or No Nuke, they see themselves as outside society.

SL: That's precisely what I find interesting about the German situation. How did the Alternative Scene come about, and what are its present possibilities for growth?

CB: Its development is parallel to the relinquishment of the concept of revolution. The movement managed to establish a strong social mini-infrastructure, especially through the network of communities in which the majority of the people involved in the movement settled after it had become clear that traditional political action had failed. As a result, all the problems of daily life and practice came to be considered primarily as political problems which had to be solved immediately, in this society, without waiting for the time when power

"Adele lost her last job at a "scene" cafe. The owner didn't want to put up with the swastika on her shirt. He forgot that she usually wore the Star of David."

Wolfgang Hagen

Atina: Why always religious schools?

Amos: Because in Cologne everything is either Catholic or Protestant. My sister had to go to the Catholic school because it was closer to home. I vigorously protested. Catholic meant the same thing to me as fascism — at least in Cologne. I still remember a picture of the Cardinal of Cologne in front of the cathedral with a whole flock of alter boys and priests. They were welcoming the Führer.

Atina: So, even as a child you had an anti-fascist rather than a Jewish consciousness?

Amos: My parents celebrated Easter and Christmas rather than Jewish holidays. One day a Hassidic child came to school, with side locks and his mother wearing a wig. His father was an itinerant Hassidic Rabbi. That was the first time we had seen such a thing. The poor boy was always tormented and I should have sided with him — at least that's what my parents said — but it was embarrassing. He was so different from me. I eventually did become friends with him. He ended up becoming a radical leftist, cutting his locks and throwing stones at the police.

Atina: Did you have a girlfriend?

Amos: My first real girlfriend was Jewish. She was the only good-looking Jewish girl my age in all of Cologne. I met her at a Jewish summer camp.

could be taken. This was the basis of a political movement that not only rejected the State and its structure but also the society which that State represents.

SL: I found in Berlin that the rejection of the term "political" did not necessarily entail a refusal of all political action. But it is clear that ideological speculations are deeply mistrusted.

CB: Traditional theories and ideologies stand little chance of success here since no one can postulate the avant-garde role of the working class as simply and naively as in the past. It's no coincidence that a book like André Gorz's *Farewell to the Proletariat* stirred up a favorable response in those circles. But this is also where the danger lies. There's a somewhat infantile notion in the alternative movement, according to which changing oneself and one's tiny social context will eventually bring a real transformation. Beside rejecting all ideology, the movement refuses to consider the possibility of changing society as a whole.

SL: How did you yourself move from direct political action to more alternative perspectives?

CB: Actually I remained very political. I belong to the "politico" alternative trend. I am all *for* political intervention. I accept numerous criticisms levelled at traditional politics, but I also feel that a new notion of politics is needed, and that the only way to give it a shape is to be a part of it.

SL: The election of an Alternative List in West Berlin last June may signal the emergence of the Alternatives as a political force. Representing extra-

Atina: Was the camp Zionist?

Amos: It was run by the Jewish congregation, which is not *per se* Zionist. Naturally there were Zionist Jewish kids there but I stayed away from them. I was opposed to the idea of Israel.

My parents wanted to raise me as a German. My father always said, "You are first of all a German and only by chance a Jew. I will not have you feel like a foreigner in your own country. You are just like the people around you."

Atina: And all this time you had it in your head to leave Germany?

Amos: Every year, I travelled with my father to England in order to participate in the Easter freedom marches. My father wanted me to gain political experience, but he had great anxiety about being involved in politics in Germany. He still does. He was afraid that his pension would be taken away. So I always planned to leave Germany. I always felt very constrained there.

Atina: How did you relate to your schoolmates?

Amos: I was never able to find out from them what their parents had done during the Third Reich. They didn't want to know. If I would say to my friends, "I am a Jew," they

parliamentary elements in Parliament is also the position of the Radical Party in Italy.

CB: The Italian radical party does indeed play an important role as a symbol.

SL: When I visited them in Rome recently, I got the impression that the Italian radicals had a much clearer idea as to which modes of action to adopt, such as referendums, etc. The Alternative List in Berlin struck me on the contrary as being rather vague, without definite vistas or objectives.

CB: Yes, but remember that the Alternatives incorporate a form of criticism of traditional politics that also addresses the Italian radicals. The *Partito Radicale* is still a gathering of personalities while the Alternatives is a gathering of movements. It's much more complicated.

SL: That point needs to be emphasized. During the anti-authoritarian struggles, the movement was dominated by personalities. We see less of that today.

CB: Yes, much less.

SL: For Germany it's a new phenomenon for no one to try to map out, or program, solutions in advance...

CB: Nor is there a claim to power on the part of charismatic leaders. Yes, that's quite true, but the absence of a strong formulation is felt profoundly during public interventions. Demands for explanation put forward by one part of public opinion remain unfulfilled because of the Alternatives' inability to define clearly their positions.

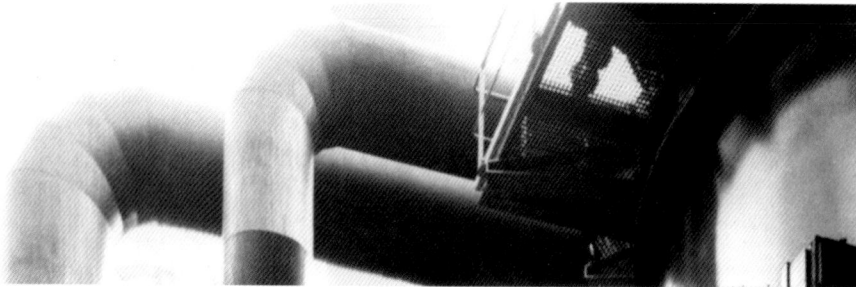

would reply, "You are not a Jew; you are a German. You are a human being just as we all are. You don't even go to the Synagogue."

Atina: It was important for you to preserve the Jewish identity?

Amos: Since I was a little exotic, they eventually accepted me as an Israeli, as an Israeli German, but never as a German Jew. Naturally, their parents knew the difference, they knew what a Jew was. My schoolmates would tell me later that their parents would make some anti-Semitic comments about me. But never to my face. After the Israeli army triumphed in the '67 war, then everyone enthusiastically exclaimed, "Aha, the Jews are still the best Germans."

Atina: How was it with the Left?

Amos: '68 was a very important year. I was studying medicine at the University of Cologne. There were many radicals. We organized the first medical students' strike in Cologne and established the first Basis Group for doctors in 1969.

Atina: Did you have any good friends in the movement?

Amos: In none of my relationships could I really talk about my uneasiness at being a

SL: Where does this inability spring from? The great period of ideological reflection is not so far behind us.

CB: The Alternatives embody after all a great break with society. The new language they developed is barely comprehensible to the public at large. This language is not specialized or complex in a scientific sense, but it belongs to another life-experience and is hardly adaptable without it. Or so we're often told.

SL: And yet the Alternative Scene in Berlin seems extremely fluid. It ranges from purely autonomous projects to small entrepreneurial forms of a neo-capitalist character. It's even difficult to say where the Alternative Scene begins and ends. No one seems to have a solid picture of what falls under its aegis, not even the authors of the yearly Alternative Guide of Berlin, which goes on for hundreds of pages. It's highly diversified, branching out in all directions.

CB: Ah yes, that dream of Guattari's, the rhizome! Actually it's the strong and the weakpoint of the Alternative Scene.

SL: No attempt is being made to analyze the movement in theoretical terms nor to define its limits strictly. Rather, there is a concerted effort to give it the widest possible space in which to grow. Is this specific to Berlin?

CB: Because of its somewhat peculiar position, Berlin attracts many young people. The movement is over-abundant there, but not at the electoral level. In Berlin 7.2% voted for the Alternatives, as against 6.5% in Frankfurt. Berlin

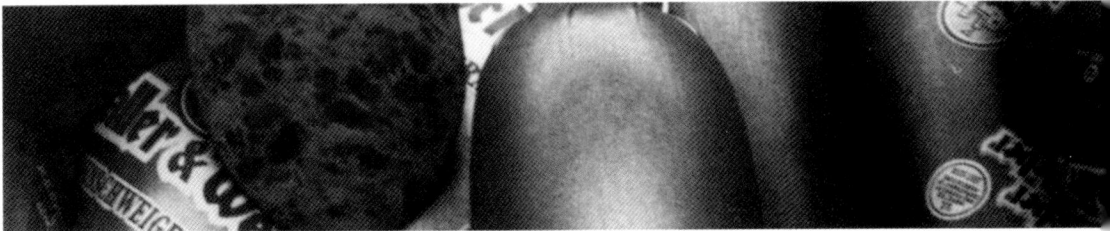

Jew in Germany. At times, I would raise the issue, but my friends and comrades would always say that I didn't understand. I wasn't looking at it right. Being a Jew was a matter of religion, it had nothing to do with what I was today. And it had nothing to do with what their parents were or had done.

Atina: How did you feel about that?

Amos: It was really schizophrenic. To be a Jew and a member of the Jewish Congregation, one has to be conservative. But if one tries to identify oneself as a Jew to Germans, one is asked, "But are you a member of the Congregation?" To leave the Jewish congregation means that one will no longer be viewed as a Jew. It's a real vicious cycle. It is difficult to maintain a Jewish consciousness and at the same time be a leftist in Germany. □

Translated by Michael Lazarin

may be a bit more advanced in this respect, but basically it's the same in all large German cities. The disintegration and search for alternatives is pretty much the same all over.

SL: The Squatters' Movement is growing rapidly in Berlin.

CB: I believe it's only an epiphenomenon that's coming strong in Berlin now because there are so many vacant houses. In Frankfurt, the occupation of houses happened in 1973. It's an important phenomenon because it's going on right now, but it doesn't offer much for the future.

SL: Don't you think that the squatters' presence not only in Berlin but also in Zurich and Amsterdam defines a new transnational situation?

CB: At present it affects all the industrial societies of Europe. Sooner or later it will strike at the United States. It is a transnational phenomenon inasmuch as it is a response to a particular transnational society. But it's an instant response, like a sheepdog answering its master. It's not a response that can go very far.

SL: What would be the base for a response that would go far?

CB: The response has to be very propositional. It must be positive, otherwise it's not an alternative. People are not going to stop living within society. Some movements express a societal crisis, and they go no further. Others can express the possibility of moving beyond that crisis. I believe that the events of Zurich and Berlin express a deep crisis and the rejection of a certain kind of politics, not a movement beyond that crisis.

JOAN REUTERSHAN

"The Future Is Female"

Two women active in the Berlin Emergency Center for Rape Victims had been looking for an apartment for months. In the *Blocksberg,* a cafe for women, they met other equally desperate women. At that time — in the Fall of 1980 — 25 houses had been taken over by squatters. Occupying a house emerged as a solution. A core group of five decided to look for fifteen women inclined to live in a feminist cooperative and willing to risk criminalization. They needed twice that number to help in preparations. The search mobilized the women's network in Berlin — the cafes, bars and bookstores, the Women's Center, the feminist art gallery and a monthly journal called *Courage.* Soon participants started holding weekly "conspiratorial meetings" in the *Blocksberg.*

The women were looking for a structurally sound house in an area where other squatters would be at hand for practical advice, or should the police interfere. The

SL: Do you think that the anti-nuclear movement could provide the necessary framework for moving beyond that crisis?

CB: Only through the anti-nuclear movement did the Alternatives experience a return to politics since there is no staying outside of the structures of a nuclear society, as everyone now realizes. Whether pro or con, we are within. To come up with a radical change that will make nuclear society and everything it entails useless is now everyone's problem. Parliamentary initiatives as well as Alternative Lists took off from there. They help us cast the problem of managing society and the State in a new light.

SL: When did the Alternative Scene and the anti-nuclear movement come together?

CB: It happened from the start. The alternative people have always been extremely propositional in the area of their experiments, and opposing nuclear technology also means opting out of certain organizational schemes. The anti-nuclear movement implies the rejection of the kind of economic growth and the type of industrialization that presently exist in Germany. The movement constitutes a strong minority that is extremely powerful nonetheless, in that it smashes the consensus of German society.

It has become very difficult to manage German society politically. Up to now it fell to the Social Democrats to integrate the various reformist elements at work in German society. The anti-nuclear movement has grown so powerful as to disintegrate the Left and center from which the Social Democrats

Squatter's Councils and store-front tenant's rights offices in Berlin neighborhoods provided information on houses in their area. The women decided to occupy the house at *Liegnitzerstrasse 5*, located in Berlin-Kreuzberg — a working class district with a large foreign worker population.

Liegnitzerstrasse 5, a house with a large street frontage and two side wings had been renovated after the Second World War. The owner, a private housing corporation, was evicting tenants. A superintendent and six legal occupants still lived in the building. Their prospective neighbors might call the police. The women decided to take the risk.

The occupation date was finally set for early January 1981. At that point the women heard that another squatter's collective, an all-male group already experienced in squatter's techniques and recently evicted from their building, had decided to move into the same house. In the Squatter's Movement no one has a claim to a building unless living in it. The women called in their supporters, donned leather jackets and confronted the male competition. Intimidated, the men retreated.

This public confrontation alerted many people of the women's intentions. Yet operations had to remain clandestine because of police informers. Successful infiltration had led to houses being boarded up and guarded by armed agents immediately preceeding a planned occupation. The women set an "official" occupation for January 7,   285

draw their main political strength. By the same token, it's the whole German system that is shaken.

SL: I assume that's what's going on right now with the debate on Euro-missiles raging around Chancellor Helmut Schmidt.

CB: The emergence of the Green Party and the Alternatives on the traditional political scene topples the political base — the three party system — on which Federal Germany was built. It's as if in the United States a new political party suddenly emerged and assumed control of 10 to 20% of the Congress.

SL: No Nukes in Germany don't all come from the Left.

CB: No, it's very complicated, but many come from the Left.

SL: What's the importance of the Protestant church in the movement?

CB: A fraction of the church plays a very important role. But it is fairly difficult to assess the strength of the various conflicting components.

SL: Greens and Alternatives are not the same either.

CB: No, they are not altogether identical. One part comes from the Social Democratic stable and a minority comes from the extreme right — but it is no more than a minority. Let's say that there's the young on the one side and on the other the world of big politics.

SL: This sounds like the French ecological movement.

CB: Correct. What's really interesting is that the electoral results are almost the

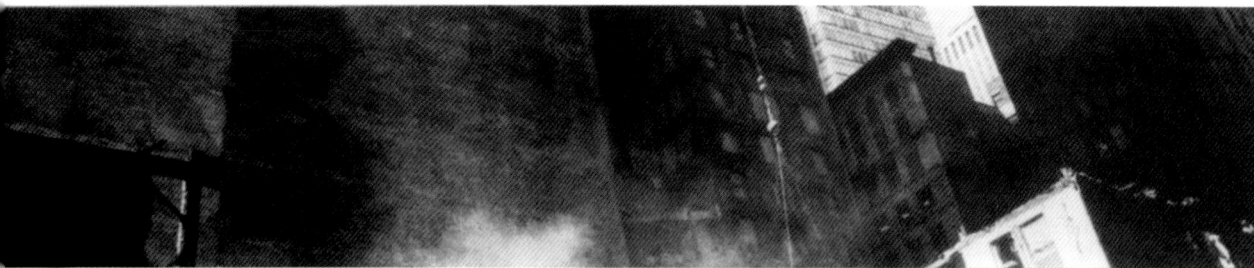

1981; only the core group and their supporters knew that it was to be two days earlier.

On the evening of January 5th, several carloads of women arrived at *Liegnitzerstrasse* 5 with sleeping bags, food, furniture, extension cords and seven bouquets of flowers which they presented to the superintendent and the tenants. They assured them that their goal was to stop the evictions, repair the house and force the owner to grant, or renew, leases.

Most tenants had mixed reactions. They were afraid of being evicted because of the occupation. Turkish workers were afraid of loosing their jobs and be expelled from the country if they had police records. The superintendent was afraid of being fired for not informing the owner and the police.

Meanwhile other women were entering the empty apartments. A few had been recently renovated and were in excellent condition. They had new windows, freshly painted walls, polished parquet floors. Others, left vacant for years, had faulty wiring and leaks. The women hung banners they had brought with them from the windows. One dubbed the building the "Witch House." "The future is female" was painted at the entrance.

One group of women stayed in the house while another drove to the cafes frequented by Squatter's movement people to announce the occupation and solicit dona-

same all over Europe, from 4 to 6%. In France the far-Left is more powerful, and there are fewer ecologists, but altogether it ends up the same.

SL: Do you think the movement will continue to grow or will it settle at this level?

CB: I think it will keep growing. In Germany we'll soon see the collapse of Social Democrats of varying persuasions and the return of the Right. That could lead to redefining a reformist political line with the prospect, hopefully, of the emergence of a new majority of ecologists and Social Democrats, but totally transformed.

SL: Where does the German anti-nuclear movement draw its strength from? Is it from the fear of total annihilation?

CB: I'm deeply opposed to playing up fear in order to stir up anti-nuclear feelings among the population. One of the major problems of bourgeois society is fear anyway. Besides, the apocalyptic consciousness runs the risk of discouraging any attempt at changing society.

SL: So what is there besides fear?

CB: Behind the surface, behind the fear of a nuclear war there looms what's been called a crisis of civilization. What we're experiencing now as a wave of pacifism, on top of the ecologist landslide now affecting Germany, and not only Germany, is primarily the expression of that crisis.

SL: Rather than a crisis of civilization, American observers talk about a crisis

tions. Some 3,000 Marks was soon collected, a generosity no doubt triggered by the fact that until then occupations had been a male prerogative. The squatter's sympathizers also welcomed the prospect of lining up the women's community firmly behind the Movement. The first night in the Witch House was spent in a mixture of exuberance and anxiety.

A second feminist house occupation followed closely. The house at *Winterfeldstrasse 37* in Berlin-Schoeneberg was an obvious choice. It was surrounded by squatter's houses. The owner had scheduled the building for demolition. One of the last remaining apartments still under lease belonged to two active feminists. That this Art Nouveau building with an entrance hall of marble and mirrors, a mahogany carved staircase, apartments with 16' ceilings decorated with plaster reliefs, was to be torn down further outraged the prospective squatters.

Renovation work was begun immediately in both occupied houses. It called for more than the usual interior decorating. The women learned the repair techniques from the Squatter's newspaper, or from women carpenters, plumbers, etc. Women members of the *Weddinger Werkstatt*, a construction collective close to the squatters, came to demonstrate how to repair electrical circuits. The wiring work was approved by a licensed electrician, which entitled them to service by the Berlin utilities company. (In

287

of German identity. They seem to be very concerned with "the new, left-wing nationalism" and point out a resurgence of old nationalistic impulses among German pacifists.[3]

CB: This is pure fabrication. The problem with today's pacifist movement is that it often formulates its refusal of a nuclear war in a terminology inherited from the 50's. This terminology is hardly adequate to the question we're now confronted with, namely: what is it about this society that needs to produce for its own security such a threatening military apparatus?

SL: The 30's terminology, or the 40's for that matter, seem to worry Americans: the existence within the movement of components appealing to *Blut und Boden*, blood and earth, family and country, all reminiscent of the heydays of fascism.

CB: I won't deny that there exists among the ecologists (but this is an altogether different question) some bizarre components, but they have nothing to do with a return of German nationalism. This is simply not true. The forces of nationalism are all in favour of the double resolution of NATO and for rearmament. I don't believe that the problem lies with what the Americans call the "spirit of Munich," i.e. a certain laxity faced with Russian totalitarianism. It is a fact, however, that the peace movement still has to prove that it doesn't just aim at de-stabilizing the political balance established by NATO, but that it can effectively contribute to de-stabilize the Warsaw Pact by establishing a real dialogue with political forces like Solidarity or Charter 78. The credibility of the peace movement in the West depends on its capacity to support similar movements now developing in the East.

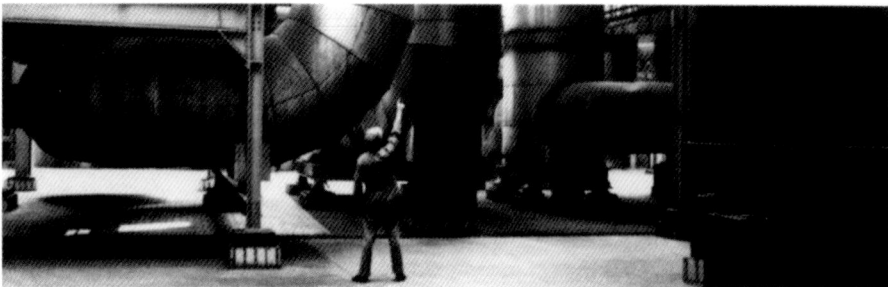

peculiarly German fashion, the publicly operated electrical concern has developed contracts for illegally occupied houses. As long as they pay, squatters are treated just like other customers.)

Taking over traditionally male construction tasks didn't prove as difficult as living up to feminist ideals of cooperative living, work and politics. The women had hoped to create an emotionally supportive environment; now they hardly had time to communicate. Chaotic living conditions, women's projects, house renovation, Squatter's Council meetings, demonstrations, interviews for feminist magazines, radio programs soon took their toll. The thought that their work on the house could be brought to naught should the owner decide to call the police, or the Senate to evict the squatters *en masse*, began to weigh on them. They harbored conflicts rather than carrying them out; many started to seek the privacy of their apartments instead of using the communal rooms.

The women squatters also had to confront various responses from their immediate communities: the verbal abuse from male tenants and some neighbors; the antagonism of the superintendent infuriated by the fact that his wife kept using the squatter's apartments to get away from him during domestic arguments.

288   The attacks of right-wing punkers were a more serious threat. Bands of young men

SL: The peace movement should help to break the deadly logic in which the two blocs are locked. Ecologists don't seem to be unanimous on this point though. Wasn't there recently within the peace movement quite a controversy about the way to deal with Reagan's visit to West Germany?

CB: Yes. Some traditionalist components of the movement led by small pro-Soviet groups confronted the Greens. The debate is still going on, but the ecologist movement as a whole definitely aims at putting an end to the confrontation between the two superpowers. And there's no doubt that it will develop in that direction.

SL: The peace movement in Germany is often perceived in the U.S. as being essentially anti-American.

CB: How could that be possible? The American way of life has been part of Germany for the last thirty years. The movement isn't anti-American, it simply rejects a certain type of technological society that leads to a Nuclear State and keeps encouraging suicidal tendencies at work in our civilization. □

April 10, 1982

Translated by Daniel Moshenberg

1. See "Italy: Autonomia," *Semiotext(e)*, III, 3, 1980.
2. *Ibid.*
3. John Vinocur, "The German Malaise," *The New York Times Magazine*, November 15, 1981.

on motorcycles occasionally roll by and throw rocks in squatter's windows. They know the occupants won't fight back for fear of the law. The squatters were put in the schizophrenic position of having to call the police when an occupied house neighboring the Witch House was badly damaged. The officers arrived late and immediately pointed to the banners hanging from the Witch House. Squatters should expect such aggression, they said. A house occupied by women was an obvious provocation to the young men.

The Minister of a Protestant church in their community, a woman active in progressive and pacifist politics in Berlin, invited the Witch House occupiers to speak at a church women's meeting. The response of the parishioners was so favorable that the minister decided to publicly support the women's occupation and serve as mediator in any negotiations. She wrote to the Berlin Senate as well as to the landlord criticizing housing policy and requesting that the women be granted leases. The parish thus became publicly a "sponsor" of the Witch House.

A few weeks after their occupation, the owner threatened the women with police eviction if they didn't leave on their own accord by March 9th. Whenever buildings are vacated, teams of thugs are usually sent with iron bars and clubs to destroy windows, heating ovens, pipes, floors, etc. The building is made uninhabitable, and the owner en-

RETO HÄNNY

Freedom for Greenland —
Melt the Pack Ice

NOTE

Quotations are for the most part not identified specifically. In an atmosphere where one can become speechless — where, in fact, attempts are made to shut people up altogether — quotes, to me, become posters against fear, belonging to everyone. I do not want to leave our HERITAGE to be administered by power, — and whoever recognizes those quotes as the tributes, which they are indeed intended to be, will perhaps continue reading. Be it the Oresteia or Hoelderlin's poems, the works of Georg Büchner or Ludwig Hohl, Achternbusch's or the poetry of a cold time: on posters and on walls there are the inscriptions of the Zurich unrest, which calls itself 'motion.'

> ...all my limbs are trembling
> when I look at the lip, the nose,
> the hollow of both eyes
> which are blind from keeping vigil

Reto Hänny is a Zurich literary ice-breaker and partisan for a Free Greenland.

titled to an official certification for demolition. The women locked the main entrance door and moved into the front to keep a close watch on the street and eventually activate the phone chain calling out supporters. The 9th of March came and went; neither police nor owner arrived.

Within the Squatter's Movement, the women's politics also gave rise to various conflicts. The women's Cafe in *Winterfeldstrasse 37* has a policy of admitting women only. As a consequence, men in the Writer's Cafe across the street refused to help out the feminist squatters when their water supply was interrupted.

By far the most intense controversy between the feminist squatters and the rest of the Movement, however, turned around the issue of "sponsorship" and negotiations with house owners. Besides pushing for an immediate legalization of existing occupations, the Squatter's Councils in Berlin made it clear that their long term goals were to negotiate with the Senate a new housing policy favoring tenants, as well as preserving the architecture and the integrity of established neighborhoods. However, increasingly harsh police actions and long jail sentences without bail against demonstrators accused of rock throwing led the Councils to break off negotiations with the Senate until amnesty for jailed squatters is pronounced. Although Berlin traditionally declares amnesty in politically charged times, the prospects had become slim now that the Chris-

the grave air of the breath
and the already dead eyelids
the tongue, blackened by the fires,
falls down along with the words
and babbles, I know not what...

Andreas Gryphius, 1616 - 1664

TIRADE

right now
where
the squares of Zurich, the streets and the alleys, on the pavement of a city that
is supposedly mine, too
— inhospitable and cold, but still the height of summer, I shudder in its
slickness, often I have the feeling of being somewhere alien and as far away as
Greenland —
and up to very recently it seemed to be dozing away in smart comfortable
satiety, to complete and definitive concrete-hard immobility, more idyllic than
the moon itself
—viewed from the Hardau, — highrises show off nicely and directly against
the sky, like charcoaled fingers swearing an oath, insignia of potentiality,
suicide chambers agglutinated into public housing, as they show on the quaint
cemented cobblestones with which the Old Town has been sanitized to death;
our town fathers are said to have been as wise, even though some might argue
in hindsight that where loose stones have long changed their positions —,

tian Democrats had taken over the Berlin City Council. Besides, any negotiation was
looked upon as treason by an increasingly radicalized Squatter's Movement.

The women from *Winterfeldstrasse 37* agree with this posiiton, but the Witch
House women do not. From the outset their lawyer, a well-known radical and feminist,
demanded that the owner extend them leases. Infighting among moderates and radicals
within the Squatter's Council, however, prevented them from pushing further their relationship with the Protestant church and the women's community. Pseudo-revolutionary
rhetoric and posturing, they felt, were paralyzing the Movement. They could no more approve of the Squatter's violent masculine style than they could tolerate police aggres-
sions.

Having created their own structures and styles in order to put their energies into
feminist politics, the women realized that they couldn't reach their goal unless they pursued the negotiations with the landlord. For the majority of the women in the Witch
House the Squatter's Movement, threatened by patriarchal reaction, had become a
means to their own end. □

suddenly there is a lot going on, yes, a hell of a lot, not to be understood pejoratively,
openly, in broad daylight
causing insomnia
intensively —

MOTION
that has overtly little to do with language, especially with a literary kind, nothing at all if observed from a safe distance, no tear gas no rubber bullets hailing down, alone, entrenched behind a desk in soothing warmth and advanced age behind a wall of flimsy years, nothing whatsoever if looked upon from a point of view hardly violated by highrises, if seen from an idyllic slope, one's glance extending over fields and forests and pastures;

but, latently, in immediate closeness experienced physically with one's own body, the sheer unreality of the encounter
— which seems to be directed so cynically, so grotesquely against all life —
adds reality to the view experienced most personally and therefore experienced even more intensely;

overcoming with languages in anger and playfulness with fantasy tight limits on the most multifarious levels, entwining piercing borne by one's body but not left alone language that
explodes
bursts
pulverizes

NANETTE FUNK

TAKE IT

Catalyzed by the squatter's movements in Zurich and Amsterdam, the West Berlin squatter's movement exploded December, 1980. Housing was the issue, style the content. A collective life style, housing for cultural space. A demand not to be met without sticks and stones, without steel and concrete, without cracking hard-nosed economic realities of speculator owned, speculator vacated, speculator controlled housing. What is this movement that forced the issue of housing into public discussion for the first time, led to extension of rent control laws, helped bring down the post-war Social Democratic party (SPD)* Berlin government?

I sit in New York, my own building about to be co-oped, steel, concrete and landlords about to break the fibers of my daily life, force me back to where I once belonged, and despairingly, I ask, "Why there, not here?"

gets things rolling
leads
towards laughter

because it stands in opposition to the crippled language of students, and especially professors, who both bear the signs of too many burdensome semesters spent in one-track single-minded oppression. Because it seeks to make room for breath withheld long enough it knocks down all confining and therefore repressing signs of consensus stretched two ways, because from inside and from below, from the atmosphere of polished coldness, the grammar of that language is recognized as being nothing but the essence of power, or, the structure of power, which, quite simply, has to be knocked down so one can regain one's breath; a stammering babble, some may say, in addition, a rude one, I don't care, but full of life, and stubbornly rejects any premature reconciliation or another cheap and frivolous annexation;

in terms of perversity, this language has a great deal more in common with Hoelderlin — whether it knows it or does not want to know it —, and no matter how mistaken this comparison may sound, to people of good taste, much more than with the domesticated, bullet-proof, imprisoned and regulated language, or un-language that officials and peace-loving citizens, employ. This can be seen most obviously in the yellow-press in which their main organ faithfully fans their flame as it both reprimands and incites them;
the contempt and the very false, and profoundly simulated seriousness that oozes out of every line in their high-carat pamphlet — brings to light ever so much more cynically the brutality hidden behind the pretense of good taste

Knowing that words count, squatters enlisted them into the struggle, calling themselves "Instandbesetzers," not "Hausbesetzers," through the art of 'zusammenhängen,' creating new words by combining the old, a long German linguistic tradition, a free space internal to the language. "Instandsetzen" *(to put in order)*, "besetzen" *(to occupy)*. Only by occupying, only by breaking the rules of private property was it possible to put in order what landlords and speculators had destroyed. In July, 1981, when Minister of Housing Rastemborski proclaimed the evacuation of eight houses by August 30, squatters planned a month long festival and 'zusammenhang' once again, calling it "Tu-Wat" *(Do-Something)*, in contrast to the "Tu-Nichts" *(Do-Nothing)*, the festival of a few years ago, a call signified not to the "leftists," but to the "Chaoten" or freaks of Europe.

Instandbesetzen is at once a battle about style and a place to have it, a battle no longer to live isolated lives, no longer to live alone in a little room with parents in authoritarian, arid, no-communication families. Instandbesetzen is a movement for a collective room of one's own, to live in houses with thirty or more people, go shopping in local outdoor markets, sit hours afterwards reading papers in Instandbesetzer cafes, go back to building the walls, installing the toilet, hearing new music in the loft down the street in Kreuzberg, sitting around arguing about anarchism and politics.

— and that not solely in the advertising section where the police seek potential job-candidates, for example in just that edition which, after all, had been delivered to its subscribers under police protection; brave guys they are looking for, at least 5'6" tall, and, after having completed a most meticulous training they are promised—at full salary as is pointed out— high-quality, multi-faceted occupations in which the emphasis is always placed primarily on human beings: yes, to kill them with cudgels and tear gas and hails of rubber bullets; a mode of reporting against which every attack is PROPER

HATRED IS ALLOWED JUST AS WELL AS LOVE, AND I CULTIVATE MINE TO THE UTMOST AGAINST THOSE WHO PRACTICE CONTEMPT. THERE EXISTS A GREAT NUMBER OF THOSE, IN THE POSSESSION OF THAT RIDICULOUS SUPERFICIALITY CALLED AN EDUCATION OR OF SOME DEAD STUFF CALLED ERUDITION, SACRIFICE THE MAJORITY OF THEIR BROTHERS TO THEIR DISTAINING EGOTISM. AGAINST THAT I TURN ITS OWN WEAPONS, HAUGHTINESS AGAINST HAUGHTINESS, RIDICULE AGAINST RIDICULE,

Buechner once wrote to his family, two years before Zurich —;

a way of delivering information
that I, for one, have long preferred to call the perfidious art of italics and quotation marks: words like Repression or even General Assembly this tabloid simply is not capable of printing without ornamentation, pressed in between quotes, italicized or otherwise twisted;

Housing was the issue, space the need, culture the content, but no culture without a space to have it. Culture not as an IT, but a DOING, a LIVING. Doing can't be done without a turf, but where's that turf when it's all been had, had by speculators who bought up the houses leaving them empty for years, had by the "worker's representative," Neue Heimat, real estate consortium of the unions owning 40% of the soon to be occupied houses? Take it, and count on those others who can't take it — the Turkish immigrant worker in too precarious legal status to dare to act, the old woman kicked out of her cheap apartment, living in an old age home down the block, seeing her old apartment locked up, held up. Take it when there's lots of support from others knowing their apartments are on the speculators block, their neighborhoods in danger of destruction.

Instandbesetzers took it in December, 1980, took it again and again, with fighting on the Kurfürstendamm, Berlin's Champs-Elysées, leaving broken glass on the street. Thousands took it, and the SPD post-war government didn't know what road to take — the high road of reasonable discourse, or the hard road to smash Instandbesetzers. Even Hans-Jochen Vogel, Helmut Schmidt's right-hand man, chief architect of Model Deutschland, flown in to salvage the situation, couldn't pull it off.

Instandbesetzers a diverse group — though mainly of Germans, not only of Ger-

faternite egalite
a heritage,
el siglo de las luces,
translated into German
have been hung by their feet
by graffitists
on their typewriters
forced into a maltreated fine phrase
idiotized, crushed —;

as an alibi
to let the clowns
in the cultural section speak
perhaps this exalted art of italics, whose full enjoyment remains a privilege of
taste: the pretense of taste as the irritating variant of normalcy —,
perhaps this art of reporting cannot get out words like repression other than in
a haywire way, because the SCARECROWS OF WELFARE, the falcons of
Goethe-street, who, one day, suddenly, fall off the beaten track, and begin to
shriek in the name of the toilers of the world.
— TOWERS OF WORDS
A HUMAN VOICE HAS GOT TO
SCREAM LOUDER THAN THEIR STRIDENCY —,
repression they probably never experienced themselves, or, perhaps they are
too dull, voluntarily, because of their selfishness, or because they do not want
to realize that they are succinctly directing repression against themselves,
harnessed in constraints that call themselves liberal democracy, or, to speak

mans, though mainly of young people, not only of young people, of working class kids
from the Märkische Viertel, Berlin equivalent of sterile city projects, drop-outs from
school, but also full-time Free University students taking classes with the generation of
'68, of eco-freaks wanting to preserve the old "Berlin mixture" of front houses, back
houses, small ateliers with courtyards in the middle for public space, of self-conscious
political types who speak the language of liberation and emancipation, and those who
speak no political language at all. A band of outsiders wanting space, working class kids
not wanting working class lives, dead end jobs, those for whom the phrase "no future"
was real, Instandbesetzers revealed a crack in the German-cum-American values — hard
work, performance principle, build a career, move upwards and onwards. Not a very
'nice' movement — wearing "funny" streaks of red down Mohican-like haircuts, breaking the law, having no jobs, wanting no jobs, outsiders the richly tufted West German
Social Democratic welfare state couldn't appease and who didn't want to be appeased,
outsiders the "rational planners" hadn't planned for.

    Instandbesetzers took it, house after house, one hundred and sixty of them, in
Kreuzberg, in Schöneberg, Wedding, Charlottenburg, took it when the law, "Bauherren
Model" ("Landlord's model") lopsidedly landed speculators subsidies up to 80% of
renovation costs, including part of the rent as well; took it, when Neue Heimat, "protec-

with the transparency of a political party's leadership which still carries those words freely on its banner: What we need is public tranquillity and the consistent enforcement of our cause, which is law and order and persistent support of the responsible power of the state;

MONEY AND POWER, POWER AND MONEY,
THAT IS FELICITY;
JUSTICE AND INJUSTICE,
THAT IS SALACITY

Power
ARE YOU SEEKING JUSTICE OR MERELY REVENGE?
whose scheme makes itself apparent in the liquidation of the other human being at a time when contradiction and deviation become a crime and all thinking freezes into a formula of law and order, hand-coloured and cut of wood;

but
WHOSOEVER HATH POWER
HATH FEAR
and
POWER
THAT IS NOT LIKELY TO ENDURE,
MUST BE PROTECTED BY SO MUCH MORE
POWER
says the Ship of Fools
and an infinite chain of revenge and counter-revenge,

tor of the workers," asked the police to kick out the children of workers occupying the houses; took it, when even *Der Spiegel* couldn't figure out who broke the law — squatters making housing liveable or speculators barricading, shutting down housing for years. Instandbesetzers took it, according to squatter's rules, deciding which houses deserved to be occupied, and damn the law. Creating cultural centers — the Kukuckcentrum, Spectrum Cafe, Bobby Sands Cafe, took it with the help of alternative mechanic collectives, printing collectives, plumbing collectives, took it with money collected from habitues of alternative cafes, with the help of "Patenschaften," literally "Godparent" groups, support groups of teachers, union members, artists, doctors, lawyers who created a moat around occupied housing, keeping the alligators at bay, pledging to sleep in when police came.

Squatters took it in the modern walled-in city held together by a wall, not a subway, a purposefully arbitrary, ugly, graffiti covered wall signifying permanent temporariness, a wall making a housing shortage a high pressure situation, making Berlin a city of no-exit, a city of no suburbs because the suburbs would be in East Germany, a city where architects come to burrow below and not just up. Squatters took it, not for the book of Mao, Lenin or even Adorno and not for the third world, but to make a world in a space threaded by images, words, sounds, and shaped to squatter's needs, on squatter's

SOLELY AN OATH, AND ITS COUNTER-OATH ALONE DO
NOT BRING ABOUT JUSTICE
and, more than 2000 years after:
FOR HOW MUCH LONGER SHALL THE FOOTSTEPS OF
FREEDOM REMAIN GRAVES? —
an indecent question, I know, I know, asked by a former resident of this barren city; —

MOTION
which is the expression, or better, the eruption of a strangled life, a life that has been lived wrongly, or not at all; an eruption of piggish courage, which is, in our time, an old word for gloom that has been piled up over the years;

but at the same time, away from alienated fathers, and their language, it becomes a search for possibilities to overcome, for the will to finally live oneself instead of being lived any further, a search which is carried by the intensity of the passion felt by those who suffer with us,

but if the gray eminences of this city were capable of displaying only the dimmest spark of the fantasy of the street, excoriated as unlawful pressure of the street — whom or what does the street press? — they would,
THE ONES WHO SIT IN THE CITY COUNCIL
THE STOUT ONES WHO SIT ON STOUT CHAIRS
THE ONES WHO DO NOT HAVE ANY OTHER REAL INTEREST
BUT TO HANG ON TO THEIR POSITION

terms. Instandbesetzers fought not to change 'society' or to change the rules in prisons, schools and not for the long march through the institutions of the '68ers. In that battle Instandbesetzers knew who won. Their actions provoked institutional reactions — union members complained about Neue Heimat's eagerness to evacuate squatters and its practice of renovating housing out of reach of its own union members; faculty at the Free University started teaching courses on the housing movement and giving lectures in occupied houses.

Instandbesetzers did it out in the open, didn't negotiate it, did it American style, committing civil disobedience in the streets, showing that breaking rules made sense, not only in Berlin with three thousand but elsewhere in the "Rechtstaat," in Frankfurt with hundreds of thousands over the expansion of the airport runways to import nuclear warheads.

BLACK TUESDAY, September 22, 1981, the police took it, Minister of the Interior Heinrich Lummer took it carrying out the evacuation of eight houses, attempting to break a style, a zone off limits to government rules. Police rushed crowds into oncoming traffic and on Potsdamerstrasse a bus driver ran down and killed Klaus Rattay, a working class youth on the move from one occupied house to another. Potsdamerstrasse, the
street of men from Sri Lanka, flooding Berlin that summer, hanging out on street corners

THESE HACK COACHMEN OF THE POWERFUL
— no reason for worrying, the one who said that is dead —
stop babbling about dialogue meant to mark the proposal off the list entrenched in their magnificent bunkers, being guarded by the police — not even one of their own anymore who dares to speak out is readmitted into their meeting; but anyway, who is upset by things like that, the following day the papers report that the council had been hindered in executing functions;
which is right, too: some of the councilmen did, indeed, appear somewhat late for supper at the 'Crown Hall' and 'Guild House' restaurants that night —;

really, if they possessed one spark of light,
THOSE WHO ARE ALWAYS OPPOSED TO CHANGE,
THOSE NON-WORKERS,
they would long ago have accepted an invitation for dialogue, which has been presented to the House, an invitation for a dialogue conducted in a language different from all languages hitherto, which all is to say that up to now the language of those peaceful citizens' administration has labeled itself again and again Chloracetophenon (CN) O — (Chlorbenzyliden) — malodinitril (CS), weapons that are destined — according to the treaties of Brussels — specifically to direct their
stifling
toxic
irritating
paralyzing
growth-regulating

with nowhere to go; Potsdamerstrasse, the street of rundown stores and tired out prostitutes.

The next twenty-four hours Berlin was a city at war, sirens wailing, evacuations the only topic of conversation, buses re-routed, police vans with squads of riot police everywhere. Evacuation as military affair.

Instandbesetzers passively resisted in the houses, fought in the streets, set up a memorial with wreaths of flowers where Rattay was killed; parents brought their children to see it all.

Public space and a space to live, a style to live, had already been a battle ground of Commune I, Commune II, the '68ers experiment in daily living spiked with fantasy and imagination. Instandbesetzers grew in the unorganized, sometimes unfriendly remnants of that alternative space, a space of bars, restaurants, bookstores, discos, a space for habitués, all counter culture types, living contentedly on unemployment insurance, not worrying about a career, much more absorbed in the next vacation in Italy or even California, the next escape from Berlin. A space where alternative values were dug in, legitimated, a space that made possible collective resistance.

No accident that the Instandbesetzer's movement became so strong in Berlin, the escape hatch from the orderliness and wealth of West Germany, the haven for West Ger-

lubrication-destroying
qualities towards military purposes only,
materials that cause injuries of the eyes and horny skin
that are carcinogenic,
lethal, although the father of our town still dares to divide them up into legal and illegal weapons,
but the thinking of administrations, the thinking of bare skulls without brains has always shown the same flexibility as a hexagonal rubber-bullet which cuts gashes in everyone who does not know how to protect himself and, in hitting the eye, blots out all sight;
an altogether different language indeed, a most grim, and at the same time, a most voluptuous one; and only this tongue, which became the language of the cobblestones, was to be understood almost terrifyingly quickly, unfortunately, I am inclined to say, IN OPPOSITION TO VIOLENCE, although this language is far from being comprehended in Zurich where, for years and years, people have been eagerly doing cosmetic patch-ups in all other respects rather than even begin to notice problems and suggestions;

instead of listening to them, instead of trying to bend an ear towards them and to extract the message thus transmitted, they now are more bewildered, shakier, and more scared than ever, frightfully awakened from their sleep BY THE BOUNDARIES THAT BEGIN TO CAVE IN —

instead of listening to them, these peace-loving bourgeois who do not even dare to acknowledge their fear, and slumbering away in front of their t.v.'s, prefer to withdraw into a fur-covered satisfaction, now suddenly cry out loud

man men escaping the army, in Berlin, the city West Germany struggles to keep alive, making it pallatable to all comers, incentives for all, but especially for Germans, even not so good Germans, in Berlin, the city where the 'freaks' come.

Post-evaucation ... The SPD* and Alternative List, * planned a censure against Ministers Lummer and Rastemborski, but withdrew it. In Fall, 1981 new occupations were immediately evacuated. Winter, never easy in Berlin, is a time of tension, anxiety only inches below the surface, Instandbesetzers suspicious of agents everywhere, preparing for the police to act out again, and the authorities counting on the cold air of winter to freeze out the Instandbesetzers, unable to afford ovens and heat.

The government now faces a dilemma. If it breaks the movement it will show that above ground resistance is impossible and only terrorism will do. If it loses the battle, it will mean that resistance can make a difference, a lesson that government doesn't want to teach in this time of Reagan hard-core nuclear penetration. □

at the sight of some smashed shopwindows as if each single one of them had
been hit personally and deeply; unable to feel their own skin anymore, the
mirage of unaffiliated shops and noble cafes has become a dear substitution for
them, a shell that must be protected —

Madness,
panicked they cried at the broken glass, before they regained their speech and
were able to draw back again, reassured
— I DEDICATE MYSELF TO THIS BLAZING MADNESS IN
ORDER NOT TO SUCCUMB TO THE DARK SIDE OF
REASON,

Madness,
shouted those who hoarded money to flee the country and the cannon
manufacturers
Madness,
shouted the illegal arms-salesmen of bloodsoaked operetta-generals;
deeply concerned about individual trade and the worldwide reputation of
Zurich, a communique says:
business, they say,
in order to secure jobs,
they say, in a country that hardly knows any unemployed:
the guest-workers are sent to their home countries as soon as the cold season
begins
Calculators
humming neonlights

HERBERT GRUHL

Doomsday in 20 Years

Q: Mr. Gruhl, aren't you exploiting the doomsday mood, too? Isn't the reason you're
painting such a horrifying picture of the future in order to cut back on social services?

HG: We won't die because of the nuclear power plants. A nuclear power plant accident
would indeed *perhaps* cause extensive damage, but it would still be regionally contained. What I'm afraid of is all the things which are associated with nuclear energy. After

During the recent Club of Rome conference at the new Conference Center in Berlin we spoke with
Herbert Gruhl, himself a member of this illustrious organization. Is it possible that this man (a former
CDU* member) is truly the 'ecofascist' a number of people accuse him of being? Or is he the in-
genious theoretician of the ecology movement, as *A Planet is Plundered* makes him out to be?
(Presentation for "TAZ"*)

industrial centers

peace within the work force

money rustles softly, like fall foliage sailing to the ground quietly in the mist, while the ocean swallows the noise of heavy boots trampling down entire continents - all those who dared to touch these noisy substitutes and smash the mirrors, all those who cry out nakedly The Kaiser is Dead, all those are being condemned as the lowest vermin, but anyway, the teargas spat in one's face tastes like insect repellent, which causes the throat to burn for days;

since the incidents that took place at the end of May between the NZZ[1] and the foyer of the opera house, which had been nailed shut
— inside they were performing La Sonnambula, the voice of the new Amina a bit unconcentrated in the first scene, I read in the paper —,
the language of the cobblestones, the only tongue to me that is clear and adequate, is ultimately a powerless answer to the bedevilment of language, to the camouflaging of problems, to the hair-splitting hassle, to the walls of servants who stubbornly obey every kind of order and advance as inexorably and undiscerningly enraged as oxen while their masters reclining in ambush celebrate their idiom Chloracetophenon —;

WE HAVE REASON ENOUGH
TO CRY,
EVEN WITHOUT YOUR TEAR GAS:
WE DON'T HAVE ANYTHING TO LOOSE,
EXCEPT OUR FEAR.

and nobody should be surprised if a plant continuously pruned, a little tree

all, nuclear power plants are not built in isolation; they presuppose industrialization of the region.

It's not so much the power plants as the reasons for their being built which primarily concern me.

Q: What time frame do you have in mind?

HG: We can't continue that way for 20 more years. In 20 years everything will be over anyway.

Before 1973 (the year of the so-called oil crisis) everyone generally assumed that economic growth would just continue indefinitely, that growth was more or less a natural process which no one could halt. You can't stop a speeding Express train: that was the prevailing view in those days. As it turned out, no one had to stop it by force; the rate of growth sank all by itself after 1973. In this situation the governments could have said: terrific, it's winding down all on its own. But this contradicted their theory, which was based entirely on the premise of economic growth. And so the German government — just like the governments in the other industrialized countries — reacted by heating up the economy again. And it worked, for a few little percentage points.

that has been carved into a crippled form, finally starts to fight back the strangled existence it has been forced into
right now
therefore I do not want to write poetry, I cannot find rhymes, I do not want to sing alone from behind the desk
— in front of the desk, on the balcony, the possibility of jumping over the railing, AWAY WITH THE DAY, PUT THE LAMP UNDER CRYSTAL SHADES AMONG THE OLEANDERS —,

and when I, while getting out of a streetcar at Bellevue early Sunday morning, am called one of those swineherd's dogs whose mug should be smashed with a crowbar because my hair is growing a few inches longer than the standard measure of one of these peace-loving citizens who is accompanied by a German shepard on a short leash, I lose my desire to write poetry,

all the more thoroughly if I have to overhear people saying at the local bar that those who demonstrate NAKEDLY AGAINST VIOLENCE should be castrated with a good blow to the balls and then thrown into the river Limmat by good athletes from central Switzerland, and that the rest should be locked up in the AJZ (Public Youth Center), so that all those S.O.B.'s can be blown high into the sky, as fireworks for the national holiday:
I do not want to understand their alien language any longer, even though it is supposed to be my mother-tongue.
NO POWER FOR NOBODY
THEREFORE TURN THIS STATE
INTO CUCUMBER-SALAD

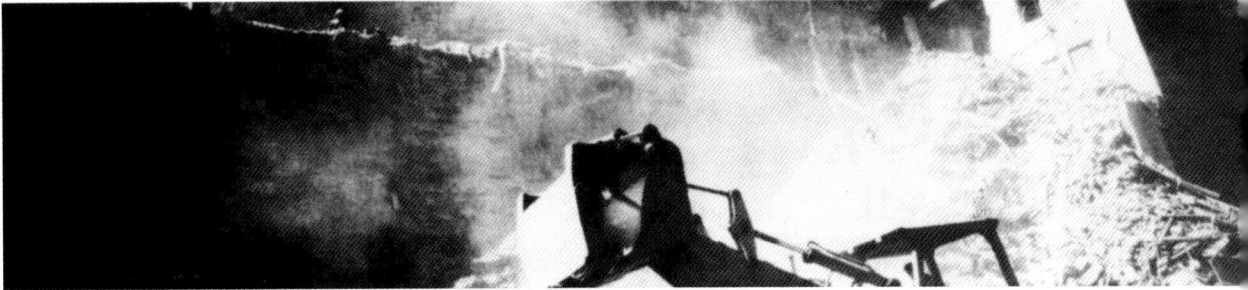

Q: Will the apocalypse of the world be nothing more than a life and death struggle of the technocrats?

HG: Of the technocrats and of those economic powers with capital which support the technocrats and want to continue business as usual. Just as the politicians want to continue business as usual.

Q: If this is the way you see it, Mr. Gruhl, then you must agree to some extent with people who want to use force to counter this growth ideology, which itself has been imposed by force.

HG: I wasn't speaking of physical force, but of money, laws, power. I do not consider brute force to be a reasonable solution. It's not acceptable for a small minority to use violence to stop the imposition by force of a growth economy, even if it's only the violence of sitting-in at a construction site. For change to occur it is pre-requisite that a large portion of the population, not necessarily a majority, already be enlightened in these matters and have attained a different level of consciousness. □

FREEDOM FOR GREENLAND,
DOWN WITH THE PACK ICE
I CAN STATE A NEED FOR LOVE
ONLY IF THERE IS A HEART

ALTHOUGH YOU DO NOT HAVE A CHANCE, TAKE IT

that is why I am writing this letter before I'm off to the street again
humming, grunting, singing,
to see for myself how the concrete acquires new cracks, to sharpen my hearing
for the creaking of the ice, before, only too soon, the manipulated petit
bourgeois set out to obscure the view in this desert of wild consumerism again

with cannons onto Dada

still just one unenlightened lawyer has
fired into the crowd
murder begins
with self-defense

therefore
DANCE ROSETTA DANCE SO THAT TIME WILL BE IN TIME
WITH THE BEAT OF YOUR NEAT LITTLE FEET
MY FEET PREFER TO BE OUT OF TIME

not yet☐

Translated by Frederike Albet-Frankel

1. Neue Zuricher Zeitung: conservative Swiss daily newspaper.

"Carlos used to say that in order to get anywhere, you have to step over dead bodies."

Hans-Joachim Klein

PAUL VIRILIO

Pure War

Sylvère Lotringer: You are one of the few French thinkers to abandon the language of philosophy or sociology for the language of war. Do you think the discourse of war is better suited to the present conflicts than political discourse?

Paul Virilio: The distinction between military intelligence and political intelligence is becoming outmoded. Georges Clemenceau gave the key phrase: "War is too serious a thing to be entrusted to the military." That was the last political word from a French politician. His statement came just at the moment of "technological surprise" brought by the First World War. From then on, the gap widened between political discourse and the increasingly technical discourse of war. I am simply reviving the ancient tradition in which the civilian possesses the same knowledge as the military man.

SL: How would you characterise this "technological surprise"?

Paul Virilio is a French urbanist whose writings on speed and war are attracting increasing attention on the other side of the Atlantic. His works include: *Bunker Archeologie* (CCI, 1975) and *L'Esthetique de la disparition* (Balland, 1980). The following interview is excerpted from a volume to be published in Semiotext(e)'s "Foreign Agents Series" (Spring, 1982) together with Virilio's *Speed and Politics* (Fall, 1982).

ALEXANDER KLUGE

The Air Raid on Halberstadt, 8 April 1945

Reporter: So you took off after breakfast?

Anderson: That's right. Ham and eggs, and coffee.

R: Well then, according to routine you started from combat airfields in the south of England?

Kunzert, a reporter born in Halberstadt,[1] who moved to the West in June 1945 when the English troops evacuated Sachsen-Anhalt, contacted Brigadier General Frederick L. Anderson of the 8th Division, U.S. Air Force in 1952 in London during a conference of the Institute for Strategic Research. They are sitting at the bar in the Strand Hotel. Anderson was one of the commanders in the air raid on Halberstadt.

PV: People came to realize that the production of arms on a traditional peacetime scale could no longer meet the demands of the military. It became necessary to create a special economy, a war economy. This was a formidable discovery, and this extraordinary machine eventually grew into a State within the State.

SL: The "technological surprise", then, announces the end of civil society.

PV: Civil society is becoming hollow, and losing its meaning. The distinction between the civil and the military is no longer very clear when there is a total engagement in a war economy, especially during times of peace.

SL: It's a Copernican revolution in the relations between strategy and politics.

PV: Absolutely—and now there is a more momentous surprise, no longer technological, as in 1914, but scientific: the appearance of the nuclear bomb. The absolute weapon moves to the center of political debate. Or more exactly, the debate is dissolved.

SL: One can still negotiate around nuclear power, but not over the absolute weapon.

PV: The gravest danger of this absolute weapon, nuclear arms, is not that it explodes, but that by its very existence it destroys all debate about the evolution of society. Its prescence is what constitutes the drama: how to kill the absolute weapon? How to destroy this weapon, present "by divine right" at the center of our society? That's the real question.

A: The Podington 92nd, the Chelveston 305th, the Thurleigh 306th, the Polebrook 351st, the Deenethorpe 401st and the Glatton 457th.

R: Instead of just listing the squadrons, can you tell me what it was like?

Anderson couldn't give a clear picture of the squadrons take-off. He stood behind one of the pilots, saw meadows and airport hangars go by and then was pressed against the back wall when the plane gathered speed. The teletype told him that the other squadrons took off at the same time. In each of the planes there are 12 to 18 men, some of them just waiting, others carrying out specific technical jobs. The entire fleet meets over the coast where some of the squadrons go into a holding pattern.

R: Then a flight over the northern coast of France?

A: Of course. We acted as if we were flying towards Nürnberg or Schweinfurt.

R: Did you have a sense of pride when you looked over a bomber formation of 300 airplanes?

A: I couldn't see it. My Mosquito, a fast wooden bomber, flew a different route — over the Netherlands, Rhine, Weser, Northern Harz, etc.

307

SL: But isn't what we classically call "war" just a smokescreen for this diffused phenomenon which is now neither war nor peace and is only partially defined in terms of deterrence?

PV: You know Clauswitz's phrase, "War is politics by other means." The total peace of deterrence is total war pursued by other means. In the era of deterrence, the constant production of arms is war. What I've called Pure War is war which perpetuates itself not by repeating war, but through infinite preparation. Quite simply, from the perspective of consumption in civil society, this infinite preparation leads to non-development. It's true not simply of the Third World, but also of the "middle power" countries of Europe; hence the debate currently raging over Euro-missiles. In fact, it will also be true of the United States. I won't mention the Soviets, since they long ago refused to follow the path of civil consumption.

SL: Marx spoke about the pauperization of the working class, which hasn't occurred; to the contrary, the proletariat has been absorbed into bourgeois society, and with it the reality of class struggle. What we are witnessing now is a relative pauperization of civil society, which goes hand in hand with the absolute growth of the military state.

PV: Absolutely. And moreover, there is with deterrence a rather extraordinary inversion: the military establishments no longer oppose anything but civil societies, and, I would say, *their own* civilian populations. What's happened in Cambodia is a small scale model, a caricature of what's taking place on a world scale. It's the military class reverting to become a sort of internal super-

R: Then German air-surveillance had only to determine the direction of this pathfinder plane to see through the ruse of the bombers flying south easterly.

A: Sure. To the extent that they were still operative, they realized that.

R: South of Fulda a change in course?

A: Towards the north east.

R: As planned?

A: Everything was planned.

R: The squadron commanders had no say in that?

A: The lead planes flew up front, but didn't determine the flight pattern.

R: What was the purpose of that?

A: I don't know. I can only describe the methods of the attack. They were all pros. First of all they had to locate the city, to "see" it. When we arrived in the Mosquitos, we saw the squadrons of bombers coming in from the south. To our right were the Harz Mountains; we could see the Brocken.[2] The planes flew over the southern portion of the city,

police. This is perfectly logical. In the climate of deterrence, the military no longer confront each other; they tend to confront only the civilian. With, of course, a few skirmishes in the Third World. The armed forces turn against their own populations. On the one hand, in order to exact the necessary budgets for war — that is, the infinite development of armaments — and on the other, in order to control society. What's taking place in Poland today is of the same order, the reversion to a state of war which is nothing more than a war against one's own population.

SL: It's the colonization of one's own territory.

PV: Yes, an endo-colonization. One colonizes only one's own population. One underdevelops only one's own civil society.

SL: The "deregulatory" politics of Reagan, as well as the colossal expansion of the American military budget, move in this direction.

PV: Reagan is already endo-colonization applied to the United States. The Welfare State, which existed in Europe and the U.S. in the 1960's, is being replaced by the State-as-destiny.

SL: Paradoxically, the coming to power of the military in the Third World is not an archaism, but a prefiguration of what's in store for the West.

PV: Latin America is the laboratory for future society, a society where control and colonization are achieved by forces of order within the country itself, though often with the assistance of foreign armies. One can easily see there the perversion of the traditional condition of "defense."

dropping a few bombs as a prophylactic measure on exit roads where the inhabitants, responding to the air raid alarm fled towards the mountains. The squadrons then regrouped at the north eastern corner of the city, over the road leading to Magdeburg. They circled twice until all the squadrons had joined the formation so that they could fly the attack in a close formation. The orders were for saturation bombing, i.e., concentration of bombs on the southern or middle section of the city. We didn't know the city, had only a map to go by and our first visual impression. From this we knew that the main streets went through the middle from west to the east, in the north small villages, to the south mountains. We didn't have time to dwell too much on the lay of the land since we still had the attack and flight back home ahead of us. We looked for the cardinal points of the city.

R: Or what seemed to you to be cardinal points?

A: We didn't know the purpose of the attack. Therefore we simply selected an efficient point to start.

R: What is that?

A: That the attack isn't blotchy.

SL: The original forms of military repression in Latin America — for example, the "desaparecidos" (the missing) — are highly exportable to Western countries. In fact, they come from there. Latin America is to American imperialism what Spain was to Nazi Germany: the occasion to test cheaply its new technology.

PV: Many people don't realize to what extent the "desaparecidos" is not a complementary technique but one that is becoming central. Why? Because it's impossible to hide anything any longer, to isolate anything in this ubiquitous and instantaneous world. It's easier to make people disappear one by one, ten by ten, even thousand by thousand, rather than enclosing millions in camps, as was the case in Nazi Germany. Disappearance is our future.

SL: What's being produced is another perversion of a traditional distinction. The direct access to power of the military class takes place indifferently in the name of reactionary or socialist ideologies, as in Chile, Cambodia, Peru...

PV: Ideology has little relevance. We're no longer in a system where political ideology dominates. We're in a system dominated by military ideology. And the only ideology is order.

SL: And the ideology of order is deterrence. But isn't deterrence itself losing its logistical value?

PV: That's true. We're now entering the second phase of deterrence. The present debate on the development of conventional armaments, on the exponential growth of the military budget, whether in the U.S., France, or the Soviet

R: What does that mean?

A: The bombing shouldn't be dispersed throughout the city. We looked for the main arteries and the exits. Also where it would really burn. You know yourself where that is in an old city. You don't have to be a medievalist to know that such cities were founded in 800 A.D. With that in mind the bombers concentrated on the corner houses so we could block the streets. Ideally a pile of rubble at the entrance and exit of every street. The trap was sprung after we opened up the houses on either side of the streets. Then followed with incendiary canisters and fire bombs, etc. Then a third and fourth wave again to detonate the houses and burn them. This led to a criss-cross effect even though we always flew along the same path. Buildings that were still intact were hard to set afire. First the roofs had to be destroyed, opening made that go down to the second or ground floor where all the flammable material was. Otherwise we didn't get area fires or fire storms, etc. My brother is an air force doctor. It's the same as treating a skin wound. You can't heal a closed or scabbed wound. I'd compare this to a scabby old city. The wound had to be opened up so that blood flowed from fresh veins before you applied the bandage.

R: After the first four waves you began again in parade formation with two more waves

Union, conveys the idea that deterrence must be generalized. And generalizing deterrence leads straight to cultural suicide. An obscurantism is beginning to pervade all levels of society.

SL: The disappearance of our civilization, if not of the human species, has ceased to be merely an intellectual speculation. For the first time, extermination on a planetary level has become a working hypothesis.

PV: General Fuller, one of the great historians of military affairs, has said that the essential feature of the nuclear era is not the destructive power of the new weapon, but its speed. It's the speed of these vectors which led in 1962 to a "hot line" between Khruschev and Kennedy, and which leads today to quasi-instantaneous decision-making.

SL: Deterrence is still a humanist category, since it implies time for reflection.

PV: But there's no longer time for reflection. The power of speed means exactly this. By the end of the century, the absolute weapon will be capable of absolute speed. There lies the real question of nuclear monarchy: today there are still Yalta agreements and confrontations between East and West, whether NATO, SEATO, the Warsaw Pact or whatever, but in my opinion they've all been surpassed by a kind of universal state. We've moved from the state to the pure state, which is the result of Pure War, that is, of the intensity of the means of destruction. The capitalist and communist ideologies are themselves in the process of being superceded by this vision of the world. The real enemy today is less external than internal: our *own* armaments, our *own* scientific power, which in reality promote the end of our own society.

to "clean up." Why did you do that?

A: In parade formation because there was no anti-aircraft fire. When there is anti-aircraft fire the planes disperse and the bombing is not concentrated. That wasn't the case here.

R: I meant after the destruction what was the purpose of flying over two more times?

A: That was routine.

R: There were rumors. On that morning at 9:30 the city's defense headquarters received a call from Hildesheim from a high ranking American officer via the civilian telephone system saying: surrender, remove the tank blockades! The mayor wasn't there to receive the call. The next in command, Detering, who was commissioner of defense, rejected this offer. Consequently the air raid began. If the mayor had gotten up earlier and had accepted the offer, the city would have been spared the bombing. If by eleven o'clock a large white flag had been raised on the left tower of the Martini Church (left as seen from the south) the bomber squadrons would have turned around. A woman is supposed to have tried to get a large cloth, six bed sheets sewn together, to the City Hall or to the Church.

A: That's nonsense. By this time the bomber fleet could never have been reached from a combat station in Hildesheim.

SL: The confrontation of the blocks, the coupling of these two imperialisms is deterrence as collusion.

PV: What's been instituted is a fatal coupling between Soviet and American imperialisms, and they are allied in the race to armaments. What end has SALT I served? It's promoted the precision of guidance systems, the miniaturization and multiplication of warheads. In other words, thanks to the SALT I agreements concerning reduction and limitation of armaments, the war machine has been further sophisticated. I think the START agreements — for the reduction of armaments and not just their limitation — will only be possible because in reality they will bring about an even greater improvement of the war technology.

SL: What's the future of pacifism, then, as it's developed out of Germany?

PV: It's not possible to understand the situation of pacifism today in relation to the danger of real wars. "The Russians are going to invade Europe," etc.

SL: You don't believe Europe is in a dangerous strategic position?

PV: I think geo-strategies are being outmoded by the laser and more sophisticated technologies. Sure, there's still the problem of military bases for the forces of intervention. But we shouldn't confuse the bases with geographic politics. That's a little like saying that the parking lots are the freeways.

SL: The European peace movement, then, relies on an analysis which is out of synch with the real logic of the nuclear war machine?

R: Is there any truth to the rumor?

A: Nothing at all. The officer would have had to telephone, via division headquarters, Army corps, the headquarters of the arm, then via General Headquarters in Reims to London, from there get connected to the Strategic Air Command, back to the Eighth Air Division, then to various airports in the south of England (in order to determine which squadrons took off and in what direction, that was all secret information, otherwise any spy could have made the call) then an appropriate command would have had to be translated into a code, etc. All this would have taken six to eight hours.

R: What would your lead planes have done, those which gave the smoke signals, for the route of the attack, if they had seen a large white flag made of six bed sheets flying from the tower of the Martini Church?

A: There was a huge formation in the air, no single leading aircraft. What was a big bed sheet supposed to mean? A trick? Nothing at all. It might have been the subject of a conversation. The planes behind were pressing on. Even if no smoke signals were given, one would have assumed that that was neglected and either made them or bombed according to what was visible.

312   **R:** But a large white flag is internationally recognized, as surrender.

PV: Yes. The real problematic is Pure War. It's not actual war, but logistical war. The word "pacifist" has a meaning, which I adopt, insofar as it is tied to a faith, one official faith confronting another. There is undoubtedly in the Polish affair or the German affair (with the Protestant churches) something of a conflict against idolatry. The believer in God protests against the divinity of the Absolute Weapon — the missile, no longer the Messiah. The nuclear age has put us closer to the apocalypse, in the sense of the extinction of the species. It's hardly surprising that religious believers are unfurling their flags.

SL: Do you see any relation between the German pacifist movement and the emergence of Polish trade unionism?

PV: The interesting side of the Polish affair is that there's a marriage of trade unionism and religious belief. There's no Walesa without the Pope. There's no trade union power over the Party without religious belief. That's the real source of Walesa's strength. He's less trade unionist than man of the cloth. He's the priest confronting the warrior. Hence the conflict between two supremacies: the supremacy of military imperialism in Jaruzelski, and the supremacy of cosmic imperialism in Catholicism. If one looks at recent events, how can one explain the fact that super-powerful armies like those of Iran or Lebanon have suddenly collapsed? It's because they've imploded, from religious conflicts within. I think Poland's of the same nature. What's interesting there, within Christianity (although the term, like most, is outmoded), in relation to the Holy War of Islam, is that Khomeini has chosen traditional Holy War — the Mullah speaking through his rifle — while Walesa and Archbishop Glemp have called for a Holy Non-war. They could have said

A: To an airplane? Let's imagine that an airplane landed on the nearby airport — the landing strip would probably have been too short for a four engine plane — and occupied the city with its 12 to 18 man crew. How could they know, whether the person who raised the white flag hadn't been taken and shot by a firing squad for "defeatism."

R: That didn't give the city a fair chance. What should a city do to surrender?

A: What do you mean? Don't you understand how dangerous it is to fly back with a load of five or four tons of explosive and fire bombs?

R: They could have dropped the bombs somewhere else.

A: In a forest, etc., etc. Before the flight home. Let's assume the units were attacked on the way home. The airfield in Hanover still had planes. We were in fact waiting for them to come. Who would take responsibility for these heavily laden geese, simply because of a white cloth? The goods had to go down onto the city. They cost a lot of money. You couldn't just throw that away, in the mountains or open fields after it was produced at such expense. How could this, in your opinion, have been reported to the higher ups?

R: You could have at least dropped a portion in open fields or in a river.

that since strikes no longer work, people should pick up arms. But no, they said they wouldn't fight. Now this is formidable. There's something there which makes one think that the ecumenicalism of Christianity is a sort of response to deterrence.

Thus, in my opinion, the Polish affair is novel particularly for throwing the religious question in the face of the military. The future of the Soviets is the same; what will happen to religion there? Because the only way to eliminate Statocracy—the military class—is through the *interior*. It's not by a mass uprising against the technocrats, against armament factories, against the nomenclaturists of Soviet war. It's got to be by a collapse of the same kind as has begun to take place in Poland. This is a supreme danger for the Soviet empire. Walesa is a "pacifist" because he has renounced terrorism, even in a time of state of war. In some ways the Polish trade unionists are lined right up with the German pacifists. They, too, have a heavy cross to carry. On the one side, the Poles "support" Soviet imperialism. On the other the young Germans, our friends, have to bear the immense burden of Naziism, which is still part of their make-up.

SL: But trade unionism *a la* Walesa is not trade unionism as it has developed in the West, as the management of society. There's been a transformation of trade unionism from a weapon of combat into a weapon of conciliation.

PV: This Solidarity-style trade unionism is hardly a trade unionism at all. That's why it went out of control. The Polish trade unionists have set themselves as a counter-power right from the start. From the outset, as pacifists, they've solicited dialogue with the politicos. And when they obtained the maximum from the State, they indirectly solicited the army. When

A: These valuable bombs? You can't hush that up. In each plane 12 to 18 men were witness to it 215 times. We didn't intend anything. We didn't know anyone down there. Why should any of us take part in some conspiracy for their sake. I could have given a command to a firing squad, everyone run for cover, airplane coming from the left, and then told the prisoner he should disappear, with the understanding that everyone would keep it quiet. But that could never happen.

R: In other words the city was erased as soon as the plans were made?

A: Let me put it this way: if a couple of our commanders of tank divisions had been in a particular hurry and had pushed forward in a brilliant maneuver over Goslar, Viennenburg, Wernigerode to reach Halberstadt by 11:30 am, that would not have changed our plans.

R: They could have signaled their presence to you.

A: Enemy deception.

R: You would have calmly destroyed your own troops?

314   **A:** Not calmly, but with some doubts. There would have been some communications

Jaruzelski came to power, Walesa said: We love our military, we're ready to talk with them. The only thing I've not understood, but which was certainly in the air, is why they never proposed Solidarity *in* the army.

SL: There was a hint in this direction with the national alliance, the fireman's academy.

PV: I imagine something like that was played out. Contrary to Kania, the army refused the "non-Party" dialogue. (The Portugese used to say, "We are a non-party revolution.") Solidarity did the same. It bypassed the Party, starting from the moment the Party began to dissolve. The Party was bypassed because it was collapsing, it no longer had any supporters. Solidarity questioned the army, but the army refused to answer. At that point, Solidarity bluntly proposed to go get the Russians. There are leaders of Solidarity saying: "We've got ten million supporters. We don't want war, we don't want to take up arms. We'll talk with the Russians, we'll talk with anyone." They're Christians, don't forget. They have an essential weapon, The Other World. What makes for the power of a Holy War? It's the lack of fear of death. It's the fact that history doesn't stop with the last beep on the encephalograph. "We'll talk with the Russians, we'll talk with the Devil if necessary." They were ready to go to extremes, which was the only way to make the army collapse. For the moment, anyway, I don't think there's any other way. To liquidate the absolute power of the army, whether in Warsaw Pact or NATO nations, I don't see any possible alternative than by making an appeal to faith. By raising the question of death again, there's a re-examination of the political. What more can politics offer on the question of death than religion? It's the ancient question, which has

which could have compromised the saturation bombing. Thank God our tank squadrons weren't magicians.

R: Did you have an idea of the purpose of this attack?

A: As I said, not really.

R: You are a cynic.

A: But I'm not dishonest. What good would it do, if I offered you my sympathy now?

R: None

The reporter refused a cup of coffee. Real hatred, here at the bar of the Strand was hard to fabricate. □

Translated by Reinhard Mayer

1. Prussian town, now part of East Germany.
2. Highest peak of the Harz mountains.

constantly been asked for all social and political formations. It's the relation to death which decides whether we exist or not. In this way, Walesa is very close to the German pacifists. What has Walesa said? "We're already dead in Eastern Europe. Our nationalities are already extinct. We exist in decline, our life is a non-life. We've got nothing to lose by confronting the enemy, the Russians, the military . . ." He's strengthened, moreover, by the statements of the French bishops: if suicide is forbidden to the individual, it's even more forbidden to a nation; a nation has no right to commit suicide. I'll rephrase it this way: does a species have a stronger right to commit suicide? Here we're back with the German pacifists again. On one side Poland, as a nation which considers itself already dead, but which doesn't want to cling to its own death and torture indefinitely, refuses suicide. Hence Walesa. On the other side, there are the Germans, who have experimented with death, having practically invented the total war, and who say they won't accept nuclear suicide. All this starts to become clear. It's very political, you see, but in the ancient sense. I can't say it better than that. □

Translated by Silvia Federici, Jim Fleming, and John Johnston.

316

ALMUT CARSTENS

History of West Berlin and the Federal Republic of Germany

1966

November 26   The "Great Coalition" formed by CDU* and SPD*.

1967

January 1   Kommune I founded in West Berlin by Dieter Kunzelmann, Fritz Teufel, Rainer Langhans, et al.

April 6   Pudding attack on Vice President Hubert Humphrey.

May 12   Expulsion of Kommune I from SDS*.

June 2   The student Benno Ohnesorg shot by a policeman during a demonstration against the Shah's visit in West Berlin.

September   Resignation of Heinrich Albertz, Mayor of West Berlin, City Administrator Wolfgang Busch and Police Chief Erich Duensing.

WHAT A STRANGE CROSS!

IT HAS HOOKS ON THE ENDS!

ALMUT CARSTENS/ FRANK MECKLENBURG

History of the Soviet Zone and the German Democratic Republic

1946

April 21-22   Founding of Socialist Unity Party of Germany.

April 23   *New Germany*, Socialist Unity Party's newspaper, first published.

1968

February 17-18   International Vietnam Congress held at the Technical University.

April 3   Arson of Kaufhaus, department store, in Frankfurt am Main as protest against Vietnam War.

April 5   Gudrun Ensslin, Horst Söhnlein, Andreas Baader and Thornwald Proll arrested and sentenced later to three years in prison for Kaufhaus arson.

April 11   J. Bachmann attempts to assassinate Rudi Dutschke, who is critically wounded. Consequently, protest demonstrations and actions against Springer* corporation arise.

June 28   Enactment of *Notstandsgesetze* (Emergency Laws)

September 12-16   At the 23rd Delegate Conference of SDS in Frankfurt am Main the Steering Committee for Women's Liberation surfaces publicly ("Free the socialist fellas of their bourgeois phallus!")

September 16   Founding of the German Communist Party in Offenbach — strong Moscow orientation declared.

October 20   Regional and local elections in Soviet Zone. Socialist Unity Party receives 47.5% of vote.

1948

February 26   End of de-Nazification of Soviet Zone.

March 9   Centralization of Soviet Zone's economy.

June 18   Beginning of Berlin Blockade. Roads and trains from West Germany to Berlin closed by Soviet troops. Berlin airlift instituted by France, Great Britain and U.S.A. to get supplies into West Berlin.

June 23   Monetary reform in Soviet Zone as a reaction to monetary reform in West Zones. West and East Germany use different currencies.

October 13   Superworker Adolf Henneke exceeds his production quota by 380%. Beginning of "activist movement" which sees work as ideology and sport.

| December 31 | Founding of the German Communist Party/Marxist-Leninist by Ernst Aust in Hamburg — Maoist, with a strong Albanian orientation. |

1969

April 1	Formation of the Socialist Bureau.
June 12	Founding of the Red Cell German Studies at the Free University in West Berlin, which became model for similar cells in FRG*.
September	During the so-called September Strike 140,000 people strike in 69 companies.
October 22	Beginning of the "Small Coalition" of SPD* and FDP.*
December	Founding of the Socialist Patient Collective in Heidelberg.

1970

| March 21 | Official disbanding of SDS. |
| March | Founding of the German Communist Party Reconstruction Organization, (which in July, 1971 becomes German Communist Party/Marxist-Leninist, Peking-oriented). |

| November 30 | Socialist Unity Party representatives to city parliament form their own governing body in East Berlin, thereby splitting Berlin politically. |

1949

May 12	End of Berlin Blockade.
October 7	Founding of German Democratic Republic (GDR)
	During the year 125,245 people flee from Soviet Zone and GDR to the West.

1950

July 6	Recognition by the GDR of the Oder-Neisse Line as the boundary between Poland and GDR.
September 29	GDR becomes a member of COMECON.
October 15	Elections in the GDR: 98.44% vote, of which 99.7% support government.

1951

October 31   First Five-Year Economic Plan.

1953

May 28   Announcement of increased production quotas.

June 16   Construction workers in East Berlin strike to protest increas-
                      ed production quotas.

June 17   Peoples' rebellion in East Berlin and the GDR put down by
                      Soviet troops.

                      During the year 391,390 people flee form GDR to the West.

1956

January 18   Formation of National People's Army and Ministry of
                      Defense.

March 4   Walter Ulbricht, head of the Socialist Unity Party, explains in
                      New Germany: "Stalin is not a classical Marxist."

April 3	Andreas Baader is arrested in West Berlin.
May 14	Freeing of Baader during a visit to Free University library — one library employee wounded.
September 29	Robbery of three West Berlin banks by RAF,* netting 220,000 DM.
October 8	Arrest of Horst Mahler.

1971

September 15	Petra Schelm, RAF activist, is shot by police in Hamburg.
December 4	Georg von Rauch shot by police in West Berlin.
December 8	Occupation of a vacant nurses' residence in West Berlin, dubbed Georg von Rauch House.

1972

January 28	Formulation of *Berufsverbote** by urging of SPD.
February 2	Bomb thrown on British Yacht Club in West Berlin, killing a shipbuilder.
March 2	Thomas Weisbecker is shot by police in Augsburg.
March 11	First inter-regional Women's Congress in Frankfurt am Main, attended by 400 women from 36 groups; men excluded.

1958

November 10	Khruschev's Ultimatum: the Allies should pull out of Berlin.

1959

April 24	First Bitterfeld Culture Conference held with motto: "Take up your pen, comrades! Socialist Nationalist Culture needs you!"
September 1	New educational program offers possibility of completing *Arbiter* and vocational training at same time.

1960

April 15	Karl-Marx Stadt (former Chemnitz) is last region to become officially economically socialized.

1961

August 13	Berlin Wall is built.
	From beginning of the year until August 159,730 GDR citizens flee to the West.

May 11	Bomb attack on Headquarters of 5th U.S. Corps in Frankfurt am Main, killing one American officer.
May 15	Bomb attack on Federal Judge Wolfgang Buddenberg, wounding his wife.
May 24	Bombing of U.S. Army in Europe Headquarters in Heidelberg, killing three soldiers.
June 1	Arrests of Jan-Carl Raspe, Holger Meins and Andreas Baader in Frankfurt am Main.
June 7	Arrest of Gudrun Ensslin in Hamburg.
June 15	Arrest of Ulrike Meinhof and Gerhard Müller in Hanover.
September 26	Formulation of law to train Federal Border Patrol as federal policemen.

1973

March 1	Opening of Women's Center in West Berlin.
June	Founding of Communist Union of West Germany (Maoist).

1974

May 7	Resignation of Willy Brandt, resulting from disclosure of GDR* spy Günter Guilleaume.

May 9	First public women's festival of the autonomous women's movement in West Berlin, attended by 2000 women.
June 5	Ulrich Schmücker, member of June 2nd Movement, shot in West Berlin.
October	Introduction of Neighborhood Patrols in West Berlin.
November 9	Holger Meins dies in prison as a result of hunger strike.
November 10	Attempted abduction and assassination of West Berlin Supreme Court President Günter von Drenckmann.

1975

February 23	20,000 people occupy construction site of an atomic reactor planned by Wyhl.
February 25	Supreme Court rejects allowing abortions in the first trimester; protests in FRG and West Berlin.
Feburary 27	Abduction of Peter Lorenz, West Berlin CDU politician, by June 2nd Movement, before Senate elections.
March 3	Ingrid Siepmann, Verena Becker, Gabrielle Kröcher-Tiedemann, Rolf Heissler and Rolf Pohle released from prison in exchange for Peter Lorenz.

1963

Christmas	West Berliners allowed to visit relatives in East Berlin.

1964

March 12-13	Sharp attacks on Prof. Robert Havemann, physicist and critic of GDR.
August 21	Law establishing that there is no limitations on Nazi and WWII war crimes.

1965

December 15	*New Germany* begins campaign against Wolf Biermann, GDR composer and balladeer.
December 10	East Berlin edition of *Berlin Newspaper* attacks writer Stefan Heym.

1966

April 1	GDR Academy of Sciences expels Robert Havemann.

April 24	Attack on the German Embassy in Stockholm, taking hostage of Embassy employees to be exchanged for 26 GDR prisoners. Two hostages shot, explosion in Embassy building kills RAF members Ulrich Wesse and Siegfried Hausner.
July 30-31	Two bank robberies in West Berlin by June 2nd Movement, "signed" by Mallomar cookies left at scene.
December 21	Attack on OPEC Conference in Vienna.

1976
May 9	Ulrike Meinhof found hanged in Stammheim Prison.
Pentecost	Anti-Repression Congress of the Socialist Bureau in Frankfurt am Main; 20,000 participate.
July	First Feminist Summer University in West Berlin.
September	First issue of *Courage*, feminist journal.
November 13	Wolf Biermann stripped of GDR citizenship and refused re-entry into GDR.

1977
January	First issue of feminist journal *Emma*.
February 19	50,000 people demonstrate against the proposed atomic reactor in Brokdorf and Itzehoe.

1967
August 28	Introduction of five-day week (43 and ¾ hours).

1968
June 10-11	Passport and visa required of Federal Republic of Germany and West Berlin citizens to enter GDR.
August 20-21	Troops of GDR National People's Army take part in invasion of Czechoslovakia.

1970
March 19	Erfurt, GDR. Leaders from East and West Germany, Stoph and Brandt, meet for first time since their republics founded.
March 26	Brandt and Stoph meet in Kassel, FRG.

1971
May	Honecker becomes first secretary of Socialist Unity Party.

April 7	Generalbandesanwalt (Attorney General) Martin Buback, his chauffer and a policeman are shot by RAF commandos.
April 28	Gudrun Ensslin, Andreas Baader and Jan-Carl Raspe receive life sentences.
April 30	First Walpurgisnacht (Halloweeen) demonstration under the motto, "Women recapture the night."
July 30	Banker Jürgen Ponto shot during alleged abduction attempt by RAF commando.
September 5	National Business Association President Hans-Martin Schleyer abducted, his chauffer and three policemen killed.
October 13	In conjunction with Schleyer abduction, four Palestinians hijack a Lufthansa jet with 82 Germans and 5 occupation troops aboard. Same demands for freeing hostages as for return of Schleyer — release of 11 FRG political prisoners, including Baader, Ensslin, and Raspe (plus release of two Palestinians from Turkish prison, and $15 million).
October 17-18	After pilot of hijacked jet shot in Aden, plane lands in Mogadishu and boarded by GSG-9 personnel (FRG

1972

| June 3 | Transit agreement between FRG and GDR on travel routes between FRG and West Berlin. |

1973

June 12	GDR seeks UN recognition.
June 15	FRG seeks UN recognition.
August 1	Walter Ulbricht, GDR's most important official, dies.

1974

May 2	Establishment of permanent consulatory relations (de facto embassies) of GDR in Bonn/FRG and of FRG in East Berlin.
Summer	Writer Siegmar Forst sentenced to 4½ years in prison for visa application.
December 9	U.S. opens embassy in East Berlin, capital of GDR.

special border patrol); three Palestinians killed, hostages freed.

October 18   Jan-Carl Raspe, Andreas Baader and Gudrun Ensslin found shot or hanged in Stammheim Prison cells; Irmgard Möller seriously injured.

October 19   Hans-Martin Schleyer found shot in Mulhouse after RAF report.

November 17   Attorney Klaus Croissant turned over to FRG by French officials.

1978

January 27-29   TUNIX meeting in Technical University in West Berlin attended by 25,000. A celebration of anti-psychology (Cooper), urban Indians, gays, philosophers (Foucault, Guattari, Glucksmann), communes, university freaks, artists, the unemployed, prison groups, dropouts, under the motto, "We want everything and we want it now!" A heterogeneous resistance movement is formed to organize a departure from "Model Germany."

June 30   Rudolf Bahro, author of *The Alternative*, a book critical of GDR, sentenced to 8 years in prison for anti-socialist and subversive activities.

Summer	"S.O. 36"in West Berlin (Kreuzberg) becomes for a year the place for artists and performers.
December	Third International Russell Tribunal on Human Rights in FRG.

1979

February	Squatters occupy first factory loft in Waldemar Street, West Berlin.
March 31	100,000 demonstrate in Hanover against proposed storage for nuclear waste in Gorleben.
April 17	First issue of leftist radical daily *Tagszeitung* (TAZ).
October	Release of Rudolf Bahro from prison, departure from GDR to FRG.
December 24	Death of Rudi Dutschke as delayed consequence of 1968 assassination attempt.

1980

May 3	5,000 occupy proposed nuclear waste storage facility in Gorleben. Proclaim Free Republic of Wendland.
September 9	According to Housing Official Harry Ristock, 225 dwelling apartments in West Berlin occupied by squatters.

1975

February	Siegmar Forst kept in solitary confinement despite severe illness.
July 30 to August 1	Governments of FRG and GDR endorse declaration of "Conference of Security and Cooperation in Europe" in Helsinki/Finnland.
October 20 to 25	World Congress for International Women's Year is held in East Berlin with some 2000 representatives from 135 countries attending.
December 16	Expulsion of GDR-correspondent of FRG news magazine "Der Spiegel," Jörg Mettke.

1976

March 14	Refusal of accreditation of three Western press correspondents at Industry Fair in Leipzig/GDR.

December 12	First big street fight resulting from squatters' demonstration in West Berlin.
1981	
March 13	First national squatters' congress in Münster.
May 12	162 new houses occupied by West Berlin squatters.
May 26	National "decentralized action" day for squatters, second street battle in West Berlin following police searches of occupied houses.
September 13	60,000 demonstrate in West Berlin against visit of Secretary of State Alexander Haig.
October 10	Largest demonstration in FRG history: 265,000 demonstrate for peace, against NATO rearmament agreements in Bonn.
1982	
June 10	Mass demonstration in Bonn during President Reagan's visit.

Translated by Dagmar Stern

May 27	Decision to raise minimum wages and minimum annuities and measures to assist working mothers.
November 3	Writer Reiner Kunze expelled from GDR Writers' Association.
November 13	Polit song writer and performer Wolf Biermann stripped of his GDR-citizenship while touring in West Germany.
November 26	Writer Robert Havemann placed under house arrest.
December 22	Expulsion of correspondent of West German TV Lothar Loewe.
1977	
January 1	Under new GDR-emigration regulations, tourists from West-Germany treated like any other foreigners.
August 23	Arrest of GDR-critic Rudolf Bahro following publication of excerpts from his *Alternative* in news magazine "Der Spiegel."

GLOSSARY

Alternative List Non-ideological party formed end of 70's by several opposition groups: leftists, ecologists, members of Citizen's initiatives, etc. Only exists in West Berlin. For first time elected to West Berlin parliament in 1981 by 7½% of electorate.

Alternative Scene Loose network of old New Left, youth movement, feminist, squatters, etc. Includes restaurants, bookstores, cinemas, communes, "banks," collective enterprises, etc.

Anti-Authoritarian Name given to 60's anti-establishment youth movement.

Movement That's where "it all began."

Autobahn West German highway.

Baader, Andreas Founder of Red Army Fraction (RAF), together with Ulrike Meinhof, Gudrun Ensslin, Horst Mahler, etc. Found dead in Stammheim prison in 1977.

Berufsverbot 1972 law barring leftists from public service jobs.

October 7 Confrontation between youth and police following a pop concert in center of East Berlin.

1978

January 1 Authorities close East Berlin "Spiegel" office after it publishes a manifesto signed by East German "League of Democratic Communists."

May 29 to 31 Hermann Kant elected chairperson at GDR Writer's congress.

June Youth riots in Erfurt/GDR.

June 30 Rudolf Bahro sentenced to 8 years in prison.

July 7 Nico Hubner refuses military enlistment. Subsequently sentenced to 5 years in prison.

September 1 Despite protests of numerous members of clergy, of whom several are arrested, military education introduced to 9th and 10th grade curricula.

Brandt, Willy	Chairman of Social Democrats. Chancellor of Federal Republic of Germany until 1974. Resigned after spy scandal.
CDU/CSU	"Christian Democratic Party," founded after WWII by Konrad Adenauer. Conservative party in power from 1949 to 1966.
	"Christian Social Party," headed by Franz-Joseph Strauss. Bavarian section of CDU.
Ensslin, Gudrun	Founding member of RAF and girlfriend of Andreas Baader. Found dead in Stammheim in 1977 together with Baader and Raspe.
Extra-Parliamentary Opposition (APO)	Name given to 60's Anti-Authoritarian movement.
FDP	"Free Democratic Party." Liberals. Nationwide party with less than 10% of electorate. Shares power with SPD since 1969.
FRG	"Federal Republic of Germany," founded in 1949. A product of East-West Cold War politics. Known as West Germany.
GDR	"German Democratic Republic," founded in 1949. A

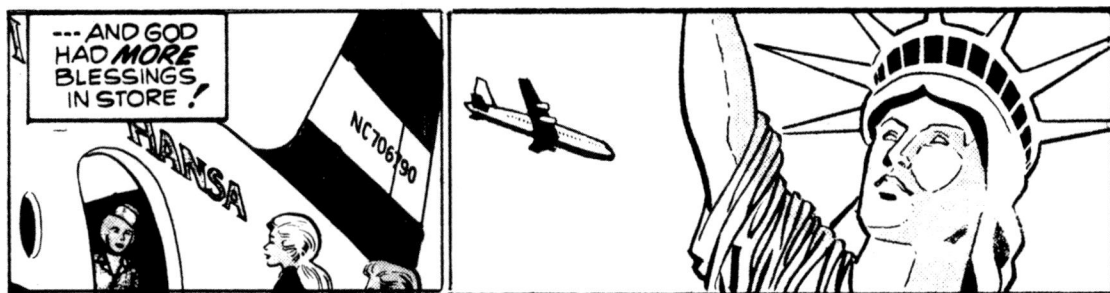

1979

April	Repressive measures against several writers.
June 7	Expulsion of 9 writers from Writers' Association.
June 28	Modifications of Criminal Law, increasing penalties for political offenses.
October	Bahro released from prison and deported to West Germany.
November	Arrest of 13 workers in Thuringen region after demonstration protesting increases in food prices.

1980

February 2	Protests against Soviet invasion of Afganistan. Several participants arrested.
March 25	Bombing of Red Army monument in Karl-Marx Stadt.

	product of East-West Cold War politics. Known as East Germany.
Green Party	Political party formed out of several organizations: ecologists, Citizen's Initiatives, old New Left, etc. Elected to parliament of several regional states.
Hitler	Title of film by Hans-Jürgen Syberberg.
Kreuzberg	Section of West Berlin mainly populated by Turkish and German workers.
Kudamm	Main street in West Berlin. Short for "Kurfürstendamm."
Kommune I	First commune founded by APO in late 60's.
June 2nd	During 1967 demonstration against Shah's visit in West Berlin, student Benno Ohnesorg shot by police.
June 2nd movement	Underground movement active in West Berlin since mid-70's. Originally advocated forms of "Fun Guerrilla." Later involved with international terrorism.
KPD	German Communist Party, with strong pro-Soviet orientation. Forbidden in 1956. Reborn in late 60's as DKP.
Mecklenburg	Area of East Germany.
Meinhof, Ulrike	Journalist in 60's. Founder of RAF, together with An-

1981

December	Schmidt(FRG) and Honecker(GDR) meet in GDR at Lake Wehrbellin.
December	Writers from East and West Germany meet in East Berlin to discuss peace movement.

1982

February 13	Peace demonstration in Dresden on anniversary of bombing of Dresden in 1945. ☐

	dreas Baader, Gudrun Ensslin and Horst Mahler. Found hanged in Stammheim cell in 1976.
Mogadishu	On October 17, 1977 Lufthansa plane hijacked by Palestinian commando lands in Mogadishu, Somalia. Offer to exchange passengers for RAF prisoners. German task-force storms plane and frees passengers. The following day, RAF prisoners found dead in Stammheim cells.
NDP	"National Democratic Party," or neo-Nazi.
RAF	"Red Army Fraction." Anti-imperialist armed group founded in 1969 by Andreas Baader, Gudrun Ensslin, Horst Mahler, Ulrike Meinhof and others.
Schleyer, Martin	President of the National Employer's Association. Also Manager of Personnel for Mercedes-Benz. On September 5, 1977 kidnapped by RAF. Offered to be exchanged for Baader, Ensslin and Raspe. Found dead on October 19, 1977. During Nazi period, S. was member of SS. Organized Nazi students in Austria and Bohemia (now Czechoslovakia). Also right-hand of Heydrich, head of SS security service.
Schmidt, Helmut	Chancellor of Federal Republic of Germany since 1974. Leader of Social Democrats and advocate of "Modell Deutschland."

Schwerin	Town in East Germany.
SDS	"Social Democrat Students" association until mid-60's. Expelled from SPD for role in Extra-Parliamentary Organization.
SPD	"Social Democratic Party." Founded in 1863 and banned during Hitler period. Stands as model for social democracy. In power since 1966. Its chairman is Willy Brandt. Helmut Schmidt is member of SPD.
Spontis	"Spontaneist" wing of Anti-Authoritarian movement. Still active in Frankfurt.
Springer press	Sensationalist chain of tabloids and magazines. Focus of many protests for coverage of 60's and early 70's anti-war movement.
Stammheim	High security prison in South-West Germany, near Stuttgart.
Strauss, Franz-Joseph	Chairman of Christian Social Party (CSU), Bavarian ally of Christian Democrats. Head of Bavarian government. Represents extreme-right in West Germany.
Tagszeitung ("Taz")	Leftist daily newspaper founded in 1979. Corresponds to *Liberation* (France) and *Lotta Continua* (Italy).

GOD WILL KEEP IN PERFECT PEACE ALL THOSE WHO TRUST HIM... SEE ISAIAH 26:3

BACK ISSUES

Volume III (1978-80)

Nietzsche's Return, No. 1
Schizo-Culture, No. 2

Michel Foucault, Robert Wilson, Guy Hocquenghem,
William Burroughs, Lee Breuer, David Cooper,
John Giorno, Kathy Acker, Richard Foreman, Gilles Deleuze,
John Cage, Jack Smith, Jean-Francois Lyotard,
Douglas Dunn, etc.

Italy: Autonomia, No. 3

Sylvère Lotringer, Christian Marazzi, Mario Tronti,
Sergio Bologna, Toni Negri, Guy Debord, Félix Guattari,
Judith Malina, Lia Magale, Gilles Deleuze, Oreste Scalzone,
Franco Piperno, Dario Fo, Leonardo Sciascia, Paul Virilio,
Renato Curcio, etc.

Volume IV (1981-   )

Polysexuality, No. 1

Francois Peraldi, Pierre Klossowski, Roger Caillois,
Paul Verlaine, Duncan Smith, Jean Pouillon, Arthur Rimbaud,
Terence Sellers, Alain Robbe-Grillet, Félix Guattari,
Jean-Francois Lyotard, Gilles Deleuze, Tony Duvert,
William Burroughs, Roger Moody, Georges Bataille,
John Preston, Jason Klein, Jacques Lacan, Roland Barthes,
Paul Virilio, Guy Hocquenghem, Sylvère Lotringer, etc.

Large Type Series

Loving Boys, No. 1

Michel Foucault, Sylvère Lotringer, Kate Millet,
Mark Blasius, Mark Moffet.

PHOTO CREDITS

Rainer Berson: 13. 281. 293
German Information Center: 4. 5. 38. 81. 82. 83. 84. 85. 87. 88. 91. 92. 94. 96. 97. 106. 108. 112. 113. 117. 120. 121. 122. 123. 124 .127 .128. 129. 130. 131. 143. 149. 150. 151. 152. 157. 167. 168. 169. 170. 176. 178. 179. 183 a, b. 192. 193. 196. 198. 199. 201. 202. 203. 206. 207. 212. 214. 215. 216. 219. 220. 221. 223. 224. 227. 229. 230. 231. 234. 236. 238. 249. 254. 257. 263. 267. 275. 277. 282. 284. 288. 295. 301. 302. 304
Eric Guichard: 14. 15. 30. 100. 222. 247
Robin Holland: 43
Lisa Kahane: 261. 273. 274. 278. 287. 292. 296
Michael Kipp: 62. 90. 173
Peter Knopp: 256
Sylvère Lotringer: 291
Michael Oblowitz: 8. 9. 10. 11. 12. 13. 14. 15. 93. 97. 115. 185. 193. 218. 225. 232. 233. 251. 253. 283. 286. 289. 303. 304
Renke Reinders: 102
Marcia Resnick: 228. 235. 237. 239. 240. 242. 243. 245. 246. 248. 250. 285.
Henri Ries: 8b. 16. 18. 19. 21. 23. 24. 25. 28. 31. 32. 33. 34. 35. 37. 39. 40. 41. 42. 44. 45. 46. 47. 48. 49. 50. 51. 52. 53. 54. 55. 56. 57. 58. 59. 60. 61. 63. 64. 65. 66. 67. 132. 135. 136. 137. 155. 160. 161. 162. 164. 165. 189. 209. 241. 255
Christa Schnepf: 103
Harry Shunk: 16. 17
Paul Virilio: 265. 290. 306. 307. 308. 309. 310. 311. 312. 313. 314. 315
Wolfgang Volz: 9. 10. 11. 12. 26
Werner Wille: 110. 126. 175. 190